SHAKESPEARE'S WIFE

SHAKESPEARE'S WIFE

GERMAINE GREER

M<small>c</small>CLELLAND & STEWART

This edition published by McClelland & Stewart in 2008

Published simultaneously in the U.S.A. by HarperCollins Publishers in 2008
First published in the U.K. by Bloomsbury Publishing Plc in 2007

Library and Archives Canada Cataloguing in Publication

Greer, Germaine, 1939–
    Shakespeare's wife / Germaine Greer.

ISBN 978-0-7710-3582-1 (bound)

    1. Hathaway, Anne, 1556?-1623 – Marriage. 2. Hathaway, Anne,
1556?-1623 – Influence. 3. Shakespeare, William – Marriage. I. Title.

PR2906.G74 2008   822.3'3   C2007-906296-2

We acknowledge the financial support of the Government of Canada
through the Book Publishing Industry Development Program and that of the
Government of Ontario through the Ontario Media Development Corporation's
Ontario Book Initiative. We further acknowledge the support of the Canada
Council for the Arts and the Ontario Arts Council for our publishing program.

Printed and bound in the United States of America

McClelland & Stewart Ltd.
75 Sherbourne Street
Toronto, Ontario
M5A 2P9
www.mcclelland.com

1   2   3   4   5   12   11   10   09   08

To Professor Anne Barton
'Whose every work . . .
Came forth example and remains so, yet'

CONTENTS

INTRODUCTION

*considering the poor reputation of wives generally, in particular the
wives of literary men, and the traditional disparagement of the wife
of the Man of the Millennium*

Anyone steeped in western literary culture must wonder why any
woman of spirit would want to be a wife. At best a wife should be
invisible, like the wives of nearly all the great authors schoolboys used
to read at school. If Homer, Aesop, Plautus, Terence, Virgil, Horace
and Juvenal had wives they have been obliterated from history. The
wives who are remembered are those who are vilified, like Socrates'
Xanthippe and Aristotle's Phyllis. Until our own time, history
focussed on man the achiever; the higher the achiever the more
likely it was that the woman who slept in his bed would be judged
unworthy of his company. Her husband's fans recoiled from the
notion that she might have made a significant contribution towards
his achievement of greatness. The possibility that a wife might have
been closer to their idol than they could ever be, understood him
better than they ever could, could not be entertained.

If Xanthippe had never existed, bachelor dons would have had to
invent her. Among the scant references to her is the story told in the
Phaedo of how, when she came with Socrates' three sons to visit him
when Socrates had been sentenced to death for corrupting the youth
of Athens and ordered to commit suicide by drinking hemlock, she
so annoyed the great man with her lamentations that he sent her
home again, so that his last hours could be spent in rational discussion
with his disciples. No historian has ever shown the slightest interest
in what became of Xanthippe and her three small children after
Socrates' suicide. Such mundane matters are beneath the consideration of great men and their biographers. To protest that Socrates'

chosen martyrdom brought catastrophe on the four innocent people who depended on him would be merely womanish.

As Lisa Jardine pointed out in 1983: 'Renaissance scholars from Richard Hooker to Francis Bacon are credited with scolding wives. Society seems to find it irresistible to characterise the "unworldliness" of the male intellectual and academic in terms of his failure to control the women in his life.'[1] Hooker and Bacon did rather well out of their wives, who were both wealthy. By 1588, when Richard Hooker married Jean Churchman, the protestant reformers had all but succeeded in eliminating the Pauline notion of wedded life as inferior to virginity. Even so, the woman who bore Richard Hooker six children, and brought him the financial security that made it possible for him to become the leading apologist of the Anglican Church, is known to us only as a scold.

Bacon was married in 1606, when he was forty-five, to a fourteen-year-old heiress called Alice Barnham, whom he had singled out for the purpose when she was only eleven years old. It was well known that Francis Bacon preferred boys to women, and kept a series of young male menials for his pleasure. In the circumstances, the young Viscountess St Albans could be thought to have had every right to behave badly. She seems to have endured her grotesque marriage without complaint until she became involved with John Underhill. A 'Mr Underhill' is listed in 1617 as a 'Gentleman-in-Waiting' at York House, where Viscount St Albans and his childless wife lived in state. In 1625, when Bacon was revising his will, in which he left the princely sum of £200 to a young Welsh servingman called Francis Edney, he added a codicil, revoking his legacies to Alice 'for just and great causes' and leaving her 'to her right only'. In a pointed gesture, a mere fortnight after Bacon's death, Alice Bacon married John Underhill in a public ceremony at St Martin's in the Fields.[2] Of the miserable story of the marriage of a trusting child to a middle-aged pederast, all that has come down to us is Bacon's view of marriage: 'He that hath a wife and children hath given hostages to fortune, for they are impediments to great enterprises, either of virtue or of mischief.'[3]

Some such idea lies behind the almost unconscious certainty shared by all (male) observers that, if a man of genius is to realise his potential, he must put his wife away. Shakespeare could not have been great if he had not jettisoned his wife, but if he is to be great, she must be shown to have got her just deserts. Many English men of genius followed the example of the earliest-known Greek philosopher:

> Thales Miletus was . . . held to be the first man that had the name of wise attributed unto him, being afterwards reckoned one of those seven who only were of the Grecians called wise men; he being importuned by his mother Cleobulina to take a wife whilst he was young, always answered her that it was yet time enough; and afterward, being grown in years and urged by her more earnestly, he told her, that it was (then) past time, and too too late, this grave man meaning hereby that it was not good to marry at all.[4]

This advice was reiterated in every generation. While the church ruled the academic establishment, all teachers were necessarily celibate but, even after the Reformation, when the reformers preached that it was a man's duty to his maker to take a wife, many artists and intellectuals chose, or perhaps were constrained by their poverty, to remain unmarried, if not exactly celibate. Literature was a particularly laddish enterprise, the province of young bachelors who usually gave it up when – or if – they married. Christopher Marlowe, Thomas Kyd, Thomas Nashe, Michael Drayton, all died unmarried. Any literary figure who bucked the trend and took a wife is usually commiserated, beginning with Geoffrey Chaucer who, we are told, 'could not have been happy in his marriage'.[5]

Thomas Moore, writing in defence of his friend Byron's appalling treatment of his clever wife, is one of the first to decide on little or no evidence that Shakespeare hated his wife.

> By whatever austerity of temper or habits the poets Dante and Milton may have drawn upon themselves such a fate, it might be expected that, at least, the 'gentle Shakespeare' would have stood exempt from the common calamity of his brethren. But, among the very few facts of his life that have been transmitted to us, there is none more clearly proved than the unhappiness of his marriage.[6]

There is no evidence that Dante's wife, Gemma Donati, who was better connected than he, made his life miserable; it is simply assumed that he would have been happier with his muse, Bice Portinari – as if it were the job of a muse to run a household and produce children. Gemma bore Dante at least four children; we should not be surprised to find that neither she nor they inspired a single line of poetry. When Dante was exiled in 1302, his wife of seventeen years chose to remain with her children in Florence.

Milton's marital infelicity is legendary in every sense of the word; he was thirty-four when he married seventeen-year-old Mary Powell, a few weeks before the outbreak of the Civil War. His wife's family were royalists, and she judged it best to return to them until the future should be less uncertain. This perfectly sensible response to a confused and dangerous situation is supposed have prompted Milton to write *The Doctrine and Discipline of Divorce* and therefore it is assumed that, when Mary returned to the marital household in 1645, he wished she hadn't and that their life together thereafter was miserable. Whatever the case, conjugal relations were promptly resumed. Mary's first child was born in July the next year; a few days after bearing her fourth in May 1652, she died. Milton's first experience of marriage was not so disastrous that he did not contemplate a second; he was already losing his sight when he married Katherine Woodcock in November 1658 and fifteen months later she died in childbirth. So far marriage to Milton would seem far more punishing for his wives than for him. Milton married a third time at the advanced age of fifty-five because he was in need of a live-in carer. The woman chosen for him by his doctor was a poor relation of his own, twenty-four-year-old Elizabeth Minshul, who lived to spend the inheritance which was her only reward, and probably inadequate to support her for the fifty-three years that remained of her life after the poet's death in 1674.

By doing the right thing, by remaining silent and invisible, Ann Shakespeare left a wife-shaped void in the biography of William Shakespeare, which later bardolaters filled up with their own speculations, most of which do neither them nor their hero any credit.

Her given name and approximate birth date were known from her tomb in Holy Trinity Church Stratford; Shakespeare's first biographer, Nicholas Rowe, supplied her maiden surname, and there matters rested until 1790.

> Previous biographers had not worried much about the poet's conjugal relations, nor (when they did evince curiosity) had they necessarily assumed his disaffection with Anne. In *The Modern Universal British Traveller*, which antedates Malone's *Supplement* by one year, the 'Biography of Warwickshire' confidently informs us that Shakespeare 'lived very happy' with his wife, and, after he made some money minding horses, fetched her to London.[7]

It was in 1790 that Edmond Malone published an observation originally made by William Oldys in the margin of the entry on Shakespeare in his copy of Langbaine's *Account of the English Dramatic Poets* (1691) that Sonnets 92 and 93 'seem to have been addressed by Shakespeare to his beautiful wife on some suspicion of her infidelity'.[8] William Oldys, who was born in 1696, had no special knowledge; his impression was based on his reading of Sonnets 92–5 which in the edition of 1640 bore the sub-title 'Lover's Affection'.[9] Oldys had as little reason to believe that Ann was beautiful as later commentators to believe that she was plain. At this early stage it looks as if Ann is being recruited into the ranks of the beautiful faithless wives; the allegation of infidelity would be made again and again, but for most scholars the mere fact of her being older than her husband made her unattractive.

Shakespeare's will was published as early as 1752, in the third volume of Theobald's *Works of Shakespeare*; as it became better known, it too was interpreted as evidence of Ann's utter failure as a wife. James Boswell, struggling with the mass of material left by Malone, is probably the first to suggest that Shakespeare's 'affections were estranged from her either through jealousy or some other cause'.[10] For others the disparity in age was enough in itself to discredit her. In *Shakespeare: A Biography* (1823), Thomas De Quincey, the first rhapsodist of bardolatry, remarked: 'Neither do we like the spectacle of a mature young woman, five years past her majority, wearing the semblance of having been led astray by a boy who still had two years and a half to run of his minority.'[11]

Ann made no 'spectacle' of herself and offered no 'semblance' whatsoever. With such semantics De Quincey turns her into a designing woman. He also decides that Shakespeare went to London to escape 'the humiliation of domestic feuds'. When the marriage bond of Will Shakespeare and Ann Hathaway with its tell-tale date only six months before the christening of their first child was found and published in 1836, bardolaters were scandalised. To the early Victorians Ann stood revealed as a lustful, designing woman who entrapped an innocent young man.

> [John] Britton entertains grave misgivings about Anne's morals. He points to the burial on 6 March 1590, of 'Thomas Green *alias* Shakspere' and, supposing without good reason that this Green was a child, adds: 'The inference of which this circumstance is susceptible must be obvious.' To Britton, apparently, belongs the distinction of being the first to suggest that the woman who bore the dramatist three children also mothered a bastard.[12]

Everybody who meddles with Shakespeare biography readily accepts that the Bard was unfaithful to his wife and excuses him for it, but infidelity on the part of his wife is sufficient to justify estrangement.

When Shakespearean master-sleuth Halliwell-Phillipps published the entry of a marriage licence between a William Shakespeare and Ann Whateley of Temple Grafton in 1887 it was immediately assumed that (old, ugly) Ann Hathaway prevented William from marrying his (young, lovely) true love. The plays were trawled for evidence that Shakespeare bitterly regretted his marriage, and so little was found that scholars from De Quincey to Stephen Greenblatt were constrained to parrot Orsino in *Twelfth Night*:

> Then let thy love be younger than thyself,
> Or thy affection cannot hold the bent . . . (II. iv. 36–7)

– as if Shakespeare were no smarter than Orsino and the whole play was not about the wooing of a woman by a boy.

Moore interprets the scant details of Shakespeare's domestic life as evidence that he disliked his wife:

> The dates of the birth of his children, compared with that of his removal from Stratford, – the total omission of his wife's name in the first draft of his will, and the bitter sarcasm of the bequest by which he remembers her afterwards – all prove beyond a doubt both his separation from the lady early in life, and his unfriendly feeling towards her at the close of it.[13]

Joseph Hunter credits the misery of living with Ann Shakespeare as the motive force of the Bard's entire career: 'It seems but too evident, that this was a marriage of evil auspices, and it may have been one principal cause of that unsettled state of mind in which the poet left Stratford, about four years afterwards.'[14]

No one has ever undertaken a systematic review of the evidence against Ann Shakespeare, while every opportunity to caricature and revile her has been exploited to risible lengths. In Joyce's *Ulysses*, Stephen Dedalus dreams of an Ann Shakespeare disfigured by age and guilt: 'And in New Place a slack dishonoured body that once was comely, once as sweet, as fresh as cinnamon, now her leaves falling, all, bare, frighted of the narrow grave and unforgiven.'[15] Cinnamon is not used fresh and women don't grow leaves. In *Nothing Like the Sun* Anthony Burgess has a sexually experienced Ann taking advantage of a drunken boy who is then forced to marry her: 'Armed with a dildo this Anne lures her boy husband into strange sexual rites and later cuckolds him with his brother Richard on the second-best bed.'[16] Journalist Anthony Holden, retelling the story in 1999, prefers his Ann 'homely'.

> It is hard to believe that this ambitious young dreamer [Shakespeare], already aware that there was a world elsewhere, way beyond rural Warwickshire, was so enamoured of a homely wench eight years his senior . . . as to want to marry her. Or did the local farmer's 26-year-old daughter, only a month after her father's

death, set out to catch herself a much younger husband by seducing him?[17]

Stephen Greenblatt is not a novelist or a journalist but a renaissance scholar, yet even he follows the tradition of Guizot who believed that Shakespeare developed a positive aversion to his wife:[18]

> When he thought of the afterlife, the last thing he wanted was to be mingled with the woman he married. Perhaps he simply feared that his bones would be dug up and thrown in the nearby charnel house – he seems to have regarded that fate with horror – but he may have feared still more that one day his grave would be opened to let in the body of Anne Shakespeare.[19]

Greenblatt labours the point, for which he has no better evidence than the doggerel quatrain on what purports to be Shakespeare's gravestone. Ann fares no better at the hands of women: according to Diana Price, . . . 'one might speculate that the Hathaways got wind of the Shagspere–Whateley licence, and Anne Hathaway's father escorted Mr. Shagspere by pitchfork to the altar'.[20]

One might, but one probably should not. The film *Shakespeare in Love* presents Shakespeare as psychologically damaged by his early marriage:

> Dr Moth: You have a wife and children?
> Will: Ay . . . I was a lad of eighteen, Anne Hathaway was a woman half as old again . . .
> Dr Moth: And . . . your marriage bed?
> Will: Four years and a hundred miles away in Stratford. A cold bed too since the twins were born. Banishment was a blessing.
> Dr Moth: So now you are free to love.
> Will: Yet cannot love nor write it.[21]

In his discussion of the film in *Shakespeare in Psychoanalysis* (2001) Philip Armstrong continues the cod psychoanalysis:

. . . half a mother and half a wife, no longer a wife since a mother two times over, Anne Hathaway (never seen in the film) provides the figure whose union with and simultaneous distance from her husband/son embodies a version of that Oedipal drama diagnosed in Shakespeare, and identified as the source and theme of all his work, by Sigmund Freud, Otto Rank and Ernest Jones.[22]

The bewildered reader of the endless traducing of the invisible woman of Stratford might ask as Master Lusam does in *How to choose a good wife from a bad*:

> But on what root grows this high branch of hate?
> Is not she loyal, constant, loving, chaste,
> Obedient, apt to please, loth to displease,
> Careful to live, chary of her good name,
> And jealous of your reputation?
> Is not she virtuous, wise, religious?[23]

All biographies of Shakespeare are houses built of straw, but there is good straw and rotten straw, and some houses are better built than others. The evidence that is always construed to Ann Hathaway's disadvantage is capable of other, more fruitful interpretations, especially within the context of recent historiography.

There is one resounding exception to the rule that the wives of great men must all have been unworthy. It does not apply to the wives of protestant reformers. The housewife superstars of reformed religion were women like Anna Zwingli, Katherine Melancthon, Idelette Calvin, Anna Bullinger and the amazing Wibrandis Rosenblatt. Käthe Luther is as silent as Ann Shakespeare; though she wrote many letters, only one survives. The marriage of the dowerless ex-nun Katherine von Bora and the ex-monk Martin Luther was arranged; they were handfasted privately and publicly blessed and feasted two weeks later, a pattern that can be discerned in the Warwickshire marriages of Ann Shakespeare's contemporaries. Käthe then took over the vast ex-monastery the Elektor Friedrich had given her husband, filled it with orphans, teachers, students, refugees and guests, brewed the ale they drank, grew the vegetables and fruit they ate, raised and slaughtered her own animals and made their butter and cheese – and bore six children, and nursed her demanding husband through his many ailments physical and mental.

Ann Hathaway had no gossip magazines to keep her posted on the day-to-day lives of such role models. She found her role model where Käthe Luther found it, in her Bible.

She girdeth her loins with strength and strengtheneth her arms.

She seeth that her merchandise is good; her candle is not put out by night.

She putteth her hands to the wheel, and her hands handle the spindle.

(Proverbs, xxxi: 17–19)

CHAPTER ONE

introducing the extensive and reputable family of Hathaway alias Gardner of Shottery together with the curious fact that one of their kinsmen was a successful playwright for the Admiral's Men

Shakespeare's wife was identified as long ago as 1709, when Nicholas Rowe informed the readers of his edition of the plays: 'His wife was the daughter of one Hathaway, said to have been a substantial yeoman in the neighbourhood of Stratford.'[1] There were many Hathaways within a day's ride of Stratford. Hathaways farmed in Bishopton and Shottery in Warwickshire, and in Horton, Bledington, Kingscote and surrounding districts in neighbouring Gloucestershire. There were also tradesmen called Hathaway in London, Banbury and Oxford, and one or two claimed the rank of gentleman. The Hathaway horde was so numerous in fact that the Shottery family into which Ann was born used a distinguishing alias. They were known mostly as Hathaway alias Gardner, and sometimes as just plain Hathaway or just plain Gardner.

In the medieval period such aliases served to distinguish between people with the same surname by specifying the region or town they came from or the trade they followed. Perhaps an earlier Hathaway had indeed been a gardener. Sometimes, when there was no male heir, a female descendant's husband might inherit on condition that he assumed her family name as an alias. The point of aliases is still being disputed by genealogists; although during Ann Shakespeare's lifetime the use of aliases became less consistent, it was a generation or two before it faded out altogether. We know that Ann's grandfather John Hathaway was already using the alias, so it is not something we are likely ever to unravel. For years nobody realised that the 'Jone Gardner of Shottery' who was buried in Holy Trinity churchyard in

1599 was the same person they had already identified as Ann Shakespeare's stepmother.[2] In 1590 a 'Thomas Greene alias Shakespeare' was buried in Holy Trinity Church Stratford, sending historians off on a wild-goose chase for a woman called Greene giving birth to an illegitimate Shakespeare, or vice versa, for the alias was occasionally used for *de facto* wives and to denote descent on the wrong side of the blanket.

The Christian name of the woman who married William Shakespeare in 1582 is as unstable as her surname. The only evidence that Richard Hathaway alias Gardner of Shottery had a daughter called Ann is a reference in his will to a daughter called Agnes. Scholars have demonstrated convincingly that in this period Agnes and Ann were simply treated as versions of the same name, pointing out dozens of examples where Agnes, pronounced 'Annis', gradually becomes 'Ann'. Richard Hathaway left a sheep to a great-niece he calls Agnes, though according to the parish record she was actually christened Annys; in 1600 she was buried as Ann. Theatre manager Philip Henslowe called his wife Agnes in his will but she was buried as Ann. Ann's brother Bartholomew called a daughter Annys, but she was buried as Ann. The curate William Gilbert alias Higgs who wrote Hathaway's will married Agnes Lyncian, but she was buried as Ann Gilbert.[3] This is not simply serendipitous. Agnes was the name of a fourth-century virgin martyr of the kind whose lurid and preposterous adventures are the stuff of *The Golden Legend*, justly ridiculed by protestant reformers.[4] Ann (or Hannah) was the solid biblical name of the Redeemer's grandmother. It is only to be expected that as protestantism gained hearts and minds Agnes would be silently driven out by Ann. We may accept that the child born Agnes Hathaway grew up to be Ann Shakespeare.

The brass plate set in the stone over her grave next to William's in the chancel of Holy Trinity Church Stratford tells us that Ann Shakespeare 'departed this life on the sixth day of August 1623 being of the age of 67 years'. We have no evidence to corroborate this information. If the funeral plate is correct she was born in 1556, eight years before her husband. Engravers do make mistakes; the figures 1 and 7 are easily confounded in the calligraphy of 1623, but as all Ann's family was baptised at Holy Trinity, where the registers began to be kept in obedience to the royal edict of 1558, we must conclude that she was born before the register began to be kept, and not afterwards. So 1556 it is.

Our best evidence that Agnes Hathaway alias Gardner of Shottery is the woman who married Will Shakespeare in 1582 is the will made in 1601 by her father's shepherd Thomas Whittington. Whittington is identified in Richard Hathaway's will: 'I owe unto Thomas Whittington my shepherd four pounds six shillings eight pence.' Twenty years on, when he made his will in 1601, Whittington identified Ann as Shakespeare's wife:

Item I give and bequeath unto the poor people of Stratford forty shillings that is in the hand of Ann Shakespeare wife unto Mr William Shakespeare and is due debt unto me being paid to mine executor by the said William Shakespeare or his assigns according to the true meaning of this my will.[5]

The Hathaway family house is supposed to be the one that is now known as Ann Hathaway's Cottage, though indeed it was never hers. This twelve-roomed farmhouse, known to the Hathaway family, if not to the bardolatrous public, as Hewlands Farm, is built on stone foundations, of timber-framed wattle-and-daub. The oldest part of the dwelling, thought to date from the late fourteenth century, consists of a hall of two twelve-foot bays reaching to the timbered roof, constructed around two oaken crucks that are pinned together to form the peak of the roof. Before the Great Rebuilding of the 1560s, all the members of the household would have slept in the hall, around an open fireplace from which the smoke escaped through an opening in the thatch.[6]

Ann's paternal grandfather, John Hathaway alias Gardner, acquired the copyhold of Hewlands Farm in 1543 and it was probably he who modernised the house by installing stone fireplaces in each of the two bays of the hall, one eight feet across and the other eleven. The stone hearths were also the supports for stout oak bressemers supporting an upper floor which was divided into separate connecting rooms. On the ground floor, next to the hall, there was a kitchen with a huge domed bread-oven. A dairy or buttery has also survived. An east wing was added to the main building later, probably by Ann's brother, Bartholomew Hathaway.

Shottery, to the west of Stratford, was then a cluster of farms worked by tenants of the manor; in 1595, we find the more substantial of them growing wheat, barley and peas on arable holdings of as much as 200 acres, but in 1581 the average holding would have been rather smaller and the farming more mixed. Hewlands Farm, which then stood right on the edge of the Forest of Arden, was typical in that it consisted of pasturage for sheep as well as cultivated yardland. Yardland or virgate was the name given to bundles of strips of land suitable for cultivation; the area of a yardland could be anything from twenty to forty-six acres. In 1595 Joan Hathaway's half-yardland amounted to no more than fifteen acres, so we should probably assume that Richard Hathaway farmed thirty acres or so. He may have held other lands which he had devised to his son and heir before his death, but, even if he didn't, his holding can be described as substantial, though he was a rung below a yeoman or freeholder.

The family had been well established in the district for generations. A John Hathaway appears as an archer on the muster rolls (lists of citizens eligible for military service) in 1536. He also served at different times as beadle, constable and affeeror (assessor of sums owed) to the parish. He was one of the fifteen citizens from whom were selected the Twelve Men of Old Stratford (one of several manors that comprised the borough of Stratford) who presided twice a year at the Great Leet, when tenancies were arranged and transferred, debts paid and rents adjusted. In the subsidy of 1549 John Hathaway's annual income in goods was valued at £10, one of the highest valuations. In 1556, as well as Hewlands, he held another house and yardland described as 'late in the tenure of Thomas Perkyns', and another toft and yardland known as Hewlyns. John Hathaway probably died before his son Richard took possession of Hewlands Farm. Richard is first named in the records as assessed on an annual income of £4 in goods in 1566–7. Following what seems to have been a Hathaway family custom of partible inheritance, with the greater share going to the younger son, John Hathaway's estate had probably been split between Richard and his elder brother George Hathaway alias Gardner who was also farming in Shottery.

At the time of his death in 1581, Ann's father had eight living children. The eldest son was Bartholomew, who, like Ann, was born before the parish registers began to be kept. A boy was christened Richard on 4 January 1562; by the time his father made his will this child had apparently perished. Next came Catherine, who was christened at Holy Trinity on 22 October 1563. It is usually assumed that the mother of these children then died, but no wife of a Richard Hathaway or Gardner appears in the Stratford burial register and no second marriage has turned up in the Stratford registers or anywhere else. The sole evidence for the supposition that Hathaway married twice is that the woman Hathaway was married to at the time of his death was called Joan, and the 'filia Richardi Hathaway alias Gardner de Shotery' who was christened 'Joan' on 9 May 1566 is assumed to be her first child. We don't know for certain how many wives Richard Hathaway had. If Ann, born in 1556, was his first child, and William, born in 1578, his last, we are presented with a child-bearing career of twenty-two years, which would not be unusual, let alone impossible, for one woman. Ann's friend Judith Sadler bore her first child in 1580 and her last in 1603.

For no very good reason then, Ann, her brother Bartholomew and Catherine are taken to be the children of the first wife, and Joan, Thomas, Margaret, John and William the children of the second. Thomas 'the son of Richard Hathaway' was christened on 12 April 1569, Margaret 'daughter to — Gardner of Shotrey' on 17 August 1572, John 'son to Richard Hathaway' on 3 February 1575, and William 'sonne to Richard Hathaway of Shottrey' on 30 November 1578. All the births in the Hathaway family are separated by three years, more or less, except for the births of Richard and Catherine, which are separated by only twenty-two months. The circumstances of Richard Hathaway's birth and putative death are a puzzle. There is no Richard Hathaway buried at Holy Trinity between January 1562 and September 1581; instead we have two Richard Hathaways each called 'filius Richardi Hathaway alias Gardner', one buried on 29 March 1561 and the other three days later. These are usually taken to be twins, one of whom inherited the name from the other, but the repetition might as easily be a scribal error. If Hathaway's wife had

borne and buried premature twins in March 1561, she could have
produced another child by January 1562, but neither it nor she is
likely to have been strong or healthy. The likeliest time for both to
have died is January 1562, which still gives Hathaway time to find a
new wife and get her pregnant by the beginning of 1563. This
reproductive scenario is grim, to be sure, but it is not at all unusual. In
1662 Ann and Bartholomew would have been too small to be taken
to the fields or left alone in the house; with no one to do the woman's
share of farm work, Hathaway had to find a new wife without delay.
The riddle may one day be resolved, but at this stage we have no idea
who Ann Shakespeare's mother was or when she died.

In the summer of 1581, Ann's father fell ill. On 1 September he called
the curate William Gilbert and dictated his will. The preamble is
conventional and protestant: 'first I bequeath my soul unto almighty
God, trusting to be saved by the merits of Christ's passion, And my
body to be buried in the church or church yard of Stratford
aforesaid . . .'[7] To each of his sons Thomas and John, Richard left
a portion of £6 13s 4d to be paid to them at the age of twenty years.
Thomas was twelve and a half, John six and a half. The youngest boy
was to get more: 'Item I give and bequeath unto William my son ten
pounds to be paid unto him at the age of twenty years'.

Again we encounter what seems to be a local or familial variant of
the custom of gavelkind, the ancient system by which all male
children inherited some part of the estate and the youngest son more
than the others. It is usually associated with Kent, but also with nearby
Wales. As it happened, Thomas may not have lived to collect his
portion, for the will is the last we hear of him.

Hathaway then turns to his daughters: 'Item I give and bequeath
unto Agnes my daughter six pounds thirteen shillings four pence to be
paid unto her at the day of her marriage', with the like to Catherine.
Edgar Fripp interprets these bequests as evidence that both girls were
already betrothed.[8] Much as I would like to be able to prove that Will
and Ann were already recognised as future spouses on 1 September
1581, more than a year before their marriage was solemnised, I'm
afraid that Fripp gets it wrong. The leaving of marriage portions in
wills is a promise of cash to be raised from the estate in the event of a

marriage. With £6 13s 4d or ten marks, Ann had exactly the same cash portion as Will's mother when she married John Shakespeare. Though Mary Arden's father too described himself as a mere husbandman, Mary inherited a landed estate as well as the cash. Ann too may have had lands settled on her by deed during her father's lifetime, and may have been a better catch than we know. If lands farmed by Richard had been left by Ann's mother's family to the heirs of her body they would have passed directly to her children at the time of her death and would not have been Richard's to dispose of.

If Catherine ever married it was not in Stratford.[9] As far as we can tell she was not buried in Stratford either, so we should probably conclude that she found work, and hopefully a life, elsewhere. As Joan is not mentioned in the will, we should infer that she is dead, but no record of her burial has ever been found, unless she is the 'child of Goodman Hathaway's' who was buried on 5 September 1572. The youngest daughter Margaret was to receive her portion when she reached the age of seventeen rather than on her wedding day, which suggests that she was not likely to marry, perhaps because she suffered from some infirmity or deformity. Her father's will is the last we hear of her. Thus three of Richard Hathaway's daughters disappear from history, leaving us with only Ann. The combined legacies, amounting to more than £40, are a lot to raise from a husbandman's estate, especially as the crop from half the yardland was to be reserved for Hathaway's first-born son Bartholomew, who was already farming somewhere on his own account, possibly near Tysoe where he was living in 1583.

> Item my will is (with the consent of my wife) that my eldest son Bartholomew shall have the use commodity and profit of one half-yard land with all pastures and meadowing thereto belonging with the appurtenances to be tilled, mucked and sowed at the charge of Joan my wife, he only finding seed during the natural life or widowhood of the same Joan my wife to be bestowed, severed from the other of my land for his commodity and profit. And my will is that he, the same Bartholomew shall be a guide to my said wife in her husbandry, And also a comfort unto his brethren and sisters to his power. Provided always that if the said Joan my wife shall at any time or times after my

decease go about to disannul or take away from my said son Bartholomew the foresaid half yard land with the appurtenances, so that
he do not enjoy the commodity and profit of the same according to
the true meaning of this my last will and testament, then my will is that
the said Joan my wife shall give deliver and pay unto my said son
Bartholomew within one year after any such denial, or discharge the
sum of forty pounds of lawful English money

This rather cumbersome arrangement suggests that, unusually, Joan
and her children would remain in Richard Hathaway's house, rather
than giving way to the son and heir; Joan would be responsible for the
management of the rest of the Hathaway farmlands with Bartholomew's help. In most parts of England in exchange for a third portion
of the estate, a widow would have been expected to vacate the house
but, perhaps because Thomas, Margaret, John and William were still
so small, Joan was allowed to remain there. A match for Bartholomew
had already been concluded; on 25 November, only three weeks after
his father's death, he married Isabel Hancocks of Tredington. Wherever he took his bride home to, it was not to Hewlands Farm, where
Joan remained farming on her own account until her death in 1599.
The will goes on: 'Item: I give and bequeath unto every of my
godchildren four pence apiece of them'. We don't know who
Richard's godchildren may have been, or how many of them there
were. It is possible that children of John Shakespeare may have been
among them. In September 1566 John Shakespeare stood surety for
Richard Hathaway in two actions, and was called on to pay debts for
him to a Joan Biddle and a John Page. Later, in 1579, Hathaway and
John Shakespeare would both be mentioned in the will of Roger
Sadler as debtors to his estate. On 15 April 1569 the Shakespeares'
second daughter was christened Joan, perhaps after Richard Hathaway's wife, though it seems as likely that she was named for her aunt
Joan, Mary Shakespeare's sister. In 1574 a son received the name
Richard. Perhaps Richard Shakespeare too became one of the
unspecified number of godchildren to whom Richard Hathaway
left four pence apiece in his will. If this was indeed the case, William
Shakespeare and Ann Hathaway were related to each other within the
prohibited degrees of spiritual consanguinity.

'Item: I give and bequeath unto Agnes Hathaway and Elizabeth Hathaway daughters unto Thomas Hathaway a sheep apiece of them'. Agnes Hathaway, not quite four years old, and Elizabeth, not quite two, were daughters of Hathaway's nephew Thomas, the youngest of the seven children of his elder brother George, who had died eight years before, being buried in Holy Trinity on 25 September 1573. Why Richard should have singled out Thomas's very small children for special remembrance is not known. Perhaps Thomas had been part of the workforce at Hewlands before his marriage. He must still have been sheep-farming otherwise there would have been small point in giving his little girls their own sheep. He may have become alienated from the rest of his family in the matter of religion and have found sympathy and support from his uncle. Thomas's children and grandchildren were to remain close to Ann and her daughters all their lives, unlike Ann's half-brothers John and William Hathaway.

It is typical of the provident Hathaway family that spouses had been found for four of George's children before he died. Philippa married Laurence Walker at Holy Trinity in 1567; John married Margery Round of Snitterfield in 1568; their son christened at Holy Trinity on 14 December 1573 was called Richard. George married Ann Heaton of Loxley in 1570 and Alice married Henry Smith of Banbury in 1572. The other three were also able to marry after their father's death, which suggests that they too had been left adequate portions. Thomas married Margaret Smith (probably the sister of Henry) in 1575; in 1579 Ann married William Wilson who was to become a Stratford alderman in 1592, and a few months later Frances married David Jones, the man who produced the Whitsun pastoral that was played in Stratford in 1583; the accounts of the Corporation for that year list 'thirteen shillings and fourpence paid to David Jones and his company for his pastime at Whitsuntide'.[10] By these marriages Ann was connected to a significant proportion of the settled population of Stratford and the surrounding district.

The fact that Richard Hathaway made his wife rather than his eldest son his executor and residuary legatee reinforces the notion that she was a second wife and rather younger than he. Joan would remain in Shottery where she is recorded as holding a half-yardland in 1590, and running a household of six in 1595. It was not until well after her death in 1599 that Bartholomew took possession of Hewlands Farm. Historians who imagine that Ann and Bartholomew were running Hewlands Farm together after Richard Hathaway's death are simply wrong.[11]

The overseers of the will, who received twelve pence each for their pains, were Hathaway's neighbours, forty-three-year-old Stephen Burman and thirty-year-old Fulke Sandells. The Warwickshire Corn Enquiry of 1595 lists four Burman households in Shottery of which Stephen Burman's with a hundred acres under barley and sixty acres under peas and a household of fifteen people was the largest.[12] Fulke Sandells seems to have been primarily a sheep-farmer, with only twenty acres of barley and eleven acres of peas in 1595. The will was witnessed by the curate William Gilbert, Richard Burman, John Richardson and John 'Hemynge'. Gilbert served as under-schoolmaster at the grammar school at various times from 1561–2, and was appointed curate on £10 a year in 1576, a position that he held until his death in 1612. He was also paid £1 a year to maintain the town clocks. John Richardson was a substantial member of the Shottery community; when he died in 1594 his goods, including wheat, barley, peas, oats and hay in the barns, five cows, three heifers and a bullock, four horses and mares, and 130 sheep were appraised at £87 3s 8d. Of most interest to us is John Hemynge or Hemmings. A John Hemmings, hayward of Shottery, baptised seven children in Holy Trinity between December 1563 and September 1582, including another John. What nobody knows is in what way if at all these John Hemmingses are related to the John Hemmings who together with Henry Condell edited the Folio edition of Shakespeare's plays. Fripp believes that John Hemmings to be the son and heir of George Hemmings of Droitwich, but the evidence is rather less than conclusive.

No servants, except the shepherd Thomas Whittington, are mentioned in Hathaway's will. As Catherine was neither married nor buried in Stratford, it seems likely that she had gone into service. If Ann was still living in Shottery, she may have been making herself too useful for her own good. Joan Hathaway, with the running of the farm to consider, may have been only too happy to leave the cooking and washing, brewing and baking to Agnes–Ann. Indeed, we might think of Ann as in much the same situation as Cinderella, except that she is older rather than younger than the other children.

The match between William Shakespeare and Ann Hathaway was an alliance of two substantial families in a close-knit community where everybody knew everybody else's business. Husband and wife would remain in contact with both their extended families, who continued to live in houses that were within walking distance of each other, worshipping at the same church, christening and burying their children in the company of their own kith and kin.

The connection of the Hathaway clan with the theatre may extend to more than the marriage of Frances Hathaway with a local impresario and the coincidence of the name Hemmings. A playwright with the same name as Ann's father, Richard Hathaway, spelt as it is spelt in the will, 'Hathway', was one of the stable of playwrights retained by Philip Henslowe, owner–manager of the Rose Theatre, to furnish plays for the resident company, the Admiral's Men. Because so few of these plays found their way into print, Henslowe's diary is virtually our sole source of information about him. The *Dictionary of National Biography* tells us that Richard Hathway was almost certainly connected to the Warwickshire Hathaways but can give no grounds for the belief.

As Hathway's professional career is rather more typical than Shakespeare's, it makes sense to give a detailed account of it. We first hear of Hathway in 1598 when he writes an entry dated 11 April in Henslowe's 'diary' (actually a memorandum book) acknowledging receipt of twenty shillings as an advance for 'The Life of Arthur King of England', 'to be delivered on Thursday next following after the date hereof'.[13] This, the only play for which Hathway was solely responsible, secured his membership of Henslowe's crew of writers; he was paid not, as some think Shakespeare was, by being given shares in the company but in cash. The full sum was lent to the company by Henslowe the following day. 'Lent unto the company the 12 of April 1598 to pay Master Hathway in full payment for his book of King Arthur the sum of four pounds'.[14] Henslowe did not give the title 'Master' to all his playwrights; it seems to have been reserved, though not consistently, for playwrights who were 'sharers', that is, share-holders in the theatre.

Hathway is supposed then to have worked with Anthony Munday on 'Valentine and Orson'. In January 1599 he, Robert Wilson, Michael Drayton and Munday received a payment of £4 on account to produce a play called 'Owen Tudor'. On 16 October 1599 Thomas Downton acknowledged receipt of £10 'to pay Master Munday, Master Drayton, Master Wilson and Hathway for the first part of the life of Sir John Oldcastle and in earnest of the second part for the use of the company'. So successful in performance was *The First Part of the true and honourable history of Sir John Oldcastle, the good lord of Cobham* that Henslowe gave ten shillings to 'Master Munday and the rest of the poets' 'as a gift'.[15] This is the only play associated with Hathway that ever found its way into print. When *Sir John Oldcastle* was licensed by the Stationers' Company in August 1600, though a 'second part' was mentioned in the entry, all that the licensee, Thomas Pavier, managed to print was a first part, originally issued anonymously, and then reissued with Shakespeare's name on the title-page. Ironically enough, when seven new plays were added to the second issue of the 1664 edition of the Shakespeare Folio, *The First Part of the true and honourable history of Sir John Oldcastle* was one of them.

In 1600 Hathway contributed a fluent if rather uninteresting encomium 'Of the Book' to *Belvedere or the Garden of the Muses*, a printed commonplace book compiled for John Bodenham, a wealthy London tradesman who furnished funds for the collection and publication of poems in anthologies.

> The sundry beams proceeding from one sun,
> The hive where many bees their honey bring,
> The sea to which a thousand rivers run,
> The garden where survives continual spring,
> The trophy hung with diverse painful hands,
> Abstract of knowledge, brief of eloquence,
> Aiding the weak, preserving him that stands,
> Guide to the soul and ruler of the sense,
> Such is this volume, and the freight hereof,
> However Ignorance presume to scoff.[16]

On 14 June 1600 Hathway with Munday, Drayton and Thomas Dekker furnished Henslowe with the script of the first part of 'The Fair Constance of Rome' for a full payment of forty-four shillings, and received an advance of twenty shillings to write a second part. Henslowe records an advance of forty shillings to Masters Rankins and Hathway on 3 January 1601 for 'a book called Hannibal and Scipio';[17] Hathway's receipt of the same date also appears: 'Received by us Richard Hathway and William Rankins in part of payment for the play of "Hannibal and Scipio" the sum of forty shillings'.[18] Also that year the duo produced 'The blind Beggar of Alexandria' featuring Henry VIII's clown Scoggins and the poet John Skelton as characters, against an advance of thirty shillings paid on 26 January, and further payment of forty shillings on 25 February and a final payment of eighteen shillings on 8 March.[19]

Sixteen days later Hathway was commissioned with Rankins to write 'a play called The Conquest of Spain' with an advance of ten shillings, was paid a further five shillings on 4 April, twenty shillings on 11 April and another four shillings on 16 April, all of which seems to indicate that he was delivering the play in dribs and drabs. This play was eventually rejected by the company: the entries relating to it in the 'diary' are cancelled. An undated letter to Henslowe from Samuel Rowley that can be found among the Alleyn MSS at Dulwich College throws a rather disturbing light on the situation:

M Henslowe, I pray you let Master Hathway have his papers again of the play of John of Gaunt and, for the repayment of the money back again, he is content to give you a bill of his hand to be paid at some certain time as in your discretion you shall think good. Which done you may cross it out of your book and keep the bill or else we'll stand so much indebted to you and keep the bill ourselves.[20]

Hathway had clearly been paid the money and spent it, for he was obviously unable to return it when the play was rejected. Henslowe must have been satisfied with his IOU for Hathway continued to write for the Admiral's Men, but then Henslowe was only too happy to keep his playwrights in debt to him, because it increased the pressure on them to produce playtexts on demand. In October

Henslowe paid advances totalling forty-three shillings for 'The Six Clothiers of the West', to Hathway, William Haughton and Wentworth Smith.[21] An undated entry in Hathway's hand records receipt of a payment 'in earnest' of forty shillings for a second part 'of the six clothiers'.[22] On 6 January 1602 Henslowe paid a first advance of fifty shillings to Hathway and Smith for 'Too Good to be True, or the Poor Northern Man', but by 7 January Henry Chettle had joined them for a further £3 10s in full payment.[23] On 17 November 1602, Hathway, Day and Smith received £6 in full payment for 'A Book called as Merry as May be'.[24] On 4 November 1602 Henslowe paid Hathway an advance of forty shillings for 'The Black Dog of Newgate', but a marginal note records it as 'John Day's Comedy' and the second payment of forty shillings is recorded as to Hathway, Day, Smith 'and the other poet'. A final payment of forty shillings was made on 20 December.[25] 'The Black Dog of Newgate', part 1, was acted by Worcester's Men in 1602, while 'The Boast of Billingsgate' on which Hathway worked with Day (for two payment of forty shillings) in March 1603 was played by the Admiral's Men.[26] Hathway seems to have had some part in 'The Fortunate General: a French History' acted by Worcester's Men that year, and worked with Day and Smith on a companion piece, 'The Unfortunate General', acted early in 1603. Henslowe records two payments of thirty shillings to Hathway and Smith 'in earnest' of a play he calls 'Unfortunate Generall French History' on 7 and 10 January 1603 and two more of forty shillings on 16 and 19 January to Hathway, Smith and Day for the same play.[27] We last hear of Richard Hathway, playwright, as one of the authors of the second part of 'The Black Dog of Newgate' with 'John Day and Master Smith and the other poet', for a total of £7 paid on 29 January and 3 February.

Then Hathway disappears from the record, annihilated possibly by the plague of 1604. He would not be the only kinsman of William Shakespeare who struggled to make a living in the London theatre and failed. What chills is the recollection that, in 1598, Francis Meres in *Wit's Treasury* had named Richard Hathway as one of the best comedy-writers of his day. Though he had a hand in no fewer than nineteen plays Hathway is nowadays utterly forgotten. Henslowe became a very wealthy man, while his writers toiled ceaselessly to avoid destitution and imprisonment for debt, often without success. In 1600 Henslowe was obliged to lend Hathway's colleague William Haughton ten shillings to secure his release from imprisonment in the Clink. Henry Chettle was continually in debt to Henslowe and in 1599 was imprisoned in the Marshalsea for debt. On 3 March 1607 he was so desperate for money that he pawned his playscript and gave Henslowe the pawn ticket instead.

A week before the Shakespeares were granted their special licence from the Consistory Court at Worcester, a similar licence was granted by the Bishop of London to the Curate of St Bartholomew near the Royal Exchange for the marriage of Richard Hathway of the parish of St Lawrence Jury, gentleman, and Ann Maddox of London, maiden, with only one announcing of the banns.[28] A gentleman who was of an age to marry in 1582 is frankly unlikely to have taken to writing for the stage sixteen years later, but in 1598 Meres wrote as if Hathway was already an established writer. It is not impossible, of course, that Richard Hathway, gentleman, came down in the world and was eventually forced to make use of his education in writing for the stage. This is after all what befell Robert Greene and Thomas Nashe. A good deal more work would have to be done tracing the Hathaways and their affines before we could rule out – or in – a connection of the Warwickshire Hathaways with the stage. What is curious is that most commentators are so convinced that the playwright Hathway could have no connection whatever with Shakespeare's wife that they do not trouble themselves to eliminate the possibility, which remains.

CHAPTER TWO

introducing the Shakespeare family, with particular attention to the Bard's mother and her role in the oft-told story of the downfall of John Shakespeare

Most accounts of Shakespeare's family concentrate on the catastrophic downhill career of his father, from its high point in 1568 when he was Bailiff of Stratford to its nadir when he was unable to put his nose outside the house for fear his creditors would seize his body in lieu of payment and drag him off to prison. In the reign of Elizabeth, if the existence of a debt had been proved in a court of law, and the debtor still refused payment, creditors had the right of summary arrest of the debtor who would languish in prison till he found someone who could pay what he owed or until he died, whichever happened sooner. This right was seldom exerted, because most people realised that a man in gaol can do little to satisfy his creditors. Even so, John Shakespeare spent years under virtual house arrest; having turned all his assets into ready cash, which sank into a morass of debt and defalcation, he had barely a house to hide his head in.

John Shakespeare's tortuous tale is well known; no one has ever looked at those events from the point of view of his wife. Studies of genius tell us that for gifted boys mothers are far more influential than fathers. Richard III explains the precociousness of the little Duke of York as the effect of his mother's influence.

> O, 'tis a parlous boy,
> Bold, quick, ingenious, forward, capable.
> He is all the mother's, from the top to toe.
> *Richard III*, III. i. 154–6

Mary Shakespeare was the person who taught the most eloquent Englishman who ever lived the use of his native tongue. The first metres Shakespeare ever heard were chanted by her. As a young woman her charm was sufficient to win her father's most valuable property, to the disadvantage of her seven elder sisters, but by 1582, when Ann Hathaway would have encountered her as a prospective mother-in-law, the bitterness of Mary's disappointment may well have eclipsed her charm.

In the 1550s when he first came a-wooing John Shakespeare seemed the ideal choice for an eventual paterfamilias. First and foremost he was a glover, a trade protected by law. The incorporation of Stratford in 1553 afforded local tradesmen great opportunities for accumulating power. By 1556 John Shakespeare was already one of two official ale-tasters, whose job it was to check not only that the ale and beer on sale were wholesome but also that loaves were the correct weight. In 1558 he was sworn one of the four constables responsible for law and order. The next year he took on the job of setting fines at the Court Leet, and soon after was elected a burgess. In 1561 he was elected one of two chamberlains who administered borough property and revenues, a job he held for years, even through the visitation of the plague in 1564, when he was elected alderman. John Shakespeare married late – he was past seventy when he died in 1601, and the earliest we can date his marriage is about 1557.[1] The bride he chose was Mary Arden, youngest daughter of his father's landlord in Snitterfield. Misogynist tradition can be relied upon to credit a mother with all the qualities that a wife lacks. Mary Shakespeare is therefore assumed to have been comely, virtuous and adoring. When she married John Shakespeare, Mary Arden was much younger than her husband, and, as her father's favourite, with a succession of older sisters to indulge her, she was probably spoiled rotten.

Though Mary Shakespeare's father, Robert Arden, described himself as a husbandman, he built up a considerable estate. To the freehold he inherited in Snitterfield, he added another that he acquired from the heirs of William Harvey, and latterly the lands brought to him by Agnes Hill, the young widow of John Hill of Bearley, whom he married in 1548. The relevant records of Arden's parish church, St John the Baptist in Aston Cantlow, have not survived, but we know from Arden's will that he had children by a former wife or wives; at the time of his death he had eight daughters of his own, and four rather younger stepchildren.[2] In 1550 (probably at the time of his marriage to Agnes Hill), Arden conveyed the house and land in Snitterfield to trustees; he and his wife were to have the use of it for their lives, whereafter it was to be divided among three of his married daughters, Joan Lambert, Agnes Stringer and Katherine Edkins.[3] Joan was married to Edmund Lambert and was living at Barton on the Heath (fifteen miles south of Stratford), where she would remain for the rest of her life. Her husband was buried at Barton in April 1587, and she in November 1593. Agnes Arden had been the widow of John Hewyns of Bearley when she married Thomas Stringer (also of Bearley) in October 1550. She died before 1569. Katherine Arden was married to Thomas Edkins of Wilmcote. The Harvey freehold was also placed in a trust to be divided in due course between three of his younger daughters, Margaret Webbe and Joyce and Alice Arden. Margaret was married to her father's brother-in-law, Alexander Webbe of Bearley.

The preamble of Robert Arden's will drawn up in November 1556, has been interpreted as an indication that the Snitterfield Ardens were Catholics.

> The document gives a picture of traditional rural society only a few years before William was born, and is thoroughly Catholic with its appeal to the Angels and the Virgin Mary 'and all the blessed company of saints'. Henry VIII's reformation had so far touched this part of Warwickshire only lightly. In keeping with most of her friends and neighbours, Mary Arden would have been brought up in a highly ritualised, old-fashioned English country Catholicism.[4]

This is part of Michael Wood's version of the elaborate argument that seeks to prove that Shakespeare was as Catholic as the pope. This 'part of Warwickshire' had in fact been transformed by 'Henry VIII's reformation'; the dissolution of the monasteries had destroyed a complex system of land tenure and ancient traditions of land use, leaving tithelands and many common pastures vulnerable to annexation by neighbouring landlords, and the poor unprotected. The Catholic college and guild of

Stratford had been replaced by a corporation in 1553; the Corporation was a closed oligarchy of sturdy protestants, into which no professed papist could dream of intruding. In 1559 the Corporation refused to pay the Vicar of Holy Trinity because of his popish practices; he retired to Wiltshire and for two years the cure lay vacant.[5] More important, as far as doctrine went, than 'Henry VIII's reformation' (which remained doctrinally incoherent) was the consolidation of the church under the clerics and the earnest reforming boy king, Edward VI. In 1556, however, everyone who was not prepared to play the heroic martyr was a Catholic. If the wording of Arden's will had been unusual, we might have to give it special significance, but in fact it is the formula in use in the third year of the reign of Bloody Mary. Suffice it to point out amid all the modish brouhaha about Shakespeare's Catholicism that John and Mary Shakespeare baptised all their children in Holy Trinity Church and all of them, bar one, were buried there. John may have been presented for failing to attend church, but the reason was understood at the time to be 'fear of processes', that is, fear of arrest for debt.[6]

Mary Arden, Robert Arden's youngest child, was left the estate in Wilmcote, which was called Asbyes, and 'the crop upon the ground sown and tilled as it is', as well as the traditional ten marks in cash for her dowry. Arden also appointed Mary one of his two executors, which was less 'a clear sign of her ability' than a response to the fact that she was present, whereas her elder sisters were either married or in service. As an executrix she was in a better position to carry out the precise provisions of the will despite any disgruntlement on the part of her in-laws. As we shall see, the Lamberts and the Webbes soon managed to reclaim the Wilmcote properties for themselves. It may be that the will was contrived this way because negotiations were already in hand for Mary's marriage with John Shakespeare; Shakespeare's acquisitions of freehold property in Stratford may also have been made with an eye to a marriage. In the same year that Arden made his will, Shakespeare bought a freehold 'garden and croft' in Greenhill Street and a house and garden in Henley Street, which became the Woolshop, the eastern part of the 'birthplace'.

Arden was relatively well off; after his death in 1556 his goods, which were valued at £77s 11s 10d, included oxen, bullocks, kine, weaning calves, horses, sheep, swine, poultry and bees, as well as 'the

bacon in the roof'. Agnes Arden remained at Wilmcote, where she
died in 1580. After Richard Shakespeare's death, the Webbes lived in
the house at Snitterfield having leased it from Agnes Arden in 1561.
When Alexander died in 1573, Margaret was made his executrix;
John Shakespeare and Agnes Arden's son John Hill were overseers of
Webbe's will and drew up his inventory. Margaret Webbe then
married a second husband, Edward Cornwell. Elizabeth would
eventually marry a man called Scarlett; she had a son John who
was old enough to sell his share of the land in Snitterfield to Robert
Webbe in March 1581, by which time Elizabeth was dead. In 1595
John Scarlett was head of a household of fifteen persons in Aston
Cantlow. The next to youngest daughters, Joyce and Alice Arden,
probably died unmarried, for their sisters eventually inherited their
reversionary rights in the Snitterfield estate.

If my interpretation of the coincidence of Robert Arden's legacy
and John Shakespeare's investment in property is correct, John
Shakespeare and Mary Arden were probably married in the church
of St John the Baptist in Aston Cantlow in the spring of 1557.
Nothing is known of the wooing of Mary Arden by the son of her
father's tenant, nor is there any indication of why the farmer's
daughter chose an artisan to marry rather than a farmer. If she had
the skills expected of a farmer's daughter, they would have stood her
in small stead when it came to helping her husband run his gloving
business. Perhaps it was Mary's dearest ambition to escape from the
tedium of the country into the bustle of the town. In town Mary
could dress to be seen and go gadding with her gossips. Emanuel van
Meteren wrote of city wives in the 1580s: 'They are well-dressed,
fond of taking it easy, and commonly leave the care of household
matters and drudgery to their servants. They sit before their doors,
decked out in fine clothes, in order to see and be seen by the passers-
by.' Their time was spent:

> walking and riding, in playing, at cards and otherwise, in visiting their
> friends and keeping company, conversing with their equals (whom
> they term gossips) and their neighbours, and in making merry with
> them at child-births, christenings, churchings and funerals; and all this
> with the permission of their husbands as such is the custom.[7]

Compared to the heavy workload shouldered by a farmer's wife, life as a glover's wife should have been easy. Instead of Mary's having to rise early to milk her cows or (more likely) ewes, milk, along with butter, cheese and eggs, would have been brought to her door. With alehouses and bakeries in every street, she had no need to brew or bake. When it was time to wash the beds, three or four times a year, the laundress would have come to collect the linen. In Stratford Mary would have seen her sisters and their families more often than if she had been living in the country, whenever they came in from Aston Cantlow or Snitterfield or Wilmcote to market and her country cousins would have been only too happy to accept a job in her household or the glover's shop if it meant living in town. When her husband became an alderman in 1565, Mary's happiness must have been complete. She had lost her first two children, Joan and Margaret, but her third, William, was a bonny boy who had survived the visitation of plague that raged for six months of the first year of his life.

The fact that John Shakespeare held high office in the Corporation has been treated as a sign of his success in business, when it was more probably the cause of his failure. Other Stratford businessmen did not share his eagerness for promotion and preferred to pay a fine rather than give their time and energy unpaid to the Corporation. William Smith, haberdasher and mercer, refused to take up the alderman's place vacated by John Shakespeare in 1586, and would not pay the fine of £3 6s 8d either.[8] Thomas Dixon alias Waterman, keeper of the Swan Inn, was sued in Chancery in 1571 for refusing to serve as an alderman and when he did accept an alderman's place in 1584 and was elected bailiff, he once again refused the office and incurred another fine.[9] Shakespeare's neighbour Abraham Sturley twice refused to serve on the Corporation.[10] John Shakespeare took on a succession of onerous public offices, and overstretched himself in business to the point of breaking; perhaps his courtship of his father's landlord's daughter is of a piece with the temerity that made him acquire freehold property before he had a wife, and to indulge in wool-dealing on a large scale rather than concentrating on his gloving business.

The marriage manuals warned men against marrying a woman richer and better connected than themselves on the ground that the

wife who had come down in the world would never rest easy but
would be constantly comparing her present state with what might
have been. The woman John Shakespeare chose for his wife was
proud of her descent from one of the oldest Warwickshire families,
the Ardens of Park Hall, but her pride seems misplaced, for no direct
relationship with the Arden Hall family can be traced. Mary Shakespeare may have been something of a social climber, goading her
husband to seek gentility rather than agreeing to work beside him at
his chosen trade.

Whittawing and glove-making was a smelly, messy business. When
glover William Hobday died in Stratford in December 1601, his
inventory included:

> 202 dozen of sheep's leather in the pits . . .
>   [that is, softening in a solution of dung or urine]
> 19 of bucks' leather in the pits . . .
> 16 calfskins in the pits . . .
> ten doeskins in the hair . . .
> six horsehides ready dressed . . .
> two dozen of deer's leather and 15 Irish skins
> 13 dozen of calves' leather ready dressed
> 104 dozen of sheep's leather and 104 dozen of lambs' leather ready
>   dressed
> five dozen and odd of sheep's leather that is tanned
> Half an hundred of sheep's leather in the alum and eight dozen of
>   lining with seventeen dogskins and other broken leather . . .[11]

Suppose that Mary gradually weaned Shakespeare off the whittawing
and glove-making business and encouraged him to deal in wool
instead, neither of them was experienced enough in commerce to
realise that the world was changing. The wool trade was gradually and
rather patchily coming under government control; stern punishments
would soon be meted out to traders who were found to have evaded
government regulation.

The Holy Trinity parish register shows the baptism of a 'Joan
Shakespeare daughter to John Shakespeare' on 15 September 1558. It
also shows another 'Joan the daughter of John Shakespeare' who was

baptised on 15 April 1569. The explanation usually given is that the older Joan must have died and her name been recycled for a later-born sister, as was not uncommon. But the burial of the older Joan does not appear in the register. Another explanation could be that there were two Joans born eleven years apart to two Johns, one of whom moved away. Further support for this view comes from the fact that the elder Joan's christening on 15 September 1558 is followed by a gap of more than four years in births to anyone called John Shakespeare. Margaret Shakespeare, christened on 2 December 1562, may have been our John Shakespeare's first-born child; she is followed by William in April 1564, Gilbert in October 1566, Joan in April 1569, Ann in September 1571, Richard in March 1574, and then a hiatus before Edmund in 1580. Six births in the first twelve years of marriage, with a seventh after six years, is a fairly typical reproductive career of the period, when lactation was the usual limiting factor, either because it depressed ovulation or because abstinence was practised while a mother was breast-feeding, or both. A longer interval, caused by the mother's declining fertility, is more likely to appear between the second-last and the last child than between the first and the second. If our suspicions about the two Joans are correct, Shake-speare's parents could have married at any time after Mary's father's death in November 1556 and before Margaret's birth at the end of November 1562. If Mary was of age when she proved her father's will in 1556 she must have been born in about 1540. She was thus only eighteen years older than her eldest son's wife, and she was at least ten years younger than her husband who was probably born before 1530, given the fact that he became a householder in 1552.

We can only imagine Mary's terror for her newborn son William when, within two months of his birth, plague broke out in Stratford and raged until the end of the year. Somehow the Shakespeare family escaped the mortality. What followed seems to have been a happy time, as John Shakespeare's affairs prospered and he rose steadily through the ranks of the Corporation. In 1568 he was elected to the highest office, that of bailiff. With it came the rank of justice of the peace, with the task of issuing warrants, investigating and deciding cases of debt and violation of by-laws, and negotiating with the lord of the manor. He was also almoner, coroner, escheater and clerk of the market. In Dekker's play, *The Shoemakers' Holiday*, when Simon Eyre becomes Sheriff of London, he gives up shoe-making, saying to his wife:

> See here, my Maggy, a chain, a gold chain for Simon Eyre. I shall make thee a lady. Here's a French hood for thee. On with it! On with it! Dress thy brows with this flap of a shoulder of mutton to make thee look lovely. Where be my fine men? Roger, I'll make over my shop and tools to thee. Firke, thou shalt be the foreman. Hans, thou shalt have an hundred for twenty . . . How dost thou like me, Marjorie? Prince am I none, yet I am princely borne . . .[12]

When it was John Shakespeare's turn to step down as bailiff, he went on giving his time to the Corporation, serving as deputy to the new bailiff. In January 1572 he rode with him to London on Corporation business, which suggests that he was not spending much time in his glover's shop.

Perhaps because he had borrowed money to purchase the freeholds that were part of his marriage settlement, John Shakespeare put himself under pressure to make money fast. In his eagerness he cut too many corners. In 1570 he was prosecuted for usury because he had illegally lent two sums, £80 and £100, at a swingeing £20 interest in each case. In 1572, on information supplied by a criminal and professional informer called John Langrake, John Shakespeare was prosecuted for dealing in wool. As a whittawer, who bought sheep-skins to whiten and soften for sewing, he also had access to fleeces, which he had been storing in his woolshop and selling on for twenty years. By 1572 he had built up a considerable business, unmindful of the fact that, as dealing in wool was the monopoly of the Merchants of the Staple, he had been trading illegally. He was charged with buying two and a half tons of wool in Westminster for £140 and a ton and a quarter in Snitterfield at the same rate. Three of the four charges remained unproven − but the cumulative effect of the prosecution and subsequent process on John Shakespeare's business career was to be disastrous. Wool shortages in the 1570s had led to a suspicion that illegal traders were buying up the clips and withholding them from the market until prices rose. In October 1576 the Privy Council called all wool brokers to testify before it, with the result that in November all dealing in wool was suspended. Traders identified as illegal were ordered to post bonds of £100 as surety against any further infringement of the law. John Shakespeare was ruined.

If Mary Shakespeare had been an astute businesswoman she might have been able to slow down or even halt John Shakespeare's downhill career. In all discussions of the woeful succession of court cases, fines, defaultings and confusion that is John Shakespeare's professional history, he is treated as a lone man, because most scholars have assumed that in the late sixteenth century wives played no part in the family business. An Elizabethan wife was first and foremost a helpmeet.

> The realm of work was . . . divided into two parts. What the man did was definite, well-defined, limited – let's call it A. What the woman did was everything else – non-A. So the realm of work was divided without residue . . . According to this, for example, if a man was a glover, his work was clearly defined and anything else that had to be done to keep the home fires burning was his wife's duty. If he became ill, and could do less and less, then she must do more and more, supervising the apprentices, seeing that the orders were fulfilled; or even by some employment, like taking in washing, she must supplement a failing business.[13]

Deloney gives an example in his tale of a draper whose business failed.

> Thus lay the poor draper a long time in prison, in which space, his wife which for daintiness would not foul her fingers, or turn her head aside for fear of hurting the set of her neckerchief, was glad to go about and wash bucks at the Thames side, and to be a char-woman in rich men's houses, her soft hand now hardened with scouring and, instead of gold rings on her lily-white fingers, they were now filled with chaps, provoked by the sharp, lye, and other drudgeries.[14]

The Stratford mercer Richard Quiney was in London on Corporation business for most of the autumn of 1598. His father wrote to him on 20 October: 'Your wife [is] careful and maketh all means she can to satisfy both your credits.'[15] In fact Bess Quiney was sending her husband goods to sell, twenty and thirty pounds of cheeses, large and small, at a time, and tobacco, as well as homemade foods for himself. She was also borrowing and lending money, and managing her rental property. On 18 November Quiney's colleague Abraham Sturley wrote:

> Also she would have you buy some raisins, currants, pepper, sugar and some other groceries if the price be reasonable and that you may have carriage reasonable . . . I wish you to remember you shall receive from your wife by Greenaway [the carrier] 12d. She has been selling wheat and malt and by borrowing discharged Mr Coles, Shaw and others and is very careful for to pay her borrowed money. She hath 7d but 20 shillings of Mr Parsons also she hopeth that my Lady Greville hath writ to Sir Edward concerning the £20 which he hopeth Sir Edward hath allowed you.[16]

In Stratford cash was always in short supply. Nobody took the risk of carrying cash between Stratford and London; instead Stratford merchants usually bought from London merchants on credit that was reciprocated for London merchants in Stratford. Bess Quiney regularly ran out of ready money and had to borrow, and her husband did too. The difference was that they never borrowed more than they knew they could repay. John Shakespeare's situation would perhaps have been less grave if, while he was working unpaid for the Corporation, Mary had been running the gloving business, filling his orders, organising the preparing of skins and the manufacture and delivery of gloves, and keeping his accounts. If she had been playing her part, it's hard to believe that John Shakespeare could have so overstretched himself as to lose everything, including the estate she brought him. It looks very much as if, in John Shakespeare's case, nobody was minding the shop. It may have been Mary's distaste for the messy manual labour of gloving and whittawing that convinced John to earn more money faster and less filthily by dealing in wool. All the other successful businessmen in Stratford hedged their investments by diversifying, but they were careful not to neglect their core business.

Mary was certainly pregnant half the time and feeding an infant the other half, but so were all the other Stratford wives who had to run the family business when the goodman was away, including Bess Quiney. Mary may have been delicate and have struggled through her pregnancies, but the record does not support such an impression. Either Mary endured eight pregnancies over twenty-four years, or, if we discount the earlier Joan, seven pregnancies over nineteen years for five surviving children. The two who died did not die in the perinatal period; Margaret died at five months old and Ann just before her eighth birthday. As reproductive careers go, this is less intensive and shorter than most. Ann Shakespeare's friend Judith Sadler was to endure fourteen pregnancies over twenty-four years and only seven of her babies lived beyond infancy. If Mary Shakespeare did not assist her husband in the management of his affairs it was not pregnancy and childbirth that impeded her, nor yet ill health.

In 1572 John Shakespeare brought an action in the Court of Common Pleas in Westminster against a glover in Banbury who owed him £50, and won for once. When he and another were then sued by one Henry Higford of Solihull for defaulting on repayment of a loan and found liable for £30, they were unable to pay. The debt was still outstanding in 1578. Such ducking and diving may have been typical of an emerging merchant class that bought cheap often on credit and bided its time before selling dear. John Shakespeare's brother Henry was another who was extremely slow to pay his debts and he died a relatively wealthy man, but John Shakespeare was sailing far too close to the wind. By 1577 he was staying away from meetings of the council of aldermen. When the council agreed to a levy to pay for equipping soldiers, they assessed Alderman Shakespeare at a mere burgess's rate of three shillings and four pence. More than a year later he still hadn't paid it.[17] In 1578 he incurred a fine by failing to show up for the vote on election day but was excused payment.[18] When it was agreed that all the aldermen should pay four pence towards poor relief, he was excused again.[19] Everybody knew he was broke.

The presumption that Will stayed at school until he was fifteen is simply that, a presumption. The records of the King's New School of Stratford-upon-Avon have not survived. Schoenbaum's 'reasonable

enough supposition that William was apprenticed in his father's shop'
after he left school is not as reasonable as it might seem.[20] There was
little point in giving a boy a grammar school education if the ultimate
intention was to apprentice him to a manual trade. Will was unlikely
to have been apprenticed to his father, because the master was
expected to exercise a degree of rigour in dealing with his apprentices
that was incompatible with fatherly feeling. Apprentices were often
whipped or beaten; it would not have done for the child's mother to
be a witness to such correction. It seems moreover that in 1579, when
his son was fifteen, John Shakespeare, being a defaulting debtor, was
in no position to take an apprentice. If Will had been apprenticed to a
fellow glover, he would have been indentured for seven years, during
which time he was not free to pay his addresses to any woman. As a
junior apprentice he would have been held to a full-time regimen of
menial tasks and could not have been wandering off to Shottery
whenever he felt like it – supposing his father had been able to find
him a master in Stratford and had had the cash needed to pay for the
indentures and for his board and lodging, which he probably didn't.
There is never any suggestion at any point in the Shakespeare family
history of Mary's participation in deciding her children's futures.
What is odd is that there appear to have been no decisions made. The
family seems to have been left to drift.

In 1576 or so, with his world crashing round his ears, John
Shakespeare made an application for a grant of arms. He had been
Master Shakespeare ever since his election as an alderman, but this did
not entitle his wife to the title Mistress, which as a descendant of the
Park Hall Ardens she may have believed she deserved. One of Mary's
motives for urging Shakespeare to put so much time into working for
the Corporation could have been her awareness that, according to the
experts,

> If any person be advanced into an office or dignity of public admin-
> istration, be it either ecclesiastical, martial or civil, the herald must not
> refuse to devise to such a public person, upon his instant request, and
> willingness to bear the same without reproach, a coat of arms, and
> thenceforth to matriculate him, with his intermarriages and issues
> descending, in the register of the gentle and noble.[21]

Though this first attempt was abandoned, Robert Cook, the Clar-
enceux King of Arms, drew a paper 'pattern' or sketch of the
Shakespeare coat which would show a spear of gold 'steeled argent'
on a bend sable on a field of gold; the crest was a silver falcon gentle
'displayed', that is, with wings spread, holding a spear or on a wreath
of gold plaited with sable. A copy of the paper sketch was probably to
be seen somewhere in the house at Henley Street, while the children
were regularly regaled with tales of the Shakespeares' 'valiant service'
under Henry VII, and how closely they were related to the grand
Ardens of Park Hall. The more desperate their circumstances, the
more Mary would have clung to her dream of gentility.

Mary would have been feeling dark enough in November 1578
when her husband was obliged to mortgage part of her inheritance,
the house and fifty-six acres of land in Wilmcote, without the galling
awareness that the person who lent them the £40 on the property was
her eldest sister's husband, Edmund Lambert. As Lambert and Edward
Cornwell, Mary's sister Margaret's second husband, had already gone
surety for Shakespeare for £5 borrowed from Roger Sadler, which he
had failed to repay, Lambert was probably confident that when the
repayment date came around Shakespeare would default, the property would be forfeit and he, Lambert, would remain in possession. At
the same time the Shakespeares conveyed another eighty-six acres to
associates of Robert Webbe, son of another of Mary's sisters, for a set
period after which it was to be returned for the use of the heirs of
Mary's body. In 1579 the Shakespeares also surrendered their ninth
part of the two houses and a hundred acres in Snitterfield, which they
sold to Robert Webbe for £4.

At Michaelmas 1580 Shakespeare failed to repay the £40 borrowed
on Asbyes and the Lamberts remained in possession. It was tough
enough for Mary to realise that her inheritance was all but gone,
without the knowledge that the £40 raised from the mortgage had
disappeared as well when the Court of Queen's Bench fined Shakespeare the huge sum of £20 for failing to appear to find security for
keeping the Queen's Peace, and then made him pay up another £20
when two men for whom he had gone surety failed to appear.[22] John
Shakespeare may have been unwise in both his borrowings and his
lendings, but in normal times he would have got away with it. What

made the difference was that by 1580 the midlands were sliding into
economic recession. The most likely cause of John Shakespeare's
inability to pay his debts was that his clients had defaulted on debts
owed to him; clearly his colleagues still considered him an honourable
man, for they gave him every chance to recover, and did not remove
him from the list of aldermen and elect another in his place until
September 1586. This by the way is proof, if proof were needed, that
John Shakespeare was not a Catholic but a full member of the
reformist brotherhood. No tolerance whatever was extended by
the Corporation to papists who defaulted.

Six or seven years before Mary needed to begin worrying about
having no property to offer with a son in hopes of making a good
match, Will pre-empted her by impregnating Ann Hathaway and
marrying her forthwith. William's marriage was probably felt by Mary
as a severe blow. She and her children were slipping in the world, as
her sisters' families prospered, some of them at her expense. In 1587
Edmund Lambert died, still in possession of Asbyes. John then
embarked on legal action, not to recover the property from the heir,
John Lambert, but for an additional £20 which he said had been
promised him in return for delivery of unencumbered title. The
unpleasantness would drag on almost to the end of his life; in 1597 the
case was heard in Chancery, and again in 1599. Such legal action was
costly, not only in money (for both sides) but also in ill feeling.

Marriage was far from universal in Elizabethan England but, even
so, the Shakespeares' making no attempt to find a wife for any one of
three boys, especially after their son and heir had made what might be
regarded as an unsuitable match, is peculiar. Gilbert would have
attained his majority in October 1587; unless his father really and truly
had no money whatsoever Gilbert must have been a worthwhile
marriage prospect for someone. If Mary had been on good terms with
her sisters and their progeny, she would have had hundreds of possible
candidates from whom to choose a likely girl for her boys. If on the
other hand her sisters and their husbands regarded John Shakespeare as
a jumped-up wastrel who had impoverished his wife and children,
they would have been reluctant to match any of their daughters or
nieces with any of his sons. Mary Shakespeare was to find wives for
none of her sons; her daughter was left to find a husband for herself.

Most of Shakespeare's heroes and heroines are motherless. The few mothers who do appear in Shakespeare's plays are anything but motherly, from the cannibal mother Tamora in *Titus Andronicus* to the neurotically affected mother of Juliet, the mother of Richard III who curses her womb and the Countess of Rossillion in *All's Well* who simply dislikes her son. At best mothers are ineffectual, like Queen Elizabeth in *Richard III*, Lady Faulconbridge in *King John* and Lady Macduff, and at worst depraved, like Gertrude and Lady Macbeth.

CHAPTER THREE

of Ann Hathaway's looks and demeanour, of age at marriage in the 1580s, the courtship of older women by younger men and whether Shakespeare's wife could read

We know from the stone over Ann Shakespeare's grave that she was born eight years before her husband. What we shall never know is how or when she and Shakespeare met, though we do know that their parents had known each other since the 1550s. It is assumed that she was the mover in the courtship, simply because she was older. To Katherine Duncan-Jones,

> it seems more likely that her father's death left the unmarried Agnes or Anne . . . without much parental care or control, and as a mature and spirited country girl she exploited her freedom to consort with the local youth. A combination of boredom with the sexual curiosity natural to his years led to Shakespeare's dalliance with her, and to what was probably his first experience of sex.

For some reason Duncan-Jones chooses to exaggerate Shakespeare's immaturity: 'In the early modern period puberty occurred, on average, four or five years later than it does today. Some boys of eighteen or nineteen were still able to sing treble.' There is, of course, no reason to believe that Shakespeare's vocal cords were undeveloped or that the boys she refers to were not singing falsetto. Will did impregnate Ann after all, and, according to Duncan-Jones, in very short order. 'Ann was unlike many young women of her age not only in being unmarried, but also in being to some extent free and independent.'[1]

Ann was also like many young women of her age in being unmarried. About 20 per cent of her female contemporaries would die without ever having been married, so spinsters of twenty-six were not at all rare. Unmarried women over the age of twenty-one were all 'free', in the sense that they could earn money and keep or spend it as they chose, as married women could not, and they could marry without waiting on their parents' wishes. In Elizabethan England there were probably more women over the age of twenty-one who were fatherless than whose fathers were still living. As for the suggestion that Ann was 'to some extent . . . independent', she could have been a girl of independent means, if property had been entailed on her by her mother's family, but such an arrangement would have left a paper trail that has yet to be discovered.

Even if Ann did have some property of her own, as a husbandman's daughter she would not have been expected to pass her life in idleness. As small children she and her brother would have been sent into the fields to scare away birds from the crops, and perhaps even to pick stones out of the soil. At an early age she would have learnt how to milk her father's ewes –

> Each shepherd's daughter with her cleanly pail
> Has come afield to milk the morning meal.[2]

What the family did not drink for breakfast, together with what she milked in the evening every day from April to October, would have been fermented until it separated to curds and whey. The whey was the family's usual drink; the curds were made into cheeses, soft for immediate consumption and hard for keeping.

Before 1534 the making of hard cheeses was done in the cool vaults of the monasteries; after the dissolution farmers took over the cheese-making themselves with rather variable results. In the 1580s cows were still a relative rarity in Warwickshire compared to sheep, but Ann may well have had a cow or two to take care of. Though the herding of the animals was mostly men's work, women could do it at a pinch. Milking and the preparation of milk products on the other hand was exclusively women's work. Ewes the milkmaid could handle by herself; if she was dealing with a cow, she needed a cowherd to hold the halter to control the beast. Women also looked after the smaller creatures, the chickens, ducks and geese.

> My love can milk a cow
> And teach a calf to suck
> And knows the manner how
> To set a brooded duck[3]

Most of Hathaway's neighbours would have fattened a pig or two each year on skim milk, root vegetables and the acorns and chestnuts of the woodlands and commons. If the jobs connected to her home farm were covered, a girl was as likely as a boy to be placed out to service on someone else's farm. For all we know Ann never lived at the house in Shottery, for she could have been placed in service as a girl of six or seven. It is only in the halcyon imagination of bardolaters that Ann could have sat around for twenty-six years waiting for a boy to set her cap at.

One very heavy task that always fell to women was laundry. The bigger the family, the more babies to appear, the heavier the work. Washing was not done weekly, because the linen took too long to dry. It was mostly, though not only, in the summer that smocks and sheets, bed- and childbed-linen were washed and thrown over bushes and on to the grass to bleach in the sun. Farmer's daughters were dressed in a fashion that displayed their industry and expertise. While women of higher rank, citizens' and merchants' wives, wore heavy gowns of dark coloured stuffs, the milkmaids dressed in white shifts, under skirts of red flannel or sheep's russet, and stiff waistcoats of buckram or durance, scrubbed dazzling white, with a white neck-erchief or scarf under a broad-brimmed straw hat.

> Upon her back she wore
> A fustian waistcoat white.
> Her body and her stomacher
> Were fastened very tight . . .
> Her neckerchief of Holland sure . . .[4]

In *Greene's Vision*, Tomkins the wheelwright falls in love with a 'maid that every day went to sell cream in Cambridge'.

A bonny lass she was, very well tucked up in a russet petticoat, with a bare hem and no fringe, yet has she a red lace and a stomacher of tuft mockado and a partlet cast over with a pretty whip, and dressed she was in a kerchief of holland for her father was a farmer. Her girdle was green, and at that hung a large leather purse with fair threaden tassels, and a new pair of yellow gloves, tufted with red raw silk very richly . . .[5]

Milkmaids were stout and straight, strong enough to carry two bulky wooden pails suspended from a yoke across their shoulders, and sure-footed enough not to slop the precious milk out of the pails as they travelled over the uneven ground. Spilt milk was a disaster, and milkmaids wept piteously over it, afraid of being beaten.[6] In the long days of summer, when all her morning chores were done, the farmer's daughter could drive her cows and sheep to pasture, and lie with her gossips in the deep grass, watching her animals graze, singing songs and telling stories to pass the lazy time till the next milking.

> Oh the wench went neatly,
>   Methought it did me good
> To see her cheery cheeks
>   So dimpled o'er with blood,
> Her waistcoat washèd white
>   As any lily-flower.
> Would I had time to talk to her
>   The space of half an hour.[7]

Supposing Ann was living at Hewlands at the time of her father's death, it was up to her stepmother whether she remained working there as an unpaid family- and farm-servant or left home to work elsewhere. As she and Shakespeare were not married in Stratford, and marriages generally took place in the parish where the bride was resident, it seems likely that at the time of her wedding Ann was not living in Shottery. Some commentators think that she had decamped to Temple Grafton. Perhaps she had found work in a Gardner household or with kin of her mother's in another parish.

Most versions of what befell William go more or less like this: 'Sometime that August, after wandering the mile or so west down the rural footpath to the tiny village of Shottery, the worldly eighteen-year-old committed an indiscretion that would profoundly affect the rest of his life. Was it a careless roll in the hay . . .?'[8] As we have seen the Shakespeares and the Hathaways knew each other, so there is no need to suppose that one day, quite by chance, Shakespeare wandered too close to Shottery and got snared by 'a homely wench'. Ann was no wench; even if she had been in service, she would have been employed at a higher rate than a mere wench. Landholders were of higher status than glove-makers, especially glove-makers who were broke and had lost their own land. How hard is it to believe that eighteen-year-old Shakespeare was so enamoured of a twenty-six-year-old that he wooed her and ultimately won her? As an elder sister Ann probably spent much of her time looking after her younger siblings. When she walked the Hewlands cows to Shottery common, the younger children would have come with her to play on the green under her watchful eye, as she and the other Shottery girls sang and dittied through their favourite ballads.

> The lark that tirra-lirra chants,
>   With hey! with hey! the thrush and the jay,
> Are summer songs for me and my aunts
>   While we lie tumbling in the hay.[9]

If Ann wasn't living in or near Stratford from September 1581 till after her marriage, the roll-in-the-hay hypothesis becomes more difficult to sustain. Still, a boy may walk many a long mile in search of somewhere to sow a wild oat. As for the suggestion that Ann was hanging around Stratford 'consorting with the local youth', if she had behaved in such a way in a God-fearing rural town like Stratford with a population of less than 2,000 she would have found herself up before the Vicar's Court in less time than it takes to sow a wild oat. If any such baggage had attempted to embroil Alderman Shakespeare's son, his friends on the Corporation would have run her out of town. A good deal of effort was expended by the Corporation in ridding the town of women of ill repute. When Richard Quiney was sworn in as Bailiff of Stratford in 1592, one of his first acts was to appoint a committee 'to discover and notify the presence, with a view to their removal from the borough, of undesirable women'.[10]

The lament of the maiden for whom no husband has been found by parents or friends is a cliché of ballad literature, as for example in *I can, I will no longer lie alone* (1612–13).

> 'Tis my cruel friends have me o'erthrown . . .

> What though my parents strive to procure
> That I should a maiden still endure?
> Do they what they will, I must have one.
> I can nor will no longer lie alone.[11]

At twenty-six Ann Hathaway is thought to have been just such a caricature, desperate for a husband, any husband.

> A blithe and bonny country lass . . .
> Sat sighing on the tender grass
>   And weeping said, 'Will none come woo me?'
> A smicker boy, a lither swain . . .
> That in his love was wanton fain
>   with smiling looks came straight unto her.

> Whenas the wanton wench espied . . .
> The means to make herself a bride,
>   she simpered smooth like bonny bell.
> The swain that saw her squint-eyed kind . . .
> His arms about her body twined,
>   and said 'Fair lass, how fare ye? Well?'

> The country-kit said, 'Well, forsooth . . .
> But that I have a longing tooth,
>   a longing tooth that makes me cry.'
> 'Alas,' said he, 'What garrs thy grief?' . . .
> 'A wound,' quoth she, 'without relief.
>   I fear a maid that I shall die.'

'If that be all,' the shepherd said . . .

'I'll make thee wive it, gentle maid,

   and so recure thy malady.'

Hereon they kissed with many an oath . . .

And 'fore God Pan did plight their troth,

   and so to the church apace they hie.[12]

In this ballad, 'Coridon's Song', by Thomas Lodge, published in *England's Helicon* (1600), responsibility for the clapped-up marriage is equally distributed between the needy maid and the opportunistic boy. Post-Victorian commentators are not so even-handed; the presumed mismatch between Ann and Will is seen as entirely down to Ann, who is taken to have been well past her sell-by date, because the received wisdom was that early modern Englishwomen married in their early teens. When Peter Laslett published his ground-breaking work *The World We Have Lost* in 1965 it contained many surprises, not least of which was the age at which Elizabethans married: 'We have examined every record we can find . . . and they all declare that, in Elizabethan and Jacobean England, marriage was rare at these early ages and not as common in the late teens as it is now.'[13]

What Laslett and the Cambridge Group found when they examined a thousand licences issued by the Diocese of Canterbury between 1619 and 1660 was that the commonest age of brides was twenty-two, and the average mean age even higher, twenty-four. Further research has come up with a mean age at marriage of twenty-six or -seven for early modern Englishwomen and twenty-eight for men.[14] What was remarkable about Ann Hathaway's wedding is not that at twenty-six she was so old, but that her husband was so young. As Laslett's researchers found of their original thousand cases, 'Only ten men married below the age of 20, two of them at 18, and the most common age was 24 . . .'[15]

The mating of younger men with older women, though unusual, occasioned no outrage in the sixteenth century. Indeed, for apprentices, far from their families, kept on hard rations and often beaten, marrying the master's widow was the kind of dream-wish that fuelled many ballads and popular romances.[16] In Part II of Thomas Deloney's *The Gentle Craft* we find an elaborated tale of the Widow Farmer's love for William, the most menial of her servants. William has dared

to woo his mistress quite aggressively and has been demoted to the
scullery for his pains, a punishment which he bears in good part
because he truly loves her. Widow Farmer invites her friends and
suitors to dinner. All her other menservants are called to the table,
only to be dismissed for their cockiness and insolence when they
refuse the menial job of fetching the oysters. Up from the scullery
with the oysters comes William in his greasy work clothes. Widow
Farmer takes his grubby hand in hers, kisses him and presents him to
the company as her chosen husband.

> Then did she set her black man by her white side and, calling the rest of
> her servants (in the sight of her friends) she made them do reverence
> unto him, whom they for his drudgery scorned so much before. So,
> the breakfast ended, she willed them all next morning to bear him
> company to the church, against which time William was so daintily
> tricked up, that all those which beheld him confessed he was a most
> comely, trim and proper man, and after they were married, they lived
> long together in joy and prosperous estate.[17]

In another of Deloney's novellas, *Jack of Newbury*, Jack begins life as
John, servant to a wealthy widow who is being courted by three men of
substance. She tells John that she loves another, who is none of the three,
and he advises her: 'For your body's health, your heart's joy and your
ears' delight, delay not the time, but entertain him with a kiss, make his
bed next yours and chop up the match in the morning.'[18] The widow,
piqued, responds that if he had announced to her that he wanted to
marry, she would not be so indifferent. He gives the answer that Will
might have given if Ann had directly or indirectly proposed to him:

> It is not wisdom for a young man that can scantly keep himself to take a
> wife; therefore I hold it the best way to lead a single life, for I have
> heard say that many sorrows follow marriage, especially where want
> remains, and beside, it is a hard matter to find a constant woman, for as
> young maids are fickle, so are old women jealous.[19]

Winter comes and with it a hard frost; the widow sups with John
and gives him sack to drink; then she puts him to bed in his master's

feather bed, slips in beside him and stays all night. In the morning she bids him fetch a link and light her way to the chapel, where she is to meet a bridegroom. As he stands with her in the winter-dark chapel John realises that the expected bridegroom is none other than himself. The widow gently reminds him: 'Stand not strangely, but remember that you did promise me on your faith not to hinder me when I came to the church to be married, but rather to set it forward: therefore set your link aside and give me your hand'.[20] After some only-to-be-expected vicissitudes, 'they lived long together in most godly, loving and kind sort, till in the end she died, leaving her husband wondrous wealthy'. Sir Sidney Lee might be shocked by the widow's forward behaviour but Shakespeare and his contemporaries were by no means so hidebound. The extraordinary career of theatrical impresario Philip Henslowe was made possible only by his marrying in 1577 the widow of the Earl of Montague's bailiff, whose servant he had been.[21]

In *The Two Gentlemen of Verona* we do not know how old Silvia is, or how young Valentine might be, but we do know that Silvia, besides being Valentine's social superior, is maturer and wiser than he, whether she is chronologically older or not. As even his servant Speed can figure out, Sylvia teaches Valentine how to woo her.

> My master sues to her, and she hath taught her suitor,
> He being her pupil, to become her tutor . . .
> Herself hath taught her love himself to write unto her lover.
>
> (II. i. 129–30, 158)

Rosalind too, in *As You Like It*, undertakes to teach the boy Orlando how to love her.

In *Twelfth Night*, the 'youth' Cesario is sent to woo 'a virtuous maid, the daughter of a count that died some twelvemonth since'. Orsino assumes that because Cesario is a boy he will succeed in his suit where his own has failed.

> She will attend it better in thy youth
> Than in a nuncio's of more grave aspect . . .
> For they shall yet belie thy happy years
> That say thou art a man. Dian's lip

Is not more smooth and rubious. Thy small pipe
Is as the maiden's organ, shrill and sound . . . (I. iv. 27–8, 30–3)

When Cesario makes a disturbance at her gate Olivia asks her
majordomo: 'Of what personage and years is he?' (I. v. 150). And
Malvolio makes answer:

Not yet old enough for a man, nor young enough for a boy. As a
squash is before 'tis a peascod, or a codling when 'tis almost an apple.
'Tis with him in standing-water, between boy and man. He is very
well-favoured, and he speaks very shrewishly. One would think his
mother's milk were scarce out of him. (151–6)

The supposed boy achieves access where no man could, but there is
nothing bashful in his suit. He describes what he would do to win
Olivia from her obduracy.

Make me a willow cabin at your gate,
And call upon my soul within the house.
Write loyal cantons of contemnèd love,
And sing them loud even in the dead of night.
Halloo your name to the reverberate hills,
And make the babbling gossip of the air
Cry out, 'Olivia'! (I. v. 257–63)

Though Olivia doesn't marry her original boy lover, who is a girl in
disguise, she does marry her twin Sebastian who can be no older than
she. There is no good reason to suppose that William wooed Ann
after Cesario's fashion; the most we can conclude from the evidence
of *Twelfth Night* is that the idea of a youth seducing a woman in
mourning didn't paralyse him with horror or drown him in bitter
reflection.

Scholars desirous of separating Shakespeare from his pesky wife
have taken for granted that all her life she could neither read nor
write. They want her, need her to have had no inkling of the
magnitude of her husband's achievement.

Of course most of the women in his world had little or no literacy, but the commonness of the condition does not change the fact: it is entirely possible that Shakespeare's wife never read a word that he wrote, that anything he sent her from London had to be read by a neighbour and that anything she wished to tell him – the local gossip, the health of his parents, the mortal illness of their only son – had to be consigned to a messenger.[22]

Greenblatt can see no one to help Ann keep in touch with her husband beyond an Elizabethan version of a courier service. He imagines that any letter of Shakespeare's would have to have been read by a 'neighbour'. If Shakespeare wrote at all, he would have written as Richard Quiney did, to a kinsman or a close friend, who had the duty of reading the letter to his wife and of penning her response. Abraham Sturley used to sign himself off to Quiney as writing 'at your own table in your own house', with Elizabeth Quiney beside him, virtually dictating what he was to write.[23] At least one of Shakespeare's brothers was fully literate and should have kept Shakespeare informed of the health of his parents. Ann's brother could read and write, as could her elder daughter Susanna.[24] Ann did not have to depend on the kindness of strangers or on professional messengers, who did not exist. Early modern letters were not private, but designed to be read aloud, in company. Truly intimate matters were deemed unsuitable for a letter.

Certainly it is possible, even entirely possible, that Ann could not read. It is also possible, given the absolute absence of evidence to the contrary, that she was blind. She may have been illiterate when Shakespeare met her, and he may have spent the long hours with her as she watched her cows grazing on the common, teaching her to read. In his plays he is very well aware of the erotic dimension of the teaching situation, whether it's Henry teaching Katharine English, or Rosalind teaching Orlando how to make love.

Ann's staunchly protestant family would have had her taught to read if only so that she could read her Bible every day. Without a growing passion for reading the Reformation could never have happened. Catholics thought the way to salvation lay through ritual and prayer; protestants put their faith in a book. By the 1580s people who couldn't read were sensible of a spiritual as well as a social disadvantage. In the winter, when there was little or no work for children in the fields, even the humblest farming villages would set up a dame school, where a woman who could read would teach children who couldn't. The Bible Ann read was probably the Geneva Bible, small in format, low in cost and aggressively marketed up and down the country.[25]

In early modern England most of the people who could read were unable to write. Until the study of literacy began in earnest in the 1960s it was generally assumed that only men who had attended a grammar school were able to read or write, and that everyone else bar a few privately educated ladies could do neither. Then to her surprise Margaret Spufford began to come across evidence of pedlars selling 'little books' up and down the country. She also found the observations of a Jesuit in gaol in Wisbech in the 1580s and 1590s who looked on horrified as large groups of puritans read aloud from their Geneva Bibles: 'Each of them had his own Bible, and sedulously turned the pages and looked up the text cited by the preachers, discussing the passages among themselves to see whether they had quoted them to the point, and accurately, and in harmony with their tenets.'[26] Thomas Daynes, Vicar of Flixton in Suffolk, was disgusted to see that his parishioners brought their copies of the Book of Common Prayer to church with them, and instead of listening to his puritan harangues went on 'looking in their books'.[27]

David Cressy found a sharp rise in the number of schoolmasters listed by visitations in rural Essex and Hertfordshire from 1580 to 1592.[28] One fifth of the villages in Cambridgeshire had a schoolmaster licensed continuously from 1570 to 1620 but the provision of teaching varied enormously from county to county and even parish to parish. In some places farmers clubbed together and pooled their resources to endow a local school.

Between 1580 and 1700, 11 per cent of women, 15 per cent of labourers and 21 per cent of husbandmen, could sign their names, against 56 per cent of tradesmen and craftsmen, and 65 per cent of yeomen . . . There was . . . 'general and substantial progress in reducing illiteracy' among all social groups except labourers in the late sixteenth century . . .[29]

In the dame schools girls were taught to read and sew, knit and spin, boys to read, write and cast accounts. We have no idea how many dame schools there were in England in the early modern period but there must have been many more than there were schools where boys were taught by graduates. When Christ's Hospital was founded in 1552, girls as well as boys were admitted; the girls would be taught to read and sew but not to write. Reading was essential if women were to follow their daily devotions, reading the approved verses of the Bible and the psalms allotted for the day; sewing provided for the woman and her family.

Claire Cross, working on the spread of Lollardism in the early sixteenth century, was vividly aware of the importance of women in the process.

> It may be that considerably more women than the churchmen suspected acquired the ability to read in order to peruse Lollard books. Certainly a reverence for books characterizes women in a majority of communities, and in several, Lollard women took a major part in organizing book distribution. As mothers and grandmothers they had unique authority over impressionable children, and far more women than have been recorded may have been responsible for helping educate succeeding generations in heresy.[30]

John Rhodes published in 1588 *The Countryman's Comfort* for 'the poor Countryman and his family who will ask these vain questions, sometimes saying: "What shall we do in the long winter nights? How shall we pass away the time on Sundays? What would you have us do in the Christmas holidays?" '[31]

Though there was a Bible in every husbandman's home, there was also literature of more light-hearted kind. Spufford found that there was a mass of literature produced for the delectation and information of the masses, mostly little books or chap books that cost two pence:

> The reappearance of a great number of popular songs of satisfying content and artistry . . . in the half-century or so after 1550, is a form of phenomenon a little like the phenomenon of the Great Rebuilding and is very likely related to it. The same upsurge of spending power in

the countryside that enabled the yeomanry to rebuild their houses, also permitted them to send their sons to school and to free them from the labour force. Children of less prosperous men could perhaps only be spared from school until six or seven, when they were able to become useful wage-earners and so only learned to read.[32]

The sabbatarian Nicholas Bownde lamented in 1595:

> In the shops of Artificers, and cottages of poor husbandmen . . . you shall sooner see one of these new ballads, which are made only to keep them occupied . . . than any of the psalms, and may perceive them to be cunninger in singing the one than the other. And indeed, the singing of ballads is very lately renewed . . . so that in every fair and market almost you shall have one or two singing and selling of ballads.[33]

The ballad sellers were often women. As early as 1520 Oxford bookseller John Dorne noted in his day-book that he was selling up to 190 ballads a day at a half-penny each.[34] Ann probably sang ballads as she worked, much to the annoyance of those who thought like Miles Coverdale that 'women at the rocks and spinning at the wheels should be better occupied than with "hey nonny-nonny – hey trolly lolly" and such-like fantasies'.[35]

Autolycus, the pedlar in *The Winter's Tale*, sells literature to both sexes.

> He hath songs for man or woman. No milliner can so fit his customers with gloves. He has the prettiest lovesongs for maids, so without bawdry, which is strange, with such delicate burdens of dildoes and fadings, 'jump her and thump her', and where some stretch-mouthed rascal would, as it were, mean mischief and break a foul gap into the matter, he makes the maid to answer, 'Whoop! Do me no harm good man'. (IV. iv. 192–200)

In *The Merry Wives of Windsor* Slender recalls that he has lent his book of riddles to Alice Shortcake (I. i. 185).

Writing depends upon materials, pen, ink and paper. Goosequills

were easy enough to come by, but ink and paper were expensive. As
Greenblatt points out, 'A pack of paper that, neatly folded and cut,
yielded about fifty small sheets, would have cost at last fourpence, or
the equivalent of eight pints of ale, more than a pound of raisins, a
pound of mutton and a pound of beef, two dozen eggs or two loaves
of bread.'[36] However, the number of women who could write may
have been greater than we think. We don't know how many women,
lacking a writing master, copied the characters they saw in the books
they read. Women's handwriting in the period is very different from
men's. Where men had two hands, a formal hand and a rapid scrawl,
both cursive, most women put their thoughts down in a single not
quite joined-up script. Their spelling was often phonetic, often wildly
inconsistent. As women were the members of the family who moved
away when they married, they were the ones who were duty-bound
to write regularly to their parents, guardians and siblings, no matter
how challenging a task they found it. Letters received had to be
answered by return of post, that is by the same time the following
week. To leave a letter unanswered was a serious discourtesy. Most of
this prodigious activity has left no trace because families did not keep
women's letters, deeming them merely personal and domestic
whereas men's letters, which dealt with political, legal and financial
matters and might be produced in the all too common event of
litigation, were carefully filed.

In the fourth song from Sir Philip Sidney's *Astrophil and Stella*,
published in 1591, the amorous shepherd tries to coax his nymph to
lower her guard:

> Your fair mother is abed,
> Candles out and curtains spread.
> She thinks you do letters write.
> Write, but first let me indite.[37]

Sometimes grown women learnt to write. In *Westward Ho* (1604), the
city wives Mistress Honeysuckle and Mistress Wafer are also being
taught the use of the pen: 'we come to acquaint thee with an excellent
secret: we two learn to write . . . Yes, believe it, and we have the
finest schoolmaster, a kind of Precisian, and yet an honest knave

too . . .'[38] Mistress Tenterhook is amazed. Master Honeysuckle interrogates the 'mechanical pedant', actually a bankrupt merchant in disguise, who claims to have been teaching married women to write for thirteen years: the exchange is possibly indebted to Malvolio's unwittingly obscene description of Olivia's hand in *Twelfth Night*.

> I trust ere few days be at end to have her fall to her joining, for she has her letters *ad unguem*: her A, her great B and her very C, very right, D and E delicate, her double F of a good length but that it straddles a little too wide, at the G very cunning.
>
> Her H is full like mine, a goodly big H.
>
> But her double L is well, her O of a reasonable size, at her P and Q neither merchant's daughter, alderman's wife, young country gentlewoman or courtier's mistress can match her.
>
> And how her V?
>
> U, sir, she fetches up U best of all. Her single U she can fashion two or thee ways, but her double U is as I would wish it.[39]

Obviously, teaching a woman to write is sexy. Did a penniless teenage boy, with nothing to his name but a grammar school education, unfold the mystery of writing as one stratagem for winning a quiet, sensible country girl? What else did he have to offer? Not a lot, as we shall see.

CHAPTER FOUR

of what is likely to happen when a town boy with nothing to his name beyond a way with words woos a serious young woman of good prospects

One thing young Will Shakespeare had to offer was poetry. Even some of Ann's most determined traducers think this truncated sonnet was penned by Will Shakespeare for her:[1]

> Those lips that Love's own hand did make
> Breathed forth the sound that said, 'I hate'
> To me that languished for her sake,
> But, when she saw my woeful state,
> Straight in her heart did mercy come,
> Chiding that tongue that ever sweet
> Was used in giving gentle doom,
> And taught it thus anew to greet:
> 'I hate,' she altered with an end
> That followed it as gentle day
> Doth follow night, who like a fiend
> From Heaven to Hell is flown away.
> > 'I hate' from hate away she threw
> > And saved my life, saying 'not you'.

If Will wooed Ann in one poem, he almost certainly wooed her in others. The syntax of this sonnet, No. 145 in Thorpe's collation, is so baggy that the sense becomes almost dropsical; fourteen lines are needed to convey a single fatuous idea that the beloved said 'I hate' (boo!) and then 'not you' (hurrah!). The complex rhyme scheme closes each four-stressed end-stopped line with a definite clunk. Amid this elephantine tiptoeing we arrive at 'hate away' which has been interpreted by the Shakespearean cryptologists as 'Hathaway', which goes as near to prove as anything does in these cloudy regions that the poem is about Ann Hathaway, if not addressed to her. If it is, then according to her husband, Ann Shakespeare's heart was merciful, her tongue ever sweet, and her judgment gentle. What is more, it was not the woman who seduced the boy, but he who 'languished for her sake', to the point of death, it would seem, and only then did she succumb to his importunity, and so save his life.

Ann had good reason to resist Will's advances: he was too young; he had been trained to no trade that we know of, and his family, having nursed pretensions beyond their means, had run into serious financial trouble. For all we know, Richard Hathaway might have forbidden Ann to countenance Will's suit and she may have been constrained, like Portia, to respect her father's wishes. Perhaps there was another contender for her hand, the son of one of her Shottery neighbours, a Sylvius to her Phoebe, a Will to her Audrey. If Ann Hathaway had suitors, they would have been farmers' sons of more or less her own age, whom she had known since they were children. The life of a husbandman was unlivable without a wife, and Ann probably had what it took to be a good one, which was not great beauty but good health and capability. A well-known song from Campion's second *Book of Airs* celebrates the country girl.

> Joan can call by name her cows
> And deck her windows with green boughs
> She can wreaths and tutties make
> And deck with plums a bridal cake
> Is not Joan a housewife then?
> Judge true-hearted honest men . . .

> Joan is of a lovely brown
> Neat as any in the town,
> Hair as black as any crow
> And does nimbly trip and go . . .

> Happy is their hour and time
> Who can give sweet Joan the wine.[2]

Country people believed that their way of managing the rampant sexuality of young people was the right way. The key to the sequence of events was continuity.

> When did Perseda pastime in the streets,
> But her Erastus over-eyed her sport?
> When didst thou with thy sampler in the sun
> Sit sewing with thy feres but I was by?
> When didst thou go to church on holidays
> But I have waited on thee to and fro?[3]

Boys and girls were guided by their parents into propinquity as they grew up together and then by degrees into intimacy.

> Between the acres of the rye,
> With a hey and a ho and a hey nonny no,
> These pretty country folks would lie,
> In spring-time, the only pretty ring-time.
> When birds do sing, hey-ding-a-ding ding,
> Sweet lovers love the spring.[4]

Once the relationship was recognised by friends and neighbours it could not easily be broken off. A girl who was abandoned by a recognised swain was damaged goods. A girl who dumped a faithful lover was a jilt. The pattern of Ann's life should have been as much as ten years courting with one or other of her country swains, then marrying when the opportunity for housekeeping arose, once there was land for him to work, beasts for him to keep and a sheep or two for her. Instead she cast herself away upon a brilliant boy with nothing. 'When parents have a long time beaten the bush, another oft, as we say, catcheth the bird . . .'[5]

We know from contemporary legislation that educated boys were considered a risk to simple country girls.[6] In *As You Like It* Touchstone is a city wit who makes a speciality of wooing silly country girls like Audrey, the goatherdess, and has done since he was a boy. He reminisces about an earlier love: 'I remember the kissing of her batler, and the cow's dugs that her pretty chapped hands had milked, and I remember the wooing of a peascod instead of her, from whom I took two cods and giving her them again, said with weeping tears, "Wear these for my sake"' (II. iv. 45–50). 'Batler' was the name given to the wooden paddle that was used to thump the washing. Touchstone fancies himself a poet: 'I am here with thee and thy goats, as the most capricious poet, honest Ovid, was among the Goths . . .' (III. iii. 6–7). The schoolboy reference to the *Tristia* means less than nothing to Audrey. Touchstone laments: 'When a man's verses cannot be understood, nor a man's good wit seconded with the forward child understanding, it strikes a man more dead than a great reckoning in a little room. Truly, I would the gods had made thee poetical' (III. iii. 9–13).

Audrey is not poetical, as it turns out, but other country girls were. In the twenty-first century we tend to imagine seducers as older men, but the typical Elizabethan seducer was a boy. In 1609 Shakespeare's sonnets found their way into print, and with them a narrative poem about the wooing of a country girl by a devilishly clever boy who, as soon as he has won her, abandons her. Those who find it hard to imagine a teenage seducer might be surprised at the description of the villain of 'A Lover's Complaint':

> 'His browny locks did hang in crooked curls,
> And every light occasion of the wind
> Upon his lips their silken parcels hurls . . .

> 'Small show of man was yet upon his chin.
> His phoenix down began but to appear,
> Like unshorn velvet on that termless skin . . .

> 'His qualities were as beauteous as his form,
> For maiden-tongued he was, and thereof free . . .'

This young male is still an adolescent and yet a sexual predator. The woman he has seduced and abandoned seems older, and not simply because her grief has aged her:

Upon her head a plaited hive of straw,
Which fortified her visage from the sun,
Whereon the thought might think sometime it saw
The carcase of a beauty spent and done.
Time had not scythed all that youth begun,
Nor youth all quit, but in spite of heaven's fell rage
Some beauty peeped through lattice of seared age.

So odd is this poem that scholars have been reluctant to attribute it
with certainty to Shakespeare, some preferring George Chapman.
The sole authority for the attribution to Shakespeare is the printing of
the sonnets published by Thomas Thorpe, which has been thought to
have been both unauthorised and inaccurate. In fact Thorpe was an
editor careful enough to satisfy the demands of Ben Jonson. Duncan-
Jones is just one scholar who has questioned whether the printing of
the sonnets really was unauthorised.[7] If we deny the poem's authenticity as a work of Shakespeare we lay ourselves open to questioning
the authenticity of some or even all of the sonnets, several of the
themes of which are revisited in this highly sophisticated poem. It
would be unwise in the extreme to interpret the poem as in any way
autobiographical, but it should be sufficient to convince those
nineteenth-century schoolmasters who could not entertain the
thought of a precocious boy seducing an innocent countrywoman
that the sixteenth century found the idea completely plausible.

Young as he is, the young man in 'The Lover's Complaint' has
been wooed by many; the country maid has heard of his conquests
and his 'foul adulterate heart' and has held herself aloof. His suit relies
upon a lying argument: he maintains that he has behaved so badly
with other women because he has never truly loved anyone but her.
She has no sooner fallen for it than he is gone, but so bewitched is she
by him that if he were to return to her she would forgive him all his
perfidy.

We may assume perhaps that the teenage Shakespeare was attractive; in later life he was described as a well-shaped man of charming
manners. The boy seducer of 'The Lover's Complaint' has something
in common with young Master Fenton in *The Merry Wives of Windsor*.
As the landlord of the Garter Inn has it: 'He capers, he dances, he has

eyes of youth; he writes verses, he speaks holiday, he smells April and May' (III. iii. 46). He is of the same breed as Falstaff's younger rivals, the 'lisping hawthorn buds that come like women in men's apparel and smell like Bucklersbury in simple time' (III. iii. 66–8). Fenton (whose Christian name we never learn) writes verses. And the maid he writes them to is called Ann.

> Never durst poet touch a pen to write
> Until his ink was tempered with love's sighs.[8]

Young lovers in Shakespeare's plays all behave in much the same way. They don't eat and don't sleep, but mooch around on their own in the forest or down by the river, carving names in the bark of trees and making up songs and sonnets. In *Love's Labour's Lost*, the young lords who join the King of Navarre in his academy no sooner glimpse the ladies in the park than they fall to rhyming. In this they are led by the ludicrous phony Armado, who addresses his effusions to a milk-maid who cannot read: 'Assist me, some extemporal god of rhyme, for I am sure I shall turn sonnet. Devise, wit, write pen; for I am for whole volumes in folio' (I. ii. 172–4).

The satirist Berowne is the next to turn poet, gnashing his teeth to think that he is being driven by mere lust, 'the liver vein, that makes flesh a deity, a green goose a goddess; pure, pure idolatry'.

> When shall you see me write a thing in rhyme?
> Or groan for Joan? or spend a minute's time
> In pruning me? When shall you hear that I
> Will praise a hand, a foot, a face, an eye,
> A gait, a state, a brow, a breast, a waist,
> A leg, a limb—? (IV. iii. 179–84)

But he falls for it anyway. Ultimately all the young lords in *Love's Labour's Lost* woo the ladies in verse, but the ladies remain unimpressed. The princess is unmoved by 'as much love in rhyme as could be crammed up in a sheet of paper' (V. ii. 6–7); Rosaline makes mock of Berowne's hyperboles; Katharine reacts more sharply to the 'thousand verses' she gets:

> A huge translation of hypocrisy,
> Vilely compiled, profound simplicity. (V. ii. 51–2)

The ladies set out to teach the young gentlemen a lesson. Stung by their mockery Berowne eschews versifying:

> O never will I trust to speeches penned
> Nor to the motion of a school-boy's tongue . . . (V. ii. 402–3)

Ultimately the clever young lords are all rejected by the ladies, and the play of mock wooing ends in confusion. Was Shakespeare sending himself up in this early play? Was he remembering his own callow wooing? There are those who would say yes, and that the play is yet more evidence that in marrying Ann he made a disastrous mistake.

In *As You Like It*, the 'young and tender' boy, the 'youth' Orlando turns poet for Rosalind, hanging poems on trees and carving her name in their bark.

> O Rosalind, these trees shall be my books,
> And in their barks my thoughts I'll character,
> That every eye which in this forest looks,
> Shall see thy virtue witnessed everywhere.
> Run, run, Orlando, carve on every tree
> The fair, the chaste, the unexpressive she. (III. ii. 5–10)

Did seventeen-year-old Shakespeare do as much? He was probably capable of this kind of thing:

> From the east to western Ind,
> No jewel is like Rosalind.
> Her worth being mounted on the wind,
> Through all the world bears Rosalind.
> All the pictures fairest lined
> Are but black to Rosalind.
> Let no face be kept in mind
> But the fair of Rosalind. (III. ii. 86–93)

And so forth. The tetrameters, the metre of doggerel, are bad in truth, and savagely mocked by Touchstone.

> Sweetest nut hath sourest rind;
> Such a nut is Rosalind.
> He that sweetest rose will find
> Must find love's prick and Rosalind. (III. ii. 107–10)

Rosalind remarks a tad sourly that some of the verses 'had in them more feet than the verses would bear'. But this is before she knows that the writer is 'young Orlando'. Jaques too decries his attempts: 'I pray you mar no more trees with writing love-songs in their barks.' And Orlando, like a shrewish boy, snaps back: 'I pray you mar no more of my verses with reading them ill-favouredly' (III. ii. 255–6). In Jaques's famous description of the seven stages in the life of man, the lover, 'Sighing like furnace, with a woeful ballad Made to his mistress' eyebrow' comes directly after the schoolboy, which would suggest someone rather younger than eighteen. Commentators on Shakespeare's life have tended to assume that there was no time for a proper courtship, because Shakespeare was so young when he was married, but he could have been making a nuisance of himself and disfiguring the trees round Shottery for years before Ann finally stooped to his lure. Elizabethans recognised no interim period between child and adult; there was no concept of adolescence or of teenage. According to Roger Ascham: 'from seven to seventeen, young gentlemen commonly be carefully enough brought up: But from seventeen to seven and twenty (the most dangerous time of all in a man's life and most slippery to stay well in) they have commonly the rein of all license in their own hand . . .'.[9]

Ann's could have been the crime of cradle-snatching as described in *The Golden Book of Christian Matrimony*: 'When a wicked subtle and shameless woman enticeth an ignorant young man from his father, which with great expenses, travail and labour hath brought him up, when she blindeth him with love and at the last getteth him away under the title of marriage.'[10] If Will Shakespeare had been a young man with prospects there might have been some point in entrapping him, but he wasn't. The family's disgrace was known to everyone in

Stratford even before John Shakespeare became involved in a violent quarrel with four of his neighbours, against whom he was forced to take out an injunction 'for fear of death and mutilation of his limbs'. Will was certainly young and witty, possibly handsome, but he had nothing else to offer the kind of girl who, as a sober, industrious, patient, frugal wife, would help him repair his family's ruined fortunes. Perhaps Will was like Bassanio in *The Merchant of Venice*, a gambler in love, risking his whole future on winning a wife. And perhaps the quiet woman of Hewlands Farm was like the doyenne of Belmont, constrained by her dead father's will to seek a better match than a penniless boy. Bassanio is worse than penniless; after squandering his own fortune he has entered over ears in debt.

> 'Tis not unknown to you, Antonio,
> How much I have disabled mine estate,
> By something showing a more swelling port
> Than my faint means would grant continuance.
> Nor do I now make moan to be abridged
> From such a noble rate, but my chief care
> Is to come fairly off from the great debts
> Wherein my time (something too prodigal)
> Hath left me gaged. To you Antonio
> I owe the most in money and in love,
> And from your love I have a warranty
> To unburthen all my plots and purposes
> How to get clear of all the debts I owe. (I. i. 122–34)

In case we have not quite grasped the nature of the case, he reiterates:

> I owe you much, and (like a wilful youth)
> That which I owe is lost . . . (146–7)

Shakespeare, of course, was 'a wilful youth'. Bassanio gambles, and he wins the prize, the mistress of Belmont, who seems a great deal wiser and more mature than he is himself.

'Hanging and wiving go by destiny,' according to the proverb, but, unlike Portia's father, Elizabethans were not content to leave such an important matter to luck. To make a difficult matter more difficult a sea-change was happening in the basic concepts that ruled wedding and wiving, as we can see from the case of Mary Darrell and the clergyman–poet Barnabe Googe which was submitted to the arbitration of the Archbishop of Canterbury in 1563. Mary was originally sought in marriage by John Lennard, of Chevening, near Tunbridge Wells, for his eighteen-year-old son Sampson. Lennard claimed to have been first approached by the Darrells who proposed their daughter as a match for his son, and that, far from being averse to the match, Mary showed as much eagerness as feminine modesty would permit. The Darrells praised young Lennard, who stood to inherit a fortune, insisting on his suitability for their daughter; Lennard demurred, perhaps because he considered his boy too young. Lennard interviewed Mary several times:

> I had divers talks with the maid for my son in his absence and yet no more than she was glad of, and then delivered me by her parents . . . at our last talk, hearing her mild and loving answers with full consent to have my son, who I know loved her entirely, and therefore I having good liking in me that he should be her husband, nature wrought in me to lay my right hand on her breast and to speak thus in effect: 'Then I see that with God's help the fruit that shall come of this body shall possess all that I have, and thereupon I will kiss you.' And so indeed I kissed her. I gave her after this silk for a gown (she never wore none so good), and she, in token of her good will, gave my son a handkerchief and, in affirmance of this, her father wrote a letter to me by her consent . . .[11]

To a modern sensibility Lennard's behaviour is repellent. The courting of Mary Darrell had reached the stage of a match concluded, with letters and tokens exchanged. Because Lennard's son had not been present the agreement was not a full contract, but a pre-contract, which would have to be formally set aside before a contract with any other party could be entered into. It may seem peculiar that the lover himself had apparently not asked the lady for her hand – indeed he might never have spoken with her at all – but a modest young woman was supposed, not to see for herself whether she fancied a given man, but to acquiesce in the choice of others, in this case both sets of parents. When Lennard visited the Darrells at Bartholomewtide he told Mary and her parents that he had heard talk that she was to be married, which surprised him.

> They all three answered me, and others for me, very often, that it was not so and that Master Googe was but a suitor. To prove that to be true, the parents sent me a letter sent to Master Googe of late wherein she termeth him to be but a suitor and prayeth him to leave his suit, and the parents still say that he hath no hold of her, except by secret enticement, against their will, he hath caught some word of her, a thing odious to God and not to be favoured by man.[12]

Part of the 'secret enticement', as here alleged, was Googe's writing of poems to Mary. A similar situation is complained of in *A Midsummer Night's Dream* when Egeus appears before Theseus:

> Full of vexation come I, with complaint
> Against my child and daughter, Hermia.
> Stand forth, Demetrius. My noble lord,
> This man hath my consent to marry her.
> Stand forth, Lysander. And, my gracious Duke,
> This man hath bewitched the bosom of my child.
> Thou, thou, Lysander, thou hast given her rhymes,
> And interchanged love-tokens with my child.
> Thou hast by moonlight at her window sung,
> With faining voice, verses of feigning love,
> And stol'n the impression of her fantasy . . .
>
> (I. i. 22–31)

What Archbishop Parker decided to do when confronted with the case of Barnabe Googe and Mary Darrell was to remove Mary from her parents' house and make her a ward of the court while the case was considered. The ecclesiastical authority decided for the lovers, and denied the claim of both the Lennard and the Darrell families. On 5 February 1564 Barnabe and Mary were married, and went on to have eight children.

In *A Midsummer Night's Dream*, Lysander defends his claim in unambiguous terms:

> You have her father's love, Demetrius.
> Let me have Hermia's. Do you marry him. (93–4)

He gets his laugh before Egeus snaps back:

> Scornful Lysander! True, he hath my love,
> And what is mine, my love shall render him,
> And she is mine, and all my right of her
> I do estate unto Demetrius. (95–8)

This is now serious. Egeus has invoked the law of *feme coverte*, which explicitly denies a woman's agency and treats her as a 'chattel' or movable possession of her father or husband. Lysander comes back with an argument that church authorities would have understood. All things being equal, there is nothing to choose between Demetrius and him; this being the case the lady should have the casting vote.

> I am, my lord, as well derived as he,
> As well possessed. My love is more than his,
> My fortunes every way as fairly ranked . . . (99–101)

Hermia meanwhile has sounded a new note: she will accept a life of celibacy rather than marry a man to 'whose unwished yoke [her] soul consents not to give sovereignty' (81–2). The idea of winning the *soul*'s consent by courtship is new; in his response to Hermia, Theseus reinforces the underlying concept of marriage as a spiritual partnership by describing his marriage day as 'the sealing day' between his love and him 'For everlasting bond of fellowship' (84–5).

The Googe story ended happily, but the seduction of country girls by wandering poets did not always end so. In *Love's Labour's Lost*, the dairymaid Jaquenetta is described by Costard as 'a true girl'. It is her misfortune to be seduced by the posturing fool Armado. The child Moth rails against him, to no avail:

. . . to jig off a tune at the tongue's end, canary to it with your feet, humour it with turning up your eyelids, sigh a note and sing a note, sometime through the throat as if you swallowed love with singing love, sometime through the nose as if you snuffed up love by smelling love, with your hat penthouse-like over the shop of your eyes; with your arms crossed on your thin-belly doublet like a rabbit on a spit, or your hands in your pocket, like a man after the old painting, and keep not too long in one tune but a snip and away. These are compliments. These are humours. These betray nice wenches, that would be betrayed without these . . . (III. i. 9–23)

Poetry was almost certainly part of Shakespeare's armamentarium as a lover, and he would surely have deployed it as part of his courtship of Ann Hathaway, but the truth of the matter could be anything but pleasant. It should not be forgotten that, when his gloving business was thriving, John Shakespeare employed women to sew up the gloves, putting together the cut-out skins or 'tranks'. The thought that the son of the house might have seduced one of the girls working in his father's workshop may be unattractive but it is a more usual, if less romantic, scenario than the one that has Will waylaying a milkmaid on her way to pasture and chanting woeful ballads to her eyebrow. Women in service have always been vulnerable to the sexual advances of their employers and their sons. The church courts took a particularly dim view of sexual exploitation of servants, because employers and their wives were considered to stand *in loco parentis*. If it was known in Stratford that Will Shakespeare had made one of his father's workers pregnant, it would have been more shame to him than to her, and that circumstance alone could explain why his parents did not refuse their consent to his marriage. It would have been the worse for him because she was not a stranger but the daughter of a respected parishioner. The possibility should not be altogether discounted. However, even as early as 1582, John Shakespeare was probably no longer working as a glover.

CHAPTER FIVE

of the making of a match, of impediments to marriage and how to overcome them, of bonds and special licences and pregnancy as a way of forcing the issue, of bastards and bastardy, and the girl who got away

We don't know whether Ann Hathaway's 'friends' ever made any effort to find her a husband. She may have had a swain before Will came into the picture. In *As You Like It*, even Audrey the goatherdess has a twenty-five-year-old swain whose name, amusingly enough, is William. When challenged, William readily confesses that he loves Audrey but, disconcerted by Touchstone's meretricious eloquence, he gives way to him without a struggle.[1] We are not told how long William had been courting Audrey in his wordless and good-natured fashion; we watch helpless as the opportunist Touchstone, who has met Audrey and wooed her between one scene of the play and the next, wins her away from William and probably ruins her life.

Though Ann's friends would have understood that negotiating a match for her was part of their duties under her father's will, they were under no obligation to initiate the process. In reserving a marriage portion for Ann out of his estate, her father may have provided a disincentive rather than an incentive for finding her a husband. The widowed mistress of Hewlands Farm could have valued Ann too much as a maiden aunt, working unpaid to support the household, to set about scraping together the cash to cover her dowry bequest. Ann may well have become resigned to the idea that she was destined to work as an unpaid servant in someone else's household for the rest of her life, until the boy from Stratford began accosting her as she went about her daily tasks. She would probably have thought him too young; he may have taken it upon himself to prove to her that he was not.

Tudor marriage negotiations were often broken off for months at a time as parents and friends wrangled over the precise arrangements for the disposal of property or the rights of any children in the property of either parent and so on back and forth. The death of a father necessitated a complete rejigging of all the terms of the agreement. The fact that no marriage contract between Will and Ann has survived doesn't mean that there wasn't one. Sandells and Richardson would have been involved in the negotiations from the outset, possibly long before the death of Richard Hathaway. If this was the case, negotiations would have been abandoned when Hathaway fell ill. A pregnancy might have been the only way the young couple could get them started again.

Holden's view is that, after the mythical 'roll in the hay', 'the autumn of 1582 saw Anne Hathaway telling her late father's friends that she was pregnant by young Will Shakespeare . . .'[2] The implication is that Ann was informing on her lover to men who would grab the figurative shotgun and prod him down the aisle with it. All we know for sure is that Fulke Sandells, the overseer of Ann's father's will, and John Richardson, one of the witnesses, both men of substance, acted for the couple in securing a special licence and putting up the bond that would enable them to marry with a single calling of the banns. Both parties to a marriage were legally required to call the banns, that is, to announce the intended marriage in both parish churches on three successive Sundays, and to ask anyone who knew of grounds why the marriage should not proceed to come forward and state the case. The banns might not be called during Advent and Christmastide. In 1582 Advent Sunday fell on 2 December and Christmastide ended on the octave of the Epiphany, 13 January. Applications for special licences were relatively common; in 1582 the Consistory Court of Worcester granted ninety-eight of them. Puritan reformers inveighed against what they saw as the survival of a popish scheme to wring money from the faithful, and argued that solemnisation of marriage should be performed throughout the liturgical year, without penalties.

That November the banns could have been called on any of four

Sundays, 4, 11, 18 and 25 November, and on the Feast of St Andrew, 30 November. If the banns were not called before the special licence became necessary, we should probably conclude that it was because the match had not been agreed. Nobody would have committed the huge sum of £40 required for the bond if it could have been avoided or if there was the slightest chance of forfeiting it. Ann did not need to argue her case to anyone; she was a spinster and at her own disposal, but only misogyny would assume on the available evidence that she was pushing for the marriage and Will was resisting.

With them to Worcester Sandells and Richardson had to take a slew of supporting documentation, all which would have had to be sworn and notarised, including an allegation giving correct names and addresses of both parties plus evidence of the consent of parents or guardians in the case of the minor, William. Being at her own disposal Ann would have signed the allegation for herself or, more likely, made her mark. She and William's parents would also have been required to sign a statement that to the best of their knowledge there was no legal impediment to the marriage, no prior contract and no question of consanguinity. The £40 bond, 'quadraginta libris bone et legalis monete Anglie', was to indemnify the court in case of a challenge; the £40, the price of a middle-sized house, would become payable only in the event that the marriage was invalid. Neither the bride nor the groom was required to attend the court. The bond itself was written in Latin with an English explanation of the terms:

The condition of this obligation is such that if hereafter there shall not appear any lawful let or impediment by reason of any precontract consanguinity affinity or by any other lawful means whatsoever but that William Shakespeare of the one party and Ann Hathaway of Stratford in the Diocese of Worcester maiden may lawfully solemnise matrimony together and in the same afterwards remain and continue like man and wife according unto the laws in that behalf provided and moreover if there be not at this present time any action suit quarrel or demand moved or depending before any judge ecclesiastical or temporal for and concerning any such lawful let or impediment. And moreover if the said William Shakespeare do not proceed to solemnisation of marriage with the said Ann Hathaway without the

consent of her friends. And also if the said William do upon his own
proper costs and expenses defend & save harmless the Right Reverend
Father in God Lord John Bishop of Worcester and his officers for
licensing them the said William and Ann to be married together with
once asking of the banns of matrimony between them and for all other
causes that may ensue by reason or occasion thereof that then the said
obligation to be void and of none effect or else to stand & abide in full
force and vertue[3]

Once the special licence had been obtained and only one proclamation of the banns was required it could be made at the door of the
church on the day of the marriage itself.

The amount of money at risk seems higher than would be required
simply to enable a marriage with only one asking of the banns. It has
always been assumed that Ann had no other suitor than Shakespeare;
if negotiations for a marriage with someone else had been begun
before Ann's father's death, and had reached a stage of commitment,
we would have another motive for speed and privacy in the circumstances. Ann's brother Bartholomew married three weeks after his
father's death; in his case the commitment had reached its final stage
and the marriage went ahead regardless. Bartholomew's son and
daughter were later to marry a sister and brother, and Ann may have
been in line for a sensible marriage with one of her brother's brothers-
in-law before she fell in love with a boy genius.

There is another possible impediment to the marriage of Will and
Ann. If Richard Hathaway stood godfather to Richard Shakespeare,
and/or Joan Hathaway to Joan Shakespeare, Will and Ann would
have found themselves within the prohibited degrees of spiritual
consanguinity. Godparents were treated within the canon law as
parents; in the eyes of the church their children and their godchildren
were spiritual brothers and sisters and could not marry without special
dispensation from the bishop's court. The doctrine of spiritual affinity
had occasioned a very satisfactory flow of revenue to the ecclesiastical
courts and was bitterly resented by the populace. It was hard enough
finding suitable mates for one's children without running into a
web of affinity that effectively rendered all the neighbours ineligible.[4] Spiritual consanguinity or 'cognatio spiritualis' as a 'diriment

impediment of marriage', that is, grounds for dissolving a marriage already celebrated, had been attacked by Luther. In England the reform of the canon law was long in coming; neither the Henrician Canon nor Cranmer's proposed reform of the canon law was ever put into effect. The Elizabethan settlement, which held that 'no prohibition, God's law except, shall trouble or impeach any marriage outside Levitical law', did not address itself specifically to the question. Whether or not spiritual consanguinity was still in force seems to have been a matter of custom.

What is actually a very ambiguous situation is seen by modern commentators as an open-and-shut case: 'The distinct impression given by the bare documentation of these subsequent events is that these two worthies strong-armed young William over to the consistory court at Worcester, some twenty miles from Stratford, before he could flee his obligations.'[5] There is no evidence that Shakespeare was ever at the Consistory Court at Worcester. He had no role to play in the negotiations and his presence was not required. There was nothing for him to sign, and as a minor he was not qualified to sign. There was no hearing. He was not to be questioned. Ann would not have been required to be there either. Holden elaborates his untenable case: 'It has even been suggested that Sandells and Richardson obtained the licence on their own initiative, with or without the knowledge of Shakespeare's father, to ensure that the father of Anne Hathaway's future child duly became her husband.'[6]

There is nothing, it seems, that ignorance and prejudice will not suggest when it comes to the marriage of Ann Hathaway. Holden's nonsense is derived from the nonsense of the great Sir Sidney Lee, who did not scruple to invent what he did not know about the law governing marriage in the sixteenth century.

The prominence of the Shottery husbandmen in the negotiations preceding Shakespeare's marriage suggests the true position of affairs. Sandells and Richardson, representing the lady's family, doubtless secured the deed on their own initiative, so that Shakespeare might have small opportunity of evading a step which his intimacy with their friend's daughter had rendered essential to her reputation. The wedding probably took place without the consent of the bridegroom's parents – it may be without their knowledge – soon after the signing of the deed.[7]

Of this there was not the slightest possibility. For anyone under age to marry without parental consent was considered a heinous sin, to which the Consistory Court could never have made itself a party. Will's full consent was necessary too; if he was married according to the order in the Book of Common Prayer, he would have been asked once whether he would and again whether he did take Ann to be his lawful, wedded wife. Yet his great champions would rather believe that he perjured himself than that he honestly and truly took Ann Hathaway to have and to hold. Certainly there could have been opposition to the match, on either side or both sides, especially if a more suitable match had already been mooted. It may have been opposition to their marriage that persuaded the young people to pre-empt the ceremony, and force the issue by chancing a pregnancy, as others had done before them and were to do after them.

In 1595 Shakespeare's patron, the Earl of Southampton (the same who is thought to have had a fully acted-out homosexual relationship with the Bard), fell seriously in love with one of the queen's maids of honour, the Earl of Essex's beautiful cousin Elizabeth Vernon. Over the next three years he wooed and won her, of necessity surreptitiously, for the queen was notoriously unwilling to countenance the wedding of her maids of honour, especially with any courtier she wanted to keep as one of her own devotees. In 1598 when the affair became known, the infuriated queen banished Southampton from Whitehall and ordered him to accompany Secretary Cecil on an official trip to France. On 1 February Rowland White wrote to Sir Robert Sidney:

My Lord of Southampton is much troubled at her Majesty's strange use of him . . . Master Secretary hath procured him licence to travel. His fair mistress doth wash her face with too many tears. I pray God his going away bring her to no such infirmity as is, as it were, hereditary to her name.[8]

At this juncture, the twenty-five-year-old Southampton, abetted by the Earl of Essex and clearly determined to have Elizabeth as his wife at any cost, took the desperate step of consummating the relationship. By 12 February when White wrote to Sidney again, Elizabeth Vernon was pregnant: 'My lord of Southampton is gone and hath left behind him a very desolate gentlewoman that hath almost wept out her fairest eyes.'[9] The fairness of Elizabeth's eyes is evinced by a series of portraits, which show her to have been a classic Elizabethan beauty with blooming cheeks and lips, dark-grey eyes and masses of auburn hair. It was not until August, when royal attention was distracted by the obsequies for Lord Treasurer Burghley, that Southampton was able secretly to cross the Channel and solemnise his marriage.

> Mistress Vernon is from the court and lies in Essex House. Some say she hath taken a venue under the girdle and swells upon it, yet she complains not of foul play but says the Earl will justify it. And it is bruited underhand that he was lately here four days in great secret of purpose to marry her and effected it accordingly.[10]

Southampton then returned to Paris, hoping that his pregnant countess would escape the queen's wrath at least until after her delivery. By 3 September the queen had been informed of the clandestine wedding and commanded Southampton's immediate return from Paris, but he failed to comply. He was probably with his wife when she was brought to bed of a daughter, Penelope, at the beginning of November, and on 11 November he was imprisoned in the Fleet, where he remained until he was needed to support Essex in quelling the Irish Rebellion. Despite the vicissitudes of Southampton's career, which included another four-year period of imprisonment, the couple would go on to have four more surviving children.

If the impregnation of Ann Hathaway had been accidental rather than part of a deliberate strategy, Shakespeare could have evaded marriage with her, just as Lucio evaded marriage with Kate Keep-Down in *Measure for Measure*. Mistress Overdone tells us that Lucio seduced Kate under a promise of marriage, which is presumably how Kate ended up working as one of her whores at the Bunch of Grapes tavern, with Mistress Overdone paying for raising her child. Later in the play Lucio tells the disguised duke that he once appeared before him for getting a wench with child. The duke asks, 'Did you such a thing?' (IV. iii. 165). Lucio answers casually: 'Yes, marry, did I; but I was fain to forswear it; they would else have married me to the rotten medlar' (166–7).

Even after promises of marriage, prolonged cohabitation and a pregnancy, it was easy for a man to evade marriage if he chose. Every year women brought fatherless children to be christened at Holy Trinity. On New Year's Day 1580 Joan Rodes brought her baby son to be christened John, and the curate wrote beside the entry in the register, as was the rule, 'bastard', in Latin, 'notha' or 'nothus'; the entry for the child's burial in November reads simply 'Jone Rodes Bastard'. Two weeks later, Julian Wainwright brought to the font the second of her four illegitimate children, a daughter Sybil. How she managed to defy the authorities and continue living in Stratford with her children as an unmarried mother until her death and burial in Holy Trinity on 11 January 1593 must remain a mystery. The most likely explanation is that she was under the protection of a gentleman so powerful that the Corporation and the church had no option but to countenance her insolence. Nearly all the other unwed mothers appear in the record once and then disappear. In July 1581 Anne Breame brought her illegitimate daughter Elizabeth to be christened. In April 1582 Margery Foster christened her illegitimate son Richard, in September Alice Baker her illegitimate daughter Joan; in October Sybil Davis of Luddington buried a bastard son she had called Francis; in November Alice Smith had her son christened Humphrey. All of these mothers, except perhaps Julian Wainwright, should have been pressured by the women who assisted them in their labour to name the men responsible. If they had weakened, the father's name would have been written in the register instead of theirs. Perhaps the parish midwives were remiss that year and the women were spared the ordeal.

Pregnant women did not always have to be tortured or terrorised before they would name a father for their child. On 26 January 1581, the curate at Holy Trinity recorded the baptism of Margaret, 'bastard daughter to Thomas Raynolds'. We are reminded of the shepherd who is Joan of Arc's father:

I did beget her, all the parish knows.
Her mother liveth yet, can testify
She was the first fruit of my bachelorship.[11]

The surviving records of the Stratford Vicar's Court tell us of Joan Dutton, a pregnant stranger detected in the house of William Russell; in court she alleged that she had been made pregnant by 'a certain Gravenor, servant of Master Greville of Milcote'. She was 'ordered to perform penance . . . clad in a sheet'.[12] In 1606 a heavily pregnant Anne Browne alias Watton named Hamnet Sadler's nephew John Sadler as the father of her child; though the citation had been pinned to his house door, he did not appear and was excommunicated.[13] Ann bore a daughter called Katherine; John went to London to seek his fortune.

Once a father had been named, he would be expected to support the child. In some cases the mother would be allowed to keep it until it was weaned or even longer, before it was transferred to the custody and the household of its father. In many cases the unwed mother who named the father stood to lose her child for ever. In 1606 in the Stratford Vicar's Court Margaret Price named Paul Bartlett as the father of her child. He was ordered to do penance but 'proffered five shillings for the poor of the parish'. He was already maintaining the child. As for Margaret, the court book says simply, 'She went away.'[14] Most of the women in her situation didn't wait to be formally ostracised but left of their own accord, many to try their luck in the brutal, anonymous world of the London stews. Bartholomew Parsons appeared in court a month before his son by the widow Alice Atwood was born and promised to maintain him. He offered ten shillings 'for the use of the poor of the parish'.[15] What became of Widow Atwood is not known. In 1608 Thomas Burman admitted that he was the father of the baby Susanna Ainge was carrying; his penance too was remitted in return for a payment of ten shillings.[16]

If Shakespeare had denied paternity, Ann could have been punished for being 'unlawfully pregnant', possibly publicly whipped, certainly made to stand in front of the congregation on a Sunday, clad in nothing but a white sheet. When her time came the midwives would have refused to help deliver her until in extremity of fear and pain she screamed out the name of her child's father, in which case Shakespeare too would have been disgraced, especially if she died, a deathbed statement having force in law. Faced with such evidence one wonders how Greenblatt could allow himself to say that 'an unmarried mother in the 1580s did not, as she would in the 1880s, routinely face fierce, unrelenting social stigmatization'.[17] What the unmarried Elizabethan mother had to face was persecution so intense that it verged on savagery. Where the ecclesiastical courts were concerned,

> What aroused most parochial concern and accounted for the great majority of prosecutions was 'harbouring' pregnant women, that is receiving them, giving them shelter until they had given birth . . . the basic source of parochial concern was the fear that the bastard child, and perhaps the mother as well, would burden the poor rates.[18]

In 1592, Thomas Kyrle was presented to the Stratford Vicar's Court for 'encouraging in his house a certain pregnant woman'. He did not appear and was excommunicated.[19] In 1608 John Phelps alias Sutton was presented at the Vicar's Court for 'receiving his pregnant daughter' who had given birth two months earlier, naming a John Burrowes as her child's father.[20] Though premarital pregnancy was so common as to be normal, bastardy was not tolerated. The commonest motive for infanticide was illegitimacy.[21]

If Shakespeare's parents had remained obdurate in refusing their consent to the marriage of Will and Ann, the match would not have been made and Ann would have been strumpeted, regardless of what Will thought about the matter. If he chose, he could have persuaded his parents that she had been free with her favours, that he was one of several sexual partners she had had that summer. In Measure for Measure Angelo justifies his failure to marry Marina not only because her dowry was lost at sea,

> but in chief
> For that her reputation was disvalued
> In levity . . . (V. i. 218–20)

When Bertram in *All's Well that Ends Well* is confronted by Diana who claims that he has taken her virginity, he replies:

> She's impudent, my lord,
> And was a common gamester to the camp. (V. iii. 190–1)

Will could have produced henchmen to swear that they had enjoyed Ann, and she would have been consigned to a life of whoredom. He could have pleaded prior contract with some other woman. He could have run away, to London, or to sea, or to the wars. He would not have been the first or the last to escape a bastard being fathered on him by doing so. If John and Mary Shakespeare had thought their son was to be married to a whore, they could have stopped the marriage dead, and sent Ann away sorrowing.

With Shakespeare's biographers so eager to traduce his wife, it is surprising that no one has ever alleged that the child Ann bore in May 1583 was not his. The point could never be proved, as can none of the other allegations made about Ann Hathaway, one of which is that, when he was forced to marry her, Will was actually in love with another woman. The evidence for this is an entry in the Bishop of Worcester's register, under the date 27 November 1582, the day before the issue of the bond for Ann and Will's marriage recording the issue of a licence for a marriage 'inter Wm Shaxpere et Annam Whateley de Temple Grafton', between a William Shakespeare and Ann Whateley of Temple Grafton.[22] These days the entry is thought to be a scribal error. If it is it is an odd one. The bishop's register was copied by a professional scribe from the rougher lists made by the clerk officiating at the time. The substitution of one word for another, of Whateley for Hathaway, might be a simple misreading of a scribbled original, or the carriage of a word over from another entry, but the simultaneous introduction of Temple Grafton, instead of Shottery or Stratford, does strain credulity. It may simply be that the scribe copied the beginning of one entry, getting as far as the 'Annam', say, and when he looked up again picked up an 'Annam' in the following entry, so writing the beginning of one entry and the end of another.

There could have been two William Shakespeares in the diocese of Worcester marrying two Anns at much the same time and both in need of a special licence. This possibility did not seem incredible to Sir Sidney Lee, but it hasn't found favour with anybody else much. There were lots of Shakespeares in Warwickshire c.1580 and lots of them were Williams. Half a dozen William Shakespeares of marriageable age can be found in Rowington in the 1580s. William was a preferred name among the Shakespeares of Oldiche too; one of the brothers of John Shakespeare the corviser (shoe-maker) who lived in Stratford for a time, and baptised three children there, was a William. William Shakespeares were common also at Wroxall. Thomas Shakespeare of Alcester left a young son William when he died in 1539; Christopher Shakespeare of Packwood names a son William as one of the overseers of his will in 1557; a William Shakespeare was named as an overseer in the will of John Pardie of Snitterfield in 1579. Other William Shakespeares there were, aplenty.

There were also Whateleys in Warwickshire, though fewer than Shakespeares or Hathaways. A William Whateley baptised a son and a daughter at Holy Trinity in the 1560s. Alderman George Whately (or Wheatley) who acted as bridge warden for many years and was elected Bailiff of Stratford in 1583, had no connections with Temple Grafton. He was born in Henley-in-Arden, where in 1586 he endowed an elementary school for thirty children. He was buried in Holy Trinity Stratford in the pestilential summer of 1593. Whateley was a successful wool draper, whose house 'with glass windows in the hall, parlour and upper chamber, and bee-hives in the garden' stood opposite the Shakespeares' in Henley Street.[23] (He had two brothers who were Catholic priests on the run.) None of his children by his wife Joan who died in Stratford in February 1579 was christened in Stratford. On 19 May 1582 another George Whateley, almost certainly the alderman's son, took Mary Nasson to wife at Holy Trinity. He could have had a sister or cousin Ann living in Temple Grafton. Three of George Whateley's children were subsequently baptised in Stratford, none of them an Ann. The only other child of Alderman Whateley's who can be traced in the Stratford records is an unmarried daughter Catherine, to whom the Corporation leased a house on the High Street in 1598.

Ann Hathaway could have been living in Temple Grafton, three and a half miles to the west of Shottery, and a good five miles from Stratford, but not for the reasons adduced by Park Honan:

> Gossip and rumour, in themselves, could cause an alert court to summon a pregnant woman and her lover, and as Anne's condition became obvious it could have attracted attention, so she may have left Hewlands by November. But the evidence is unclear, in any case: her November locale is given as 'Temple Grafton', in a Worcester entry that errs with her surname . . . If she huddled there William perhaps felt obliged to ask for his father's consent to marry, and his mother's willingness to share a home with his bride.[24]

Honan begins by assuming that the William Shakespeare of the entry in the Bishop of Worcester's register is identical with our William Shakespeare; the possibility of two William Shakespeares seeking special licences at the same time is not to be considered. Then, he assumes that in copying the original register the scribe made a single mistake, getting the name wrong but the place right. It is actually harder to do this than to join half of one line to half of another. For the eye to return to the right line and not note the mistaken surname is almost impossible. For Honan Ann Whateley is a mistake for Ann Hathaway but Temple Grafton is not a mistake. Temple Grafton is the hamlet where she is to be found 'huddled'. A small hamlet in Elizabethan Warwickshire was not an easy place to hide in; as a stranger newly arrived in the district Ann would have been conspicuous. Any suspicion that she might be pregnant would have brought her to the attention of the authorities. A woman in search of anonymity and invisibility in 1582 would have had to travel a lot further than three or four miles.

If Ann Hathaway was living in Temple Grafton, it places her courtship by William Shakespeare in a very different light. It is usually assumed, and, given the fact that the men who acted for her in the securing of the licence were the same men of Shottery who witnessed her father's will, it is most likely, that she was until her marriage a member of the Hathaway household in Shottery. If she was not, it would not have been because she was in the early stages of pregnancy, but because she was working to support herself. It was quite usual in

Tudor England for children to be sent away from home, to live and work in the households of relatives or even of complete strangers. About half the children apprenticed to learn crafts and trades in London in this period were girls. Instead of working as an unpaid farm servant for her own family in Shottery, Ann could have been apprenticed to a skilled craftswoman or artisan somewhere else, but it is more likely to have been in a busy market town like Stratford than in sleepy Temple Grafton. At twenty-six Ann would have been long out of her indentures.

One scholarly tradition treats the entry in the Bishop of Worcester's transcript as evidence that Ann and Will were married in Temple Grafton. The parish registers of the ancient church of Temple Grafton, built by the Knights Templar in Saxon times, do not begin until 1612. The Vicar of Temple Grafton in 1582 was John Frith, who was, according to a puritan survey of the Warwickshire clergy, 'an old priest and unsound in religion. He can neither preach nor read well. His chiefest trade is to cure hawks that are hurt or diseased, for which purpose many do usually repair to him.'[25] In 1580 Bishop Whitgift's officers had had to require Frith to indemnify the church against any litigation arising out of marrying without licence anyone 'at any times prohibited by the ecclesiastical laws'. If Frith was a Catholic and married Will and Ann as Catholics, we might wonder why they put themselves through the laborious business of the bond in the first place. It seems rather that Ann Whateley of Temple Grafton has nothing to do with the case.

If Ann Whateley is another Ann altogether but the William the same, we could decide that Ann Hathaway rescued her lover before he made a terrible mistake, and found himself yoked for life to the wrong Ann. For all their frantic fantasising, this possibility never occurs to the Shakespeareans, who have never swerved in their conviction that it was the woman Shakespeare married who was the wrong one. For them 'Ann Whateley' must have been the love of his life, simply because she got away. Anthony Burgess lets his fantasy rip.

> It is reasonable to believe that Will wished to marry a girl called Anne Whateley . . . Sent on skin-buying errands to Temple Grafton, Will

could have fallen for a comely daughter, sweet as May and shy as a fawn. He was eighteen and highly susceptible. Knowing something about girls he would know that this was the real thing. Something, perhaps, quite different from what he felt about Mistress Hathaway of Shottery.

Burgess has decided that Ann Whateley, about whom we know nothing, is beautiful, sweet and shy; he calls Ann Hathaway 'Mistress' for no other reason than that it makes her sound forbidding, spinsterish, schoolmarmy even. The 'something different' that Shakespeare feels is 'the real thing'. The argument could as easily be reversed; Ann Hathaway could have been the real thing, Ann Whateley the decoy. Burgess and most of his ilk prefer to believe that Shakespeare married the wrong girl. 'But why, attempting to marry Anne Whateley had he put himself in the position of having to marry the other Anne? I suggest that, to use the crude but convenient properties of the old women's-magazine morality stories, he was exercised by love for the one and lust for the other . . .'

Burgess is not at all troubled by the thought that Will had had sex with Ann Hathaway without loving her, and he clearly doesn't care whether Ann loved Will, as I'm sure she did. Burgess thinks that Ann Hathaway allowed Will to make love to her simply because she was easy, and that Will took advantage simply because he was incontinent.

> I consider that the lovely boy Will probably was – auburn hair, melting eyes, ready tongue, tags of Latin poetry – did not, having tasted Anne's body in the spring, go eagerly back to Shottery through the early summer to taste it again. Perhaps Anne had already said something about the pleasures of love in an indentured bed, away from cowpats and the pricking of stubble in a field, and the word *marriage* frightened Will as much as it will frighten any young man.[26]

Burgess's calendar is askew. Ann's baby, born in May, must have been conceived in the third or fourth week of August. The association of stubble with spring or early summer is not one a country person would make. Cowpats are found in stubble only after the cows have been let into the fields after the harvest. If Titania could find a bank where the wild thyme grows, we might conclude that Ann and Will could too. England was not then farmed every inch; all around Stratford there were hay and water meadows, and grazing commons, and fallow land, plus wilderness and wood. Shakespeare loved the summer meadows, where the young courting couples wandered in the deep grass and lay down together.

>   When daisies pied and violets blue
>   And lady-smocks all silver-white
>   And cuckoo-buds of yellow hue
>   Do paint the meadows with delight . . .
>
>   When shepherds pipe on oaten straws
>   And merry larks are ploughmen's clocks,
>   When turtles tread and rooks and daws,
>   And maidens bleach their summer smocks . . .[27]

Burgess prefers his imaginary Anne Whateley, 'chaste, not wanton and forward'. He is neither the first nor the last to stigmatise Ann Shakespeare as promiscuous. She has been accused of adultery with two of her brothers-in-law, and a visiting preacher, on no evidence whatsoever. 'Will gave in, with bitter resignation, and was led to the slaughter, or the marriage bed. The role of the honourable Christian gentleman was being forced on him.' We may wonder how flattering Shakespeare would have found Burgess's estimate of his character. If any of this had been said in his hearing, he would have been obliged to challenge Burgess in defence of his own honour, to say nothing of his wife's.

CHAPTER SIX

of handfasts, troth-plights and bundling, of rings, gauds and conceits,
and what was likely to happen on the big day

At some stage in the wooing, wedding and bedding of Ann Hath-away, the couple committed themselves by taking each other's right hand and uttering the words of marriage in the present tense, Will saying 'I take thee Ann to be my wife' and Ann 'I take thee William to be my husband'. Once they had done this they were married, whether the event had been witnessed or not. There were other sacramental signs, the exchange of rings and other tokens, the kiss, but the words were what constituted the sacrament. Even if consummation did not follow, the mere saying of the words between two parties was sufficient to render them ineligible for a match with any other party. If the couple cohabited after a handfasting or troth-plight, regardless of whether they had said the words in the present tense or mistakenly in the future tense, they were fast married:

> If the parties betrothed do lie together before the condition be performed; then the contract for the time to come is without further controversy sure and certain, for . . . it is always presupposed that a mutual consent as touching marriage, has gone before.[1]

Scholars annotating the passage in *The Winter's Tale* in which Leontes suggests that his virtuous wife Hermione deserves a name 'As rank as any flax-wench, that puts to it Before her troth-plight' have generally failed to understand the importance of that 'before'. The difference between 'before' and 'after' was the difference between fornication and matrimony.

This situation could only too easily be manipulated by unscrupulous people anxious to set aside valid marriages or to evade their responsibilities. The only remedy was the setting aside of clandestine matches whether valid in the sight of God or not, and requiring marriage to be celebrated publicly according to the laws of God and man before it could be accepted as legally binding. The Council of Trent, acting on the certainty that *de occultis non scrutantur*, 'what is secret may not be examined', demanded the presence of two witnesses as a condition of valid matrimony. For English protestants the situation remained confused until the Hardwick Marriage Act of 1754. Till then 'making all sure' in marriage required a belt-and-braces approach.

The action of *Cymbeline*, one of Shakespeare's most mysterious plays, known to us only from the Folio, turns on a 'handfast'. Imogen, destined by her father for marriage with the brutish son of his second wife, takes pre-emptive action by handfasting herself to Posthumus Leonatus, 'a poor but worthy gentleman'.

> She's wedded,
> Her husband banished, she imprisoned. All
> Is outward sorrow . . . (I. i. 7–9)

The courtier who gives us this information at the beginning of the play is anxious that we should understand that Imogen is truly married: when he refers to Posthumus as 'he that hath her' he immediately corrects himself – 'I mean that married her . . .' (18). The queen plots against Posthumus' loyal servant Pisanio, because he is 'the remembrancer' who will remind Imogen 'to hold The handfast to her lord' (I. vi. 77–8). With Posthumus out of the way, Imogen is treated by her father and stepmother as if she were still eligible. She and Pisanio are the only ones aware that Cloten is 'A foolish suitor to a wedded lady That hath her husband banished' (I. vi. 2–3). Cloten upbraids Imogen:

> Your sin against
> Obedience, which you owe your father, for
> The contract you pretend with that base wretch,
> One bred of alms, and fostered with cold dishes,

> With scraps o'th'court, it is no contract, none,
> And though it be allowed in meaner parties
> (Yet who than he more mean?) to knit their souls
> (On whom there is no more dependency
> But brats and beggary) in self-figurèd knot,
> Yet you are curbed from that enlargement, by
> The consequence o'the crown . . . (II. iii. 108–18)

Those who comb Shakespeare's work for possible disparagement of his life with Ann might snatch at the hint that they had nothing but 'brats and beggary', but the person making the judgment is not Shakespeare but Cloten, the brutish villain of the piece.

In *Romeo and Juliet,* when Juliet inadvertently declares her love to Romeo, and he returns it, she describes what has passed between them as a contract. Some of the things she has said could be construed as constituting a troth-plight:

> be but sworn my love,
> And I'll no longer be a Capulet . . .
> Romeo, doff thy name,
> And for thy name which is no part of thee
> Take all myself. (II. i. 77–8, 89–91)

Romeo replies with a version of the words of the handfast: 'I take thee at thy word' (91). Juliet has committed herself unwittingly, thinking herself to be alone. Nothing about this interchange could possibly bind either of them, except perhaps Juliet's belief that she is so bound:

> Fain would I dwell on form, fain, fain deny
> What I have spoke, but farewell compliment.
> Dost thou love me? I know thou wilt say 'Ay',
> And I will take thy word. At lovers' perjuries
> They say Jove laughs. O gentle Romeo,
> If thou dost love, pronounce it faithfully . . . (130–5)

Romeo attempts to swear and fails; nevertheless Juliet considers herself contracted:

> Well, do not swear. Although I joy in thee
> I have no joy in this contract tonight.
> It is too rash, too unadvised, too sudden . . . (158–60)

As she turns to go, Romeo stops her: 'O wilt thou leave me so unsatisfied?' (167). She replies, 'What satisfaction canst thou have tonight?' (168). He explains: 'Th'exchange of thy love's faithful vow for mine' (169). Juliet believes that her vow has already been given. 'I gave thee mine before thou didst request it . . .' (170). When she returns she instructs him to arrange the solemnisation of their wedding.

> If that thy bent of love be honourable,
> Thy purpose marriage, send me word tomorrow
> By one that I'll procure to come to thee,
> Where and what time thou wilt perform the rite . . . (185–8)

'The rite' is eventually performed off-stage by Friar Lawrence. Romeo promises to tell him 'when and where and how We met, we wooed and made exchange of vow . . .' even though, as far as the audience has witnessed, neither of them has made a vow. What is more, no banns have been published and parental consent has not been and will not be given. By the end of Act II scene ii of *Romeo and Juliet*, Juliet is already hopelessly compromised. The friar, 'a ghostly confessor and a sin-absolver', the like of whom had not been seen in England for more than fifty years, is hardly as cheery and reassuring a character as he is usually played. Juliet is to be shriven – an exotic concept for most of Shakespeare's audience – then married in short order. Romeo, whose vow-making has been anything but satisfactory, tells the friar that his job is to join their hands 'with holy words'. The friar's answer would have chilled many an anxious parent to the bone.

> Come, come with me, and we will make short work,
> For by your leaves you shall not stay alone
> Till holy church incorporate two in one. (II. iv. 35–7)

It is the same meddlesome friar who advises Romeo to consummate his marriage before fleeing to Mantua where he will live till they
can find a time to 'blaze', that is, publicly proclaim, the fact of the
marriage and reconcile the friends of both parties. Verona is and is not
the Warwickshire of the 1590s; what Romeo and Juliet do was
identified with the bad old days, but the anxieties evoked by their
wilfulness were real and present to Shakespeare's audience. Scandals
arising from secret or invented handfastings, troth-plights and weddings occurred every year, and cruel and tyrannical proceedings by
parents were not uncommon either. To Shakespeare's audience
Capulet's contemptuous treatment of his daughter would have been
every bit as shocking as her impetuosity.

In his search for an explanation of the high incidence of premarital
pregnancy in early modern England, Laslett came across the Proceedings of the Registry of the Archdeaconry at Leicester, July 1598:

> The common use and custom within the county of Leicester . . . for
> the space of 10, 20, 30 or 40 years past hath been and is that any man
> being a suitor to a woman in the way of marriage is upon the day
> appointed to make a final conclusion of the marriage before treated of.
> If the said marriage be concluded and contracted then the man doth
> abide the night the next following after such a contract, otherwise he
> doth depart without staying the night.[2]

Again and again in the record we find rather confusing references to
the fact that, after the contract to marry is concluded, it is made
binding by the beginning of cohabitation, before solemnisation can
take place. In *The Christian State of Matrimony* (1543) Heinrich
Bullinger deplores the practice: 'in some place there is such a manner,
well worthy to be rebuked, that, at the handfasting, there is made a
great feast and superfluous banquet, and even the same night are the
two handfasted persons brought and laid together, yea, certain weeks
before they go to the church'.[3]

If the couple do not sleep together after the troth-plight it is not
consummated and may, with difficulty and at considerable expense,
be set aside by an ecclesiastical court. The separation of wedding from
the solemnisation of matrimony was not, as we might think, a division

of the civil contract from the sacrament, as happens in Europe today, when couples marry in the town hall and then go to church. Rather it is a separation of the actual wedding from the public recognition of that wedding. Under the old dispensation, the actual contract of matrimony, the wedding, had taken place in the church porch; the bridal couple then entered the church not for the wedding but for the nuptial mass, when their union was blessed.

The protestant reformers who drew up the Book of Common Prayer during the brief reign of Edward VI brought the wedding into the church, so that the spouses uttered the words of both the pre-contract and the contract before the altar in full view of their families, friends and neighbours. This was the ideal, but it was far from the real. For several generations local custom had filled the doctrinal void and was not so easily abandoned. Besides, nothing could alter the underlying tenet that if a man told a woman that he was taking her to be his wife, and she replied in kind, in the present tense, they were married in the sight of God. When Edward VI died and Mary acceded to the throne, the Book of Common Prayer was thrown out, and the attempt to make publication of the banns and the church wedding itself a condition of the validity of marriage was abandoned. Catechisms like the Bishop of Lincoln's *Wholesome and Catholic Doctrine Concerning the Seven Sacraments* (1558) reiterated the old Catholic canon law:

> although the solemnisation of Matrimony and the benediction of the parties married is made and given in the face of the church by a priest, yet the contract of matrimony wherein this sacrament consisteth, may be and is commonly made by the layman and woman which be married together. And because for lack of knowledge how such contracts ought to be duly made, and for omitting of such things as be necessary to the same, it chanceth oftentimes that the parties change their minds and will not keep that promise of marriage which seemed to have passed between them before, whereupon cometh and groweth between such persons and their friends great grudge and hatred and great suit in the law.

The good bishop then goes on to supply the correct form of words for the contract, and goes to on to reassure the faithful that 'the parties so contracting may without scruple or evil conscience for so much live together in godly and chaste matrimony to the good will and pleasure of almighty God'.[4]

Laslett is tempted to interpret pre–solemnisation cohabitation as a sort of 'trial marriage', which is a little misleading. If the contract itself was valid, in that there was no legal impediment, the only way the trial marriage could fail would be if one or other partner was incapable of sexual intercourse. This too would become a matter for the ecclesiastical court, which could order an examination of either party or both parties. Hence the rage and disgust of the puritans at the antics of the learned clerics in what was known to the common people as the 'bawdy' court.

> This court poulleth parishes, scourgeth the poor hedge priests, loadeth churchwardens with manifest perjuries, punisheth whoredoms and adulteries with toyish censures, remitteth without satisfying the congregation, and that in secret places, giveth out dispensations for unlawful marriages, and committeth a thousand suchlike abominations.[5]

The matters that came before the church courts were:

> so handled that it would grieve a chaste ear to hear the bawdy pleading of so many proctors and doctors in those courts, and the sumners, yea, and the registrars themselves, Master Archdeacon and Master Chancellor are even fain to laugh it out many times, when they can keep their countenance no longer. An unchaste kind of dealing of unchaste matters: when folk may not marry, what degrees may not marry . . .[6]

The assertion by the likes of Anthony Holden that Ann's pregnancy was the result of a single 'roll in the hay' is more revealing of their own attitudes than of the social context of Ann's pregnancy. Elizabethans were not hillbillies. The marriage prospects of their children were matters of the highest importance. Young people were never unobserved by their neighbours and kin. Demographic historians would not take Nicholas Breton's Countryman as a reliable observer of what really went on, but his is certainly a description of a bucolic ideal, to which village elders could aspire.

. . . at our meetings on the holy days between the lads and the wenches, such true mirth at honest meetings, such dancing on the green, in the market house or about the may-pole, where the young folks smiling kiss at every turning, and the old folks checking with laughing their children, when dancing for the garland, playing at stool ball for a tansy and a banquet of curds and cream, with a cup of old nappy ale, matter of small charge with a little reward for the piper, after casting of sheep's eyes and faith and troth for a bargain, clapping of hands, are seals to the truth of hearts, when a pair of gloves or a handkerchief are as good as the best obligation, with a cap and a curtsey hie you home, maids to milking, and so merrily goes the day away.[7]

At such gatherings a young woman who was not spoken for would have found it difficult to steal away with an unattached boy, but space was made for young people known to be courting, so that they could be together unobserved, even to the extent of leaving them together in the family house in the dark. The likelihood is that Ann Hathaway and young Shakespeare were known to be courting months before her father's friends applied for a special licence for them to marry. Further evidence of a tradition in parts of England of bedding the couple first and going to the church in the morning can be found in the well-known ballad of *The Northamptonshire Lover*:

> The damsel, this perceiving
>   And noting his behaviour,
> Thought fit to entertain him,
>   Possessed of all her favour,
> Which he enjoyed with full consent.
>   So unto church they go,
> Where he espoused the maid he loved,
>   Fa lero lero lo.[8]

Ann's enemies among the bardolaters have seen a rejection of his own youthful behaviour in *Measure for Measure*, in the harsh treatment meted out to Claudio, who seems to have done pretty much as he did in 1582.

> upon a true contract
> I got possession of Julietta's bed.
> You know the lady. She is fast my wife,
> Save that we do the denunciation lack
> Of outward order. This we came not to
> Only for propagation of a dower
> Remaining in the coffer of her friends,
> From whom we thought it meet to hide our love
> Till time had made them for us, but it chances
> The stealth of our most mutual entertainment
> With character too gross is writ on Juliet. (I. iv. 133–48)

There was nothing sinful in Claudio's and Julia's cohabitation, because, having said the words of the *sponsalia per verba de praesenti*, they would have been married in the eyes of God. The 'denunciation of outward order' is merely the making public of the state of affairs to enable its recognition in law. When Isabella hears of the pregnancy she simply cries, 'O let him marry her,' which would have been the reaction of most of the audience. Lucio, the whoremonger, tells her that Angelo has 'picked out an act' under which the punishment for fornication is death. When the disguised duke comes across Julia, he asks her if their 'offenceful act' was mutually committed, which, as we have seen, is enough to sanctify it, but the duke interprets the fact as increasing Julia's burden of guilt: 'Then was your guilt of heavier kind than his' (II. iii. 30). Julia takes the burden upon herself:

> I do repent me as it is an evil,
> And take the shame with joy. (37–8)

Measure for Measure was written in 1604–5; bedding before wedding had been roundly condemned from the pulpit for years and by then the protestant reformers were beginning to see a result. More and more vicars' courts all over the country were summoning newly-weds to face charges of fornication if their first child was born within forty weeks of the wedding, and punishing them by the same public humiliation and fines that had earlier been imposed for fornication and adultery. Public perceptions were changing; although the average

age of marriage was the highest ever recorded, premarital pregnancy and bastardy were both disappearing from parish registers.[9] The full extent of this step-change in public mores has yet to be charted, much less explained. Claudio's behaviour and Angelo's summary justice would have been judged differently by different sections of Shakespeare's audiences whether at court or in the public theatres. *Measure for Measure* squarely confronts the shift in moral perception together with the distressing truth that more and more women fleeing disgrace in the church courts or actually driven out of town by the parish authorities for 'unlawful pregnancy' were arriving in London every week to swell the ranks of prostitutes.

The solemnisation of the marriage of Ann Hathaway and William Shakespeare is not to be found in any surviving register, which doesn't mean that they were married hugger-mugger by a hedge-priest. The issuing of the special licence itself suggests that the wedding of Will and Ann was to be properly solemnised, *in coram populo*, before a congregation, and by a priest with the authority to perform the ceremony. We could hope that, though it was out of season, they treated themselves to a village wedding. Ann may even have heard the bridesmaids singing *The Bride's Goodmorrow* as she opened her shutters on that dark November morning.

> The night is past and joyful day appeareth
>   Most clear on every side.
> With pleasant music we therefore salute you,
>   Good Morrow, Mistress Bride.
> From sleep and slumber now wake you out of hand.
>   Your bridegroom stayeth at home,
> Whose fancy, favour and affection still doth stand
>   Fixed on thee alone.
> Dress you in your best array!
> This must be your wedding day.[10]

Traditionally, the wedding celebrations took a whole summer's day, beginning with the waking of the bride by her maids and ending after sunset. At sun-up the village girls would form a procession and walk to the bride's house, singing as they went. Having roused the bride and dressed her they would then escort her on foot through the village to the church. In the epithalamium that he wrote for his own wedding with Elizabeth Boyle in 1594, Spenser conflated popular custom with the classic form; though he summoned the Muses to be bridesmaids, their duties are recognisable as those of English girls.

> Early before the world's life-giving lamp
> His golden beam upon the hills doth spread,
> Having dispersed the night's uncheerful damp,
> Do ye awake and with fresh lustihead
> Go to the bower of my beloved love,
> My truest turtle dove;
> Bid her awake . . .
> Bid her awake therefore and soon her dight [i.e. dress]—
> And while she doth her dight,
> Do ye to her of joy and solace sing,
> That all the woods may answer and your echo ring.[11]

It was the maids' job to arrange the bride's gown and hair, which would be worn spread on her shoulders for the last time. As a married woman she would put it up and cover it with a kerchief. Spenser gives us an idea of the costume of a bride of the 1580s:

> Clad all in white, that seems a virgin best . . .
> Her long loose yellow locks like golden wire,
> Sprinkled with pearl and pearling flowers a-tween,
> Do like a golden mantle her attire,
> And being crowned with a garland green,
> Seem like some maiden queen.[12]

Ann is unlikely to have dressed in white, but she would have had a new gown for the occasion. When widowed Jack of Newbury took a second bride she appeared before the company of local gentry,

> attired in a gown of sheep's russet and a kirtle of fine worsted, her head attired with a biliment of gold, and her hair as yellow as gold, hanging down behind her, which was curiously combed and pleated, according

to the manner in those days. She was led to the church between two
sweet boys, with bride-laces and rosemary tied about their silken
sleeves.[13]

Sometimes the bridesmaids prepared the way to the church, so that
the bride did not sully her slippers:

> As I have seen upon a bridal day,
> Full many maids clad in their best array,
> In honour of the bride come with their flaskets
> Filled full with flowers, others, in wicker baskets,
> Bring from the marsh rushes to o'erspread
> The ground whereon the lovers tread.[14]

Sometimes the groom too was woken with music; in *The Merchant
of Venice* the music Portia will have played while Bassanio considers
the caskets will be such:

> As are those dulcet sounds in break of day,
> That creep into the dreaming bridegroom's ear
> And summon him to marriage. (III. iii. 51–3)

The groom too had new clothes for the occasion: '[The groom's]
house was as full of lusty gallants that took care to set out their
bridegroom all new from top to toe, with a pair of green garters tied
cross above the knee and a dozen of crewel points that set off his hose
very fair.'[15] The groom then walks to the bride's house with his
attendant knights, 'fresh boys' 'in their fresh garments trim' with the
musicians, the pipe, the tabor and the excited crowd.

> The whiles the boys run up and down the street,
> Crying aloud with strong, confusèd noise . . .[16]

Among the garlands brought by the maids should be a special one
for the bride, according to Spenser, 'of lilies and of roses Bound true-
love-wise with a blue silk riband'.[17] The onlookers begin to applaud
as the groom's party approaches and at last the bride appears:

> Forth, honoured groom; behold not far behind,
> Your willing bride, led by two strengthless boys . . .[18]

The wedding was above all a celebration for the neighbourhood. Rather than bringing presents the guests brought flowers and herbs, and were rewarded by the bride with tokens, usually twopenny gloves.

> All things are ready and every whit prepared
>   To bear you company.
> Your friends and parents do give their attendance
>   Together courteously.
> The house is dressed and garnished for your sake
>   With flowers gallant and green.
> A solemn feast your comely cooks do ready make,
>   Where all your friends will be seen.
> Young men and maids do ready stand
>   With sweet rosemary in their hand . . .[19]

With all this clamour anyone in the neighbourhood who didn't already know that a marriage was toward would join the throng that was bringing the bridal pair towards the church. Such a village wedding was as public as could be, with all the neighbours, as well as the couple's parents and the ubiquitous 'friends' who had made the match and drawn up any settlements, as witnesses. What happened next was ordained by the Book of Common Prayer: 'At the day and the time appointed for solemnization of Matrimony, the persons to be married shall come into the body of the Church with their friends and neighbours . . .' The main plot and all the sub-plots of *As You Like It* are driven by the theme of marriage; the finale of the play is a four-fold wedding at which Hymen himself officiates and everybody sings the 'wedlock' hymn:

> Wedding is great Juno's crown,
> O blessed bond of board and bed.
> 'Tis Hymen peoples every town;
> High wedlock then be honourèd.

> Honour, high honour and renown
> To Hymen, God of every town. (V. iv. 139–44)

Nearly all the marriages in Shakespeare's plays are two-stage affairs, consisting of contract or 'wedding' and solemnisation or 'matrimony'. As Fripp remarks, 'The domestic contract was the binding ceremony, marriage in church was the concluding rite.'[20] The earliest of the Shakespearean two-stage marriages is that of Katharina and Petruchio in *The Taming of the Shrew*. The first stage, the church wedding, is thoroughly sabotaged by Petruchio. Though he himself had arranged it, he evidently doesn't consider it a true wedding, for after it he doesn't permit himself to exercise the rights of a husband.

He is so late in coming to collect his bride that Katharina storms off in tears.

> He'll woo a thousand, 'point the day of marriage,
> Make feast, invite friends, and proclaim the banns,
> Yet never means to wed where he hath wooed. (III. ii. 15–17)

The 'goodly company' stays to witness Petruchio's arrival bizarrely accoutred. He goes to 'bid good morrow' to his bride and together they proceed to the off-stage church, where he indulges in a bout of sacrilege.

>   when the priest
> Should ask if Katharine should be his wife,
> 'Ay, by gogs-wouns,' quoth he, and swore so loud
> That, all amazed, the priest let fall the book,
> And, as he stooped again to take it up,
> The mad-brained bridegroom took him such a cuff
> That down fell priest and book, and book and priest.
> 'Now take them up,' quoth he, 'if any list.' (III. iii. 31–8)

Katharina, we are told, merely 'trembled and shook'. 'After many ceremonies done', Petruchio called for wine, 'quaffed off the muscadel And threw the sops all over the sexton's face'.

This done, he took the bride about the neck,
And kissed her lips with such a clamorous smack
That at the parting all the church did echo. (50–2)

The sound of music warns the people on stage that the bridal
couple is on its way back from the church, but when he arrives
Petruchio refuses to enjoy 'the great store of wedding cheer' and drags
his rebellious wife off to the country where he refuses to consummate
the marriage. The second stage of the wedding is when Petruchio,
satisfied that Katharina now respects and trusts him, asks her to kiss
him 'in the midst of the street', *in coram populo*, like any puritan.

In *Twelfth Night*, Olivia gives Sebastian a pearl as a love-token, and
then turns up with a priest, but even in this rather popish case the
marriage is divided into two parts, the first private and the second public:

> Now go with me, and with this holy man,
> Into the chantry by. There before him
> Plight me the full assurance of your faith,
> That my most jealous and too doubtful soul
> May live at peace. He shall conceal it
> Whiles you are willing it shall come to note,
> What time we will our celebration keep
> According to my birth. (IV. iii. 23–31)

The troth-plight in the chantry is clandestine, and chantries are a
feature of the old religion. If Shakespeare was the Catholic so many
scholars think he might have been, he might well have married Ann
by the rites of the Catholic Church. For a Catholic marriage to have
been valid after the Council of Trent, there would have to have been
another witness besides the priest, but as there would have been no
opportunity to publish the banns in a parish church, the marriage
could not have been valid in English law. The only solution would
have been another ceremony, with all the appropriate legal safe-
guards. Without these the Shakespeares' children would have been
illegitimate and Ann deprived of her rights. Probably, though not
certainly, the marriage of Will and Ann was solemnised according to
the ritual set out in the Book of Common Prayer.

The rites are done, and now, as 'tis the guise,
Love's fast by day a feast must solemnise.

The season for marriages has always been supposed to be the summer solstice but the register of Holy Trinity Stratford tells a rather different story. The most popular month by far for weddings in the 1580s was October, followed by November. Together these two months accounted for more than a third of the total number of weddings. May was next, on a par with January, with June rather a long way behind. From 1580 to 1590 not a single wedding was celebrated on Midsummer Day. November days are short. Ann and Will would not have had to wait out an endless twilight as the couples have to do in *A Midsummer Night's Dream* before they could be bedded. If they had followed the custom, Ann would have been conducted to her bride bed and undressed by her maids, who were entitled to keep her garters. Will would have been undressed by his bride boys who would carry off his points, the ties that secured his codpiece, to keep for talismans. Perhaps none of this happened at the Shakespeares' November wedding but, if it did not, it would not have been because the bride was pregnant or because they were in a hurry. In *Romeo and Juliet*, Juliet's father decides to marry her off to Paris at a mere thirty-six hours' notice, but the feasting is not scamped. Twenty cooks are hired, spices, dates and quinces brought from the pantry and the musicians already playing when the nurse goes to give the bride good-morrow. If Will and Ann could give their neighbours no wedding feast, it would have been simply because there was no one to pay for it. Ann's parents were dead, Will's parents were broke and they needed every penny they could scrape together for somewhere to live.

CHAPTER SEVEN

*considering how and where the Bard and his bride set up house, of
cottages and cottaging, and of how they understood their obligations
to each other*

At the end of *Shakespeare the Man* (1973) A. L. Rowse has the temerity to
exercise his imagination on what passed through Shakespeare's mind as
he lay dying: 'And so back to earlier scenes, the pretty country folks in
the acres of rye on the way to Shottery, bringing a bride in over the
threshhold of the crowded old home in Henley Street . . .'[1] Carrying
the bride over the threshhold makes very little sense if the house you are
carrying her into is not yours, and hence not hers. Rowse's fantasy has
more to do with the mores of the early-twentieth-century urban
working class than with rural Warwickshire in the sixteenth century.
Fripp too is almost foolhardy in his certainty that Shakespeare brought
his pregnant wife to live with his parents and brothers and sister:

> It was the custom in Stratford, as elsewhere, for the eldest son to make
> his home under the parental roof, and if the Poet and his wife had lived
> elsewhere than at the Birthplace . . . it was contrary to custom, and we
> should probably have a hint of it.[2]

But Fripp is wrong. It was not the custom in Stratford or anywhere
else in sixteenth-century England for married children to live with or
off their parents. The conclusion Laslett draws from the evidence of
the Cambridge Group is quite uncompromising:

> The rule is as follows: no two married couples or more went to make
> up a family group . . . When a son got married he left the family of his
> parents and started a family of his own. If he was not in a position to do

this, then he could not get married, nor could his sister, unless the man who was to take her for his bride was also in a position to start a new family.[3]

Despite all the work that has been done on English family building patterns since Fripp wrote, Greenblatt simply follows him, with the difference that 'the crowded old home' has become a 'spacious house':

> In the summer of 1583 the nineteen-year-old William Shakespeare was settling into the life of a married man with a new-born daughter, living all together with his parents and his sister Joan, and his brothers, Gilbert, Richard and Edmund, and however many servants they could afford in the spacious house on Henley Street.[4]

John Shakespeare was not a nineteenth-century captain of industry but a Tudor artisan. The house in Henley Street may have been 'spacious' but if Shakespeare was still working as a glover it should also have been the site of the workshops where his workmen treated the stinking skins. The piles of skins were bulky and more room had to be found for the various pits where the skins were treated and the tubs in which they were soaked. When the skins were cut out and ready, space had to be found for the workmen and -women who sewed them. Then there were the bales of wool and other farming produce that Shakespeare dealt in. Any servants kept by the Shakespeares would have been employed in the business, not in domestic niceties. Nursemaids and ladies' maids were not to be found in the houses of Tudor tradesmen.

The atmosphere in the Shakespeare house cannot have been improved by the fact that John Shakespeare had been on bad terms with his neighbours for years. We shall probably never know what convoluted set of circumstances led to his punishment by the Court of Queen's Bench in 1580 – if indeed it was he. In Trinity Term a 'John Shakespeare of Stratford, yeoman' was fined the swingeing sum of £20 when he failed to appear to provide surety for 'keeping the peace towards the Queen and all her people'; he also forfeited sureties of £10 each for two other men, John Audeley of Nottingham, hatmaker, and Thomas Cooley of Stoke, yeoman.[5] Michael Wood thinks that what connected the three was religion, and that they had been singled out as Catholic recusants.[6] The matter remains mysterious; we don't know why John Shakespeare preferred to jettison so much money, as much as he had made on the mortgaging of the principal part of his wife's inheritance, rather than show his face in the Court of Queen's Bench. Nor do we know why he was referred to as a 'yeoman' when he was supposed to be a glover.

In Trinity Term 1582 John Shakespeare was obliged to petition in the Court of Queen's Bench for sureties of the peace against four of his neighbours, Ralph Cawdrey, William Russell, Thomas Logging and Robert Young 'for fear of death and mutilation of his limbs'.[7] Ralph Cawdrey, then serving as Bailiff of Stratford, had been running his butcher's business in Bridge Street since 1541. In 1559 he had been fined for fighting with Mary Shakespeare's brother-in-law Alexander Webbe of Bearley, and in 1560 he was fined for an affray with one 'Greene of Wotton'. Why he should have been one of the people threatening to cudgel John Shakespeare in the summer of 1582 we shall probably never know. Rowse assumes that he owed them all money.[8] By September the affair seems to have blown over, for Cawdrey was present when John Shakespeare attended the council meeting on 5 September and voted for his friend John Sadler to be chosen bailiff, his first appearance in the council chamber in six years.

Some time before July 1582 one of John Shakespeare's properties had been leased to William Burbage who, finding the arrangement unsatisfactory, demanded to be released from the contract and the return of the £7 he had paid for the lease.[9] The Court of Common Pleas appointed three Stratford businessmen as arbitrators. Two lived in Henley Street: one, Alderman Nicholas Barnhurst, a rambunctious puritan woollen draper, represented John Shakespeare, the other, Alderman William Badger, a Catholic woollen draper, represented Burbage. The third, neutral member of the committee was John Lytton. The three met at St Mary le Bow in London and found for Burbage. It was decided that John Shakespeare should present himself at the Sign of the Maiden Head in Stratford on Saturday 29 September between the hours of one and four in the afternoon,

to sign the quittance and repay the money. He did not show up. The
debt was to remain unpaid for ten years.[10]

Fripp believes that the difficulties with the letting were caused
directly or indirectly by Will and Ann's wedding:

> To his father's house in Henley Street, according to the custom in
> Stratford and elsewhere, Shakespeare would bring his wife. In antici-
> pation of this additional household, changes were made which seem to
> have been disturbing to the tenant (as we have supposed) of part of the
> house on the west, William Burbage.[11]

Despite his tireless examination of the Stratford records Fripp had no
idea which of John Shakespeare's properties was leased to Burbage; he
had deduced that Burbage had leased part of Henley Street because he
already assumed that Will and Ann would have been expected to live
there and interpreted the difficulty that arose in 1582 as a result of their
need for accommodation. He also recognises that Will and Ann
constituted an 'additional household' and his way of reconciling that
is to assume that a self-contained apartment was set aside for the newly-
weds and it was this that incommoded Burbage. If this was already
understood before July 1582, Will and Ann must have been
already betrothed, which does seem unlikely. As well as the 'fine'
or fee for the lease, Burbage would have been expected to pay ten
shillings a year in rent, on part of one or other of Shakespeare's
properties. The fact that two of the arbiters had Henley Street
connections is the best evidence that the premises involved were
there. In 1592 when Shakespeare was finally forced to give Burbage
back his money, he was required to pay thirty-six shillings in damages
as well. The likeliest cause of the litigation is that Burbage considered
that the conditions of his lease had been breached and the arbitrators in
the case obviously agreed with him. The ground for the confusion
probably lies in the fact that the lease to Burbage was not the only lease
demised by Shakespeare on the Henley Street property. Robert
Bearman, who probably knows more about the Stratford archives
than anyone else on earth, makes another observation that really does
knock the idea of the 'spacious house in Henley Street' firmly on the
head. Referring back to the litigation with Burbage, he observes:

The arbiters have instructions that the money should be paid back 'at the sign of the Maiden Head' ('apud signum de le maiden hedd') in Stratford, the inn name by which part of the Henley Street property later became known. It could be, then, not only that John, hard pressed for cash, had mortgaged part of his main residence for cash but also that part of it had been leased for use as an inn.[12]

If this is so, then, even if John, Mary, Joan, Gilbert, Richard and two-year-old Edmund were still rattling around in the double house in Henley Street in November 1582, plans were already afoot to turn the freehold into cash. By 1590 the house in Greenhill Street was gone as well, so we should probably guess that within a few months of their son's untimely marriage the Shakespeares were reduced to roosting in a pair of rooms at the back of the Maiden Head, hard by the Gild Pits (the town dump). Turning the property into an inn was not as bad an idea as it might seem. Inns were where all business was transacted; as a wool brogger Shakespeare needed to meet clients from all over England and beyond, and an inn, where messages and goods could be left and collected, where the scriveners based themselves, which functioned on occasion as a bank, would serve his turn. As it was someone else's business to run it and keep it clean, John Shakespeare could concentrate on his business, if in November 1582 he still had any business.

The Maiden Head, which was leased to Lewis Hiccox, was no hole in the wall. The inventory made after Hiccox's death in 1627 lists no fewer than thirteen beds, variously disposed in a 'hall', a 'parlour', a 'lodging chamber', a 'room over the cellar', a 'best chamber', a 'stairhead chamber', a 'three-bed chamber', a 'servants' chamber', a 'further parlour' and a 'room overhead'. Even more significant is that the unexpired remainder of the lease is valued as part of the estate: 'Item one chattel and lease of the houses in Henley Street of the demise and grant of William Shakespeare gent. for 63 years . . .'[13] It would seem from his inventory that Hiccox occupied rather more than half of the double property, and the high value of the lease confirms such an impression. The lease sold to Hiccox in 1601 must have been for ninety-one years; what should surprise those people who believe that by 1601 William Shakespeare was a very rich man is that once he had become the owner of the freehold he apparently made no attempt to rescind the lease and restore the house to his mother and brothers. There may have been very little he could do, if the terms of the original lease had been faithfully observed by the tenant and his rent paid on time. If this was the case, then John Shakespeare had effectively disinherited his son. If, on the other hand, Shakespeare offered Hiccox a new long lease and pocketed the fine himself, we should probably infer that he needed the money.

One of Will's reasons for getting married at the age of eighteen might have been a profound desire for a quiet home of his own where he could think straight.[14] Philoponus, in Philip Stubbes's *Anatomy of Abuses*, lamenting the irresponsibility of boys who marry young, takes it for granted that even the youngest would set up housekeeping on their own:

> And besides this you shall have every saucy boy of ten, fourteen, sixteen or twenty years of age, to snatch up a woman and marry her, without any fear of God at all, or respect had, either to her religion, wisdom, integrity of life, or any other virtue, or, which is more, without any respect how they may live together with sufficient maintenance for their callings and estate. No, no – it maketh no matter for these things. So he have his pretty pussy to huggle withal, it forceth not, for that is the only thing he desireth. Then build they up a cottage, though but of elder poles, in every lane end, almost, where they live as beggars all their life . . .[15]

The opportunity to set up housekeeping for themselves was interpreted by some of the ballad-writers as an incentive for premarital sex (italics mine):

> Faith, boys and girls, and knaves and trulls,
>   There can be no dividing.
> They must be matcht and will be pitched,
>   *Somewhere to have a biding.*
> 'Tush!' quoth old Rule, 'Man, you're a fool.
>   Don't those so that have riches?
> But now they'll prevent the impediment,
>   For down goes cloak, and bag and breeches.[16]

(The reference to preventing an impediment is also germane.)

John Shakespeare's affairs were in such disarray in the autumn of 1582 he was in no position to offer his teenage son and pregnant bride free board and lodging. In the late Elizabethan household food accounted for nearly half of all outgoings; the relative cost of food can be assessed from the fact that workers who were not fed by their masters received double the rate of pay offered to workers who were given meals. A man who had been assessed as having no goods whatever that could be distrained to pay his debts could not afford to take on numerous servants (as Greenblatt supposes) or invite his son's family to eat him out of house and home.

The puritan divine William Whateley of Banbury, who often preached at Stratford, admonished the young man seeking to marry:

> When thou art married, if it may be, live of thyself with thy wife in a family of thine own, and not with another in one family, as it were, betwixt you both . . . The mixing of governors in an household, or subordinating or uniting of two masters or two dames under one roof doth fall out most times to be a matter of much unquietness to all parties. To make the young folks so wholly resign themselves unto the elder as not to be discontented with their proceedings, or to make the elder so much to deny themselves as to condescend unto the wills of the younger . . . [is] in the common sort of people altogether impossible. Whereof as young bees do seek unto themselves another hive, so let the young couple [seek] another house . . .[17]

Joan Hathaway might have been able to feed her stepdaughter and stepson-in-law from the yield of her half-yardland but she would not have been expected to do so. If Will was not prepared to take over the work of a husbandman, it would have been folly to have offered him houseroom at Hewlands Farm. The matrimonial bed stood in the parlour at the top of the stairs; Richard Hathaway's widow was hardly likely to have handed it over to the newly-weds, and even less likely to send them to sleep with the younger children. We may conclude that it is as unlikely that Ann brought Will to live at Shottery as that he brought her to Henley Street. If the worst came to the worst and the newly-weds could not find a home of their own the chances are they would each have returned to the house of their parents to live apart until some habitation could be found for them. In *The Witch of Edmonton* by Dekker, Ford and Rowley, Frank Thorney has not the wherewithal to set up house with his pregnant bride, Winifred, who must go to live with her uncle. She laments:

> You have discharged
> The true part of an honest man. I cannot
> Request a fuller satisfaction
> Than you have freely granted, yet methinks
> 'Tis a hard case, being man and wife,
> We should not live together.

When Frank tells her that he will visit her once a month she wails:

> Once every month?
> Is this to have a husband?[18]

It was because married people were expected to set up housekeeping on their own that the age at marriage in Elizabethan England was so high:

> marriage was an act of profound importance to the social structure. It meant the creation of a new economic unit as well as a lifelong association of persons previously separate and caught-up in existing families. It gave the man full membership of the community, and added a cell to village society. It is understandable, therefore, that marriage could not come about unless a slot was vacant, so to speak, and the aspiring couple was to fill it up. It might be a cottage which had fallen empty, so that a manservant and a womanservant could now marry and go to live there as cottagers. For the more fortunate it would be a plot of land which had to be taken up and worked by some yeoman's or some husbandman's son, with his wife to help him. It might be a bakery, or a joinery, or a loom which had to be manned anew. This meant that all young people ordinarily had to wait before they married, unless they were gentlefolk, though they might well have to wait even then for rather different reasons. Therefore the age at marriage would necessarily tend to be high . . .[19]

Ann is typical of Laslett's early modern bride; it is her husband who is the exception to the rule, being himself a minor, with a mother who has a two-year-old child and could still produce more. The presence of another breeding woman in the house would have been unusual, if not positively indecorous.

On the day of her marriage Ann should have received the ten marks promised her in her father's will and Will should have matched it with ten marks of his own. Twenty marks would have been more than enough to cover the rent of an adequate dwelling. The most costly item of furniture would have been the marital bed. If the newly-weds had found a plot of four acres or more to buy, they would have had the right to erect a cottage on it, and they might still have got some change out of their twenty marks. There is at least a chance that for a year or two or even more Will and Ann experienced love in a cottage. Nowadays a 'cottage' is thought of as a detached dwelling with a particular kind of garden and roses round the porch. 'Ann Hathaway's Cottage' is just such a cottage, with an inappropriate garden that is more Helen Allingham than Shakespeare. An Elizabethan cottage is an altogether humbler habitation, built on waste land or a road verge, with no rights to the surrounding land. People driven off the land by changes in land tenure and use had no option but to find shelter where they could. The authorities struggled to control the situation. In 1589 a new statute was passed: 'No man may at this day build such a cottage for habitation unless he lay unto it four acres of freehold land, except in market towns or cities or within a mile of the sea, or for habitation of labourers in mines, sailors, foresters, sheepherders &c'.[20]

In August 1599, Lady Margaret Hoby 'walked with Mr Hoby about the town to spy out the best places where cottages might be builded';[21] as diligent landlords the Hobys were apparently intending to provide basic accommodation for the poorest of their employees, and at the same time to reduce the likelihood of their squatting in inconvenient places and unsuitable buildings. Some private landlords in Stratford did build cottages for rent; in 1614 or so Philip Rogers, a Stratford apothecary, leased a group of five cottages from Richard Lane and sub-let them to poor inhabitants.[22]

If Ann's cottage had been thrown up on the banks of the Avon she might have made her living as the family of Dekker's Patient Grissill did. The action of the play, originally performed by the Admiral's Men in 1603, is patently incredible, which makes it all the more important that the circumstantial detail be familiar. Grissill lives with her father in a cottage by a river; with Babulo, the comedy hired help, they make a living by gathering osiers and plaiting them into baskets. Her sole possessions are her straw hat, her threadbare russet gown and her earthen pitcher in which 'many a good mess of water gruel' has been made. When her scholar brother Laureo turns up, lamenting that he has been forced by poverty to abandon his university studies, his father makes the best of it:

> Welcome, my son. Though I am poor
> My love shall not be so. Go, daughter Grissill,
> Fetch water from the spring to seethe our fish
> Which yesterday I caught. The cheer is mean,
> But be content. When I have sold these baskets
> The money shall be spent to bid thee welcome.[23]

It is Grissill's fate to be married to a marquess and dressed in silks, and then persecuted and rejected. When she is clothed once more in her russet and sent back home, with her pitcher and her twin boy and girl, her father simply says as Ann might have, 'We'll work to find them food' (IV. ii. 90). It is only proper to point out that basket-makers are never mentioned in the Stratford muniments, but it stands to reason that there must have been some living along the Avon, anywhere where there was a 'rank of osiers by the murmuring stream'.[24] Baskets are not the kinds of wares that are hawked from place to place; traditionally they are made on the spot and to order. The young Shakespeares are unlikely to have survived by basket-making, unless like Janiculo they had hired help. People who lived on the other side of Stratford near the heath made 'besoms' or birch-brooms to sell. Even the poorest of householders in the 1580s could find people poorer than themselves who would work for a relatively small proportion of what they earned, sometimes for no more than a pallet in an outhouse and belly-cheer.

The main action of *As You Like It* takes place in the 'Forest of Arden' which is ostensibly in France but occasionally recognisable as

Warwickshire. When Rosalind disguised as Ganymede hears from Corin the shepherd that his master has put up for sale 'his cote, his flocks and bounds of feed' she asks him:

> I pray you, if it stand with honesty,
> Buy thou the cottage, pasture and the flock,
> And thou shalt have to pay for it of us. (II. iv. 89–91)

Corin thus becomes their agent and buys the dwelling, the pasturage and the flock with the ladies' gold (III. v). The cottage is referred to several times, once as 'a sheepcote fenced about with olive trees',

> down in the neighbour bottom.
> The rank of osiers by the murmuring stream,
> Left on your right hand, brings you to the place. (IV. iii. 79–81)

Perdita lives in what is several times referred to as a cottage (*The Winter's Tale*, IV. i. ii). The first two scenes of Act IV are set in 'the shepherd's cottage', scene iii on 'a road near the shepherd's cottage'.

What are described as cottages in late-sixteenth-century Warwickshire are usually three-roomed dwellings made of lath and plaster, consisting of a 'hall' (not necessarily spacious), a lower chamber and a single upper chamber, which was often used as storage space for corn, malt, cheeses and bacon. The central feature of the hall was the open hearth where the cooking was done. With luck there would have been a chimney, otherwise the smoke simply made its way out through the thatch, annihilating lice, flies and fleas as it went. Windows were few, small, and unglazed; in bad weather or when the inhabitants were out, the window spaces were shuttered and barred from within. Except for the timber floor of the upper chamber or soller, the floors were either earthen or paved. All the water for cooking and bathing had to be carried in heavy wooden buckets from the nearest well or stream.

The Stratford archives give us no clue whatsoever to the whereabouts of Will Shakespeare and his family in the 1580s. If they had been tenants of the Corporation, their whereabouts would have been a matter of record, but they were not. If they had been private tenants they would have been as hard to pick up as Lewis Hiccox was in Henley Street. If they bought land by private treaty or squatted on vacant land, they would probably have escaped notice altogether. Where changes in land tenure had resulted in depopulation, cottages and farmhouses stood empty; Ann and Will could have squatted or acquired some kind of tenancy in the environs of Stratford. All we can say with a degree of certainty is wherever they found a home it was within the boundaries of the parish, because when their first child was born Will and his friends brought her to the font at Holy Trinity.

Ann Shakespeare was probably clearer about her duties as a wife than her boy husband was about his own role. She had learnt from her Bible that wifehood was the female's highest calling, instituted by God in the time of man's innocency, that is, in Paradise, before the Fall: 'House and riches are the inheritance of the fathers but a prudent wife is of the Lord' (Proverbs, xix: 14). In Sir John Davies's thumbnail sketch, we may see perhaps Ann Shakespeare's role model:

> The first of all our sex came from the side of man.
> I thither am returned, where first our sex began.
> I do not visit much, nor many when I do.
> I tell my mind to few, and that in counsel too.
> I seem not sick in health, nor sullen but in sorrow.
> I care for somewhat else than what to wear tomorrow.[25]

Women themselves had even more rigorous expectations of wives, if we are to judge by this chorus from Elizabeth Cary's closet *Tragedy of Mariam*:

> 'Tis not enough for one that is a wife
> To keep her spotless from an act of ill,
> But from suspicion she should free her life,
> And bare herself of power as well as will.
> 'Tis not so glorious for her to be free
> As by her proper self restrained to be.[26]

Stephen Greenblatt argues rather quaintly:

> It is, perhaps, as much what Shakespeare did not write as what he did
> that seems to indicate something seriously wrong with his marriage . . .
> though wedlock is the promised land toward which his comic heroes
> and heroines strive, and though family fission is the obsessive theme of
> the tragedies, Shakespeare is curiously restrained in his depictions of
> what it is actually like to be married.[27]

Greenblatt then lists fascinating glimpses of spousal interaction in
Shakespeare's plays, Goneril and Albany arguing, Kate Percy rejected
by Hotspur, Edmund Mortimer and his Welsh wife unable to
communicate, Portia and Brutus ditto. The inference seems to be
that other authors do show us happy married life and the communion
of spouses. There is almost no literature in any language known to me
in which we are shown around a functional marriage. Though
marriage is the happy ending of most works with happy endings,
we are not invited to hang about and watch the spouses interacting.
We get inside marriages only when they are dysfunctional. Then the
sacredness of marriage, its shared privacy, its skinless intimacy can be
dissected, the awfulness of the symbiosis drawn out and displayed like
the living guts of the dying heretics on Tower Hill. Shakespeare is not
Edward Albee or John Updike. Besides, despite his public profession,
he seems to have been a very private man. It is not simply that we
have no letters from him to Ann or vice versa; we have no letters from
him to anyone. We assume that his sonnets are private, but in fact we
can't be sure that he was writing them in his own persona.

It seems as likely that Shakespeare protected Ann's privacy as that he
was so alienated from her he couldn't bring himself to write about
husbands and wives at all. Greenblatt sees that Shakespeare understood
something of what Ann had to endure during his long absences, and
gives the obvious example of Adriana's outcry in *The Comedy of Errors*:

> How comes it now, my husband, O how comes it
> That thou art thus estrangèd from thyself? –
> Thyself I call it, being strange to me
> That, undividable, incorporate,
> Am better than thy dear self's better part.
> Ah, do not tear thyself away from me,

> For, know, my love, as easy mayst thou fall
> A drop of water in the breaking gulf,
> And take unmingled thence that drop again
> Without addition or diminishing,
> As take me from thyself, and not me too. (II. ii. 122–32)

Greenblatt comments: 'The scene in which these words are spoken is comical, for Adriana is unwittingly addressing not her husband but her husband's long-lost identical twin. Yet the speech is too long and the pain too intense to be altogether absorbed in laughter.'[28] This is true, as far as it goes. Greenblatt does not notice that Adriana's figure of the drop in the ocean is part of an important image cluster in the play, which is by no means as uniformly funny as he thinks, unless you think having people sentenced to death, robbed, hounded and driven to distraction is good for a laugh and nothing else. A closer look at a play that wears its profundity lightly will tell us much more about Shakespeare's attitude to marriage.

The play opens with an aged father on trial for his life; Egeon, a Syracusan merchant, has fallen foul of the Ephesian authorities who have placed an embargo on trade with Syracuse. Any merchants who, cannot raise sufficient 'guilders to redeem their lives' will be executed:

> if any Syracusan born
> Come to the bay of Ephesus he dies,
> His goods confiscate to the duke's dispose
> Unless a thousand marks be levied
> To quit the penalty and to ransom him.
> Thy substance, valued at the highest rate,
> Cannot amount to a hundred marks,
> Therefore by law thou art condemned to die. (I. i. 18–25)

There is nothing very amusing about any of this, especially to anyone who knew what persecution John Shakespeare was enduring at the hands of capricious authority back in Stratford. Egeon answers:

> Yet this is my comfort: when your words are done
> My woes end likewise with the evening sun. (26–7)

The duke is moved to a minimum degree of mercy.

> Yet will I favour thee in what I can.
> Therefore merchant I'll limit thee this day
> To seek thy health by beneficial help.
> Try all the friends thou hast in Ephesus.
> Beg thou, or borrow, to make up the sum,
> And live. If no, then thou art doomed to die. (49–54)

We don't see Egeon again until the final scene of the play. He is brought on 'barehead with the headsman and other officers', bound, as if on his way to execution. He stands silent as Adriana pleads with the duke to order the abbess of the nearby convent, where her errant husband has found sanctuary, to open the gates. Egeon does not speak until he has seen his son's long-lost twin, whom of course he takes for the son he knows. He pleads with him to pay his ransom, and is denied. His prospects of survival having withered away, the gate of the convent suddenly opens to reveal the abbess with the other Antipholus. She is the *deus ex machina*. She is also Egeon's wife. As she originally presented him with twins, she presents them now on stage together for the first time. The words of redemption are spoken by her.

> Whoever bound him, I will loose his bonds,
> And gain a husband by his liberty. (V. i. 341–2)

The wife who redeems her husband does so by remaining faithful to her bond, even in the absence of fellowship, comfort and intimacy. The compact between spouses is a spiritual one; remaining faithful to it is what constitutes salvation. This is a hard doctrine; only the abbess knows how hard.

> Thirty-three years have I but gone in travail
> Of you, my sons, and till this present hour
> My heavy burden ne'er deliverèd.
> The duke, my husband, and my children both,
> And you the calendars of their nativity,

> Go to a gossips' feast and joy with me
> After so long grief, such felicity. (403–9)

Greenblatt might object that this is nothing but a conventional schema, typical of an older kind of didactic play, that he is entitled to ignore it and concentrate on interchanges that might strike him as belonging to the stuff of theatre rather than ritual. Perhaps, perhaps. What should be obvious is that Shakespeare did not think in twentieth-century clichés. We are not dealing here with representations of folk as 'happily married', but as truly married. For Shakespeare marriage was a demanding and difficult way of life – if anything, more demanding and more difficult for wives than for husbands. Even before the abbess appears to redeem her husband, the wronged wife Adriana steps in to do something similar for the man she thinks is her husband, bound as a madman and pursued for debt. When the arresting officer protests:

> He is my prisoner. If I let him go,
> The debt he owes will be required of me (IV. iv. 118–19)

she answers:

> I will discharge thee ere I go from thee.
> Bear me forthwith unto his creditor,
> And, knowing how the debt grows, I will pay it. (120–2)

When we first meet Adriana she is distraught because her husband does as he pleases, ignoring her needs and demands; her younger sister, who has yet to assume the yoke of marriage, presumes to tell her her duty. The audience can see very clearly that Adriana rails because her husband doesn't turn up for dinner and that her husband turns up less and less because when he does he gets an earful. In *The Comedy of Errors* Shakespeare dramatises the growing misunderstanding and alienation of spouses who begin their married lives with unrealistic expectations by poising the 'before' against the 'after'. The courting of Luciana by the unmarried Antipholus is the before; the after is the painful conflict that has arisen between the married Antipholus and Adriana, who laments:

> What ruins are in me that can be found
> By him not ruined? Then is he the ground
> Of my defeatures. My decayèd fair
> A sunny look of his would soon repair . . . (II. i. 95–8)

> Thou art an elm, my husband, I a vine,
> Whose weakness married to thy proper state
> Makes me with thy strength to communicate . . . (II. ii. 177–9)

Though Luciana is critical of Adriana's destructive state of mind, she is also ready to exhort her sister's husband to behave better. Strangely, when she confronts the man she thinks is Adriana's husband she proceeds on the assumption that he is unfaithful to her sister and tells him to conceal it:

> Alas, poor women! Make us but believe
> (Being compact of credit) that you love us.
> Though others have the arm, show us the sleeve.
> We in your motion turn, and you may move us.
> Then, gentle brother, get you in again.
> Comfort my sister, cheer her, call her wife . . . (III. i. 21–6)

Of course Luciana is speaking to the unmarried Antipholus, who then to her horror begins to court her, calling her:

>   mine own self's better part,
> Mine eye's clear eye, my dear heart's dearer heart,
> My food, my fortune, and my sweet hope's aim,
> My sole earth's heaven, and my heaven's claim. (III. i. 61–4)

When Luciana beetles off to inform her sister of this turn of events she describes his hyperboles as 'Words that an honest suit might move'. Antipholus's eulogy of a wife as the helpmeet and pledge of salvation comes from the same psalm, cxxviii, to which Adriana refers in her lament. Though this paradisaical communion between spouses cannot happen on earth, it is what will characterise their relationship in heaven, according to the protestant champions of marriage.

Marriage, to all, whose joys two parties be,
And doubled are by being parted so,
Wherein the very act is chastity,
Whereby two souls into one body go,
It makes two one, whilst here they living be,
And after death in their posterity.[29]

Even before the mystery of her husband's strange behaviour has been solved, Adriana recovers her balance as a wife, with the aid of some rough talk from the abbess. We never see Adriana and Antipholus of Ephesus kiss and make up. Greenblatt, who hasn't noticed the aged spouses at all, thinks this odd and significant.

The situation seized Shakespeare's imagination, as if the misery of the neglected or abandoned spouse was something he knew personally and all too well. Amid the climactic flurry of recognitions, the play does not include, as it would have been reasonable to expect, a scene of marital reconciliation.[30]

That was because, even for the most rhapsodic panegyrists of marriage, the perfect union of spouses is not of this world but the next. Time and again Shakespeare confronted the two-in-one paradox of marriage, knowing it to be a contradiction in terms while celebrating its saving grace and power. Greenblatt goes on to discuss the one interchange between Leontes and Hermione in *The Winter's Tale* which seems to him to have the right touch of conjugal familiarity. In this play, as in *The Comedy of Errors*, an errant husband is saved by his wife; Hermione preserves unbroken the integrity of their union by removing herself from him who would have destroyed it, and making herself dead to the world, living as chaste and cloistered a life as the abbess. Will and Ann too seem to have lived most of their married life apart, unable even to communicate with each other. For all that, Ann, at least, was true to her bond.

CHAPTER EIGHT

of pregnancy, travail and childbirth, of christening and churching, and the society of women

Ann conceived forty weeks and a few days before her baby was christened on Sunday 26 May, Trinity Sunday, 1583, that is, in mid- to late August. At the time her friends made their trip to the Consistory Court at Worcester she was between twelve and fourteen weeks pregnant. In the weeks that had elapsed since her missed period she and Will had told her friends and his parents of their situation, secured his parents' consent, and taken advice from their local curate or the vicar himself as to how to proceed. Even if they guessed that a trip to the Consistory Court would be necessary they could not have known how much and what kind of paperwork would have to be prepared, if the journey was not to be fruitless. Officers of the court visited Stratford from time to time, but from the wording of the bond it seems that it was signed in Worcester. If Ann's pregnancy was no sooner verified than the arrangements for a marriage began to be put in place, we ought at least to consider the possibility that what has been assumed by almost all observers to have been an unfortunate accident was anything but.

Anthony Holden's version of events is more or less typical:

> Whatever Will's feelings, two of the late Farmer Hathaway's close friends, Fulke Sandells and John Richardson, came knocking on the door of the Shakespeare home in Henley Street that autumn demanding that the son of the house do the right thing by their deceased friend's homely daughter. Or so we may surmise . . .[1]

There were no pregnancy tests in 1582; Ann's pregnancy, especially behind the wooden busk that women then wore, would not have been evident. And if it had been, no shame would have attached to bride or groom on that score. Elizabethan parish registers show many christenings within three or four months of the parents' marriage, and the register of Holy Trinity is no exception. Of the twenty couples who were married there in 1582, five do not appear again in the register, probably because the brides have gone to live in their husbands' parishes elsewhere. Of the remaining fifteen brides, five were pregnant at the time of the solemnisation. Joan Slye, who married George Careless on 16 March, bore a son who was christened Nicholas on 13 June the same year, three months later. Joan Atford who married Robert Hall on 14 June bore a daughter who was christened Elizabeth on 5 November, less than five months later. Mary Mason, married to John Smith on 14 October, bore a son who was christened John on 21 January, three months later. In at least one case we may suspect the activities of the church court, intervening to regularise an irregular union; Margaret Meadowcraft bore and buried a bastard daughter, Frances, in January 1577; when she was married to (another) Robert Hall on 4 November she was pregnant again and bore a daughter who was christened Grace on 18 June the following year. Anne Such and Richard Sutton, who were married on 9 November 1582, were Ann's neighbours in Shottery. Their first child, a boy called John, was buried at Holy Trinity on 10 June 1583. Margery Field (sister of the printer of *Venus and Adonis*) married the Stratford dyer Robert Young on 16 October 1586; the couple's first child was baptised on 10 May 1587. As long as the solemnisation had been understood to be following on, it could have been delayed until the penitential season was over, without Ann's pregnancy being much more visible or any more shocking than it was in November.

For an honest woman, who was not free with her favours, premarital pregnancy was no disgrace at all. When Laslett's researchers took the trouble of comparing the register of marriages with the register of christenings in the same parish, they were surprised to see just how many of the christenings of first children occurred within nine months of marriage. They didn't have the luxury of comparing parish registers all over England so they couldn't come up with an overall figure, but in some parishes nearly a third of all first-borns were christened within eight and a half months of the solemnisation of marriage.

More than half of those babies who arrive early had been conceived within the three months before the marriage ceremony and not earlier . . . these first results of study show that premarital pregnancy was common in England, so common in Colyton and Wylye that it hardly seems possible that the affianced couple was everywhere expected to maintain chastity until after the church celebration was over.[2]

Thomas Deloney gives us a more reliable insight into Elizabethan attitudes to pregnancy in *Jack of Newbury*. While he was a house-guest of Jack's, a gentleman called Sir George Rigley seduced one of Jack's maidservants under the promise of marriage. When she found herself with child and reminded him of his promise, Rigley replied:

'Why thou lewd paltry thing, comest thou to father thy bastard upon me? Away, ye dunghill carrion, away! Hear you, good housewife, get you among your companions and lay your litter where you list, for if you trouble me any more, by Heaven I swear, thou shalt dearly abide it', and so, bending his brows like the angry god of war, he went his ways, leaving the child-breeding wench to the hazard of her fortune, either good or bad.[3]

Jack, who as the woman's employer stood *in loco parentis*, chose to believe his maidservant's word against the gentleman's. Determined that his guest should not dishonour his house he contrived an almost Shakespearean ruse. He told Rigley that he had chanced upon a rich young widow who, because she thought she might be pregnant by her late husband, was refusing all suitors. He advised Rigley to woo her, win her and bed her. Rigley proffered his suit to the supposed widow, who was actually the maidservant disguised in a French hood, and was accepted. The marriage was solemnised at the Tower of London without delay. When Rigley realised how he had been tricked, 'he fretted and fumed, stamped and stared like a devil'.

'Why!' quoth Master Winchcomb, 'What needs all this? Came you to my table to make my maid a strumpet? Had you no man's house to dishonour but mine? Sir, I would you should well know, that I account the poorest wench in my house too good to be your whore, were you ten knights, and, seeing you took a pleasure to make her your wanton, take it no scorn to make her your wife, and use her well too, or you shall hear of it.' And 'Hold thee Joan,' quoth he, 'there is a hundred pounds for thee. And let him not say thou camest to him a beggar.'[4]

Shakespeare's feelings about premarital pregnancy can perhaps be deduced from his treatment of Jaquenetta's pregnancy in *Love's Labour's Lost*. It is announced at the Masque of the Nine Worthies, in front of the whole company including the king and princess. Costard, who would have liked Jaquenetta for himself, shouts out to Armado, playing the role of Hector: 'Fellow Hector, she is gone. She is two months on her way . . . Unless you play the honest Troyan, the wench is cast away. She's quick. The child brags in her belly already. 'Tis yours' (V. ii. 666, 667–8). Costard threatens Armado with whipping, the penalty for fornication. Armado, who is a complete fraud, as poor as Shakespeare must have been in 1582, unable even to afford a shirt, eventually vows 'to Jaquenetta to hold the plough for her sweet love three year'. Jaquenetta is not rendered unworthy of Armado's love simply because she is pregnant by him. Theirs will be a crazy mésalliance, but the person who must bear the blame for that is not Jaquenetta but the poseur who besieged her with letters dotted with Latin tags, with songs and sonnets and 'whole volumes in folio'. Who knows but with Jaquenetta's help the fake gentleman might well make an honest farmer? Was Ann Will's Jaquenetta? According to Anthony Burgess, Will's discourse was garnished with Latin tags.[5] Was he more like Armado than Romeo?

It should not be thought that because his wife was pregnant Shakespeare was excluded from the usual pleasures of a honeymoon. According to the seventeenth-century midwife Jane Sharp,

. . . so soon as a woman conceives the mouth of the womb is most exactly shut close, yet can they lie with men all that while, and some women before others will take more pleasure and are more desirous of their husband's company then than before, which is scarce seen in any other female creatures besides, most of them being fully satisfied after they have conceived, but it was needful for Man that it should be so, because polygamy is forbidden by the laws of God.[6]

Ann had probably assisted at the births of Joan Hathaway's children at Hewlands Farm, so she knew the drill. She would have had her childbed-linen ready. Some of it would have been left to her and her sister Catherine by their mother. In 1665 or so Lady Elizabeth Hatton wrote to her son Christopher whose wife she thought (correctly) was pregnant:

> If my guess be true tell her if she will make me a grandmother I have a little shirt and head cloths and biggin which I have kept by me that was the first that my mother wore and that I wore and I am very sure that you wore and have ever since laid it up carefully for your wife.[7]

More childbed-linen would have been given or lent to Ann by her stepmother Joan Hathaway and perhaps by Mary Shakespeare too. And some of it Ann would have acquired or made for herself. Childbed-linen consisted of bed-linen and clothing for both mother and child. The mother needed forehead cloths, caps, open-fronted shifts suitable for breast-feeding, and skirts, the baby caps, bibs, belly-bands (to tie down the umbilicus), bigons or biggins (bonnets), dimity waistcoats and 'a fine holland little pillow'. When Ann felt her labour pains beginning she would have sent someone to fetch the midwife, and her married women friends, her gossips, as well. Midwives were usually recruited from the ranks of sober matrons who could be trusted to examine pregnant and newly delivered women, and to testify in the Vicar's Court. In many parishes the midwife was licensed by the bishop or the vicar acting on his authority, but Stratford doesn't seem to have been one of them. No midwife is referred to in the surviving act books of the Vicar's Court. Still, helpers there must have been. Ann would not have been left to labour alone.

If Will had been away from home, word would have been sent to him, for it was generally expected that a husband be on hand during his wife's labour, even though he was not required to render any service to her during it, and there was no question of his actually witnessing parturition. When the midwife arrived she would super-vise the closing of all the doors and windows of the dwelling and the drawing of the shutters. All cracks in the walls would have been stuffed with rags, because draughts were believed extremely dangerous to both mother and newborn. A large fire would have been made on the hearth, with no other light in the room, for it was thought that a woman might become deranged if she was exposed to bright light during labour. Ann's clothing would have been loosened and she would have been encouraged to eat a large knob of butter. Meanwhile, the childbed-linen would be warming on her bed or on straw laid near the fire.

> When the patient feels her throes coming, she should walk easily in her chamber, and then again lie down, keep herself warm, rest herself and then stir again, till she feels the waters coming down and the womb open. Let her not lie long abed, yet [if] she may lie sometimes and sleep to strengthen her, and to abate pain, the child will be the stronger.[8]

When the midwife arrived she may have brought with her a birthing stool. In his version of Eucharius Roesslin's *The Birth of Mankind*, first published in 1545, Thomas Raynaldes makes clear that the use of the stool was spreading into England from continental Europe.[9] By the time Ann gave birth, use of the 'groaning stool' was widespread. Where it was not in use the labouring woman used a bed spread with straw to protect it from soiling by blood, faeces or lochia. 'Take notice that all women do not keep the same posture in their delivery. Some lie in their beds, being very weak; some sit in a stool or chair, or rest on the side of the bed, held by other women that come to the labour.'[10]

The midwife did not simply attend to physical requirements of the labouring woman.

> Also the midwife must instruct and comfort the party, not only refreshing her with good meat and drink, but also with sweet words, giving her good hope of a speedful deliverance, encouraging and enstomaching her to patience and tolerance, bidding her to hold in her breath so much as she may, also striking gently with her hands her belly above the navel, for that helpeth to depress the birth downward.

Good meat and drink included specially sustaining broths or caudles as well as strong beer. Midwives also knew how to support the perineum: 'And if necessity require it let not the midwife be afraid nor ashamed to handle the places, and to relax and loose the straits (so much as shall lie in her) for that shall help well to the more expedite and quick labour.'[11]

As labour went on, care was taken to refresh and sustain the labouring woman:

> If her travail be long the midwife must refresh her with some chicken's
> broth with the yolk of a poached egg and a little bread, or some wine
> or strong waters, but moderately taken, and withal to cheer her up
> with good words and stroking down her belly above her navel gently
> with her hand, for that makes the child move downwards. She must
> bid her hold in her breath as much as she can, for that will cause more
> force to bring out the child.[12]

Midwives were prepared to take action in cases where the child presented feet first or sideways: 'If the head of the child do not come forth first, the midwife then must turn the child that the head may come forth first, and let the midwife anoint her hand with oil olive.' If the midwife did not succeed in manually turning the child, both mother and child remained in 'great peril'. If the contractions looked as if they were weakening, various herbal preparations would be used to provoke them. 'Also if the woman be in extreme labour, let her take the juice of dittany a dram with the water of fenugreek, or else take of Serapine an ounce, and drink it at three times with the water of cherries, and keep the woman moderately in a temperate heat.'[13]

When the child was fully born the umbilical cord was cut. Sympathetic medicine required that it be cut short for girls and long for boys. The newborn Susanna would have been held by the fire and bathed in warm water, and the vernix removed by the application of a mixture of oil, milk and warm water. The end of the cord was anointed, the cord knotted and a band tied around the belly to hold the knotted end of the umbilical cord in place. Over Susanna's head would have been tied a biggin, under which would be placed a compress to protect the fontanelle and keep the brain warm. And, unless Ann was an exceptional mother, Susanna would have been tightly swaddled, on a board, with her arms bound to her sides.

Ann meanwhile would have first had to expel the afterbirth and might even have been made to sneeze to bring it away faster. If sneezing failed, stimulants would have been prescribed. Then she would have had her belly rubbed with oil of St John's Wort, and been swathed in linen. She would not have been allowed to drift off to sleep, but kept awake for four hours, and given broth or caudle to rebuild her strength. For two days she should eat no meat and then be encouraged to nibble white meat and sip spiced wine to bring her to her full strength. She would not have been allowed to give her baby the breast because it was thought that 'those unclean purgations cannot make good milk. The first milk is naught . . .'[13] The baby would have been fed on weak warm water gruel through the narrow end of a cup made out of a sheep's horn.

As Ann had borne a girl she was expected to remain confined within her house for forty days. 'If the child be a boy she must lie in thirty days, if a girl forty days, and remember that it is the time of her purification, that her husband must abstain from her.'[14] The most dangerous time in the infant's life was its very first day. Once they had both got through that, Ann had only to keep Susanna safe from thrush, infectious diseases like smallpox, measles and chicken pox, whooping or 'chyne' cough, the yearly visitations of epidemic disease, nutritional deficiencies like rickets and scurvy, and infestations of intestinal worms, lice, fleas and itch mites. Ann was the more successful in protecting Susanna because she breast-fed her, as all mothers of her class did.

The fountains of the earth are made to give water and the breasts of women are made to give suck. Every beast and every soul is bred of the same that did bear it, only women love to be mothers and not nurses. Therefore if their children prove unnatural they may say, 'Thou followest thy mother for she was unnatural first in locking her breasts from thee and committing thee forth like a cuckoo to be hatched in the sparrow's nest.' Hereof it comes that we say 'He sucked evil from the dug', that is, as the nurse is affected in her body or in her mind, commonly the child draweth the like infirmity from her, as the eggs of a hen are altered under the hawk. Yet they which have no milk, can give no milk, but whose breasts have this perpetual drought?

Forsooth it is like the gout. No beggars may have it but citizens or gentlewomen.[15]

When forty years later Susanna and her husband decided to write an epitaph for Ann in which her feeding of her daughter from her own breasts is lauded, they were consciously or unconsciously suggesting that she had always been a gentlewoman, for whom to consent to suckle her own child was to do something unusual, even heroic. In being everything to her tiny daughter, Ann did what every country-woman of her class did, right or wrong. If Susanna had suffered from strabismus, Ann would have licked her eye straight.

Women who had recently given birth could not attend the church ceremonies until they had been purified or 'churched', so Susanna would have been carried to the church on the first Sunday after her birth by the midwife, there to meet her godparents. Her father would have been allowed to witness the ceremony but he played no part, and he was under no obligation to attend. According to the first prayerbook of Edward VI, with the child would be brought the chrisom, a white linen cloth which would be laid upon her after she had been dipped in the font and before she was anointed with chrism. If she died before her mother was churched the chrisom would be her winding sheet; if she was spared her mother would bring it as an offering when she came for churching. The second prayerbook makes no mention of the chrisom and deletes the prayer that should accompany the laying of it on the child, but we know from contemporary images and grave portraiture that infants who died within the first weeks of life are usually portrayed wearing it. Though the child would no longer have been anointed with holy oil and spittle and salt, she would still have been wrapped in white linen as a sign of her new status as a baptised Christian. Then the midwife and her godparents would have carried her back home to a party, to which Ann's gossips would have brought cakes and ale.

During the forty days of her lying-in, Ann would have had to do nothing but rest and play with her baby, while Will or his deputy carried out the household chores. On the forty-first day of Susanna's life, Ann would have gone to Holy Trinity to be churched.[16] Churching may have been a humiliating ritual, but it was also an occasion for great cheer. The best ale was laid on in quantity. This was one occasion when husbands waited on their womenfolk, pouring their ale and cutting their meat. The women meanwhile talked.

> Many women, many words; so fell it out at that time, for there was such prattling that it passed. Some talked of their husbands' frowardness, some shewed their maids' sluttishness, others deciphered the costliness of their garments, some told many tales of their neighbours, and to be brief, there was none of them but would have talk for a whole day.[17]

Ann probably breast-fed Susanna for about a year. Even before she had finished weaning her, she was pregnant for the second time. Lactation is nowadays known to suppress ovulation;[18] this effect is often reinforced by an embargo on sexual intercourse with a wife who was breast-feeding, but seldom in Britain, where it was considered unfair to the husband. The pattern of births in Stratford in the 1580s as revealed by the parish records shows us that, except in cases of infant death, births to each mother were usually two years apart, implying a year's breast-feeding with a new pregnancy beginning soon after weaning. For some reason Katherine Duncan-Jones assumes that Ann continued breast-feeding all through her second pregnancy and even considers that 'she may have attempted to feed all three children'.[19] Certainly the nurse in *Romeo and Juliet* weaned Juliet at the age of three, by putting wormwood on her breast, not a method that could be used by a woman with other babies to feed.[20]

Ann had no way of knowing in 1584 that she was pregnant with twins.

> It may be discerned but with some difficulty that a woman will have more than one child by their heavy burden and slow motion, also by the unevenness of their bellies, and there is a kind of separation made by certain wrinkles and seams to shew the children are parted in the womb, and if she be not very strong to go through with it in her travail, she is in danger, both she and her children.[21]

Just how dangerous twinning was can be seen from the Holy Trinity registers. Robert Bearman has counted thirty-two sets of twins baptised at Holy Trinity between 1560 and 1600; he looked to see how many of these infants were buried within three months and came up with eighteen sets of twins surviving. However, the burial register also contains records of twins who were never publicly baptised, including some who were buried as nameless. This gives a higher total for only eighteen sets of survivors. Even then we can't be sure that more of these children did not die outside the parish, as twins are more likely than other children to be put out to nurse. All we can say with certainty is that no burials are recorded for them at Holy Trinity.

Jane Sharp believed that the mother had a better chance of surviving the birth of identical twins.

> If the twins be both boys or both girls she will fare the better. Yet one is found by frequent examples to be more lusty and longer-lived than the other; be they both of one sex, or one a boy and the other a girl, that which is stronger increaseth, but the weaker decays or fails by reason of the prevailing force of the other.[22]

If her mother's family had a history of twinning Ann might have expected it but, as we don't know what her mother's name was, we have no way of investigating the matter. There is some evidence in the family history that twins were not uncommon among the Hathaways. In the Holy Trinity parish register for 1561 the burial of two individuals both called 'Richardus filius Richardi Hathaway alias Gardner' is recorded on 29 March and on 1 April. This is usually interpreted as reflecting the burial of newborn twins, one of whom inherited his father's name from the other.[23] Rose, daughter of Ann's kinsman Thomas Hathaway, bore twins in 1602. Sixteenth-century gynaecologists were not at all sure how multiple births came about.

> [That] twins are begot at the same act of copulation is held by all ancient and modern writers, for the Seed (say they) being not cast into the Womb all at once divides in the womb and makes more children. Another reason they give is that the womb when it has received the seed shuts so close that no more seed can enter.

The truth of this belief is obvious to us today but the sixteenth century
was not so sure:

> nor do all authors agree that twins are begotten at the same time, for all
> the Stoic philosophers hold that they are begotten at several times and,
> if you read the treatise of Hermes, he will tell you that twins are not
> conceived at the same minute of time, for if they were conceived at
> once they must be born at once, which is impossible.

The notion persisted that women could conceive by successive acts of
intercourse: 'All authors allow of a superfetation, that is, the woman
may conceive again when she hath conceived of one child before she
be delivered of that . . .' For moralists the conclusion was obvious;
superfetation was caused by the persistence after conception of
inordinate sexual desire in the woman.

> Some say it is a virtue and a prerogative given to women, but they are
> those that call vice virtue. The truth is that Adam's sin lies heavy upon
> his posterity . . . and for this the curse of God follows them and
> inordinate lust is a great part of this curse, and the propagation of many
> children at once is an effect of this intemperance. Hippocrates forbids
> women to use copulation after conception but I may not wrong the
> man so much.[24]

Ambrose Paré was of the opinion that identical twins were conceived
by a single act of copulation and fraternal twins by superfetation.

Marital love was expected to be chaste not only in that it did not allow
of sexual activity with any other partner, but also because it restrained
sexual activity within marriage. In the epithalamium in the Old Arcadia
(1590) Sir Philip Sidney banishes lechery from the bride bed:

> But thou foul Cupid, sire to lawless lust,
>   Be thou far hence with thine empoisoned dart,
> Which though of glittering gold shall here take rust,
>   Where simple love, which chasteness doth impart,
>   Avoids thy hurtful art
> Not needing charming still,

Such minds with sweet affections for to fill,
Which being pure and plain,
O Hymen long their coupled joys maintain.

Ann would have heard as often as any other parishioner at Holy Trinity the dissuasives against whoredom in marriage. If married love is to be pure chastity, a wife must comport herself with a certain reserve, as Imogen did with Posthumus, showing that though she chose him for herself it was for esteem of him rather than base desire.

Me of my lawful pleasure she restrained,
And prayed me oft forbearance, did it with
A pudency so rosy, the sweet view on't
Might well have warmed old Saturn, that I thought her
As chaste as unsunned snow.[25]

Those who believe with Greenblatt that Shakespeare felt revulsion for his wife's body might want to believe too that he was shocked and disconcerted by the birth of fraternal twins, and ready to believe that her prolonged agony during the birth was the direct outcome of excessive lust, his or hers or both.

Even in the twenty-first century stillbirth and death within the first week of life are four times more common in twins than in singletons; the incidence of cerebral palsy is five times higher in twins. Twins are more likely to be born premature and to be of low birthweight, and their mothers run an elevated risk of pre-eclampsia and other complications of pregnancy. Nowadays the presence of twins in the uterus is first detected by ultrasound and from that point on the growth rate of twins *in utero* is carefully monitored, but in 1585 the matter was managed rather less well. Until she was heavily pregnant Ann may not have suspected that she was carrying an extra burden. The Stratford wise women, who had their own ways of detecting the presence of twins, may well have taken special care of her, advising her to rest, and to eat more than pregnant women usually should, so that her babies would be born robust and willing to compete for equal shares of her milk. And perhaps no special care was taken of her at all, so that she did not know until she had endured the pains of one birth that she was going to have to go through it a second time.

Philip Barrough, licensed as a surgeon by the University of Cambridge in 1559, is one of few sixteenth-century practitioners whose published work makes any mention of multiple births. Chapter lxiv of Book iii of his *Method of Physic*, first published in 1583 by Shakespeare's friend Richard Field, deals with 'sore travail in childbirth'. Difficult labour can ensue 'if they be two or more, and all do rush suddenly into the neck of the matrix'. 'If there be two or three or more children, and do thrust together into the neck of the matrix, you must drive back the rest into the bottom of the womb, and bring that out first that seemeth to be most ready.'[26] Jane Sharp's advice is similar: the midwife delivering twins should have prepared the birth canal 'with oil of almonds or lilies and a whole egg . . . beaten and poured into the passage to make it glib' and 'enlarge the part with her hand'.

> Now sometime it chanceth the woman to have two at a burthen, and that both proceed together headlong . . . then must the midwife receive the one after the other but so that she let not slip the one whilst she taketh the first. If both come forth at once with their feet forward, then must the midwife be very diligent to receive first the one and then the other . . . When one cometh headlong, the other footwise, then must the midwife help the birth that is nearest the issue, and it that cometh footlong (if she can) to turn it upon the head . . . taking ever heed that the one be not noisome to the other in receiving forth of either of them.[27]

The twins were born in the dead of winter. We don't know who came first, but we may guess that it was Judith. She was the twin who would survive to adulthood and old age. Hamnet may have been visibly smaller and weaker. Ann would not have been able to tell at first if he was afflicted with cerebral palsy or any of the other ill effects of a prolonged struggle in the birth canal. The double labour would have exhausted her perhaps to the point that her survival too hung in the balance. Birth was dangerous at the best of times; in Ann's time between 125 and 158 births per thousand proved fatal for the mother.[28]

If the babies were premature, as twins usually are, and of low birthweight, Ann would have faced a struggle to keep them alive. Of the three other sets of twins born in Stratford that year Mary and Joan, daughters of John Goodyear, christened on 21 February, were buried the same day. William and Catherine, son and daughter to Master William Court, baptised on 10 April, apparently survived. David Bewser's twins William and Frances were buried unchristened on 12 May.

Ann's babies were taken to be christened on 2 February. Their godparents were probably Hamnet and Judith Sadler, who lived at the corner of High Street and Sheep Street, next to the Cornmarket. Hamnet Sadler, nephew of Stratford alderman Roger Sadler who was bailiff in 1560 and 1572 and died in 1578, was, like his uncle, a baker. We are usually given to believe that, because Hamnet Sadler witnessed Shakespeare's will, the Sadlers were William's friends rather than Ann's, as if the woman who lived a few doors down from them and saw them every day was creeping around Stratford with a bag over her head. I think we may be sure that Ann and Judith Sadler were lifelong friends. As Judith Staunton of Longbridge, Judith Sadler was an heiress in her own right. She married Hamnet in Longbridge in about 1579. Her first child was christened John on 20 September 1580, and buried two months later. Her second, a girl christened Jane, was born a year later almost to the day, and her third, Margaret, was christened two years after that. When Judith and her husband met their newborn namesakes in the cold, dark church on 2 February 1585 she was pregnant for the fourth time. A second son, christened Thomas on 26 August, would live for a month.

It was against the odds that Ann would keep her twins alive. First of all she had to produce sufficient breast-milk to feed two babies. If one or other was or both babies were too weak to suck properly, her milk would have failed; in such cases the babies usually died. One option was to farm one of the babies out to a wet-nurse. Interestingly, wet-nursing was a trade followed by the wives of artisans; in the 1570s a glover's wife is listed in the records as a wet-nurse.[29] Mary Shakespeare, who had borne her last child in 1580, could conceivably have come to the aid of her son's wife, but no similar circumstance has ever been recorded. It is doubtful too whether Will and Ann could have afforded a wet-nurse.

Judging from the Dee family in the late sixteenth century, different nurses either merited or demanded different amounts in the same neighbourhood during the same period. Between 1580 and 1592 these ranged from four shillings to twelve shillings a month, plus soap and candles. Sir William Petre of Ingatestone Hall in Essex paid his son's wet nurse ten pence a week in 1550, whilst her own child was nursed by another woman for nine pence a week. Between 1602 and 1604 Sir William Herrick paid two shillings for one nurse in Surrey, and two shillings and sixpence for another in Middlesex.[30]

Both these children of Sir William's died at nurse and were buried in the parishes where they died, rather than brought home to be buried from their father's house. Such deaths of nurslings were far from uncommon. Champions of maternal breast-feeding criticised the diet of the poor women who breast-fed for money.

I pray you what else is the cause that many children nursed in the country are so subject to frets, sharpness of urine and the stone; but that their nurses for the most part eat rye bread strong of the leaven and hard cheese and drink nothing but muddy and new ale.[31]

All things considered, we may conclude that Ann Hathaway undertook the rearing of her twins herself, with the help perhaps of one of her half-sibs, who would have run errands, and done household chores for her in return for food and lodging. 'To increase a woman's milk you shall boil in strong posset ale good store of coleworts and cause her to drink every meal of the same, also if she use to eat boiled coleworts with her meat, it will wonderfully increase her milk.'[32] Like Ann, Dekker's Patient Grissill has 'two beauteous twins, A son and a daughter'. When her husband throws her out of his palace with nothing but her russet gown, her hat and her pitcher, two footmen are told 'to help to bear her children home' but she says 'It shall not need; I can bear more.' When told she must give them up, she pleads and displays her breast:

see here's a fountain
Which heaven into these alabaster bowls
Instilled to nourish them. Man, they'll cry
And blame thee that this runs so lavishly.
Here's milk for both my babes, two breasts for two . . .
. . .
I pray thee, let them suck. I am most meet
To play their nurse. They'll smile and say 'tis sweet
What streams from hence. If thou dost bear them hence
My angry breasts will swell and, as mine eyes
Let fall salt drops, with these white nectar tears
They will be mixed . . .[33]

Ann's success in rearing her twins may have been just a matter of luck. Both she and they may have been unusually strong, but it's at least as likely that Ann met the challenge and managed it, that she found ways to keep her milk supply adequate for her two babes, and to keep them both interested and feeding properly. For the forty days of her lying-in Will would have had no option but to help her, yet there are some of his admirers who want to believe that he had left her even before the twins were born, to face her ordeal alone.

CHAPTER NINE

pondering how and when it was that young Shakespeare quit Stratford, leaving wife and children to fend for themselves, and whether he dared risk his health and theirs by consorting with prostitutes

When the twins were christened in Holy Trinity Church on 2 February 1585 by Richard Barton of Coventry, the Shakespeares had been married three and a half years. Greenblatt, for whom Shakespeare was 'someone who had married a woman older than himself and then left her behind in Stratford',[1] alleges that Shakespeare 'contrived after three years' time not to live with his wife', which suggests that he left even before the twins were born. E. A. Honigman too thinks this to be the case.[2] The lost years are simply that; from the christening of the twins to Shakespeare's emergence on the London stage we have no idea what he might have been doing or where he, or he and his family, might have been. That he separated from Ann is accepted by all but a very few scholars. Some, in the tradition of De Quincey and Wilson Knight, hold that he stayed with his family only until he attained his majority in April 1585. Twentieth-century scholars suggest that he took the place in the Queen's Company left vacant by the murder of the player William Knell in June 1587.

The harvest of 1586 was poor. That autumn grain prices, always higher in Stratford than elsewhere, rose steeply. The Vicar of Stratford exhorted the faithful from the pulpit to fast twice a week and give the food they saved for the relief of the starving, to give as much in alms as they could spare, and to join in public prayers of repentance. Grain prices had been rising steadily since 1520, as demand outstripped supply; the pattern of earlier enclosures of arable land to increase available pasture for sheep reversed, as scattered parcels of pasture were enclosed and ploughed for the growing of corn. In the fertile fielden of Warwickshire the new methods of convertible cultivation using crop rotation were guaranteed to double seed-yields and eventually to bring grain prices down, but in the 1580s this desirable outcome was not yet in sight.

> The re-orientation of English agriculture from subsistence to com-
> mercial production disrupted rural communities by emphasizing the
> difference between large farmers and smallholders. Many of the latter
> failed to survive the prolonged late-Elizabethan and early-Stuart crises,
> and rural as well as urban communities faced worsening problems of
> providing poor relief and regulating masterless men. In the country-
> side, vagrants and artificers frequently squatted upon wastes in
> woodland-pasture regions, while paupers were housed in poor-law
> cottages built upon the village common.[3]

Though Stratford was a market town rather than a village, all these processes and problems can be traced through the archives. By 1600 Shottery, in the woodland-pasture area or 'arden', was home to people so poor that they had no names; when they died of privation they were buried in the Stratford churchyard as simply 'a poor boy' or a 'poor man' of Shottery.

Around Stratford, enclosures, engrossments and depopulations were gathering pace. In 1584, three years after Ann's father's death, his Shottery neighbours were called to London to testify in a Chancery case. Fulke Sandells of Shottery, 'yeoman', testified on 29 April that he and other jurors had given witness in the manor court for Old Stratford that eleven butts of land in Shottery were believed to belong to the Earl of Warwick, 'upon the report of one Hathway alias Gardner, the said Gardner being then dead'. Two days later Richard Burman, husbandman, corroborated this testimony, citing 'the report of one Richard Hathway alias Gardner deceased, and of one Roger Burman'. The land in question adjoined the moor otherwise known as Baldon Hill, which the earl claimed by a charter of AD 709. As long as anyone could remember it had been taken to be, not part of Shottery manor, but of the 'ferme ground' of Old

Stratford. Roger Burman, who, according to Sandells, had lived on the manor 'by the space of fourscore years or very near', said 'he had heard his elders say so' and Richard Hathaway 'said he heard his father say the same'. Stephen Burman too gave evidence.

The earl's claim to the land was being challenged by Francis Smith of Wootton Wawen, lord of the manor of Shottery, who had leased the land in question to Richard Woodward as part of the manor of Shottery. A meeting between the earl's agents and Master Smith in the parlour of the inn of his kinsman the vintner John Smith had ended in violent disagreement, hence the litigation in Chancery. Woodward was gradually engrossing Shottery manor by taking up all the waste, disputed and common ground and enclosing it. Husbandmen like the Hathaways and their neighbours could not survive without access to manorial wastes where they could pasture their team animals, milch kine, pigs and geese. If Smith's claim had been upheld, the Shottery farmers stood to lose many of their use-rights, so they may have been economical with the truth. The case seems to have been decided in the earl's favour, but landlords looking to fiscalise their holdings were not easily dissuaded; when push came to shove the small farmers generally had to give way. In extreme cases frustrated landholders would resort to wholesale beatings and intimidation. Despite the best attempts of the jurists to protect the ancient rights of the people, no fewer than eighty-three Warwickshire villages were depopulated, most of them before Ann Hathaway was born.

One of the longest-lived explanations of Shakespeare's sudden departure from Stratford is that he had been caught stealing vension from Sir Thomas Lucy's park at Charlcote: this is Nicholas Rowe's account of the circumstances, written in 1709, more than a hundred years after the event.

He had, by a misfortune common enough to young fellows, fallen into ill company, and, amongst them, some that made a frequent practice of deer-stealing, engaged him with them more than once in robbing a park that belonged to Sir Thomas Lucy of Charlcote near Stratford. For this he was prosecuted by that gentleman, as he thought, somewhat too severely, and, in order to revenge that ill usage, he made a ballad upon him . . . said to be so very bitter, that it redoubled the persecution against him to that degree that he was obliged to leave his business and family in Warwickshire for some time and shelter himself in London.[4]

To this account is made the objection that Sir Thomas Lucy was not licensed to impale a park, that is, to fence parkland to make an enclosure for deer, until 1618.[5] The same tradition is recollected by Richard Davies, who died in 1708, before Rowe's account was published. Shakespeare, he writes, was 'much given to all unluckiness in stealing venison and rabbits from Sir [blank] Lucy, who had him oft whipped and sometime imprisoned, and at last made him fly his native country to his great advancement'.[6]

We are not after all talking about a peccadillo. The penalties for poaching were severe, more severe if anything in time of dearth when fear of riot ran high. Then the managers of country estates increased their vigilance, even to the point of hiring armed men to protect their orchards and storehouses. It may be that Shakespeare and other young men, desperate to provide for their families and disgusted by the failure of the magnates to give of their superfluity, did raid Sir Thomas Lucy's well-provided establishment where there was a free-warren. A brace of rabbits would have gone a long way in Ann's stew-pot, but conveying a dead deer any distance from Charlcote would have been a far more challenging assignment. It would have been necessary to butcher the creature on the spot, thus ruining the meat which could not be properly bled and hung, and making the kind of bloody mess of themselves and the surroundings that would have been difficult to conceal. Still, that Shakespeare and other young toughs may have killed deer at Charlcote is just possible. Sir Thomas may have taken the opportunity afforded by his free-warren to run wild roe deer, for which he did not need to create a fenced enclosure, and Shakespeare and his mates may well have killed some, as Falstaff has apparently done before the opening scene of *The Merry Wives of Windsor*. Shallow, the landowner and a member of the Commission of the Peace for Gloucestershire, accuses Falstaff directly: 'Knight, you have beaten my men, killed my deer, and broke open my lodge' (I. i. 103–4). Falstaff is hardy enough to admit the crime. Slender, Shallow's kinsman and a member of his household, names his accomplices, the 'coney-catching rascals, Bardolph, Nym and Pistol'. Such a crime, as has been discussed earlier in the scene, amounts to 'riot', a serious offence against duly constituted authority, which might well have brought Falstaff and his gang before the Court of the Star Chamber.[7]

If Shakespeare had ever been a member of such a deer-stealing gang he had aligned himself with the most seditious elements in Warwickshire, which hardly sorts with his eventual emergence as a servant of the lord chamberlain. Stranger sequences of events could happen in Tudor England, but we need better evidence than unsupported anecdote and a reference to deer-stealing in one of Shakespeare's plays before we can decide once for all that Shakespeare was a deer-stealer. *The Merry Wives of Windsor* was first performed in 1597, more than ten years after Shakespeare's deer-stealing episode is thought to have taken place. It would have been the height of folly for Shakespeare to have risked all by making reference in a play to be performed before the queen at the Garter Feast in Whitehall Palace to a forgotten and unpunished crime of his youth. Such a pointless in-joke, if it had been understood at all, could well have put a premature end to Shakespeare's brilliant career. If as a younger man he had been identified as a ringleader of attacks on the barnyards and game warrens of local landowners, his family would have been well advised to send him out of harm's way.

In 1586 John Shakespeare had to yield up his furred gown because he had been finally struck off the list of aldermen. In the same year William was a party to attempts by his parents to raise a further £10 on the property that they had mortgaged to Edmund Lambert. As his father's son and heir, and therefore party to decisions about the disposal of family property, William simply didn't have the option of disappearing altogether. Indeed, he would have needed his father's express permission before he could absent himself for any considerable period of time. To leave Stratford for parts unknown without his father's blessing would have been tantamount to a crime. We have no option but to countenance the possibility that whenever and wherever William went, he went with the blessing of his wife and his parents.

Almost every day carters travelled in convoy taking goods and people and correspondence backwards and forwards from Stratford to

London. In term-time everybody who was anybody had business in London; in between, everybody who could get out of London did. The terms were three in number, Michaelmas, October to December, Hilary or Lent, January to March, and Trinity or Easter, April to June. The three terms each lasted eighty days; the days in between were vacation or recess; between June and October there was the long vacation or the summer recess. Lawyers, litigants, politicians, courtiers, traders, all went home from London for Christmas and Easter and for the summer, if they had homes to go to. The country folk who were obliged to spend part of the term in London, waiting for their cases to come up or their petitions to be heard in court or parliament, all except a few of the very rich, lived in lodgings. Back in the country their families worried whether they were getting wholesome food to eat, and sent homemade cheeses and pies to supplement tavern fare.

As we have no way of proving that Shakespeare was anywhere else, we cannot be entirely sure that during the so-called lost years he wasn't with his wife and children in Stratford. We cannot even be sure that Ann did not become pregnant again; all we know is that no more children of hers were christened at Holy Trinity Church, or anywhere else that we know of, and no more are mentioned in Shakespeare's will. So we assume that conjugal intercourse between Will and Ann had ceased. Even this is not a safe assumption. In giving birth to twins, Ann had run an increased risk of birth accident and post-partum haemorrhage and infection. She might have been left infertile; she might even have been left incapable of sexual intercourse. We simply don't know.

There were many wives in Tudor England who did not see their husbands for months on end. A gentleman did not normally take a wife who was 'breeding', that is pregnant or trying to become so, when he made his necessary visits to London. A woman with children was understood to be better off at home in the country than roosting in digs in the foul air of London, while her husband transacted his business. Besides, a wife was needed in the country to run her husband's affairs in his absence. We have only to think of Margaret Paston, living in rural Norfolk while her lawyer menfolk haunted the law courts and danced attendance on the king, to realise how necessary was her management of their estates in their absence.

A wife left at home by her husband could not set off on her own and go to find him without his express permission. She had no right to intimacy, or to a share of his time, or even to support for herself and her children. As long as he was living with her, her husband had a right to anything she owned or could earn, and she had no right to set any of it aside for herself or her children. If Shakespeare was unable to find suitable work in Stratford or to keep it if he found it, he and Ann both may have been aware that separation was their only chance. He could try his luck in London, while Ann, relieved of a fourth hungry mouth to find food for, looked out for herself and her children. If Will had gone for a soldier or been pressed into the army she would have had to do as much.

With John Shakespeare foundering, William may well have represented the only hope of repairing the family fortunes. When Valentine bids farewell to his friend Proteus at the beginning of *The Two Gentlemen of Verona*, he chides him gently, 'Home-keeping youth have ever homely wits' (I. i. 2). He is on his way to see 'the wonders of the world abroad'. Perhaps Ann comforted herself with the same thought as Proteus: 'He leaves his friends, to dignify them more'. (I. i. 64). Proteus' father Antonio is criticised by his brother for keeping him at home:

> He wondered that your lordship
> Would suffer him to spend his youth at home,
> While other men, of slender reputation,
> Put forth their sons, to seek preferment out,
> Some to the wars, to try their fortune there,
> Some to discover islands far away,
> Some to the studious universities . . .
> And did request me to importune you
> To let him spend his time no more at home,
> Which would be great impeachment to his age,
> In having known no travel in his youth. (I. iii. 4–10, 13–16)

Antonio pleads guilty:

> I have considered well his loss of time,
> And how he cannot be a perfect man,
> Not being tried and tutored in the world. (19–21)

Schoenbaum asks, 'Did the young husband tick off the weeks and days and months of the apprentice's statutory seven-year sentence until the fateful day of his departure from Stratford?'[8] In April of that year William had attained his majority and would have come into any bits and pieces of money or property left him by earlier bequests, supposing there were any. He would then have been free to seek his fortune away from Stratford without asking permission of his parents, but he would not have been free to abandon his pregnant wife.

Robert Greene's abandonment of his wife was so scandalous that it inspired a literary sub-genre.

> I married a gentleman's daughter of good account, with whom I lived for a while, but forasmuch as she would persuade me from my wilful wickedness, after I had a child by her, I cast her off, having spent up the marriage money which I obtained by her. Then I left her at six or seven, who went into Lincolnshire, and I to London.
>
> But O my dear wife, whose company and sight I have refrained these six years, I ask God and thee forgiveness for so greatly wronging thee, of whom I seldom or never thought till now. Pardon me, I pray thee, wheresoever thou art . . .[9]

On his deathbed Greene wrote to his wife, who had sent him word that she was in good health:

> Sweet wife, as ever there was any good will or friendship between thee and me, see this bearer (my host) satisfied of his debt. I owe him ten pounds, and but for him I had perished in the streets. Forget and forgive my wrongs done unto thee . . . Farewell till we meet in Heaven for on earth thou shalt never see me more . . .

Bardolaters are made of sterner stuff than the repentant Robert Greene. Greenblatt is sorry only for the defaulting husband, asking his reader how Shakespeare could have written Orsino's words 'Let still the woman take an elder than her' 'without in some sense bringing his own life, his disappointment, frustration and loneliness, to bear upon them'.[10] Usually when a husband abandons a wife with three small children, we are less concerned for his disappointment, frustration and loneliness than for hers. In this case, the absconding husband can do no wrong; it is the inconveniently fecund woman who has brought desertion upon herself.

Most scholars assume that once Shakespeare left Stratford, he didn't come back until he retired in 1611 or so, when he settled in at New Place as if he had never been away. Greenblatt refers airily to 'long years apart'.[11] If literary scholars were not all so desperate to get Will so far away from Ann, they would see at once that the very idea is absurd. In the sixteenth century 'living away from a wife' was a crime, punishable in both the ecclesiastical and the civil courts. In 1584 Henry Field, the tanner of Bridge Street, close friend and colleague of John Shakespeare, was presented by the churchwardens for living apart from his wife. They were both charged with being 'absent one from the other without the rule of law'.[12] By this time they had been married for more than twenty-six years and had ten surviving children, one of whom would a few years later be the publisher of *Venus and Adonis* and *The Rape of Lucrece*. If Ann had alleged desertion, Will would have been a fugitive from the law. If she did not allege desertion, it was probably because she was not in fact deserted. If Will did desert her, and she did not denounce him, she must have been protecting him. If she was, she has been given no credit for it.

Laertes is one case in Shakespeare's oeuvre of a son who insists on leaving his family and his birthplace to pursue his own ambition, having obtained his father's 'hard consent' 'by laboursome petition'. As he prepares to take ship from Denmark to France, he commands Ophelia,

> sister as the winds give benefit
> And convoy is assistant, do not sleep,
> But let me hear from you. (I. iii. 2–4)

Ophelia, like virtually all Shakespeare's female characters, can both read and write. Shakespeare's wife is not allowed to have been capable of either. Polonius, the councillor and court functionary, probably has more in common with Alderman Shakespeare than any other Shakespearean character. We can only wonder if John Shakespeare set spies on his son in London as Polonius does on Laertes in Paris in the shocking first scene of the second act of *Hamlet*. We know that there were groups of Stratford citizens busied in London and we may guess that Shakespeare would have been given contacts for them, if indeed London is where he went. What seems oddly close to home is the last instruction Polonius gives his spy: 'And let him ply his music' (II. i. 73).

Most of Shakespeare's biographers assume that when the Bard went missing he left his wife and children with his parents and brothers and sister at Henley Street. This scenario is worse than grim: son is seduced by ugly harlot, forced against his will to marry her, with no option but to bring her back to the parental home, where child is born, then twins, then he abandons everyone, his wife, his children and his parents. If this is what happened Ann's life could hardly have been worth living, for she would have been held to blame for all of it, including the desertion of his parents by the son and heir. Such behaviour would have been considered so reprehensible by all the people Shakespeare had grown up with that Will could hardly have wanted to show his face in Stratford again. Fathers overwhelmed by their responsibilities did run away; some of the destitute men who wandered the country looking for work were fathers. In burial registers in times of dearth we find entries for children who starved because their fathers went away and didn't come back and their mothers couldn't cope. Ann Shakespeare did cope.

If Ann loved Will, and we shall decide in default of evidence to the contrary that she did, she must have missed him terribly, especially in the long dark winter evenings, when she sat working by the dying fire as her children slept. No commentator on Shakespeare has ever suggested that during his absences from Stratford he missed his wife and children. Yet it is Shakespeare who gives voice to the yearning of the women who wait out the weeks and months for the return of the man they love. If he didn't miss Ann, he was vividly aware that she missed him.

In *Cymbeline*, when Imogen hears that Posthumus believes that she has betrayed him, Shakespeare puts these words into her mouth:

False to his bed? What is it to be false?
To lie in watch here, and to think on him?
To weep twixt clock and clock? If sleep charge Nature,
To break it with a fearful dream of him,
And cry myself awake? That's false to's bed, is it? (III. iv. 40–4)

We might be reminded of a theme that surfaces from time to time in the sonnets.

Being your slave, what should I do but tend
Upon the hours and times of your desire?
I have no precious time at all to spend,
Not services to do, till you require.
Nor dare I chide the world-without-end hour
Whilst I, my sovereign, watch the clock for you,
Nor think the bitterness of absence sour
When you have bid your servant once adieu.
Nor dare I question in my jealous thought
Where you may be, or your affairs suppose,
But like a sad slave, stay and think of naught,
Save, where you are, how happy you make those.
   So true a fool is love that, in your will
   Though you do anything, he thinks no ill. (57)

That God forbid that made me first your slave,
I should in thought control your times of pleasure,
Or at your hand th'account of hours to crave,
Being your vassal, bound to stay your leisure.
O, let me suffer, being at your beck,
Th'imprisoned absence of your liberty,
And patient-tame to sufferance, bide each check
Without accusing you of injury.
Be where you list, your charter is so strong
That you yourself may privilege your time
To what you will. To you it doth belong
Yourself to pardon of self-doing crime.
   I am to wait, though waiting so be hell,
   Not blame your pleasure, be it ill or well. (58)

Try as one might, these two sonnets are hard to fit into the relationship either with the young man or with the dark lady. The thought
process is very like that of a wife left alone at home, watching the
clock, trying to keep her love unpoisoned by jealousy or bitterness.

In 1613 or thereabouts, Lady Mary Wroth, niece of Sir Philip
Sidney and friend of Ben Jonson, wrote a sonnet sequence in the
person of Pamphilia to Amphilanthus, her lover, William Herbert,
third Earl of Pembroke, the father of her two illegitimate children,
and joint dedicatee of the Shakespeare First Folio.

> Dear, famish not what you yourself gave food,
> Destroy not what your glory is to save,
> Kill not that soul to which you spirit gave,
> In pity, not disdain, your triumph stood.
> An easy thing it is to shed the blood
> Of one who, at your will, yields to the grave,
> But more you may true worth by mercy crave
> When you preserve, not spoil but nourish good.
> Your sight is all the food I do desire.
> Then sacrifice me not in hidden fire,
> Or stop the breath which did your praises move.
> Think but how easy 'tis a sight to give –
> Nay, even desert, since by it I do live.
> I but chameleon-like would live and love.[13]

As his mistress (or more probably one of his mistresses), Lady Mary
had no right to the company of her lover, but a lawfully wedded
wife had no better claim to her husband's time. Almost all the
opportunities open to ambitious men required them to spend long
periods away from their families. Soon after Grace Sharington
married Anthony Mildmay in 1567, he left her at his family estate
in Northamptonshire while he went off to Paris. She was to live in
Northamptonshire for twenty years while he travelled in Europe and
sojourned in London. It was not his wife but his father, Elizabeth's
chancellor of the Exchequer, who had the power to have him
recalled from France in March 1569 in the hope that he would find
preferment at court.[14] When he didn't, Mildmay chose to join the

attempt to suppress the revolt of the northern earls rather than stay at home.[15] In 1576 Elizabeth, entirely unmindful of Mildmay's responsibilities as a husband, granted him permission to travel overseas for two years 'for his better increase in knowledge and experience of foreign language to be thereby the more able to serve [her] thereafter'.[16] He accompanied Walsingham to the Low Countries and was sent as envoy to Duke Casimir of the Palatinate.[17] When he came back in 1579 to England, instead of joining his wife he entered Gray's Inn. By March 1582 he was back in Holland,[18] and his wife was pregnant. When Mildmay was elected MP for Wiltshire in the 1584 parliament he was obliged to spend all three terms in London. In 1586 he escorted Mary Queen of Scots to Fotheringay.[19] Grace wrote in her own account of her life:

> My husband was much from me in all that time and I spent the best part of my youth in solitariness, shunning all opportunities to run into company lest I might be enticed and drawn away by some evil suggestions to stain my unspotted garment and so be robbed of mine innocency . . .[20]

In 1595 Elizabeth consented to Mildmay's taking five servants, three horses, £100 and some jewels to Germany, where he was to stay for a year to be treated at a medicinal spa.[21] In 1596, after he was knighted, he accompanied the Earl on his embassy to France, only to incur the disfavour of Henri IV who requested his recall, whereupon his diplomatic career collapsed, and he had no option but to retire to his estates and endure the company of his wife.[22]

Ann must have known by repute what London was like, known that the streets were full of whores, from the sleaziest to the most glamorous. As the long months passed, she must have worried that Will would be led astray, by a young man's urges or by ill company. Once again we may be reminded of Polonius questioning whether his son Laertes may not commit:

> such wanton, wild and usual slips
> As are companions noted and most known
> To youth and liberty. (II. i. 22–4)

Ann may have had to struggle not to think about her young husband being drawn into 'drinking, fencing, swearing, quarrelling, drabbing', 'the flash and outbreak of a fiery mind'. She might have heard the gossip from people returning from London—

> 'I saw him enter such a house of sale' –
> Videlicet a brothel . . . (*Hamlet*, II. i. 60–1)

It is painful to think of Ann bailed up by a Stratford busybody as Mistress Arthur is by Master Anselm in *How to choose a good wife from a bad*, and having to keep her countenance as she is harangued:

> I say your husband haunts bad company
> Swaggerers, cheaters, wanton courtesans.
> There he defiles his body, stains his soul,
> Consumes his wealth, undoes himself and you,
> In danger of diseases whose vile names
> Are not for any honest mouths to speak
> Nor any chaste ears to receive and hear.[23]

If Shakespeare went to London specifically to try his fortune in the theatre, he would have had to wade through the stews to get to it. In January 1587 Philip Henslowe joined forces with a London grocer to run a new 'playhouse now framing and shortly to be erected and set up' on a site at the corner of the Rose Alley and Maiden Lane, bang in the middle of the red-light district.

> 'Rose' was a street euphemism for a prostitute . . . (One of the most fashionable of Southwark's brothels, the Cardinal's Hat, owes its name to the colour of the tip of the penis.) Henslowe and Alleyn had a financial interest in brothels other than the Rose, and Alleyn's wife (Henslowe's step-daughter) may have been a partner.[24]

In *Pierce Penniless his Supplication to the Devil*, Nashe has Pierce instruct his Satanic Majesty to:

Call a leet at Bishopsgate and examine how every second house in
Shoreditch is maintained. Make a privy search in Southwark and tell
me how many she-inmates you find . . . Lais, Cleopatra, Helen, if our
clime hath any such I commend them with the rest of our unclean
sisters in Shoreditch, Southwark, Westminster and Turnbull Street to
the protection of your Portership, hoping you will speedily carry them
down to Hell, there to keep open house for all young devils that
come . . .[25]

In late-sixteenth-century London, though prostitution was ubiquitous it was hardly big business. Every alehouse had female servants
who could be had for a few pence or a dish of coals. Prostitution
supplemented the earnings of working girls but the extra earnings
were mere pocketmoney, 'sixpenny damnation' as Nashe calls it.
London was not Venice. It boasted no grand courtesans, unless we
may count Emilia Lanier such. The illegitimate daughter of a Jewish
court musician from the Veneto, in 1587 she was or was about to
become the mistress of the lord chamberlain, Henry Carey, Lord
Hunsdon.[26] Shakespeare would eventually become a member of his
company of players. It is assumed that because Emilia was half Jewish
she was swarthy; the great Venetian courtesans, some of whom were
Jewish, were usually Titian-haired, that is to say, dyed blonde. As a
courtesan Emilia was a rare bird; most of London's prostitutes were of
a different class altogether.

Ann knew, none better, how strong her husband's desires were,
and she probably also knew that any penalty he incurred for casual sex
would be brought home to her. Shakespeare too would have read the
injunction in their Bible:

> Let thy fountain be blessed and rejoice with the wife of thy youth. Let
> her be as the loving hind and pleasant roe; let her breasts satisfy thee at
> all times and be thou ravisht always with her love. And why wilt thou,
> my son, be ravisht with a strange woman, and embrace the bosom of a
> stranger? (Proverbs, v: 15–20)

The first prostitute in the Shakespeare oeuvre is Doll Tearsheet in
Henry IV, Part 2. (Her name doesn't mean that she tore up sheets, but

that her sheets are hempen.) This whore with a heart of gold plies her trade at the Boar's Head tavern in Eastcheap. Falstaff reminds us at her first entrance that, despite her merry nature and quick wit, she carries disease. Though Prince Hal who, like the young Shakespeare, is on the loose in London and well outside his father's ambit, gets up to all kinds of villainy, he exhibits no familiarity with Doll or her ilk. When Hal becomes Henry V, Doll is dragged off to prison, despite her vociferations that she is pregnant. She is unusual among Shakespearean whores in that, while she is shameless and vulgar, she is essentially a sympathetic character.

In *Measure for Measure* when Pompey learns that the prostitution industry is to be extirpated, he warns the disguised duke of the economic consequences for the city: 'if this law hold in Vienna for ten year, I'll rent the fairest house in it after three pence a bay' (II. i. 230–1). Prostitution provides the contrast both for Isabella's idealistic purity and for the misdemeanour of her brother who has cohabited with his wife before solemnisation, and is to be punished with death. The disguised duke is shocked and disgusted to learn that Lucio esteems him as a whoremaster. If Shakespeare played any part in *Measure for Measure* it was probably that of the duke, and he may have responded with particular plangency: 'I have never heard the absent duke much detected for women. He was not inclined that way' (III. i. 185–6).

Escalus, the honest councillor, describes the duke as 'rather rejoicing to see another merry, than merry at anything that professed to make him rejoice. A gentleman of all temperance.' Similar words would be used of Shakespeare by his contemporaries. Later commentators would prefer him to have had more in common with Lucio than Escalus. We have no evidence, beyond the ghostly presence of the dark lady in the sonnets, that Shakespeare was a whoremaster. Some of his writing about sex with prostitutes could be thought to suggest that he was revolted by the very idea.

The brothel in *Pericles*, the play Shakespeare is thought to have written in collaboration with the brothel-keeper George Wilkins, is one of the most wretched places in Shakespeare. The pimps are angry that they are losing custom because of a shortage of wenches. 'We were never so much out of creatures. We have but poor three and they can do no more than they can do, and they with continual action are even as good as rotten . . .' (IV. ii. 6–9). The imagery becomes more disgusting: 'The stuff we have, a strong wind will blow it to pieces, they are so pitifully sodden' (17–18). And more threatening:

> Thou sayest true. There's two unwholesome, a'conscience. The poor
> Transylvanian is dead that lay with the little baggage.
> Ay, she quickly pooped him. She made him roast meat for worms.
> (19–23)

In *Cymbeline*, when Iachimo sees Imogen for the first time, he rhapsodises on the distorted taste that could prefer bought sex to conjugal relations with such a woman.

> It cannot be i'th'eye, for apes and monkeys,
> 'Twixt two such shes, would chatter this way, and
> Contemn with mows the other. Nor i'the judgment,
> For idiots, in this case of favour, would
> Be wisely definite, nor i'th'appetite.
> Sluttery to such neat excellence opposed
> Should make desire vomit emptiness,
> Not so allured to feed. (I. vi. 40–7)

Imogen listens, uncomprehending. Ignoring her bemusement, Iachimo raves on:

> The cloyed will –
> That satiate yet unsatisfied desire, that tub
> Both filled and running – ravening first the lamb,
> Longs after for the garbage. (49–51)

Iachimo's disgust may not be Shakespeare's, and some would argue that, if it was, it could well have been self-disgust. Iachimo tells Imogen that, given a wife as superlative as she, he is astounded that her husband has become a whoremonger,

> should I (damned then)
> Slaver with lips as common as the stairs
> That mount the Capitol, join gripes with hands
> Made hard with hourly falsehood (falsehood, as
> With labour), then by-peeping in an eye
> Base and illustrous as the smoky light
> That's fed with stinking tallow . . . (I. vi. 6–12)

> to be partnered
> With tomboys hired with that self exhibition
> Which your own coffers yield? With diseased ventures
> That play with all infirmities for gold
> Which rottenness can lend nature? Such boiled stuff
> As well might poison poison? (122–7)

Such hymns of horror cannot tell us whether Shakespeare ever had dealings with the women of the stews and back alleys. In *All's Well That Ends Well*, Helen muses on the fact that her young husband who hates her has just enjoyed sex with her thinking she was someone else.

> But, O strange men!
> That can such sweet use make of what they hate,
> When saucy trusting of the cozened thoughts
> Defiles the pitchy night. So lust doth play
> With what it loathes, for that which is away. (IV. v. 21–5)

Perhaps Ann too thought bitter thoughts as she lay in her matrimonial bed alone. Perhaps she indulged fantasies of disguising herself as a boy and riding to London, to feel Will's arms about her again, only to reflect ruefully that she might find him with someone else. We can only wonder if she heard a story going round the Inns of Court in the spring of 1602. In his diary for 13 March John Manningham, a student at the Middle Temple who had it from another student, entered it so:

Upon a time, when Burbage played Richard III, there was a citizen grew so far in liking with him that, before she went from the play, she appointed him to come that night unto her by the name of Richard the Third. Shakespeare, overhearing their conclusion, went before, was entertained, and at his game ere Burbage came. Then, message being brought that Richard the Third was at the door, Shakespeare caused return to be made that William the Conqueror was before Richard the Third.[27]

Ann would have found it very difficult if, as she went about her daily business, to market or to church, the maltworms of Stratford were sniggering over such tales. Any hope that such gossip would not make it back to Stratford is, I suspect, vain, especially as Thomas Greene, Town Clerk of Stratford and Ann's star boarder at New Place, was a Middle Templar and one of Manningham's friends. Sex with a healthy city wife was relatively safe, but hard to come by.

In Middleton's *A Mad World My Masters* (1605) a female member of the audience cries out in rapture after hearing a prologue: 'O my troth! An I were not married, I could find it in my heart to fall in love with that player now and send for him to a supper. I know some i'the town that have done as much . . .' (V. ii. 33–5). A later account ironically describes a 'virtuous player': 'The waiting-women spectators are over ears in love with him, and ladies send for him to act in their chambers.'[28] If we stick to the Bard's own words about lust, we shall find nothing that makes light of lechery, or even common or garden promiscuity.

> The expense of spirit in a waste of shame
> Is lust in action, and, till in action, lust
> Is perjured, murderous, bloody, full of blame,
> Savage, extreme, rude, cruel, not to trust,
> Enjoyed no sooner, but despisèd straight,
> Past reason hunted, and no sooner had,
> Past reason hated as a swallowed bait
> On purpose laid to make the taker mad,
> Mad in pursuit, and in possession so,
> Had having and in quest to have, extreme,
> A bliss in proof, and proved, a very woe,
> Before a joy proposed, behind a dream.
>   All this the world well knows, yet none knows well
>   To shun the heaven that leads men to this hell. (129)

If Ann had not misdoubted that some fine lady of the capital would throw her modest country charms into the shade, she would have been a very unusual woman. However, she had more immediate concerns. In 1587, following on from a winter of high prices and scarcity, a 'burning ague' appeared in Stratford. Ann brought her little family through it. Somehow in these years of dearth she was finding ways to feed them the kind of nourishing food that would protect them from the yearly visitations of infectious disease.

In *Westward Ho* written by Dekker and Webster for the Admiral's Men in 1604, Mistress Justiniano is asked by her husband, who has ruined them by his prodigality, gambling, riding abroad, consorting with noblemen and 'building a summer house', and has even sold the house she lives in: 'Why do you not ask me now what shall you do?' She replies, as Ann might have done to Will in 1585, 1586, 1587 or whenever: 'I have no counsel in your voyage, neither must you have any in mine . . . Fare you well. Let not the world condemn me if I seek for my own maintenance.'[29]

CHAPTER TEN

*suggesting that, having sent her boy husband to seek his fortune,
with three small children to look after, Ann Shakespeare found work
she could do indoors, and with the help of her haberdasher brother-
in-law might even have prospered*

In considering what it might be that Ann Shakespeare did once her
husband set off for parts unknown, farming comes soonest to mind.
Ann's stepmother Joan Hathaway was one of many Warwickshire
women farming on their own account. When Elizabeth Smart of
Bishopton died in 1585, she had five flitches of bacon stored in her
house, two live pigs, two geese and a gander, twelve hens and a cock,
a cow and a heifer, as well as wheat and barley to the value of £4.[1] In
the inventory of the Hathaways' neighbour, the widow Elizabeth
Pace, drawn up by Richard Burman, John Richardson and Thomas
Burman in January 1589, we find 'three kine . . . three calves . . . five
horses and mares . . . eighteen sheep and a colt'.[2] In 1590 Roger
Burman's widowed daughter, Ann Pace, was farming her own
copyhold yardland in Shottery.[3] Ann Nash, mother of Shakespeare's
friend Anthony Nash, widowed in 1587, farmed four and a half
yardlands in Welcombe.[4] Ann would have known Roger Burman's
widow, Alice. She would farm in Shottery for sixteen years after her
husband died in 1592. When Alice died in 1608, she left, as well as
two cows, a year-old heifer and ten sheep, a crop of corn valued at
£20.[5] The Warwickshire Corn Enquiry of 1595 lists several female
heads of farming households:

> Anne Baker hath four quarters of rye, six quarters of barley and five of
> household
>   Alice Wall ten quarters of rye, fourteen quarters of barley, two

quarters of peas, thirteen acres of barley to sow and seven acres of peas, seven of household.[6]

In Shottery Joan Hathaway was one of three widows farming at the end of 1595. John Richardson's widow was preparing to sow thirty-two acres with barley, and twenty-one with peas; she had in hand nine quarters of wheat, nineteen of barley and fifteen of peas; after seed corn was taken out she had eighteen quarters left 'to serve her house and the market'.[7] Widow Burman was to sow twenty-four acres of barley and twelve of peas, to support a household of six.[8] With only fifteen acres to farm, Ann's stepmother was still well able to support her household of six.[9]

These women would not have done all the work of the farm themselves – the number in the household would have included farm-servants – but women did do heavy work. When the Avon suddenly flooded on the morning of 18 July 1588, among workers trapped by the rising waters was a young woman: 'It did take away suddenly one Sale's daughter of Grafton out of Hillborough meadow removing of a hay cock . . .'[10] The young woman had apparently been intending to shoulder the haycock and carry it, possibly the mile or two uphill to Temple Grafton. John Locke wrote in his diary about Alice George who was born in 1562:

> When she was young she was fair-haired and neither fat nor lean, but very slender in the waist, for her size she was to be reckoned rather amongst the tall than the short women. Her condition was but mean, and her maintenance her labour, and she said she was able to reap as much in a day as any man, and had as much wages.[11]

Women who were employed at harvest as 'shearers', cutting corn with sickles, got the same wages as mowers; 'we should do them an injury if we should take them from their company and not make them equal to those in wages they can equalize in work'.

If Ann had no visible means of support and couldn't go out to work, her in-laws would not have been expected to take on the responsibility. Since the enactment of the Poor Law of 1563, justices of the peace had the duty of collecting and administering funds for relief of the poor. While Ann's children were still so small that she couldn't go out to work she could either have been given a dole to live on or she and they could have been sent to separate wards in the poor house. Elizabeth Sadler, deserted wife of Thomas Sadler, son of the John Sadler who was Bailiff of Stratford in 1570, was admitted to the almshouses in 1601, her mother-in-law having agreed to raise her two sons but not to support her.[12] The same option would have been available to Mary Shakespeare, if she and her husband had been better off than they were. They could have taken Ann's children and left her to fend for herself.

> Women made up a high percentage of the settled poor people (people, not being vagrants, who received parish poor relief), sometimes outnumbering men by as many as two to one, and heading a disproportionately large number of households as widows or deserted wives. In the 1570 Norwich census of the poor, 62 per cent of the total number of adults over sixteen were women.[13]

If Ann and her family had ended up on the parish, menial work would have been found for all four of them. The worst work was picking oakum for a mere four pence a week. In 1560 the Westminster Workhouse set to work children over six but under twelve winding quills for weavers.[14]

The records of poor relief in Holy Trinity parish are incomplete, but there is no sign that Ann ever received help, which suggests that somehow she managed to support her three children. Work available to an unskilled woman was sporadic and very poorly paid. In the Minutes and Accounts of the Stratford Corporation we find entries for 'dressing and sweeping the school house' after the builders had completed its refurbishment, almost certainly women's work, for which was paid eight pence.[15] In the accounts submitted on 1 March 1576, we read that three pence was paid to 'Mother Margaret' for 'making clean before the chapel'. In the accounts for 1576 women are listed as being paid for a variety of jobs, 'for drawing of straw in the chapel garden', twelve pence, for taking food to the gardener, four pence, to Jane Salt 'for drawing of straw', three pence, to Empson's wife, for carrying straw, two pence, to the gardener's wife for drawing of straw, four pence, and to Jane Plummer for the same, two pence.[16] A 'poor woman' was paid one penny 'for bearing in of chips', and 'Conway's wife' also got a penny for carrying a load of sand.[17] Conway's wife Margaret appears in the accounts again, as the recipient of two pence for 'making clean the gaol' in 1581 and four pence for doing the same job in 1586.[18]

In the annual account for 1577 are three entries of four pence each paid to 'a poor woman sweeping before the chapel' and once again in 1578. The second and third times the payment appears in 1578 the person 'making clean without the chapel' is identified as Margaret Smith; in 1579 she is once more 'the woman that sweepeth about the chapel door' and her wages are given as sixteen pence, while 'Bennett's wife' who sweeps the Hall is paid two pence.[19] In 1580 Margaret's year's wages were twenty pence, plus an extra penny 'for sweeping the street after the tiler'.[20] The next year, her wages sank back to sixteen pence.[21] In 1582 Smith was again paid sixteen pence; in the entry for the sixteen pence paid to her the next year she is called simply 'old Margaret'. In the same account we find Alice Earl, who would be buried as a pauper In December 1596, receiving three pence for carrying lime from the Hall to the bridge.[22] By 1585 Margaret Smith, her wages still sixteen pence, has become 'lame Margaret'.[23] We find Margaret's burial on 15 May 1586 in the Holy Trinity register. By the will that William Gilbert had written for her on 11 April, Margaret bequeathed one coffer, her brass pot and whatever corn was left in her bag to Richard Holmes, to his son another coffer, and to Joan Johnston and to Isabel Barrymore a kerchief each. These legacies made and her debts paid, she bequeathed the rest of her goods movable and immovable to Agnes Holmes whom she made her sole executrix. Five shillings already in the hands of Richard Holmes were to be bestowed on the day of her funeral, probably in a feast for the poor, including her neighbours in the almshouse.[24] Margaret's will, proved on 6 July, is a dignified little document, a fitting epilogue to an ordered, frugal and useful life. With Margaret gone the chapel environs still had to be swept: in 1587 an unidentified woman received the sixteen pence and in 1588 the money was recorded as paid simply for 'sweeping about the chapel'.[25] In 1589 the rate slumped to twelve pence, paid to 'a woman'.[26] In

1591 the rate was back at sixteen pence, and once again the woman has no name.[27]

Ann could not have housed, clothed and fed three children on sixteen pence a year. She could have managed on the two pence a day she would have earned working in the fields, helping with the harvest, but the work was seasonal. The rest of the year she would have had to scratch together a pittance by cleaning, washing or cooking for her neighbours, or tending the sick or preparing the dead for burial. If she had been condemned to such drudgery, her babies would have been like the children of many other poor women, neglected, ragged, dirty, and weeping with hunger and cold. If the Bard is not to be suspected of craven and callous behaviour, we have to assume that Ann did have some sort of marketable skill. We don't know, after all, how the young Shakespeares lived before William took himself off to wherever it was that he went. He doesn't seem to have gone into the whittawing and glove-making business, nor does he seem to have begun sheep-herding or dairying or horse-breaking. If he had he probably would never have become a playwright. It seems more likely that he wandered about like Mr Micawber looking for something to turn up. All that turned up were more mouths to feed.

In our own time the fact that separations are usually initiated by women is most often explained as a consequence of the degree of economic independence they enjoy. Tudor women enjoyed a measure of economic independence that would not be equalled again until our own time. Ann Shakespeare could have been confident of her ability to support herself and her children, but not if she had also to deal with a layabout husband good for nothing but spinning verses, who had the right to do as he pleased with any money she could earn. Ten to one, if he was useless he was also restless. When the chance arose to send him off to London in the train of some dignitary or filling in for someone in a group of players, she could well have jumped at it and sent him south with her blessing.

Alison Plowden gives an admirably concise account of women's economic activity in the second half of the sixteenth century:

As a career woman the Queen was also unique, and yet for the resolute minority – whether married or single – who found themselves faced

with the necessity of earning a living, opportunities, though limited
were by no means non-existent. Apart from domestic service – often a
stepping-stone to marriage – wet and dry nursing, governessing or a
position as a 'waiting gentlewoman' in a great household, the commonest female occupations were tailoring, upholstery, millinery,
embroidery and related trades. But inn-keeping was also considered
acceptable, and there were plenty of laundresses, fishwives and other
street vendors, as well as a few wax-chandlers, brewers, bakers and
confectioners, and even some female ironmongers and shoemakers.
Some enterprising women set up as herbalists, concocting cosmetics
and perfumed washes, and, of more dubious respectability, there were
astrologers, fortune-tellers and quack medical practitioners.[28]

In Stratford, after the death of Richard Balamy, the smith who also
acted as the locksmith for the Corporation in 1580, his widow
Katharine Balamy took over the business and ran it herself with
hired labour.[29]

Female employment was universal in Tudor England; the woman
of leisure is a creature of a later era. All women worked, even if most
were no more likely to receive actual cash money than the animals in
their husbands' stalls. If she could make no significant contribution to
the family income, a single girl could not expect to keep her feet
under her father's table. She had to find work, with neighbours, with
kin, or far away, with strangers. 'Domestic service' was not a matter of
frilly caps and aprons but of hard graft, sweating in the kitchen or
brewhouse or bakery, living on hard rations. Mistress Winchcombe,
wife to Jack of Newbury in Deloney's tale, is admonished by her
gossip for feeding her servants too well:

You feed your folks with the best of the beef and the finest of the
wheat, which in my opinion is a great oversight: neither do I hear of
any knight in this country that doth it . . . Come thither, and I warrant
you that you shall see but brown bread on the board; if it be wheat and
rye mingled together, it is a great matter, and the bread highly
commended. But most commonly they eat either barley bread, or
rye mingled with pease and suchlike coarse grain, which is doubtless
but of small price, and there is no other bread allowed, except at their

own board. And in like manner for their meat. It is well known that
necks and points of beef is their ordinary fare which, because it is
commonly lean, they seethe therewith now and then a piece of bacon
or pork, whereby they make their pottage fat, and therewith drives out
the rest with more content. And thus must you learn to do. And beside
that the midriffs of the oxen, and the cheeks, the sheep's heads, and the
gathers, which you give away at your gate, might serve them well
enough, which would be a great sparing to your other meat, and by
this means you would save in the year much money, whereby you
might the better maintain your hood and silk gown.[30]

Domestic service was not always and perhaps not even often a
stepping-stone to marriage. Most of the women who went into
service did not find husbands; a woman whose employer chose not to
release her, and did not permit anyone to pay his addresses to her, was
likely to die unmarried. The more highly a servant was valued, the less
likely she was to be let go. It was a rare master who gave a marriage
portion to a servant.

As Miranda Chaytor and Jane Lewis pointed out in 1982:

not all daughters had dowries. The eldest might marry well, into a
trading family as prosperous as her father's, but the maidservants . . .
were usually her less fortunate younger sisters. [Alice] Clark's somewhat idealised account of the family business, centred on the natural-
ness of the husband–wife partnership, the equality between them and
the complementarity of their roles, overlooks the exploitation of other
household members – the younger sons and daughters, the maid
servants without dowry or prospects whose exclusion and drudgery
ensured the comfort of the prosperous few.[31]

Thomas Deloney gives a fascinating insight into how women found
work in *Thomas of Reading or The Six Worthy Yeomen of the West* (1597).
The occasion was 'a fair that was kept near Gloucester, there to be
ready for any that would come to hire them, the young men stood in a
row on one side and the maidens on the other'. The same kind of fair
or 'mop' was held at Stratford every year. In Deloney's story the
daughter of the banished Earl of Shrewsbury encounters two girls on

their way to the fair, and introduces herself. 'I am a poor man's child that is out of service, and I hear that at the Statute, folks do come of purpose to hire servants.' The girls invite her to go along with them, and she asks what kind of service she should offer.

> 'What can you do?' quoth the maidens. 'Can you brew and bake, make butter and cheese, and reap corn well?' . . .
> 'If you could spin or card,' said another, 'you might do excellent well with a clothier, for they are the best services that I know . . .'[32]

But the earl's daughter can only read and write, sew a fine seam and play the lute. In the event she becomes a personal maid, but even so she is sent out into the fields for the hay-making; 'attired in a red stammell petticoat and a broad straw hat upon her head, she had also a hay-fork and in her lap she did carry her breakfast'.[33]

In *The Two Gentlemen of Verona*, Launce has made a memorandum of the qualifications of the woman he wants to marry:

> 'tis a milkmaid, and yet 'tis not a maid for she has gossips. Yet 'tis a maid, for she is her master's maid and serves for wages . . . Imprimis: she can fetch and carry . . . Item: she can milk . . . Item: she brews good ale . . . Item: she can sew . . . Item: she can knit . . . Item: she can wash and scour . . . Item: she can spin . . . (III. i. 266–307)

The routine of a farming household was tough; the day began at five a.m. in the winter, four in the summer. Ann had probably begun working almost as soon as she could walk, wool-picking and looking after the lambs. Joan of Arc's father, in *Henry VI, Part 1*, talks of Joan's herding his lambs when she was a little girl. Sheep were often left to children in Warwickshire wills in this period. John Eliott of Luddington left a ewe sheep to each of three goddaughters in 1560.[34] Philip Wells of Shottery left a sheep to each of his brother's children when he died in 1562.[35] In 1570 Richard Hathaway's godson, Roger Burman's shepherd Edmund Cale, left two sheep to the children of Thomas Burman, and a 'little lamb' to another little girl.[36] Ann's father left a sheep each to two of his young nieces. When Simon Beard of Bishopton made his will in 1587 his daughter Mary was expecting a child, who would receive a lamb when it was born.[37] Roger Burman of Shottery, who died in 1592, left one sheep to each of the children of his son Thomas.[38] When Ann's brother Bartholomew came to make his will in 1624, he left a 'chilver sheep' to a daughter of his first son Richard, and four of the children of his second son each received one of his best ewes. As Bartholomew was then farming Hewlands, his inventory gives a pretty good idea of how they lived. When he died, in the barns and outhouses there were, as well as twenty quarters of barley, ten strikes of wheat, pulses and hay, a malt mill and a cheese press, with the hemp and flax to be used with both.[39] Ann would have learnt, as her nieces did, the proper use of both malt mill and cheese press.

Ann Hathaway would have been quite small when she learnt like her cousins to care for her own ewe lamb, which she was to rear by hand after it had been taken from its mother in April. The ewe would then be milked each day until October when she would be mated again. The lamb reared by Ann would have been mated in due course and brought forth its own lamb, and then it would have been time for Ann to learn to milk the grown ewe. The milk would be put in the dairy to separate, and she would have been taught how to skim off the cream and set it as curd cheese. The whey left to ferment would have been drunk by the family and the rest of the skim milk fed back to the lambs or used to fatten a pig. Pressing removed the last of the moisture in the curd, to make a hard cheese that would last the winter. Curds or cheese together with hard, dark bread were the healthy staples of the sheep-farming diet.

No farmer would have taken on a servant with three small children, but it was also possible for Ann to have made cheeses at home. Katherine Salisbury had in her house in Church Street at the time of her death in 1591 five flitches of bacon and twenty-two cheeses, as well as 'one dozen cheese trenchers'.[40] Her husband, Alderman Robert Salisbury, was a brewer; when he died, and her son-in-law took over the business and the main house, Katherine moved into the gatehouse, where she worked to sustain herself. Among her belongings was a malt mill.[41]

Many of the Stratford women left with children to support turned to malt-making. Two-thirds of the value of the estate of the widow

Agnes Eliott, who died in 1564, was in malt. Her inventory lists '18 quarters of malt [180 bushels], a quarter of muncorne [mixed grain]; half a quarter of malt, 2 strikes of barley [2 bushels]'.[42] In the inventory of Margaret Hathaway, the widow of Ann Shakespeare's nephew Edmund, are listed: 'one malt mill, two little grates, three wheels, one strike [a measure], three malt sieves, one peck [another measure], one try [another kind of sieve], one haircloth [used in drying malt], one winnow sheet . . . three looms [open tubs], two kivers [pails] . . .' and 'twenty-four quarters [240 bushels] of malt in two garners'.[43] Other women brewed and sold ale for a living. After Rose Reve's husband died in 1625, she worked as a brewer and as a needlewoman to support her five children. When she died five years later, the appraisers of her goods found that she had, as well all the equipment for beer-making in her kitchen and four quarters of malt in an upper room, seven hogsheads of strong beer, three of ordinary beer, six half-hogsheads of beer and four barrels of small beer in her cellar, with a impressive total value of £22.[44]

Ann could have set herself up as an ale-wife or have used her smidgin of capital and what she had learnt as the eldest daughter of a farming family to set herself up as a market trader. If she was farming for herself, she may have made enough money from the sale of her butter, cheese and cream, her eggs, honey and pies to house, clothe and feed her family and even a servant. It would have been unusual for the unsupported mother of three tiny children to attempt to support herself in any of these ways, but perhaps Ann was an unusual woman. In her Bible she would have read:

Who shall find a virtuous woman? . . .

She seeketh wool and flax and laboureth cheerfully with her hands.

She is like the ships of the merchant; she bringeth her food from afar.

And she riseth while it is yet night, and giveth the portion to her household, and the ordinary to her maids.

She considereth a field and getteth★ it and with the fruit of her hands she planteth a vineyard.

★She purchaseth it with the gains of her travail.

(Proverbs, xxx: 10–16)

Ann could have found work indoors, as a housewife or housekeeper. In the sixteenth century 'housewife' was a job description. As set out by Gervase Markham in *The English Housewife*, the inward and outward virtues to be found in a compleat housewife were:

> her skill in physic, surgery, cooking, extraction of oils, banqueting stuff, ordering of great feasts, preserving of all sorts of wines, conceited secrets, distillations, perfumes, ordering of wool, hemp, flax, making cloth and dyeing, the knowledge of dairies, office of malting, of oats, their excellent uses in families, of brewing, baking, and all other things belonging to a household.[45]

This kind of skilled work was probably not available to Ann Shakespeare until rather later in her career, when her children were able to fend for themselves. Under normal circumstances the housewife was the partner of the husband. When Thomas Tusser voiced the first version of 'a woman's work is never done', he was thinking of the woman working in her own household.

> Though husbandry seemeth to bring in the gains,
> Yet housewifery labours seem equal in pains.
> Some respite to husbands the weather may send
> But housewives' affairs have never an end.[46]

Housewives did also work in the houses of others, of widowed men for example, and of married men whose wives were too grand or too ignorant or too young to undertake the work of running the household. Girls were apprenticed to housekeepers to learn 'the mystery and sciences of housewifery' whether they had marriage in prospect or not.[47] In *The Merry Wives of Windsor*, the house of Dr Caius was kept by Mistress Quickly, 'which is in the manner of his nurse, or his dry nurse, or his cook, or his laundry, his washer and his wringer' (I. ii. 1–5). She gives us her job description: 'I may call him my master, look you, for I keep his house, and I wash, wring, brew, bake, scour, dress meat and drink, make beds and do all myself' (I. iv. 89–92).

When John Attwood died in Stratford in 1601, his daughter was indentured to the whittawer Robert Butler and his wife as a maidservant for ten years, while her brother was apprenticed to his uncle a tailor.[48] In 1606 orphaned Katherine Sumner was placed with the seamstress Jane Lummas for seven years.[49] In November 1614 Ellen Burcher, daughter of a cutler from Henley-in-Arden, was apprenticed to Richard and Susanna Holmes to learn the business of weaving bone-lace and housewifery.[50]

In Thomas Deloney's novel, designed to be read by the clothworkers of London, Jack of Newbury employed more women than men; this huge workshop is a myth but the division of labour would have been accurate.

> Within one room, being large and long,
> There stood two hundred looms full strong.
> Two hundred men, the truth is so,
> Wrought in these looms all in a row.
> By every one a pretty boy
> Sat making quills with mickle joy,
> And, in another place hard by,
> An hundred women merrily
> Were carding hard with joyful cheer,
> Who singing sat with voices clear,
> And, in a chamber close beside,
> Two hundred maidens did abide,
> In petticoats of Stamell red
> And milk-white kerchiefs on their head . . .
> Those pretty maids did never lin
> But in that place all day did spin.[51]

In London about half of all apprentices to crafts and trades were female. If Ann was a skilled worker, then it would follow that she had served an apprenticeship before she was married, possibly far from Shottery. For this her father would have had to pay a fee for her training and something towards the cost of housing, feeding and clothing her, but this comparatively small investment coupled with her own aptitude and diligence would have combined to give her another attraction to join with her dowry of ten marks in the quest for a good match. There were other skills, however, that she could have learnt at home. As the exemplary wife says in the comedy *How to choose a good wife from a bad*, the best resource for a woman with an improvident husband was her needle.

> My husband in this humour well I know
> Plays the unthrift, therefore it behoves me
> To be the better housewife here at home,
> To save and get, while he doth laugh and spend.
> Though for himself he riots it at large,
> My needle shall defray the household's charge.[52]

Spinning was a job that had always been done by unmarried women or spinsters. Women also made lace by winding linen threads on pigs' trotter-bones (hence 'bone-lace') and weaving them under and over around a pattern picked out on a bolster with pins, much as bobbin lace is still made today.

> Lacemaking . . . was work which did not depend on the man's occupation and where the woman acted as an autonomous producer, an independent wage earner in her own right. The lacemaking community of Colyton in Devon, where Honiton lace was made between about 1600 and 1740, had a preponderance of women in the population and a later than average age of marriage. Lacemakers' earning were high, probably higher than those of wool spinners.[53]

Ann could, like the gentlewomen mentioned in *Henry V*, have earned an honest living by the 'prick of her needle' and/or she could have made bone-lace. She could have, but in the 1580s there was no shortage of seamstresses or lace. The demand for knitted stockings on the other hand was growing faster than it could be met. In the midlands, where the sheep bore wool of a fine, long staple, knitting worsted stockings was a growth industry. Joan Thirsk, summarising the information in Stow's *Annals*, tell us that 'stocking knitting . . . was a handcraft among peasant communities before this period, probably for centuries before, but it developed into an industry commanding a considerable place in English domestic trade from the mid-sixteenth century onwards'.[54]

The first mention of knitting in an English document is in an act of 1563 regulating manufacturers of and dealers in 'knit hose, knit petticoats, knit gloves and knit sleeves'. Before wire-drawing was mechanised in 1566, it was impossible to make steel knitting needles. Needles were originally imported from Spain: 'The making of Spanish needles was first taught in England by Elias Crowse, a German, about the eighth year of Queen Elizabeth, and in Queen Mary's time there was a negro made fine Spanish needles in Cheapside but would never teach his art to any.'[55] Before that caps and stockings were knitted on wooden and bone needles but most hose were constructed out of woven cloth, usually cut on the bias. Henry VIII and Edward VI were both presented with knitted silk stockings from Spain.

> Just how expensive they were we may deduce from an entry in the London port book of 1567–68. Twelve pairs of silk hose were shipped from Malaga to London and valued by the customs officers at nearly £4 a pair. Since such valuations were well below, and sometimes only half, the true value, we may estimate their full worth at something nearer £8 a pair.[56]

In 1560 Mistress Mountague, silk woman to Elizabeth I, presented her with a pair of black silk stockings that she had knitted herself; the queen was so delighted with them that she never wore woven hose again.[57] According to Stow:

> In the year one thousand five hundred and sixty four, William Rider, being an apprentice with Master Thomas Burdet . . . chanced to see a pair of knit worsted stockings in the lodging of an Italian merchant that came from Mantua, borrowed those stockings and caused other stockings to be made by them, and these were the first worsted stocking to be made in England. Within few years after, began the plenteous making both of kersey and woollen stockings, so in short space they waxed common.[58]

In 1578 when Elizabeth visited Yarmouth she was treated to a display of knitting. On a specially erected stage

there stood at one end eight small women children spinning worsted
yarn and at the other end as many knitting of worsted yarn hose . . .[59]

By the time Shakespeare was writing *Twelfth Night* in 1600, knitting
had taken its place among the skills of working women: Orsino tells
Cesario to pay particular attention to the song Feste is about to sing.

> Mark it, Cesario, it is old and plain.
> The spinsters, and the knitters in the sun,
> And the free maids that weave their thread with bones
> Do use to chant it . . . (II. iv. 44–7)

Knitting was probably one of the skills Ann had acquired when she
was growing up in Shottery in the 1570s:

> Joan can spin and Joan can card,
>   Joan keeps clean both house and yard.
> She can dress both flesh and fish
>   or anything that you can wish.
> She can sew and she can knit.
>   Joan for anything is fit.[60]

The milkmaid Launce wants to marry in *The Two Gentlemen of
Verona* can knit, and Launce interprets this skill in her as being as
good as a dowry: 'What need a man care for a stock with a wench
when she can knit him a stock?' (III. i. 301–3). An odd light is cast
on the way in which knitting served as a source of income for poor
women by the discovery that, when Ann Morgan of Wells in
Somerset, who combined knitting with occasional prostitution, was
overheard bargaining with a man who asked 'Shall I lie with thee
and I will give thee a shilling?' she replied, 'No, I will have
eighteenpence for thou has torn my coat and has hindered me
the knitting of half a hose.'[61]

In early November 1598 Adrian Quiney wrote from Stratford to
his son Richard, who was in London on Corporation business,
advising him to invest in 'knit stockings':

if you may have carriage to buy some such wares as you may sell presently to proft. If you bargain with W[illia]m Sh[akespeare] or receive money there, or bring your money home you may. I see how knit stockings be sold. There is great buying of them at Evesham. Edward Wheat and Harry your brother's man were both at Evesham this day sevennight and as I heard bestow £20 there in knit hose, wherefore I think you may do good if you can have money.[62]

Quiney's excitement suggests that the demand for knit stockings was greater than the supply, so that if they could buy up large quantities at Evesham they stood to make a tidy profit.

More skilled knitters could knit finer, decorative stockings, with more stitches to the inch, as well as fancy stitches and embroidery, and for them they could charge enormous prices. Stubbes was particularly outraged by the extravagance of the hosiery affected by all classes:

Then have they nether stocks to these gay hose, not of cloth (though never so fine) for that is thought too base, but of jersey, worsted, crewell, silk, thread, and such like, or else at the least of the finest yarn that can be got and so curiously knitted with open seam down the leg with quirks and clocks around the ankles and sometime haply interlaced with gold or silver threads . . . it is now grown that everyone (almost), though otherwise very poor, having scarce forty shillings of wages by the year, will not stick to have two or three pair of these silk nether stocks or else of the finest yarn that may be got, though the price of them be a royal or twenty shillings, or more, as commonly it is . . .[63]

And that's just the men. Women go even further:

Their nether stocks in like manner are either of silk, jersey, worsted, crewell, or at least of as fine yarn, thread or cloth as is possible to be had . . . they are not ashamed to wear hose of all kind of changeable colours, as green, red, white, russet, tawny, and else what, which wanton light colours any sober chaste Christian . . . can hardly without suspicion of lightness at any time wear. And then these delicate hose must be cunningly knit and curiously indented in every point, with quirks, clocks, open seam, and everything else accordingly.[64]

If Ann were involved in the upper end of the stocking manufacture, spinning her own thread of 'changeable' or mixed colours and
knitting it into elaborate patterns, she could have earned a good living
for herself and her little ones. If she taught other women to knit up
her designs and provided them with patterns and materials, she could
have earned much more. Such goods were manufactured in the
midlands; in Stratford in 1598 the haberdasher William Smith sued
one Perry for failing to pay him for 'fustians, lace, worsted stockings,
silk buttons, taffeta &c'.[65] A cottage industry like this has to be
organised and co-ordinated; evidence of female entrepreneurs in this
field is hard to come by but there is some. In 1622 when she
accompanied her husband to Ireland, Elizabeth Cary, Viscountess
Falkland, undertook to organise a local textile industry there:

> she procured some of each kind to come from those other places
> where those trades are exercised, as several sorts of linen and woollen
> weavers, dyers, all sorts of spinners and knitters, hatters, lace-makers
> and many other trades at the very beginning, and for this purpose she
> took of beggar children (with which that country swarms) more than
> eight score apprentices, refusing none above seven year old, and taking
> some less. These were disposed to their several masters and mistresses
> to learn those trades they were thought most fit for, the least amongst
> them being set to something, as making points, tags, buttons or
> lace . . .[66]

Lady Falkland was no businesswoman and her noble project eventually failed. If Ann had tried something similar in Warwickshire with
the wives and daughters of the growing horde of landless workers, she
could well have succeeded. All sources note that agriculture was
employing fewer and fewer people in the midlands in the 1580s
and 1590s, and that the clothing trades were becoming more and more
important.[67] What we lack is any account of just how that happened. If
Ann Shakespeare had both skill and business acumen, she could have
become a wealthy woman in her own right. So far we don't know that
she did, but we don't know that she didn't either.

We can be sure that there were women in Stratford who made a
living by knitting because the Overseers of the Poor, among whom

were numbered various of Ann Shakespeare's nephews at different times, included knitting among the useful trades to be taught to orphan girls. In 1607 eleven-year-old Dorothy Mather was placed with George Davis and his wife Margaret for fourteen years as an indentured servant 'to learn to knit and weave bone lace'.[68] In the same year fourteen-year-old Elizabeth, daughter of Thomas Bayliss, was placed with Anne Curtis, widow, a knitter, to be taught 'knitting, carding, spinning and other housewifery'. In 1612–13 Widow Curtis took on thirteen-year-old Margaret Getley, to learn 'the trade of knitting and other housewifery'.[69] In 1615 Dorothy Mather's sister Katherine was apprenticed to Margery Shepherd for eight years 'to learn the art and science of knitting'.[70]

In his *History of Myddle*, the Shropshire yeoman Richard Gough mentions one house-bound woman who survived by knitting:

I knew but one of Parkes's children. Her name was Anne. She was taken in her youth by that distemper which is called the rickets. She could not go or walk until she was nineteen years of age. Afterwards her limbs received strength and she was able to walk. She learnt to knit stockings and gloves, in which employment she was very expert and industrious, and thereby maintained herself after the death of her parents . . .[71]

Elinor, widow of Richard Ralphs, one-time Parish Clerk of Myddle, is likewise described as being able to 'knit very well and thereby gets her maintenance'.[72]

In 1589 William Lee of Calverton in Nottinghamshire, graduate of St John's College Cambridge, devised a mechanical knitting machine. It was promoted at court by Shakespeare's patron Lord Hunsdon, who secured an opportunity for Lee to demonstrate his machine to the queen, in hopes that she would grant him a patent. Elizabeth refused. For one thing the worsted stockings made by his machine were too coarse, but, revealingly, she feared that recourse to the machine would throw too many knitters out of work. Lee improved his machine, increasing the number of stitches to twenty per inch, but still the queen refused.

The key to how Shakespeare's wife could have managed to make a living may be his brother Gilbert, the haberdasher. We have very few hard facts about Gilbert. We know that he was christened at Holy Trinity on 13 October 1566. He was probably named for Gilbert Bradley, John Shakespeare's fellow glover, who had been made a burgess in 1565. We have no way of knowing if Gilbert attended the Stratford grammar school, but we do know that he could write a fine italic hand, because he signed his full name as witness to the lease of a property in Bridge Street, Stratford, in 1610. In 1597 when he stood bail for William Sampson in the Court of Queen's Bench in London, he was described as a 'haberdasher of St Bride's Parish'.[73] If Gilbert had ever been apprenticed to a haberdasher it would have been in 1580 or so, and by 1587 he would have been newly out of his articles and looking to set himself up, but so far no record of any apprenticeship has turned up. There is no mention of a Gilbert Shakespeare in the registers of St Bride's parish nor is he listed as a member of the Worshipful Company of Haberdashers. He was clearly still connected with Stratford; William Sampson, the man he went bail for, was from Stratford. Gilbert was in Stratford on 1 May 1602, when he acted for his brother in the conveyancing of the land he bought in Old Stratford. On 3 February 1612 Gilbert was buried in Stratford. We have no record of his owning a shop in Stratford or in London, or of his being a householder in either place; his haberdashery business seems to have been peripatetic at best.

Nobody has ever been quite sure what a haberdasher does. In 1502 the original haberdashers who sold ribbons, beads, purses, gloves, pins, caps and toys, were amalgamated with the Guild of Hat-makers, in an odd confederation of manufacturers of one product with traders in different products. If we may believe Robert Greene, the connection between the two was not always to the customer's advantage.

> The haberdasher . . . trims up old felts and makes them very fair to the eye, and faceth and edgeth them neatly, and then he turns them away to such a simple man as I am, and so abuseth us with his cozenage. Beside you buy gummed taffeta, wherewith you line hats, that will straight asunder, as soon as it comes to the heat of a man's head . . .'[74]

Though in 1446 the Haberdashers' Company was accorded a grant of arms, and in 1448 a charter of incorporation, the business of haberdashery remains inextricably connected with merchandising all kinds of trumpery, much of it done by travelling chapmen and chapwomen. In 1550 haberdashery was thought to consist of 'French or Milan caps, glasses, daggers, swords, girdles and such things'.[75] Because of the Milan connection haberdashers were also called milliners: 'the other a Frenchman and a milliner in St Martin's, sells shirts, bands, bracelets, jewels and such pretty toys for gentlewomen . . .'.[76] In 1561 Stow lists 'mousetraps, bird cages, shoe horns, lanterns and Jews' trumps' as part of a particular haberdasher's ware.[77] In 1576 haberdashery is described as 'bells, necklaces, beads of glass, collars, points, pins, purses, needles, girdles, thread, knives, scissors, pincers, hammers, hatchets, shirts, coifs, headkerchiefs, breeches, clothes, caps, mariners' breeches . . .'.[78] 'Trash' and 'haberdash' went together. Cotgrave defines a 'mercerot' as 'a pedlar, a paltry haberdasher'.[79]

Obviously, haberdashery is closely related to the other clothing trades, spinning, weaving, wool drapery, linen drapery, tailoring, knitting, lace-making, gloving, shoe-making, hosiery. As a glover John Shakespeare would have sold some of his production to haberdashers, and he would also have needed the services of haberdashers in supplying him with yarn, braid and other trimmings as well as needles, pins and scissors for his workwomen. Mercers, hatters, hosiers and woollen drapers too would have distributed their wares with the help of haberdashers and chapmen. Stratford, not far from the point where the London road split to serve the fast-growing industrial towns of Coventry and Birmingham, was well placed to serve as a depot for luxury goods, which might explain why the town was virtually run by businessmen who called themselves mercers. Strictly speaking mercers dealt in the top end of the fabric range, in the silks and velvets which hardly anyone in Stratford was entitled to wear. The Sumptuary Law of 1597 stipulated that 'None shall wear velvet in gowns, cloaks, coats and upper garments, or satin, damask, taffeta or grograin . . . or embroidery with silk or netherstocks of silk except knights and all above that rank, their heirs apparent, those with net income of £200.'[80]

There were no knights and only one esquire among the parishioners at Holy Trinity and very few gentlemen. The wives of gentlemen who had the right to a coat of arms might wear kirtles of satin, as well as gowns of damask, tufty taffeta, plain taffeta and grosgrain, but there were hardly enough of them in Stratford to keep a single mercer busy. Mercers did sell silks and velvets to people not qualified to wear them, thus enabling them 'playerlike, in rich attires not fitting [their] estate' to counterfeit their betters and impose upon the public.[81] Mercers supplied fabrics for making up by tailors, and were so often kept waiting for their money by spendthrift gallants that the 'mercer's book' of outstanding debts was a byword. In *Measure for Measure*, among those languishing in prison is a gallant who has been put there by the mercer because he has not paid 'for some four suits of peach-coloured satin' (IV. iii. 8–9).

The senior Stratford mercer was Thomas Phillips who had been master of the Guild of the Holy Cross in 1536; his daughter Elizabeth would marry a mercer, Richard Quiney, son of another founding alderman, also a mercer, Adrian Quiney. Adrian Quiney, bailiff in 1559, 1571 and 1582, managed the sale of the guild chapel vestments in 1571. When Quiney was elected bailiff for the third time in 1571 John Shakespeare served under him as head alderman; in Hilary Term the next year they travelled together to London. Quiney's second wife, whom he married in 1557, was the widow of another Stratford mercer, Laurence Baynton, whose son followed his profession. Charles Baynton is described as a mercer 'in country term', meaning that he was also a grocer and fishmonger, in partnership with William Court, who sold everything from loaf sugar to gunpowder. Country mercers seem in fact to have dealt in all kinds of wares. Baynton sold the Corporation a pound of sugar to regale the justices in 1577[82] and in 1579 at the time of the muster sold them gunpowder, 'a pint of sallet oil' and 'a girdle and hangles'; in 1580 he sold the Corporation a girdle for John the tabor player, more 'solett oil' and thirty-nine shillings and five pence worth of sugar loaves for New Year's gifts.[83] In 1577 Adrian Quiney supplied the New Year's gifts for the farmer of tithes of Stratford at a cost of six shillings and eight pence; in 1579 he was paid sixteen pence for two ells of Southwich cloth and twice sold the Corporation twelve pounds of red lead at three pence a pound.[84] William Smith, mercer and haberdasher, also supplied the Corporation with 'red lead'. Mistress Quiney sold the Corporation a pound of ginger for twenty pence.[85] In 1581 it was Adrian Quiney's turn to sell the Corporation 'a pint of sollett oil'. In 1583 William Smith shared with Charles Baynton the duty of supplying sugar.[86]

Mercery may have been the trade these men claimed to follow, but they seem to have spent most of their time working for the Corporation, and to have been trading in land and rents rather more than in mercery. The ascription mercer was itself unstable; Humphrey Plumley, bailiff in 1562 and 1574, is described at various times as a mercer, a yeoman and a draper. One of his associates was Robert Hynd, called a chapman in 1562 and haberdasher in his will of 1588. Hynd brought goods by packhorse from Birmingham and leased a shop at Shipston on Stour. The trade of haberdasher, especially one who travelled with his wares from fair to fair and market to market, seems indistinguishable from that of chapman or pedlar. William Rogers, married to the sister of Henry Walker, mercer, who was elected Bailiff of Stratford in 1607, 1624 and 1635, is variously described as a mercer and a victualler.

The inventory of Anne Lloyd, who died in Stratford in 1617, is unusual in that it itemises articles of apparel, which have been taken by the compiler to have been her own, when usually the testator's apparel was not itemised and listed merely as such. One of the two appraisers was John Smith, son of the mercer, and it seems altogether more likely that the inventory represents Lloyd's stock in trade as a dealer. It includes a velvet cape, old taffeta and lace, a pair of silk garters, silk girdles and a grogram gown, none of which she would have been entitled to wear. Such clothing represented an important part of a gentleman's outlay and it seems that Anne worked both with the mercers and with gentlemen desirous of recouping some of the initial outlay on garments that were no longer useful. Two gentlemen owed her considerable amounts of money, amounting to nearly a third of her total estate, so she may have advanced money on the garments in her possession. In her will Lloyd left two white lace handkerchiefs to Henry Smith, mercer, who was bailiff that year, as well as two stomachers to his wife, and her brass and pewter to his daughters. She also left a scarf to Alice, wife of Francis Smith. The inventory reads like a pedlar's list, with assorted scarves, 'a mask and tiffany', aprons, skirts, purses, girdles, gloves, aprons, 'little books', a fiddle and fiddle cloth, and spectacles, to the considerable total value of £56 8s 10d.[87]

Joan Perrott seems to have been working as a dealer in mixed goods of a similar kind. In 1596 Richard Field's sister, Margaret Young, who was left with three small children when her husband died in February 1595, sued Perrott in the Court of Record claiming recompense for goods supplied to her on 25 July 1595, namely:

> a woman's gown of a sad tawny colour, faced with velvet and a velvet cape, value £5, another woman's gown of rat colour faced with taffeta, with a cape of tufty taffeta and laid about with silk lace, value £3, a kirtle of broad worsted laid about with billiment lace and fringe, value 30s, a petticoat of stammel with a bodice of durance and fringed about, value 30s, a cloak of rat's colour lined with tawny baize, value 4 marks, 2 daggers, value 6s 8d, a coverlet of red, black and yellow, value 40s, and three prayerbooks, value 10s.[88]

Perrott sold these on 25 August, to 'Mr Shakespeare one book, Mr Barber one coverlet, ii daggers, the three books, Ursula Field [Young's sister] the apparel and the bedding clothes, at Whitsuntide was twelvemonth'.[89] The court decided that Young should be 'damnified' to the value of £6 9s 6d, and pay 6d costs. Young seems to have been unable to cope with being left to rear three children on her own; in October 1595 she had been cited in the Vicar's Court for 'continually quarrelling and not attending church'.[90] She did not appear, was excommunicated and fined 2s 10d.

Avice Clarke, a single woman and a 'stranger' who died in Stratford in 1624, was a pedlar. Her inventory lists the contents of her pack, all of it haberdashery:

nine coifs of black and tawney [assessed at]	3s
six handkerchiefs	2s
eleven drawn work coifs	3s
nine coifs	2s 3d
six crest cloths	12d
six plain coifs	2s
thirteen bands	3s
six pairs of garters	3s
six pairs of gloves	10d

coarse gartering	20d
five other garters	12d
seven dozen laces	2s 4d
seven dozen points	1s
two dozen white inkles	1s
six yards of loom work	12d
one ounce of thread	8d
two dozen bandstrings	18d
one paper of handkerchief buttons	18d
nine silk points (?)	12d
pins	2d
one box of brooches	6d
eight boxes	2d
thimbles and two bound graseies	4d
forty-two yards of bone lace	4s
four and a half dozen yards of loom work lace	4s . . .[91]

Avice kept a servant called Mary Beddson, whom she remembered in her will, and she made a small legacy to Peter Woodhouse, 'chapman of small wares', who seems to have been her colleague. Such rare and precious documents give us our only glimpses of women working alongside mercers, haberdashers and pedlars. The wares that were cried by women up and down the streets of London include:

> Bands, shirts or ruffs,
> Handkerchiefs or cuffs,
> Garters, knives or purses
> Or Muscova silken muffs[92]

For an Elizabethan working girl a visit from a pedlar was one of very few opportunities for retail therapy. In the jest book of Sir Nicholas Le Strange we read of 'a gentlewoman [who] loved to bubble away her money in bone-laces, pins and such toys, often used this short ejaculation, "God love me as I love a pedlar." '[93]

Somewhere in an intricate and elastic web of retail trading of small wares, Gilbert Shakespeare plied the haberdasher's trade. It seems unlikely that he was himself a chapman or a pedlar, but equally unlikely that he kept a shop in competition with the mercery mafia who controlled Stratford. Of 232 aldermen elected to the Corporation between its institution and the Civil War, 71 were Quineys or Quiney connections; the trading network extended through the west midlands, to Coventry and Birmingham to the north and southwards to London. We have no record of Gilbert as a shopkeeper in Stratford or in London. Besides, the stock in trade of a mercer was costly, and the Shakespeares were broke. It seems more likely that Gilbert traded in a modest way in wares of local manufacture that he sold on in London, and bought imported wares in London for resale in the provinces. He seems more likely to have organised, supplied and co-ordinated groups of chapmen than actually to have been himself a pedlar.

The haberdasher's stock in trade was affordable. Most of the items in Avice's pack were made by women in their homes, who had to be supplied with their materials, and with patterns to enable them to follow the current fashion. The finished work had also to be collected and conveyed to the nearest or best market to be sold on. The matter was not as straightforward as it might seem; the overseer of this female cottage industry had to make sure that the work was clean, saleable and of good quality, and that he could hold his own against those who peddled cheap and gaudy imports at a lower price. This is the level at which one can see Gilbert Shakespeare finding his niche, especially if one of the women who was making and organising the making of merchandise for him was his sister-in-law.

Shakespeare's Autolycus in *The Winter's Tale* is a thief, stealing linen from the hedges, picking pockets, 'a snapper-up of unconsidered trifles', a haunter of 'wakes, fairs and bear-baitings'. At the sheep-shearing feast he impersonates a pedlar, equipping himself with typical haberdashery, including a large range of gloves:

> no milliner can so fit his customers with gloves . . . He hath ribbons of all the colours i'the'rainbow; points [the tags that finished the ends of the laces attaching bodices, sleeves and hose] . . . inkles [linen tapes], caddisses [worsted tapes used for tying up stockings], cambrics, lawns . . .

Autolycus sings his wares in rather more high-falutin' fashion:

> Lawn as white as driven snow,
> Cypress black as ne'er was crow,
> Gloves as sweet as damask roses,
> Masks for faces, and for noses,
> Bugle-bracelet, necklace amber,
> Perfume for a lady's chamber,
> Golden quoifs and stomachers
> For my lads to give their dears,
> Pins and poking sticks of steel . . .

Autolycus himself is neither pedlar nor haberdasher, so Shakespeare cannot be accused of pillorying his haberdasher brother as a rogue. The role he assumes as a pedlar is an attractive one that could have been an affectionate remembrance of a younger brother's brilliant career as an uncommonly gifted travelling salesman.

We have no indication at all that Shakespeare was ever aware of his brother, or ever in his brother's company as an adult, but we do know that from about 1604 Shakespeare lived in the house of a Huguenot tire-maker called Christopher Mountjoy, on the corner of Monkswell and Silver Streets in Cripplegate. This was the haberdashers' quarter; the Haberdashers' Hall was close by on the corner of Staining Lane and Maiden Lane. Tires were ornamental headdresses of twisted wire, and as such part of the haberdashers' stock in trade. Mountjoy's, which were top of the range, being of gold and silver and studded with gems, were made to order, but tires of cheaper materials would have been offered on street stalls and by travelling chapmen. It is usually thought that Shakespeare was introduced to the Mountjoys by Richard Field. Field, the original printer of *Venus and Adonis* and *The Rape of Lucrece*, was married to the widow of the Huguenot printer Vautrollier. They lived close by in Wood Street and worshipped at the French Church. If Field was embarrassed by the association with the notorious author of a mildly pornographic best-seller, it seems more likely that, ten years after their successful collaboration had come to its rather swift end, neither Field nor Mrs Field was often in contact with Shakespeare, which leaves his brother the haberdasher as the possible connection with Mountjoy.

If Ann had provided for her children during their father's absence by becoming involved in the textile industry, she would have done nothing unusual. In *The Shoemakers' Holiday* (1600), when newly married Rafe Damport, journeyman to the master shoe-maker Simon Eyre, is pressed for a soldier, his young wife wails: 'What shall I do when he is gone?' Eyre rallies her: 'Let me see thy hand, Jane. The fine hand, this white hand, these pretty fingers must spin, must card, must work. Work you bombast cotton-candle-quean, work for your living with a pox to you!'[94]

Gilbert, born in October 1566, would have reached his majority in 1587, which is about when most scholars think Shakespeare took himself off. Gilbert was never to marry.

> The state of marriage was thought a desirable one, both for mutual comfort and support, and for raising children to carry on the family name, and young men of Stratford were expected to marry once they had completed their apprenticeship. Bachelors aged more than thirty were rare; so much so that the compilers of the 1595 list of maltsters felt it necessary to explain that John Page, 'a smith by trade' was 'a man never married'.[95]

Never married men were not rare in the Shakespeare household, which contained three of them. In Shakespeare's plays brotherhood is not an easy relationship. We have only to think of Orlando's fratricidal brother, and the usurping younger brother of the exiled duke in *As You Like It*, of Richard III, of Prospero's treacherous younger brother and Sebastian plotting against his brother the King of Naples in *The Tempest*, not to mention the bastard brothers, Faulconbridge in *King John*, Don John in *Much Ado* and Edmund in *King Lear*. Brotherhood in Shakespeare is far more problematic than marriage.

CHAPTER ELEVEN

of how one Stratford boy became a leading printer, and another wrote
a sexy poem that became a notorious best-seller, being literally read
to pieces, and Ann buried her only son

All her life Ann Shakespeare could rely on the support and guidance
of her brother Bartholomew Hathaway, and never did she need it
more than in the difficult years when her children were small. He, it
will be remembered, was married three weeks after their father's
death, on 25 November 1581, to Isabel Hancocks of Tredington. He
was then farming in Tredington and Tysoe, as well as cultivating half
of the Hewlands yardland and helping his stepmother and half-siblings
to run their part of the Shottery farm. His first son, named for his
father Richard, was christened at Tysoe. In April 1583, shortly before
his sister bore her first child, Bartholomew took a lease on a house in
Ely Street and moved his family to Stratford. It is possible, but not
likely, that Ann and her family lived there with him – indeed it is
possible that she was married from her brother's house in Tysoe. One
thing we can be sure of is that Bartholomew took his responsibilities as
head of the Hathaway–Gardner family seriously. It is not inconceivable that he decided to base himself in Stratford because of
concern for his sister, by then probably his closest surviving relative.
When Bartholomew's second child was born in January of the next
year, she was christened Annys, and it seems likely that her aunt Ann
was her godmother. (When Annys was married in 1610 it was as
'Ann' Hathaway.) Two years later another boy was born and
christened John; two years later a new baby died before it could
be baptised, and two years after that, in 1590, Edmund came along.
The name is not a common one in Stratford, and it may be that he was
named for his young uncle, Edmund Shakespeare.

As Bartholomew was a constant presence in Ann's life, it is fitting to give some account of him, if only to correct the erroneous impression often given that he was some kind of dependant of Shakespeare's. He was god-fearing, hard-working and astute and could both read and write. By 1605 he was of sufficient substance to be appointed one of the four churchwardens of Holy Trinity, a position that he held for four years.[1] To be eligible for the post he had to have an income of at least £200 a year.

> These officials upon whom the administration of the church and parish so much depended, were chosen from 'the better sort', the more substantial men of the parish and the borough. Their chief duties . . . were:
> 1. to 'present' or report all offenders to the [vicar's] court;
> 2. to certify the performance of court orders;
> 3. to see that the church and church property were in good repair;
> 4. to see that the books and articles required were provided and kept in good condition;
> 5. to see that all attended church at the required times and behaved themselves there.[2]

Hathaway carried out the public services expected of a substantial citizen – as Shakespeare markedly did not. In 1586 he collaborated with Stephen, Richard and Thomas Burman in drawing up the inventory of their Shottery neighbour William Such;[3] in 1608 he led the team that drew up the inventory of the widow Alice Burman.[4] In 1616 he signed his full name to the inventory of Humphrey Allen of Old Stratford when the others involved signed by mark.[5] In 1610 Hathaway managed to buy for £200 the freehold of the land in Shottery that his family had held in copyhold since 1543. This would not have been as easy as it seems, for at the time powerful consortia were buying up all available arable land. There is no reason whatsoever for supposing that Shakespeare gave Hathaway the money for the purchase. When Bartholomew's son Richard died in 1636 he left important freehold properties in Stratford and five lands in the common fields of Old Stratford, which may have been acquired earlier by his father and transferred to him by deed before his father made his will.[6] If Shakespeare had abandoned his wife and children, Bartholomew Hathaway would have been in the best position to bring the case to the attention of the authorities; if he did not – we do not have all the records for the Vicar's Court – it must be because his brother-in-law's absence from home was condoned, and his sister was managing without him.

We don't know if, in August 1592 when the plague broke out in London with such ferocity that the theatres had to be closed, Shakespeare took refuge in Stratford or elsewhere. Stratford escaped the contagion; the parish registers show that mortality for 1592–3 remained within the normal parameters. Whether Shakespeare chose to wait it out in Stratford or not probably depends as much on where Ann and the children were living as on anything else, for he needed space and quiet to write what would turn out to be a huge best-seller, namely the housewives' favourite poem, *Venus and Adonis*. This would be the first time a work by Shakespeare would appear in print. Whether Ann could read or not, she would not have been allowed to remain in ignorance of this turn of events. Some well-meaning person would have told her that there was a book selling like hot cakes in London with her husband's name on it. Besides, the printer–publisher, Richard Field, was a Stratford man.

Field, three years older than Shakespeare, was the son of the tanner Henry Field, whose shop stood in Bridge Street. In 1579, when he was eighteen his father bound him apprentice to George Bishop, a London stationer, who agreed that he could serve the first six of his seven years of indentures with Thomas Vautrollier, a Huguenot printer in Blackfriars, who as a foreigner was not permitted to take apprentices of his own. Vautrollier may have been a Calvinist; he certainly published the first British editions of Calvin's *Institutes* in French in 1576 and 1584. In 1574 Vautrollier was awarded the patent for printing Latin school texts for ten years; in 1582 he published the *Metamorphoses* in Latin, and in 1574 had published the Latin edition of Ovid's *Fasti* that Shakespeare would later use for *Lucrece*. In 1586 Vautrollier printed Timothy Bright's *Treatise of Melancholy*, which is generally accepted as one of the sources for *Hamlet*. Vautrollier was often away running his Edinburgh printing shop, at which times his wife Jacqueline managed his London business with Field's help.

Field lived the apprentices' dream; on 2 February 1587 he was made free of the Stationers' Company. Five months later Vautrollier died and his widow, who inherited all of Vautrollier's copyrights, his presses, type and devices, took over the business. In February 1588, she married twenty-six-year-old Field, who stepped into the shoes of one of the most prestigious printer–publishers in Britain. Field printed and published *Puttenham's Art of English Poesie* in 1589. Like his master, as a printer Field was probably allowed to take only one apprentice, but there was nothing to stop him employing other people, of whom Shakespeare may for a time have been one.

The Shakespeares and the Fields certainly knew each other. After Henry Field died in 1592, John Shakespeare appraised his goods for probate.[7] It may be that when Shakespeare went to London to try his fortune, he based himself at first at Vautrollier's shop. He may have worked there as a proof-reader or assessor of manuscripts for publication, which would partly explain the curious scatter of sources that we find across the whole range of his works, which includes texts in Latin and French and texts which had never appeared in print. Vautrollier published North's translation of Plutarch's *Lives* in 1579, the same year Field joined the shop as an apprentice. Field would go on to print the second edition in 1595, then the third in 1603 and the fourth in 1607. Holinshed's *Chronicles*, another of Shakespeare's most important sources, was sold by five booksellers, of whom one was George Bishop, the stationer to whom Richard Field was originally apprenticed and for whom he was working out the last year of his apprenticeship when the volume was published in January 1587. Field maintained a close working relationship with another of the booksellers, John Harrison. When Field printed and published Shakespeare's *Venus and Adonis* in 1593, it was sold in Harrison's shop; of the twenty-seven books Harrison published between 1590 and 1596, seventeen were printed by Field.

Like all poets of his generation Shakespeare was immersed in Ovid; he certainly used Golding's English translation of the *Metamorphoses*, but he apparently knew the original Latin as well. One of Field's first independent publications was a second edition of the *Metamorphoses* in 1589. Many other major and minor sources for Shakespeare's works can be traced in Richard Field's publishing history. He published Sir

John Harington's translation of *Orlando Furioso* in 1591, and this was used by Shakespeare as a primary source of *Much Ado About Nothing*. He printed the second edition of Robert Greene's *Pandosto*, the main source for Shakespeare's *Winter's Tale*. He printed the first full edition of Spenser's *Faerie Queene*, which influenced Shakespeare in many ways, and in 1598 he printed an edition of Sidney's *Arcadia*, which Shakespeare used as a source for numerous plays, most notably *King Lear* and *Pericles*. In 1599 he printed Richard Crompton's *Mansion of Magnanimity*, which Shakespeare used as a source for *Henry V*, generally considered to have been written at about the same time.

As the Field and Shakespeare families were in contact in the months following Henry Field's death in 1592, we might ask ourselves whether Richard, being a publisher of poetry, might not have suggested that Shakespeare, cooling his heels in Stratford, should try his hand at an 'epyllion'. Since its first publication in 1589, copies of Thomas Lodge's mythical–erotic narrative poem *Scilla's Metamorphosis* had been walking out of the bookshops. Christopher Marlowe was known to be writing an epyllion of his own, an adaptation of Musaeus' story of Hero and Leander, part of which was already circulating in manuscript.

Perhaps Shakespeare penned his sixains at Ann's kitchen table; he might have read them out to her, to see if they made her blush or laugh. The household may have been rather more bookish than is usually thought. Ten-year-old Susanna could both read and write, and perhaps eight-year-old Hamnet too. The children could have been schooled together with their cousin Richard Hathaway, who could also read and write. Richard Quiney's son Richard was about to turn eleven when he wrote to his father in 1598, in Latin, so Susanna could certainly read an English text by the time she was ten.

Perhaps Shakespeare joined the train of the Earl of Southampton, and worked in peace and quiet far from Stratford. The dedication of his poem to Southampton doesn't of itself indicate that he was already enjoying Southampton's patronage. If Shakespeare followed the correct procedure, before publishing a poem with a dedication to the Earl of Southampton, he should have presented him with a copy, and waited for him to read it and give his gracious permission for it to be printed, usually accompanied by a reward of a couple of guineas or so. Because it is literally unthinkable that anyone would dare to sign a dedication to a person of Southampton's rank using an alias, the signature on the dedication is the best proof we can have that there really was a poet called William Shakespeare. The poem itself is proof that he was already a pretty good poet.

Venus and Adonis is the one work of Shakespeare's for which scholars feel almost as much distaste as they do for his wife. Year after year of multifarious shakespeareanising goes by without producing a single discussion of the work that was the Bard's principal claim to fame among his contemporaries. Scholars would rather bicker for years over corrupt texts of the plays than address themselves to this authentic and acknowledged text that Shakespeare himself saw through the press.

If Shakespeare didn't put a copy of his published poem into Ann's hands, somebody else surely would have. She may have recognised herself in the desirous older woman and her boy husband in the reluctant young man, and followed with interest the shifts in the poem's mood from stanza to stanza, enjoying the poem's lightness of touch, even as she shrank from its rampant sensuality. However matters transpired, the appearance of *Venus and Adonis* must have changed Ann Shakespeare's quiet life. Everybody was reading it; no fewer than eleven editions of the poem would appear in her lifetime and each had so many readers that only single copies of each edition have survived, the rest being read to pieces. And in every single copy could be seen the full name of the author at the end of the dedication.

What may have made life even more difficult for Ann at this juncture is that the poem was decidedly erotic. In the past erotic poetry had been reserved for the delectation of educated gentlemen, who read it in Latin and Greek. Written in the language of the people, *Venus and Adonis* was one erotic poem that would be passed from hand to hand by excited housewives. In Middleton's *A Mad World My Masters*, first performed in 1605, printed in 1608, Harebrain informs us that he has removed from his wife's possession 'all her wanton pamphlets, as *Hero and Leander*, *Venus and Adonis* – oh! two luscious marrow-bone pies for a young married wife' (I. ii. 44–6).

The disgruntled schoolmen sneered. In *The Return from Parnassus*, a self-serving play written by students at St John's College Cambridge, and staged in about 1600, in which they whinge about the decay of learning and their own poor prospects, it is the nincompoop Gullio who can quote *Venus and Adonis* by the yard. 'Let this duncified world esteem of Spenser and Chaucer, I'll worship sweet Mr Shakespeare, and to honour him will lay his *Venus and Adonis* under my pillow . . .'[8]

Having produced one best-seller, and the theatres still being closed, Shakespeare set about writing another. This time the publisher would be John Harrison, who was also preparing to acquire the copyright to *Venus and Adonis* from Richard Field. The poem must have been finished or nearly finished by 9 May 1594 when Harrison entered a 'book entitled the Ravishment of Lucrece' in the Stationers' Register. On 25 June 1594 Field sold him the rights to *Venus and Adonis* as well, probably for rather more than he had paid for them the year before. This seems to mark the end of the active collaboration between Shakespeare and Field. Field can be identified as the printer of *Love's Martyr, or Rosalind's Complaint* in 1601 only by his device on the title-page. Most of the text was by Robert Chester; the rest was by Marston, Chapman, Ben Jonson and 'Ignoto' – but the little volume also contained Shakespeare's most mysterious poem, *The Phoenix and the Turtle*. Field did not stoop to play-printing, which was generally of a lower and more ephemeral order than his elegant productions. He went on to become master of the staunchly puritan Stationers' Company in 1619 and again in 1622.

In *The Second Return from Parnassus*, Cambridge students grudgingly admitted that Shakespeare's poems were seductive:

> Who loves not Adon's love or Lucrece rape?
> His sweeter verse contains heart-robbing lines,
> Could but a graver subject him content,
> Without love's foolish lazy languishment.[9]

Lucrece was admired by the wiser sort, but was less successful than *Venus and Adonis*, which was reprinted year on year. The poem's reputation as pornography endured. Epigram 92 of *Freeman's Epigrams*, written in about 1614, instructed readers

Who list read lust, there's *Venus and Adonis*,
True model of a most lascivious lecher.[10]

In 1625 John Davies of Hereford weighed in:

Making lewd Venus with eternal lines
To tie Adonis to her lewd designs,
Fine wit is shown therein, but finer 'twere
If not attired in such bawdy gear,
But, be it as it will, the coyest dames
In private read it for their closet games.[11]

Venus and Adonis might have made Shakespeare famous but it didn't make him rich. Royalties had yet to be invented. An author who sold his copy to a publisher was paid once and once only. The copyright was the publisher's property.

Ann, who was probably as puritan as Field, might have dreaded her husband's return to the stage, but she could hardly have thought that there was a future in writing more ambitious poetry. In 1593 Spenser, acknowledged by his contemporaries as their 'principal poet', was at the height of his career, and yet Carew, Jonson and Fletcher all allege that he was living in poverty, even with a royal pension of £50 a year. Perhaps Shakespeare went back to the theatre because he was sickened by what he had seen of the life led by Southampton and his cronies. He may well have felt incapable of functioning as a flunkey poet, living as a menial in Southampton's or some other noble household. Samuel Daniel, employed by the Earl of Pembroke as tutor to young William Herbert, later co-patron of the publication of the First Folio, produced no poetry for the five years that he was in post.

Meanwhile the level of hardship suffered by the people of the west midlands, never negligible, was set to rise steeply. In 1594 the harvest failed. The weather in June had been 'wonderful cold, like winter';[12] Stow records, 'It commonly rained day and night until St James's Eve,' that is, until 24 July.[13] On the second Sunday of September, a devastating fire swept through Stratford. The dwellings of the poor, made of 'poles' filled with plaster and thatched, without chimneys, were so obvious a fire-hazard that for years the Corporation had been exhorting householders to reroof their dwellings with tile. On 7 May 1583 the Corporation had issued an order to the 'inhabitants to make sufficient chimneys in their habitations or rooms for preserving the rest of the inhabitants from the danger of fire'.[14] The poorer people didn't have the choice of tiling their roofs, because their cottage walls were not strong enough to support the added weight. The cause of the conflagration in 1594 was almost certainly the making of malt, which required drying with a fast-burning fire of straw. Among the causes of fire identified in 1583 were fires being left under kilns overnight, straw litter lying around the kiln house, and children under twelve and even the blind left to look after the fire.[15]

Within days the Stratford aldermen had been sent into the surrounding shires to collect money.[16] The rebuilding had barely begun when, a year later almost to the day, another fire ripped through the town. Not a single house remained in Wood Street; between them the two fires had destroyed 120 dwellings, more than half the housing stock, had been destroyed, as well as 80 other buildings. The cost of the damage was estimated as £12,000; some 400 people had been left homeless and destitute. Judith and Hamnet Sadler were among those whose houses had been burnt to the ground:

> the accounts of the following years and the rent roll of 1598 indicate that many buildings destroyed or damaged by fire were not immediately reconstructed but remained 'ruinous' with consequent loss of rent to the Corporation and adding to the distress of the townspeople.[17]

In November 1595, in a belated effort to ease the shortage of food grain, maltsters were bound over not to make malt. In obedience to a royal edict, an inquiry was set up to ascertain whether richer citizens were hoarding corn, waiting for prices to rise even further, while their neighbours starved. Anyone who could was taking advantage of the situation. 'Thomas Rogers, bailiff of the borough, did buy a cartload of barley, 30 October, and what more we know not, before it came into the market and did forestall the market, and he doth say he will justify it, and that he careth not a turd for them all . . .' Altogether

Rogers had in his house fifteen quarters of malt and two of barley, plus twenty quarters of malt that he claimed to be storing for his son-in-law.

> Master Parsons and Master Sturley bought of Thomas Yate of Broad Marston 15 weigh of barley at 20s a quarter. Master Parsons and Master Tovey bought of Nicholas Tybbots eight lands of wheat, 12 lands of barley . . . Master Sturley and Richard Quiney and Master Badger all these being great corn-buyers and buyers of wood and such-like . . .[18]

In fact the mercery mafia were buying up grain futures as well; they would prove to be a very good, if illegal, investment, the price of corn having gone up from seventeen shillings a quarter in 1592 to fifty shillings in 1596.[19]

> Master Richard Quiney useth the trades of buying and selling of corn for great sums. We are given to understand that he hath bought since midsummer . . . a hundred quarters of grain viz. barley and peas, his barley for 3s the strike and peas at 2s 6d the strike for twelve months day of payment . . . and hath in his house and in his barn unthrashed forty-seven quarters of barley and thirty-two quarters of malt, and peas eleven and a half quarters, and of wheat two strikes . . .[20]

And so on. Quiney could have argued that he was a merchant, and that his trade was buying cheap and selling dear, but the law was taking a dim view of engrossing in the circumstances, partly because of the mounting danger of riot. That winter mortality was higher than usual, but Ann brought her children through it. It was in the high summer of 1596 that she lost her only son.

Hamnet Shakespeare was buried in Holy Trinity churchyard on 11 August. The parish register offers no clue to what might have killed him. There were only four other burials that month, three of them newborns, the other an old man, so it was not a season of unusual sickness. After the third bad harvest in a row, the whole country was in the grip of dearth but it seems unlikely that the Bard's only son died of hunger, or one of the many diseases that attack malnourished children. The summer was the easy time, when the bills of mortality were at their lightest. In November that year mortality would rise steeply to more than double the usual rate. Over the following five months more people would die than usually died in a year, probably of the diseases of malnutrition. Hamnet's death appears unconnected.

If, as often happened with fraternal twins, Hamnet was weaker than his sister, he might have been vulnerable from birth. As Professor Duncan-Jones has it:

> It is not uncommon for one of a pair of twins to be markedly smaller and frailer than the other, having received less nourishment from the placenta before birth. Perhaps the little boy had always been rather frail. The disparity between his life-span and that of his sister, who lived to the great age of seventy, is striking.[21]

As a fraternal rather than identical twin, Hamnet would have had a placenta of his own which may not have been as efficient as his sister's, for any one of a number of reasons to do with its positioning in the uterus. Discordancy in twins is common, and was more pronounced before multiple pregnancies were diagnosed early and managed with special care. It would follow that as the weaker of the twins Hamnet could have been starved of oxygen at the time of birth. He may have suffered a birth injury; birth injuries were after all common, and commonest in multiple births, yet no thought has ever been given to the likelihood that the Bard's child was disabled. At the end of *A Midsummer Night's Dream*, thought to have been written for performance at about the time that Hamnet died, Oberon pronounces a blessing on the three marriage beds:

> So shall all the couples three
> Ever true in loving be,
> And the blots of Nature's hand
> Shall not in their issue stand,
> Never mole, hare-lip, nor scar,
> Nor mark prodigious such as are
> Despisèd in nativity,
> Shall upon their children be. (V. i. 37–44)

No one has ever considered the possibility that Shakespeare's son suffered from cerebral palsy. Instead we find airy certainties, such as that he attended Stratford grammar school, or that he was a bright and lively child, all mere supposition. Shakespeare is not the kind of writer to jerk tears with tales of crippled children. He shows scant sympathy for Richard III, who was not 'shaped for amorous tricks', but 'rudely stamped', 'curtailed of . . . fair proportion'.

> Cheated of feature by dissembling nature
> Deformed, unfinished, sent before my time
> Into this breathing world scarce half made up –
> And that so lamely and unfashionable
> That dogs bark at me as I halt by them . . . (I. i. 19–24)

Congenital deformity was construed by Shakespeare's contemporaries as evidence of sin, evil in both cause and effect. (If Greenblatt was looking for a reason for the revulsion he claims Shakespeare felt for Ann, a deformed child could fit the bill, especially if the multiple birth itself was construed as evidence of inordinate sexual desire.) Queen Margaret calls Richard an 'elvish marked, abortive, rooting hog'—

> Thou that was sealed in thy nativity
> The slave of Nature and the son of hell,
> Thou slander of thy heavy mother's womb,
> Thou loathed issue of thy father's loins . . . (I. iii. 226–9)

The damaged child slanders the womb that bore it because its disability is interpreted as evidence of the mother's sin: the same idea surfaces in a disturbing speech of Constance to her small son Arthur in *King John*:

> If thou that bidd'st me be content wert grim,
> Ugly and slanderous to thy mother's womb,
> Full of unpleasant blots and sightless stains,
> Lame, foolish, crooked, swart, prodigious,
> Patched with foul moles and eye-offending marks,
> I would not care. I then would be content

For then I should not love thee, no, nor thou
Become thy great birth, nor deserve a crown. (II. ii. 43–50)

More unnerving possibly is this utterance in the poet's own persona
speaking of his brainchild, *Venus and Adonis*: 'But if the first heir of my
invention prove deformed, I shall be sorry it had so noble a godfather,
and never after ear so barren a land, for fear it yield me still so bad a
harvest.'[22]

Perhaps Ann had succeeded in bringing her frail little boy through the
annual visitations of epidemic illness, until he hit the hurdle of
adolescence, which is often a time of crisis for spastic children. However, there is no need to posit a birth defect to explain Hamnet's death;
children of the same age died every year in Stratford, most of them boys.
The cause was usually infectious disease which, coinciding with the
growth spurt of adolescence, could be more than usually virulent.

Since Christmas 1594 Shakespeare had been a member of the new
company of players formed by Lord Hunsdon, now Lord Chamberlain. When his son sickened, he was touring with the company in
Kent; on 1 August the Lord Chamberlain's Men played the 'market
hall' at Faversham.[23] Though Peter Ackroyd tells us that 'There is
every reason to suppose that Shakespeare hastened from Kent for
Stratford, for the funeral,'[24] there is no reason to suppose any such
thing. The family had no way of knowing exactly where Shakespeare
was. The companies of players did not follow a preordained itinerary
but travelled, announced their arrival and sought permission to play. If
it was refused they travelled on. In high summer burial followed
swiftly upon death; it would have taken a messenger four days to get
to Kent, more time to track Shakespeare down, and four days to get
him back again to Stratford. If Shakespeare could not have made it in
time to take a last leave of his boy, there was no point in his coming
back at all. No one in Stratford would have interpreted his absence
from his son's simple obsequies as indicative of callousness.

Ann would have nursed her boy in his final illness, and when it was
over, closed his eyes and prepared him for burial. Her gossips would
have come to help her wash the loved body, wind it in its clean white
linen shroud with aromatic herbs tucked into it, and then watch by it
until the time came to carry it to the churchyard. As a godparent,

Judith Sadler would certainly have been there to support the bereaved mother. Six of Judith's children had died; five of them lived less than forty days, and, as they were buried before she had been churched, she could not attend their funerals. She would have followed John, her second son to bear that name, when he was buried at the age of six months. Isabel Hathaway too had lost at least one newborn child. Losing even a newborn was painful, but to lose an eleven-year-old was immeasurably worse.

There would have been no need for a bier, and coffins were a luxury demanded by few. Hamnet was probably carried on a board or table-top by his uncles or his godfather Hamnet Sadler. As Shakespeare was almost certainly not there, it was probably Ann who followed behind as chief mourner, unless John and Mary Shakespeare took that role. If Susanna and Judith had been judged old enough to participate in the ceremony, they would have walked with their mother, but if the grief of either had been judged immoderate, she would have waited at home with one or other relative until the funeral party returned. Hysterical outbursts at the graveside were to be avoided. The funerals of ordinary Elizabethans did not require togging up in black crape or cypress; the mourners would have worn their everyday clothes. Ann's habitual wear, her gown of grey russet, her headcloth and hat were nun-like enough.

More important than the arrival of distant kin to attend the short ceremony was the respect of neighbours for Goodwife Shakespeare and her family. As the procession wound its way to Holy Trinity the citizens who cared would have downed their tools and removed their caps; some would have taken off their aprons, and joined the mourners. Even though the Shakespeare family was losing the son of a son and heir they did nothing to make Hamnet's funeral special: nothing was paid for the use of the pall, or for the tolling of the bell. Once he was buried, the mourners would have returned to Ann's house, where Susanna and Judith would have served them with the traditional funeral baked meats. If she could have afforded it, Ann would have given a dole of a penny or two to each of the other mourners.

A good deal has been written about the impact of child death on parents of previous generations. For years people thought that, because child death was so common, parents were inured to it. Then came the revelation that child loss was the commonest cause of mental illness and emotional disturbance among the patients of the seventeenth-century physician Richard Napier.[25] People who believe that Shakespeare cared nothing for his wife because they can find no trace of intimacy between them ought also to register that they can find no sign of grief at the extinction of his little boy. Ben Jonson has left us poems on the deaths of a son and of a daughter.[26] Sir John Beaumont wrote beautifully on the death of his son.[27] Shakespeare may have remained silent not because he cared less, but because he cared more. Ann would certainly have cared; indeed her grief may have been terrible to behold. It would not have been the first time Shakespeare witnessed the anguish of the bereaved mother. When his sister Ann was buried on 4 April 1579, six months short of her eighth birthday, Will was almost fifteen, of an age to be intensely aware of his mother's grief, however stoically she might have borne it.

Scholars cannot agree when Shakespeare wrote *King John*. Because it is audacious and experimental they tend to place it early in his writing career, about 1590. Others have tried to connect it to 1596, the year of Hamnet's death, and still others anywhere in between. The play is remarkable for many reasons, not least the portrayal of the relationship between eight-year-old Arthur, Prince of Britain, and his mother Constance. More telling than Constance's frantic raving is the extraordinary scene in which Arthur dies. He is alone on the upper stage, on the walls of the castle. The audience learns that it is his intention to jump down, and, if he survives the fall, to run away.

> I am afraid and yet I'll venture it.
> If I get down, and do not break my limbs,
> I'll find a thousand shifts to get away.
> As good to die and go, as die and stay.

Which no sooner said the boy leaps off the wall and lies still. He stirs only to utter his *consummatum est*:

> O me. My uncle's spirit is in these stones.
> Heaven take my soul, and England keep my bones. (IV. iii. 5–10)

The audience is the sole witness of what has happened. When the other characters come on they do not see Arthur's body at first; when they do they go off on their own tangents, uselessly swearing revenge on the non-existent person who threw the boy over the battlements. There is no other coup de théâtre like this in British drama. The helplessness of the audience watching a child act his dismal scene alone is a pale reflection of parents watching a child struggle with a life-threatening illness. At the end Constance's railing against fate is irrelevant; there is only the child's struggle with the inescapable and the helplessness of the onlooker. I would never argue that Shakespeare put his own child on the stage; what seems clear to me is that he knew what a bereaved mother's anguish was like, and he knew what it was like to live with a dying child who approached his fate more bravely and serenely than either of his parents could. Ann's grief may not have been unmixed with bitterness. Perhaps her little boy had missed his young father terribly and had been pining for him. If for years Ann had had to coax the boy to get him to eat, say, she might have raged inwardly that his listlessness was all the fault of his uncaring father. There is no play in the Shakespeare canon that is anything like *The Spanish Tragedy* in which a father is driven literally mad with grief for the death of a son. In *The Winter's Tale* Leontes causes the death of his son and heir Mamillius, who dies of grief at his father's ill-treatment of his mother. When Leontes gets his wife back in the last scene of the play, the rejoicing is unalloyed by any mention of the boy who will not be coming back.

CHAPTER TWELVE

treating of the curious circumstances of the grant of arms made to William Shakespeare, and the acquisition of a compromised title to a rambling and ruinous house in a town he spent little or no time in

While Ann was still grieving the death of her son, the old business of the grant of arms to John Shakespeare, begun before her marriage and subsequently abandoned, was revived. His son and heir being dead, William Shakespeare's line was now extinct, unless he outlived his wife, married again and had a son, which was possible, given his own youth. As Duncan-Jones has it: 'Yet while there's death there's hope. Fairly naturally given the discrepancy in their ages, Shakespeare may have dreamed that he would eventually outlive Anne, and that he might one day be able, as a gentleman of substance, to make a better marriage, and beget another son.'[1]

Duncan-Jones believes that in securing his grant of arms Shakespeare was encouraged and aided by Southampton and even given money with which to suborn the heralds into countenancing a fraudulent claim. If Shakespeare had decided to leave playing and devote his time to writing verse best-sellers his quest for gentility might have made sense. To be called a gentleman could have protected him from the sneers of the university men, but it was as likely to have prompted them to further derision. A gentleman might write for the stage without losing caste, but not if he wrote for money.[2] Still, there was the troubling 'Richard Hathaway, gentleman' who may be the same 'Richard Hathway' who was writing for Henslowe. Class distinction is always volatile, and towards the end of Elizabeth's reign rich tradesmen are increasingly to be found acquiring gentle status, but Shakespeare knew that players who performed on public stages for money were 'common' by definition.

There's much confusion in the explanations of what Shakespeare thought he was up to, when he approached the Garter King-at-Arms. If he genuinely wanted gentility he had gone the wrong way about it, for he had acquired a share in the Lord Chamberlain's Company, probably on the strength of giving them his playbooks,[3] and was now back writing full-time for the commercial theatre. Still, approach the heralds he did, perhaps carrying the old design that he had known since he was twelve years old. Usually we are told that he was doing this for his father; I suspect that he was doing it for his mother. His father knew that he was a husbandman's son; it was his mother who believed that she was an Arden of the Park Hall Ardens. The notes of the family history taken at the time are full of nonsense: John Shakespeare is said to have married 'the daughter of a gentleman of worship', Robert Arden is referred to as 'esquire' and 'gentleman' when he was neither. John Shakespeare is said to have been a justice of the peace and Bailiff of Stratford 'fifteen or sixteen years past', when in fact it was a good twenty-seven years, and to have 'lands and tenements of good wealth and substance' worth £500 which he did not.

Scholars have assumed that John Shakespeare's affairs recovered in the years before his death. They point to the absence of claims against him as if it were evidence of a new-found solidity. In fact it is the opposite. Men of worth in Stratford were in and out of the Court of Record on a weekly basis. Cash being always in short supply, most transactions were conducted on the basis of consideration, which regularly resulted in confusion and misunderstanding. The Court of Record was resorted to in all cases of confusion; the bailiff, who was the presiding judge, was trusted to assess relative indebtedness and record the result. Indebtedness or 'credit' was then, as now, the basis of all economic activity; difficulties arose only when indebtedness was denied or when the debtor proved unable to pay. Everybody who was anybody owed money to somebody and was owed money in return.

If John Shakespeare is absent from the record it is not because he was prospering, but because he was inactive. If he was on an even keel it was because he had flat-lined. If William Shakespeare had been as rich as some scholars like to think he was, he might have advanced his father sums sufficient to get him going again, but, as far as we can tell, he didn't. Instead Shakespeare applied for a grant of arms. In his right mind he seems to have had special contempt for plebeians who tried to pass themselves off as gentle. Joan of Arc, La Pucelle, is a more or less sympathetic character in *Henry VI, Part 1*, until she denies her poor father, crazily asserting that she is not 'begotten of a shepherd swain But issued from the progeny of kings'. When her father sees her on the way to the pyre he cries out: 'Ah, Joan, sweet daughter Joan, I'll die with thee.' Joan's response could hardly be more shocking:

> Decrepit miser, base ignoble wretch,
> I am descended of a gentler blood.
> Thou art no father nor no friend of mine.

The poor shepherd has had to confess her once before:

> I did beget her, all the parish knows.
> Her mother liveth yet, can testify
> She was the first fruit of my bachelorship.

He pleads with her, only to be rejected again.

> 'Tis true I gave a noble to the priest
> The morn that I was wedded to her mother.
> Kneel down and take my blessing, good
> my girl. (V. vi. 6–26)

If we are to exonerate Shakespeare from the suspicion of fraud in his dealings with the Garter King-at-Arms, we have to assume that he believed in his mother's descent from a gentle family. His father had a claim on the strength of his public service, which would have been justified without the taradiddle about his father-in-law's status, which was intended to justify the eventual quartering of the new Shakespeare arms with the old coat of Arden. There is no indication that John was actually present during the interviews with the heralds, so Shakespeare, who had been more or less estranged from his family for the last ten years or so, would have been relating the family history as he understood it from adolescence. It is a feature of reiterated family myth that it invariably works to elevate the status of forebears. When he sold a strip of land to George Badger in 1597 John Shakespeare is described in the deed of sale as a 'yeoman' which is also incorrect. By birth he was a husbandman, a rung lower than yeoman. If the clerk making out the deed wrote 'yeoman', it may have been because he could not described John Shakespeare as a tradesman, which strengthens the impression that in 1597 it was a long time since he had followed the trade of glover. He clearly did not know of the grant of arms acquired in his name by his son three months before, perhaps because Shakespeare had not yet attained his final objective. Three years on, John (or rather William) Shakespeare applied to the heralds again. This time what he was after was permission to combine the Shakespeare arms with those of the Ardens. The coat was to be divided vertically, with the Shakespeare arms on the right, and the Arden arms on the left. At first the heralds assumed that Mary Shakespeare was a descendant of the Park Hall Ardens, and sketched a version of their coat, only to cancel it for a version of an older coat. In the event the attempt was abandoned.[4]

The fraud did not go unnoticed. Ralph Brooke or Brokesmouth, York herald from 1593, took it upon himself to review the recent grants of arms, in an attempt to establish just how many were based on fictitious genealogies. In a list of twenty-three dubious grants made by Sir William Dethick, Shakespeare's name was fourth. The Shakespeare grant incurred Brooke's censure both because the device was too close to the arms of the extinct Mauley family and because John Shakespeare was a 'mean person' and his son a common player. Shakespeare's old enemy Robert Greene, who as a university graduate was entitled to call himself gentleman, was particularly contemptuous of those whose 'own conceit was the Herald to blazon their descent from an old house, whose great grandfathers would have been glad of a new Cottage to hide their heads in'.[5]

John Shakespeare, who was buried five years later as Master Joannes Shakespeare, seems never to have had the benefit of the grant of arms. The title 'Master' was a reference to his service of the Corporation; the appellation 'gentleman' would have been something else. More telling still is the fact that when Mary Shakespeare was buried in 1608, it was as plain 'Mary Shakespeare, widow'. A coat of arms, especially one that was mostly gold, was a difficult thing to make use of if you could not afford to have it 'painted, embroidered, gilded or carved on . . . movables and immovables, such as trunks, furniture, bed canopies, book bindings, glass windows, seal rings',[6] as well as carved and painted above the windows and the entrance to your house. If John Shakespeare had had the golden shield with the bend sinister and the silver spear stuck up all round his fragment of a house, behind the sign of the Maiden Head, his creditors and his triumphant in-laws would have laughed him to scorn.

Scholars have been slow to abandon the notion of John Shakespeare as a rich man who left a substantial inheritance.

> The death of [Shakespeare's] father in September would have enforced some reflection. For one thing, it made him rich, by contemporary standards. His inheritance would have included the double house in Henley Street as well as some of the substantial agricultural holdings that John Shakespeare maintained to the end.[7]

William certainly inherited the freehold of the Henley Street property, but, as we have seen, most of it was leased out as the Maiden Head Inn and either the old lease still had ninety years or so to run when Shakespeare inherited in 1601 or he chose to levy a new fine and issue a new ninety-one-year lease.[8] There were no 'substantial agricultural holdings' either. At present, though the records of Worcestershire, Warwickshire and Canterbury and Chancery Lane have been exhaustively searched, we have neither will nor inventory nor letters of administration nor notice of probate for a will of John Shakespeare. Perhaps John Shakespeare's will stipulated that Mary be allowed to live out her days in what remained to them of Henley Street, but we cannot be certain that she did live out her days in Henley Street. We don't know where her three sons were living. In 1596, when Shakespeare set out to acquire his coat of arms, thirty-year-old Gilbert had not found himself a wife and there is no evidence that one was ever sought for him. Richard was twenty-three, unmarried, apparently uneducated and good-for-little. Sixteen-year-old Edmund was so devoid of prospects that he was thinking of running away to London to be a player. Instead of helping any of his brothers to a wife, Shakespeare threw his time and money away on a coat of arms that nobody believed in, and that there was no one to inherit. The Hathaways were frugal, no-nonsense people. When it came to posterity they took care for it, by matching their children with their own class, so that by the time she died Ann could see Hathaways filling the pews in Holy Trinity, while in the Shakespeare pews there were only the draggletail Hart children.

Joan Shakespeare turned up in Stratford the year before her father's death, married to a hatter (no one knows where or when) and pregnant. More nonsense is written about that too: 'Joan had married a local hatter, William Hart, but remained in the family dwelling to look after her mother.'[9] No William Hart appears in the Stratford records before the entry in the Holy Trinity register for 28 August 1600 when he brought a son to Holy Trinity Church to be christened William. We don't know when or where Joan married Hart, or even if William was her first child. We don't know where she had been for most of her life, which was probably not in Stratford. Perhaps we can discern the hand of Shakespeare's brother Gilbert in this matter, for as a haberdasher he would have had a good deal to do with hatters. In the Accounts of Edmund Tilney, Master of the Revels, 'haberdashers' parcels' were all hats and the makings of hats, while what we would think of as haberdashery was supplied by mercers.[10] Both Gilbert Shakespeare and William Hart could have supplied the Lord Chamberlain's Men with hats and other fripperies, if it comes to that.

Joan may have kept house for Gilbert in London, or she may have been in service elsewhere. Either way Gilbert could have been instrumental in making a match for her with one of his business contacts. Hart was not a Stratford man, and we cannot now know why he transferred to Stratford after he married Joan. In October 1598 Elizabeth Quiney asked her husband in London to buy 'a suite of hats for five boys the youngest lined and trimmed with silk' which is an odd thing for her to have done if the same hats could have been made to her order in Stratford.[11] In 1600 Hart was sued for debt in the Court of Record and 1601 he was sued again, which implied that he was economically active, though whether he was making hats is not clear. Hatters were less often sued than forced to sue for payment for work done. In June 1603 Joan bore a daughter Mary, in July 1605 another son Thomas and in September 1608 a third son Michael. Eight years later her husband died. It was Joan's fate to outlive all her brothers, and all but one of her children.

On 4 May 1597, less than a year after the death of his son and heir, Shakespeare bought New Place, the second biggest house in Stratford. According to the 'foot of fine' the property was handed over to him in return for 'sexaginta libras sterlingorum', £60 in silver, which seems unbelievably little, especially if the house already consisted, as it did in 1663, of ten hearths. The recorded price is usually treated as a legal fiction, although the house had changed hands not long before for only £40. Even Schoenbaum, usually so careful to arrive at the single nugget of irreducible fact, assumes what should need to be proved. 'In 1597 Shakespeare bought a fine house for himself and his family.'[12]

Big New Place certainly was but there is no evidence that it was 'fine'. The frontage of the property extended for sixty feet along Chapel Street and seventy feet down Chapel Lane. Such a extent could not well have been roofed; we must presume then that what ran along Chapel Street and round the corner was a range of buildings surrounding various open spaces or garths. The evidence also suggests that the property had never been properly maintained. The three storeys of brick and timber looming over Chapel Street right opposite the guild chapel might well have been ruinous. The title Shakespeare acquired had been in contention for more than twenty years. The rightful owners were the heirs of the Clopton family, but it was not to them that Shakespeare paid his pieces of silver. It was to be five years before he could secure even a dubious title, and yet the restoration of the building is thought to have begun immediately. If it had been Shakespeare's wife who took on the project of restoring and running this vast pile, the legal record would give no indication of the fact, because Ann was *feme coverte*. What is obvious is that in 1597 and for some years thereafter Shakespeare had enough to do as shareholder, dramaturge, playwright and performer with the Lord Chamberlain's Men, without involving himself in the restoration of a big tumble-down house a hundred miles away.

It is assumed that Shakespeare bought New Place because he could, because he was rich, but how rich was he? He had joined the

Chamberlain's Men only three years before as one of 'six or seven sharers'.

> Theirs was the overall control of income and expenditure. They would divide among themselves what remained after they had paid the wages of the hired players and musicians, the scribes, money-gatherers. tiremen, book-keepers and stage-hands, after they had covered the costs of each individual production, and after they had handed over to the theatrical landlord his agreed share of the takings.[13]

In the real world rent would be paid first rather than last, and would be payable whether the company performed or not. It makes sense for the Chamberlain's Men to embark on building their own theatre in 1598–9, only if they were finding the rent of their performing space a drain on their resources. If Henslowe's memoranda are any guide Shakespeare can only have expected £4 or £5 per playscript. His small share in the theatre may have been offered in lieu of cash. Thomson makes no mention of what appears to be the costliest item in Henslowe's theatre accounts, namely costumes. On 29 September the Admiral's Men paid Dekker and Marston £6 for the play *Civil Wars;* they then borrowed £19 from Henslowe to pay for a single garment, a 'rich cloak'. Henslowe's memoranda should suffice to illustrate how hard it was for players or poets to earn significant money in the theatre. Most of the playwrights were shareholders, because as proprietor Henslowe found it expedient to involve them in the business as a way of putting pressure on them to produce playscripts on demand. Many of them were in debt to him.

Few of Shakespeare's contemporary playwrights had more conspicuous success than Thomas Dekker.

> From 1598 until 1602 he contributed regularly and prolifically to the work of the Lord Admiral's Men. In 1602 he wrote for both the Earl of Worcester's Men . . . and briefly for the Lord Chamberlain's Men. He worked for Prince Henry's . . . Men from 1604 and for other companies, including the boys of St Paul's, after that. He pressed himself hard. Henslowe's papers show that between 1598 and 1602 he had a hand in between forty and fifty plays . . .[14]

In 1599 Dekker was arrested at the instance of the Lord Chamberlain's Men and Henslowe had to put up £3 10s to procure his discharge from imprisonment in the Counter. In 1612 he was flung into the King's Bench prison. He had just received a fee of £181 for devising a lord mayor's pageant called *Troia-Nova Triumphans*, which, though apparently high, was not sufficient to cover the costs of mounting the show. With no hope of satisfying his creditors, Dekker was to languish in prison for seven years. Henry Chettle too was arrested for debt in 1599, and Henslowe had to come to his rescue with twenty shillings. Yet we assume that, on the strength of writing forty-four plays and having a small share in the company, Shakespeare got very rich and stayed that way. The hard evidence does not bear out the assumption.

In October 1596 the Petty Collectors of the Bishopsgate ward listed seventy-three residents of St Helen's Parish who were liable for local taxes. Among them was a William Shakespeare, whose goods were assessed at £5 on which five shillings was payable in February 1597. Schoenbaum interprets this as meaning that Shakespeare was a 'householder', though what kind of housing he might have been holding is not clear, £5 being hardly enough to cover a bed and bedding, table and chair. The assessment was low but apparently not low enough, for Shakespeare did not pay it. On 5 October 1598 he was assessed again with goods still to the value of £5 and a total to pay of 13s 4d, and once again he did not pay. The collectors reported him, learnt subsequently that he had left the area, and referred the matter to a different authority. On 6 October 1600 the Exchequer records show that the 13s 4d was still unpaid.

Perhaps to buy New Place it was not necessary to be rich. In 1597 large parts of Stratford were still lying derelict after the devastating fires of 1594 and 1595. Many of the buildings destroyed belonged to the Corporation, which had rented them out at reasonable rates, but maintenance and repairs had always been the responsibility of the tenants who now had to find the money and the materials for rebuilding. Many were still struggling in 1598 when Richard Quiney travelled to London to petition the queen for tax relief, which was granted on 17 December 1598. In 1599 Abraham Sturley still hadn't finished rebuilding his house in Wood Street, burnt down in 1594.

New Place may have been standing vacant, the owner having moved
to Fillongley, near Coventry. As the house was not the property of the
Corporation it doesn't appear in the accounts; for all we know Ann,
or legally her husband, had been a tenant there ever since her
marriage. As the people of Stratford were struggling to find materials
to rebuild their houses, New Place's tiles, bricks and even timbers
must have been disappearing overnight.

New Place escaped the fires, but otherwise it seems to have been an
unlucky house. Even Sir Hugh Clopton, who built it, seems never to
have lived there. After his death the house was leased to various
tenants. In 1540 or so Leland saw it, and entered it in his memoranda
as a 'pretty house of brick and timber'.[15] In 1543 William Clopton
leased it for two lives to Dr Thomas Bentley, physician to Henry VIII,
and a former president of the Royal College of Physicians. When
Bentley died his widow brought an action in Chancery complaining
that Clopton was trying illegally to evict her; Clopton counterclaimed
that the terms of the lease had been broken because Bentley had 'left
the said manor place in great ruin and decay and unrepaired and it
doth still remain unrepaired ever since . . . to the great damage and
loss of the defendant'.[16] In 1560, Clopton's heir, another William
Clopton, in an effort to raise cash for his sisters' portions under the
terms of his father's will, and to finance his own travels in Italy, sold
and mortgaged as much of his inheritance as he could. In some of
these dealings he used the lawyer William Bott of Snitterfield as his
agent, which was, to say the least, unwise.

In 1557 Bott had acted as overseer of the will of one Hugh Porter,
even though he had mortgaged land in Hatton to Porter to the value
of £30. In 1560 he sued the Deputy Steward of Stratford for slander,
because he had accused him of accepting a fee for representing a client
in a lawsuit and then making an opponent's plea against him. In 1563
Bott sued for slander again, claiming that Roland Wheler had said to
him, 'William Bott thou art a false harlot, a false villain, and a
rebellion, and I will make thee to be set on the pillory.'[17] Bott
had no option but to try to silence Wheler, who was the principal
witness to Bott's murder of his own daughter, the first of two dastardly
crimes to be connected with New Place. According to evidence given
under oath by Wheler in the Court of Star Chamber in 1571, in April

1563 Bott had managed to negotiate a match between his daughter Isabella and John Harper of Henley-in-Arden, a minor. As part of the settlement it was agreed that if Isabella should die without issue, the lands entailed on Harper would pass to the Botts:[18]

> the said Bott having in this wise forged the said deed and so conveyed the said lands, the said Bott's daughter, wife of the said John Harper, did die suddenly and was poisoned with ratsbane and therewith swelled to death. And this deponent knoweth the same to be true, for that he did see the wife of the said Bott in the presence of the same Bott deliver to the said Harper's wife in a spoon the said poison of ratsbane to drink, which poison she did drink in this deponent's presence, the said William Bott by, and at that time leaning to the bed's feet . . .[19]

Isabella was buried at Holy Trinity on 7 May 1563. Bott was never prosecuted for her murder. In the Court of Star Chamber in 1564 Clopton testified that Bott had kept the rents he received from Clopton's tenants and forged a deed that gave him a claim to his lands. Soon after, Clopton brought a suit against Bott in Chancery for recovery of deeds and jewels. The tortuous case seems to have resulted in part from the desperate machinations of Lodowick Greville to finance his housebuilding at Mount Greville:[20]

> Bott acknowledged that he had evidences belonging to Clopton, but declared that he had delivered to Lodowick Greville of Milcote, to redeliver to Clopton, bonds dated in 1564 by which Greville promised to pay Clopton one hundred pounds and forty pounds, and a recognisance by Greville in two thousand pounds . . .[21]

Clopton was then obliged to sue Greville in the Court of Star Chamber and in Chancery for conspiring to convey his lands to William Porter by a false deed, and Bott too sued Greville in the Court of Star Chamber.[22] The Cloptons may have been hampered in the proceedings because they were known recusants, and their property at risk of confiscation whatever the outcome. The actions in the Court of Star Chamber and Chancery went on for many years with Bott's dubious title to New Place remaining for the moment unchallenged. It was not until 1720 that New Place became once more property of the Clopton family.

In 1567 Bott divested himself of New Place, selling it to William Underhill of the Inner Temple, clerk of the assizes at Warwick, for £40, and apparently retired to Snitterfield where he was buried on 1 November 1582.[23] This Underhill's heir, another William Underhill, is described as a resident of Stratford in the return of 'names and dwelling-places of the gentlemen and freeholders dwelling in the county of Warwickshire' in 1580. In 1583 Underhill acquired for a down payment of £20 a twenty-one-year lease of the tithes of Little Wilmcote but it seems that he never paid the annual rent of £3.[24] In 1588, he entertained the Recorder of Stratford at New Place, but soon afterwards moved to Fillongley in Coventry. In 1597, when the town of Stratford was suing him for the unpaid tithe rent, he sold New Place to the Shakespeares. The conveyancing had not been completed when Underhill suddenly died, of poison. By the will he managed to declare in his last moments, and left everything to his eldest son Fulke. Two years later twenty-year-old Fulke Underhill was hanged at Warwick for his father's murder. As he was a convicted felon his estate was forfeit. Shakespeare's purchase could not actually be completed until the estate was regranted to Underhill's second-born son, Hercules, when he came of age in 1602.

Though he had not actually secured title to New Place Shakespeare was duly listed on 4 February 1598 as a householder in Chapel Street ward, which doesn't of course mean that he was actually living there. In 1598 the Corporation paid 'Mr Shakespeare' ten pence for a load of stone. 'Mr Shakespeare' is assumed to have been the Bard, and the load of stone to have been 'left over from the repairs executed at New Place',[25] and therefore the restoration work must have been complete. The stone, which was used in repairs to Clopton Bridge, could have been what was left over from repairing pavements, sills and stairs around the brick and timber house, or it could simply have been removed to be replaced by something else, and the repairs to the actual structure could have gone on for years afterwards. Three years of dearth had reduced many people to penury and near-starvation even before the fires; increased demand had driven up the costs of building materials and the number of skilled building workers was unequal to the demand. The restoration of New Place would have been a challenge at any time, but at no time more than when the Shakespeares undertook it.

Shakespeare's acquisition of a townhouse is usually assumed to have been part of his gentrification project, but, if it was, he bought the wrong house. The source of gentility is land and a rent roll, not a rambling house with no land. New Place, smack in the centre of a half-incinerated market town, was not a gentleman's house but a merchant's house. Those who say that Shakespeare was country-bred and longed for the leafy lanes of Warwickshire should bear in mind that in 1597 London was still pretty rural; there were woods and green fields aplenty within a few hundred yards of the theatres on the Bankside. Besides, Shakespeare must have known that he would soon inherit the freehold (but probably not the tenancy) of the double house in Henley Street, so whose idea was it that he should take on the huge wreck of a house that dominated Chapel Street and rambled halfway down Chapel Lane?

If the scholars who have assumed that Ann and her children had been living all this while with her in-laws in the house on Henley Street are correct, Ann had been married for nearly fifteen years without ever having had a chance to manage her own household. It would have been only fair if the Bard had bethought him of her awkward situation and made a priority of finding a house for her as soon as he had sufficient cash, but not if he had switched from providing no kind of a roof over her head to overwhelming her with a dilapidated pile. If he was expecting her to fail, he was to be disappointed. Supposing the New Place project was Shakespeare's idea, he must have thought that in Ann he had the person he needed to manage the restoration of the house and get it up and running. If he had employed a steward we would probably have come across such a person in the Stratford records; if on the other hand he employed his wife as the clerk of works, all her commands and all her transactions would have been attributed directly to him.

There was nothing unusual in a woman's directing the restoration of her own house, even a house as big as New Place. When the house known as the Shrieve's House in Sheep Street, Stratford, was destroyed by the fire of 1595, and the householder William Rogers died six months later, it was his widow Elizabeth who rebuilt it. In 1599 it was listed in a Corporation survey as 'new-built', with three bays in Sheep Street, and a range of six bays on the back-side.[26] Lady Mary Wroth, wife of Ben Jonson's friend Sir Robert Wroth, raised funds for the restoration of her husband's house at Loughton Hall by direct petition to Anne of Denmark, and in 1612 it too was described as new-built.

In 1597 the affairs of the Lord Chamberlain's Men required Shakespeare's attention. In January James Burbage died, and in April his lease on the Theatre, the company's headquarter, ran out. Burbage and the landlord, Giles Allen, had been unable to agree terms for a new lease, so Burbage had decided upon a new site, the old refectory of the dissolved Blackfriars monastery, and had invested £600 in a lease, and hundreds more in refurbishing the building for use as a theatre. This money he had borrowed. According to evidence later given by the younger James Burbage his father had built the Theatre:

> with many hundred pounds taken up at interest . . . he built this house
> upon leased grounds by which means the landlord and he had a great
> suit in law, and by his death, the like troubles fell on us, his sons: we
> then bethought us of altering from thence, and at like expence built
> The Globe with more sums of money taken up at interest.[27]

The interest would have been 10 per cent per annum. Once Shakespeare became a shareholder in the theatre he would have been liable for his share of the costs of servicing the loans and fighting the various legal actions. When the residents protested to the Privy Council and the Blackfriars project was abandoned, interest was still payable on the money borrowed by Burbage. Burbage's son Cuthbert entered into new negotiations with Giles Allen and agreed to pay a much higher rent for the Theatre site, but the deal fell through when Allen refused to accept Burbage as the guarantor. For years Giles Allen pursued the Lord Chamberlain's Servants through the courts, demanding the crushing amount of £800 in damages.

At this critical juncture in the company's fortunes Shakespeare is believed to have squandered money on a huge house three days' ride from London. The acquisition of residential real estate was not at all the kind of thing that theatre people went in for. What with playing in London during the terms and touring the countryside in the vacation, few of them had any use for a permanent residence of any kind. Most of Shakespeare's colleagues in the theatre, even those who called themselves gentlemen and had a university education, lived a hand-to-mouth existence in lodgings, and spent the little money they made on good cheer. Christopher Marlowe, Thomas Kyd, John Day and Henry Chettle never became heads of households. According to Aubrey, Beaumont and Fletcher 'lived together on the Bankside, not far from the playhouse, both bachelors, lay together, had one wench in the house between them, which they did so admire, the same clothes and cloak etc. between them'.[28] Fletcher never married. Beaumont eventually gave up the theatre and married a gentlewoman who bore him one child and was pregnant at the time of his death in March 1616.

Those who did marry do not seem to have invested much time or energy in the role of paterfamilias. Robert Greene, a few years older than Shakespeare, married 'a gentleman's daughter of good account' in about 1585 and settled briefly in Norwich. When she had borne a child and he had spent her portion he abandoned her and returned to his haunts in London, where he died destitute in 1592, having signed a bond to the poor shoe-maker whose family cared for him which he begged his estranged wife to honour. Thomas Dekker, gentleman, may have been the father of a daughter christened at St Giles Cripplegate in 1594, and another buried there in 1598, and a son buried at St Botolph's in 1598, and he may not. Philip Massinger was married and had children, apparently, but nothing is known of his family. Even the most successful of Shakespeare's rivals, Ben Jonson, though like Shakespeare married in his youth and father of at least three children, lived mainly in other people's houses, at Polesworth with Goodere, and at Loughton with Sir Robert Wroth, for example, evidently at their expense, though he must have earned at least as handsomely as Shakespeare both at court and in the public theatres. Jonson lamented that he followed the muse of poetry even though she had beggared him, when he might have been a rich lawyer, physician or merchant.[29] Yet Shakespeare, who did the same, is presumed to have earned and kept a fortune. Those of Shakespeare's colleagues who acquired houses of their own looked for them rather closer to London. Thomas Middleton and his wife, the well-connected Mary Marbeck, and their single child lived at Newington Butts. The player Augustine Phillips bought himself a house in Mortlake. Condell owned a house in Fulham.

We have no clear idea of what the house that the Shakespeares bought in 1597 was like. The fine of 1597 mentions a messuage with two barns and two gardens; the version of 1602 adds two apple orchards. The restored house was pulled down in 1702, and so we have to rely on the long-distance reminiscences of people who were alive in the later seventeenth century to get any idea of what the Shakespeares ended up with. In 1737 George Vertue interviewed Shakespeare Hart, a descendant of the Bard's sister Joan Hart, and sketched what he told him. Vertue's drawing shows a house with three storeys and five gables. His caption reads, 'This the outward appearance towards the street, the gate and entrance (at the corner of Chapel Lane) . . .' He then drew a plan showing the gate and a building on either side in front of the house: 'besides this front or outward gate there was before the house itself (that Shakespeare lived in) within a little court-yard, grass growing there – before the real dwelling house, this outside being a long gallery etc. and for servants.' The long gallery would have been used for exercise in the winter months and for children to play in during inclement weather. Richard Grimmitt, born in 1683, said that to the best of his remembrance 'there was a brick wall next the street, with a kind of porch at the end of it next the chapel; then they crossed a small kind of green court before they entered the house which was bearing to the left and fronted with brick, with plain windows consisting of common panes of glass set in lead, as at this time'. Besides the little green forecourt, New Court had a big enclosed garden of at least three-quarters of an acre. This, the 'great garden', was sold off at about the time that the house was pulled down. It is there that Shakespeare is supposed to have planted the famous mulberry tree.

Mulberry trees can be in the ground for many years before they fruit, but, if the point of the planting is to rear silkworms, it doesn't matter if the trees don't fruit, as you only need fresh green leaves.

Shakespeare's mulberry tree, the bole of which when it was cut down in 1758 was a mere six inches in diameter, was probably the last surviving of a row whose leaves were originally harvested for silkworms. Everybody who could remember agreed that the tree was in the garden in Shakespeare's time, and this, later generations supposed, meant that he had planted it with his own fair hands. Malone surmises that the mulberry tree was planted in 1609 when thousands of mulberry trees were imported from France at the order of James I in a bid to establish silk manufacture in Britain.[30]

James's attempt failed, as did that of his grandson Charles II who sixty years later planted a mulberry garden at Whitehall with the same intention. Before the industrial revolution silk production, whether in China or in Europe, was a cottage industry. If, as has been suggested, Ann was involved in the haberdashery business with her brother-in-law, in the manufacture of lace and ribbons or as a knitter, teacher of knitting or organiser of outworkers, she might well have wanted to branch out into the really big money, which was in silk. The suggestion that she was involved in sericulture at New Place is given some support from the Holy Trinity register for 1611 which for the first time describes the occupation of a parishioner, one Thomas Knight, as 'silk weaver'.[31] All things considered it is unlikely that the Bard planted a single mulberry tree at New Place and rather more likely that his wife planted several.

There were grapevines at New Place too, but no one has suggested that the Bard trod his own grapes or bottled his own vintage. All the work associated with New Place, whether it was brewing or wine-making or sericulture, would have been overseen by Ann Shakespeare. If she had been unwilling or unable to extend the field of her operations, Shakespeare could never have bought the house, unless he was prepared to employ a housekeeper or a steward. As no such person appears in the record, the best guess is that Ann was both housekeeper and steward. Within months of acquiring New Place Shakespeare is listed as a holder of malt; the malt was almost certainly made by Ann or under her supervision. If she was making malt, she was probably also brewing ale, and raising pigs on the spent malt, curing her own bacon, and baking bread, for all these activities were interdependent.

> *Brew somewhat for thine*
> Where brewer is needful, be brewer thyself
> What filleth thy roof will help furnish thy shelf,
> *Else bring up no swine*
> In buying thy drink by the firkin or pot,
> The tally ariseth, but hog amends not.[32]

To make malt in this period barley, or mixed oats and barley called maslen, was soaked in water in a 'yealing vat' and spread on the floor of a 'couch house' to begin the germination process that converts the starches in the grain to sugar or maltose. For this process space was needed.

> The place may be so and the kiln may be such
> To make thine own malt shalt profit thee much.

As soon as rootlets began to emerge from the grain, the malt was swept up and put to dry on a 'kill' or 'keele', a wooden frame supporting a 'hair cloth' made of woven horse hair, which was set over a fire of straw. Straw was chosen because it does not create the kind of thick smoke that would taint the malt, which was meant to assume a golden colour. The process was dangerous, especially when carried out in a confined, poorly ventilated space. All of the fires that devastated Stratford probably involved the mismanagement of some stage of the malting or brewing process. It was essential to dry the malt thoroughly, if it was not to spoil.

> Some drieth with straw and some drieth with wood,
> Wood asketh more charge and yet nothing so good . . .
> Malt being well spared the more it will cast,
> Malt being well-dried the longer will last . . .[33]

This activity, especially if carried out on a considerable scale, required the services of maids; others were employed by the good housewife elsewhere in her establishment:

> Set some about churning, some seething of souse,
> Some carding, some spinning, some trimming up house . . .

Set some to grind malt, or thy rushes to twine,
Set some to peel hemp, or to seething of brine . . .[34]

The most skilled workers were to be found in the dairy:

Good servant in dairy that needs not be told
Deserveth her fee to be paid her in gold . . .
Keep dairy house cleanly, keep pan sweet and cold,
Keep butter and cheese to look yellow as gold.[35]

Ann could have undertaken the same enormous range of activities as her younger contemporary, Margaret, Lady Hoby.[36] As well as observing her daily routine of private and public devotions, reading and conference with her household, Lady Hoby attended women in labour, dressed wounds, prepared medicines, gardened, propagated plants, gathered and preserved fruit, made cakes and confectionery, kept bees, made candles, distilled essential oils, dyed wool, and lent money and held money.

Malt-making and money-lending were connected activities; the women who prospered as the one entered in business as the other, both holding and laying out funds for clients. We have one piece of evidence of Ann's participation in this kind of related activity. On 25 March 1601, the Hathaways' shepherd made his will. Shepherds, responsible for keeping the scattered small flocks healthy, for crutching, docking, castrating, shearing and mating them, paring their feet and delivering lambs, as necessary, made good money. According to Edgar Fripp there were no fewer than eight shepherds living in Stratford in 1600. In his will Whittington admitted a debt for 'a quarter's of an year's board' to Ann's brothers John and William Hathaway who were still living at Hewlands Farm, so he was probably one of the six people in Joan Hathaway's household in 1596. His will was witnessed by two of the creditors listed in Richard Hathaway's will of 1581, John Pace and John Barber; another witness was William Gilbert the curate who wrote the elder Hathaway's will. When he died at Shottery in April 1601 Whittington's possessions, assessed at the handsome sum of £50, included 'four score and one sheep' and eleven quarters of malt.[37] One clause in his will is of particular interest:

Item I give and bequeath unto the poor people of Stratford forty shillings that is in the hand of Ann Shakespeare wife unto Mr William Shakespeare and is due debt unto me being paid to mine executor by the said William Shakespeare or his assigns according to the true meaning of this my will.

As Whittington also listed further debts owed to him by Ann's brothers, John and William Hathaway, executors of their mother's will in which he had been left money which he had not yet received, the will might be thought to give us a picture of the Hathaway clan in 1601 as so strapped for cash that their faithful shepherd was obliged to lend them small sums that they were not able to repay in his lifetime. In fact the last person to whom a shepherd like Whittington would confide his money would be someone who was in financial difficulties. Having no households of their own to maintain, because they lived mostly with the owners of the flocks they managed, shepherds tended to accumulate quantities of cash which they had no way of keeping safe. As soon as a sizable sum had accumulated they tended to place it in the hands of a solid citizen who would be certain to repay it on demand. When Richard Cowper, also a shepherd, died in 1588, and left an estate valued at more than £37, all but £7 of it was in the hands of other people, his principal debtor being Alderman Abraham Sturley, who owed him £22.

If Whittington had not known Ann all her life, he would probably have described the money he had placed in her hands as in the hands of her husband, who would have been legally liable for it. In departing from custom, Whittington has provided us with a single scintilla of evidence that Ann Shakespeare was economically active in her own right. Even if the only money she had access to was her husband's income, Ann may have been empowered to lend and spend it as she thought fit, which would give the lie to those people who want to believe that Shakespeare's wife did not enjoy her husband's trust or respect. Not all wives enjoyed such freedom, but it was not at all uncommon. In *The Merry Wives of Windsor* Falstaff makes love to the married ladies because he believes that both of them have access to significant amounts of money. Mistress Ford, according to report, 'has all the rule of her husband's purse; he hath a legion of angels' (I. iii.

49–50). She has the key to her husband's coffer (II. ii. 263) and Ford in his jealous fit fears that if she and Falstaff get together his coffers shall be ransacked (II. ii. 281). Mistress Page 'bears the purse too: she is a region in Guiana, all gold and bounty' (I. iii. 64–5). What Whittington's will does not prove, or even suggest, is that Shakespeare ever left his family without enough to live on, so that Ann was forced to borrow.[38] It seems more likely that Ann was, like many other women in a similar position, operating as a banker. 'There be other Usurers which will not lend themselves but give leave to their wives and they play like hucksters, that is, every month a penny for a shilling . . .'[39]

Another court case relating to Ann's business dealings began in 1607 when Shakespeare sued a John Addenbrooke, seeking recovery of £6 plus damages. As far as we can tell the women who made and traded in malt and in money were usually single, either unmarried or widows, but as the dealings of married women were invariably subsumed within their husband's business activities, it may be that we have a very partial notion of women's economic activity at the turn of the sixteenth century. Even so, it seems very much more likely that it was Ann who wanted New Place, Ann who restored it and Ann who ran it than that it was Shakespeare. Perhaps it was her money that paid for it.

CHAPTER THIRTEEN

of hunger and disorder, introducing the villain of the piece, Sir Edward Greville, who contrived the foul murder of the Bailiff of Stratford, and Ann's friend and ally the young lawyer Thomas Greene

The prevailing notion of Shakespeare's Stratford is that it was a sleepy place of leafy lanes and picturesque half-timbered houses, neat and peaceful, a sort of Metroland before the event, a retirement village just waiting for Shakespeare to return and put his feet up. Nothing could be further from the truth. From the mid-1590s most Stratfordians struggled; the rich grew richer but the numbers of landless poor proliferated and even substantial citizens were menaced with destitution. The winter of 1596–7 saw the highest death-toll of the century, the cumulative effect of years of malnutrition.

The Corporation did its best to stem the tide of misery, but by all the indices, the frequency of violent death, of family breakdown, desertion and bastardy, of pauperisation and despair, the situation deteriorated. The puritan city fathers strove with might and main to keep a modicum of order as the gentry looked on, waiting for a moment of weakness. Elsewhere in Warwickshire the poor people had lost the struggle against their landlords before Ann Shakespeare was born; in the 1590s enclosures began to encroach upon the common lands near Stratford. Endless wrangling in the law courts spilled over into fighting in the streets.

The villages of Leicestershire, Northamptonshire and Warwickshire waged the fiercest struggle of all to defend their common fields and slender commons against enclosure in the sixteenth and seventeenth centuries and were the scene of the Midland Revolt of 1607.[1]

An already difficult situation was made more so by changes in local administration. After the death of the childless Earl of Warwick in 1590 the lordship of the Stratford manors fell vacant. The Corporation petitioned Lord Treasurer Burghley for the right to name Stratford's vicar and schoolmaster, and other privileges associated with the lordship, only to be forestalled.[2] Local landowner Edward Greville took out a patent in the names of two London scriveners, one of whom did a good deal of legal work for Greville's new patron, the Earl of Essex, and bought the lordship for himself. Greville is typical of the gentlemen described by a later town clerk of Stratford:

> gentlemen were naturally enemies to Corporations and the truth whereof this Corporation hath experiently tasted: all their troubles and suits proceeding from distaste proudly and causelessly taken by neighbouring gentlemen who will be satisfied with no reasonable respects except such crouching observance as standeth not with the honour of a Corporation to perform . . . who make no other use of them but as they do of their stirrups to mount their horse, so to serve their times they will bestow a salute of them or some formal compliment when they have scorn in their hearts.[3]

Properly managed, Edward Greville's estates, which extended from the Avon to the Stour, and included the substantial manors of Milcote, Weston, Welford, Coldicote and Sezincote, would have made him a very wealthy man, but he had no interest in improving them. He coveted the rich prizes that his fellow courtiers were winning with minimum effort or personal risk from patronage and speculation.

The Grevilles were a law unto themselves. Edward's ancestor John Greville of Milcote was decidedly vicious. In the Acts of the Privy Council we read that on 26 October 1541,

> Upon an information given that John Greville of Milcote in the County of Warwick should misuse his own daughter, and shot at one of his servants with a cross-bow, it was decreed that the said John Greville should be sent for to appear immediately before the Council.[4]

Greville appeared, was bound over for a surety of £500 and required to appear before the court every day, while the crown prepared its case, but no witnesses could be persuaded to give evidence and the case was ultimately dismissed. Greville's grandfather, Sir Edward Greville, married one of the co-parcenary heiresses of William Willington, a Merchant of the Staple, who had greatly enriched himself by buying up land in Warwickshire, enclosing and depopulating the villages of Barcheston and Chelmscote. When Sir Edward died in 1562, his son Lodowick, who was only twenty-two, became the head of the family. After his ambitious marriage to Thomasine Petre, daughter of Sir William Petre, Greville pillaged his estates to lavish money on the building on his Milcote estate of a huge country mansion to be called Mount Greville, while his encroachments on the rights of his tenants resulted in a succession of Star Chamber suits. In March 1576 the Privy Council wrote to Sir Thomas Lucy, Thomas Smith and John Higford, desiring them to investigate the complaints of tenants of Wellford in Gloucesterhire against Greville.[5] In January 1579, after he knocked down Sir John Conway of Arrow in a London street and laid about him so fiercely with his sword that he was likely to have cut his legs off if he had not been dragged away by Conway's attendants, Greville spent some time in the Marshalsea.[6]

The Edward Greville who became Lord of the Borough and of Old Stratford was Lodowick's second son, born in 1564. By 1588 Lodowick Greville's affairs were in such disarray that he devised a desperate plan to restore them. He had long coveted the assets of one of his wealthier tenants, Thomas Webb of Drayton, who had served him as steward. Greville invited the elderly Webb to spend Christmas with him at Sezincote, where he had him strangled in his bed by two of his servants, Thomas Smith alias Barber and Thomas Brock. He then had one of them impersonate Webb on the point of death, and dictate to the unsuspecting parson a will in Greville's favour. 'One of the assassinates [Brock] being in his cups at Stratford, dropped out some words among his pot companions that it lay within his power to hang his master.'[7] For this indiscretion Greville had Smith drown Brock. When the body floated to the surface, the murder was discovered. Smith was arrested and revealed the whole conspiracy. On 6 November 1589, after ten months in the tower, Greville came to trial. He refused to speak, and was subjected to the 'peine forte et dure', that is to say, pressed to death, on 14 November. Because he had remained silent, his estates were not forfeit and twenty-four-year-old Edward was able to inherit.[8]

According to Dugdale, when Edward was a boy, he shot an arrow straight up into the air which when it fell killed his elder brother, whereupon his father 'made a jest of it telling him that it was the best shoot he had ever shot in his life'.[9] Apparently there is no foundation in truth for this tale, but it tells us more about the feelings the Greville family inspired in the countryside than mere documentary fact could have done. Greville had the right to present the vicar to the living of Holy Trinity, and he also claimed the right to be consulted in the choice of bailiff and the appointment of the collector of market tolls. Though the Corporation duly plied him with sack and venison, pears and walnuts, wine and cakes on all prescribed occasions, he found the aldermen insufficiently subordinate.[10] When Richard Quiney was elected to the post of bailiff in 1592, Greville refused his assent; it took a letter from the Recorder of Stratford, Greville's cousin Sir Fulke Greville, to remedy the situation.[11] From 1597 when he was knighted by Essex, whom he had accompanied on the expedition to the Azores, he was Sir Edward Greville. Greville's career is comprehensible only if, as well as being endowed with an utter lack of principle, he had considerable personal charm. He wooed and won in marriage Joan Bromley, a younger daughter of Lord Chancellor Bromley and his wife Elizabeth, whose brother Sir John Fortescue was chancellor of the Exchequer. Greville pillaged his wealthy wife so efficiently that she was ultimately left with nothing but the clothes she stood up in.

The scarcity of food grain in 1597 prompted a royal proclamation forbidding the making of malt from Ladyday, 25 March, to Michaelmas, 29 September, so that there would be more grain on the market and prices could be kept down. The making of malt and brewing of ale was Stratford's chief industry. The Corporation drew up a petition to the chancellor of the Exchequer, Sir John Fortescue, Greville's wife's uncle, begging for an exemption. It is an extraordinary document:

In most humble wise beseeching your honour her Majesty's loyal servants your poor orators, the bailiff, aldermen and burgesses of her majesty's borough town of Stratford upon Avon in her Highness's county of

Warwickshire that, whereas in regard to the dearth of corn which by the Lord's hand is laid upon our land and upon our county more than many others, your honour have given commandment by your letters to the Justices of the Peace in our county to restrain malt-making generally, and, upon their sending the knowledge of your command and honour's pleasures therein we have bound our neighbours, that is to say, the citizens of Stratford entreating them not to transgress therein, which we know they are not able to endure, in that our town hath no other especial trade having thereby only, time beyond man's memory, lived by exercising the same, our houses fitted to no other uses, many servants among us hired only to that purpose and many only upon making malt for gentlemen and others maintained, besides our town wanting the help of commons to keep any cattle towards our sustenance, as all our neighbour towns have to their great comfort, neither is it a thoroughfare, and beside that we have endured great losses by two extreme fires which have mightily decayed our said town, having burnt in the thirty-sixth and thirty-seventh year of her Highness's reign a hundred and twenty dwelling houses, and con-sumed £12,000 and upwards in goods, the means whereof we have 400 people that live only upon relief at our doors in that our abilities cannot better provide for them.

The drafter of the petition, who was probably Richard Quiney, here seems to pause for breath, and a curious aside. Moreover many badgers inhabiting the woodland near us.[6] Then he rattles on:

Poor men with great charge of wives and children live by portage of our malt into other counties . . . all which will feel the want with us, that in consideration hereof it might please your Honour to enlarge us, with some toleration to your Honour's best beseeming and to leave the allowance unto us, adjoining Sir Edward Greville with us that it may the better appear we desire to satisfy that beseemeth our duties to you and our country and safeguard of our poor neighbours' estates whereunto we are also bound. And that it might please you also to give order to our Justices for the counties to restrain all farmers and husbandmen inhabiting in our county not to convert their own barley into malt as they have done and do to the great hindrance of all our markets and the utter spoil of our town . . .[12]

While Richard Quiney was in London about the business of presenting the petition, his friend Abraham Sturley wrote to him often. He never mentions Ann Shakespeare, but in a letter of 24 January 1598 he makes a suggestion that may have originated with her.

> It seemeth by him [Quiney's father, Adrian] that our countryman, master Shakespeare, is willing to disburse some money on some odd yard-land or other at Shottery or near about us. He thinketh it a very fit pattern to move him to deal in the matter of our tithes. By the instructions you can give him thereof and by the friends he can make therefore, we think it a far mark for him to shoot at and not impossible to hit. It obtained would advance him indeed and would do us much good.

Since the Act of Suppression, tithes were no longer collected from the faithful but were due to the secular authorities who rented out rather than farming the tithelands within their jurisdiction. The Corporation had rented the tithes to William Underhill, who did not pay the rent and had forfeited them. It now needed to rent them out again to raise capital for poor relief. As far as we can tell, Shakespeare made no move towards acquiring the tithelands at this stage; indeed, we might suspect that the person interested in acquiring yardland at Shottery at the beginning of 1598 was Ann, who was probably born there, rather than her husband.

Sturley's letter continues:

> You shall understand that our neighbours are grown, with the wants they feel through the dearness of corn (which here is beyond all other countries that I can hear of dear and over dear), malcontent. They have assembled together in a great number, and travelled to Sir Thomas Lucy on Friday last to complain of our maltsters, on Sunday to Sir Fulke Greville, and Sir John Conway – I should have said, on Wednesday to Sir Edward Greville first.

The artisans of Stratford had walked to Milcote and back on 18 January, to Charlcote and back two days later, and made the round trip to Beauchamps Court and Arrow two days after that, to protest the cost of grain. They probably heard nothing but fair words, if that, and returned in rebellious mood.

> There is a meeting here expected tomorrow. The Lord knoweth to what end it will sort! Thomas West returning from the two knights of the woodland came home so full that he said to Master Baily that night, he hoped within a week to lead some of them in a halter, meaning the maltsters; and I hope, saith John Grannams, if God send my Lord of Essex down shortly, to see them hanged on gibbets at their own doors.[13]

Public disorder on the streets of Stratford would have meant punitive sanctions for all concerned, particularly the Corporation for failing to keep the queen's peace. It would also have led to the defeat of Richard Quiney's petition and obliterated any possibility of the new charter that the Corporation had decided was necessary if the decay in the town's fortunes was to be repaired. On 25 January the High Sheriff of Warwickshire warned the Privy Council of increasing unrest in the countryside and requested that the price of malt be fixed, to prevent profiteering. The Privy Council declined to act. Instead, the bailiff and his officers set about binding over the citizens to refrain from making malt, and an inquiry was set up to identify the worst offenders. The result of the inquiry came down on 4 February 1598; in Chapel Street ward William Shakespeare was listed as holding ten quarters of malt.[14] In fact he was in London; the malt was Ann's business. Ann had been in New Place for little more than six months, but she was already holding ten quarters, that is, eighty bushels of malt. Of the thirteen householders listed in Chapel Street ward only two held more. Ann Shakespeare's activities would have been legal as long as she could demonstrate that the malt she held was needed for brewing ale for her own household.

Ale was as nutritious as plain water was dangerous; every housewife of substance was expected to be able to direct the long and cumbersome process to a good end-product. To make ale, malt is ground in a mill or 'quern' and then mixed with hot water in a mashing vat. A complex chain of sugars is released from the malt, which dissolves in the hot liquor to become wort. The wort is drawn off, leaving spent grains behind and put into a boiler with a convex bottom to be boiled for between one and two hours, until the solids coagulate and the ale clears. Then the liquid is sieved or 'boulted', the spent hops are strained out and wort poured into shallow tubs or trays to cool, before being run into a fermenting tun or 'gyl' and yeast or 'barme' added. When fermentation is complete the ale is racked and left to settle.

All households of any size brewed their own ale, which was drunk in preference to water at all times of day. An establishment the size of New Place would have had a purpose-built brew house, with a double-bottomed mashing vat, a fermenting vat, a cooler, troughs and a mauling board, and a 'boyling lead'. Ann's eighty bushels of malt would have made ten hogsheads, that is about 600 gallons, of good ale and the same quantity of small beer. The good ale was made of two mashings of the same malt, and small beer from a third. Baking was inseparable from brewing, for barme from the process was used to raise the dough. The appearance of her husband's name in the list of malt-makers is enough of itself to place Ann Shakespeare in the first rank of Stratford housewives, along with the likes of Bess Quiney. No one else by the name of Shakespeare held any corn or malt whatsoever.

On 27 September 1598 the Corporation was obliged to issue a resolution to control alehouse-keepers who:

> thorough their unreasonably strong drink, to the increase of quarrelling, and other misdemeanours in their houses, and the farther and greater impoverishment of many poor men haunting the said houses, when their wives and children are in extremity of begging; and also for that most of the said tippling-houses are very dangerous for fire by reason of the straitness to lay fuel in.[15]

As nobody carried money back and forth between London and Stratford, the matter was usually managed by raising money in London and paying it back in Stratford or vice versa, but trying to work such a system with Sir Edward Greville was a high-risk business. On 25 October 1598, extremely strapped for cash, Quiney wrote out in a fair hand a letter to Shakespeare:

Loving countryman, I am bold of you as of a friend, craving your help
with £30, upon Mr Bushell's and my security, or Mr Mytton's with
me. Mr Rosswell is not come to London as yet and I have especial
cause. You shall friend me much in helping me out of all the debts I
owe in London, I thank God, and much quiet my mind, which would
not be indebted. I am now towards the court in hope of answer for the
despatch of my business. You shall lose neither credit nor money by
me, the Lord willing, and now but persuade yourself so as I hope and
you shall not need for fear but with all hearty thankfulness I will hold
my time and content your friend, and if we bargain further you shall be
the paymaster yourself. My time bids me hasten to an end an so I
commit this to your care and hope of your help. I fear I shall not be
back this night from the court. Haste! The Lord be with you and with
us all. Amen. From the Bell in Carter Lane, the 25 October, 1598.
Yours in all kindness.[16]

This has been interpreted as evidence of a friendship between the
two men, when in fact it is the opposite. The approach is tentative;
there is no reliance whatsoever on mutual trust or a gentleman's word.
Instead sureties are offered, as if to a stranger, and two of them,
Mytton and Rosswell, were henchmen of Greville's. (The other was
Quiney's son-in-law.) In the event, though Quiney sealed the letter
and addressed it, he decided not to send it. It remained among his
papers where it is to this day. The tone of that letter to Shakespeare
offers an absolute contrast to the warmth of the correspondence with
his father and Abraham Sturley, both members of the puritan
brotherhood. When Quiney communicated to Sturley his belief that
he could raise cash from Shakespeare, Sturley replied on 4 November
that he 'would like of it as he could hear when and where and how'.[17]

Quiney's petition was successful and his expenses were eventually
paid by the Exchequer. There is no mention in the extremely detailed
account Quiney submitted of any loan from Shakespeare. At the Hall
of 23 April 1600, the Corporation decided that, in view of the
ongoing cash shortage, the sergeants were to have the toll corn they
collected in lieu of wages.[18] Greville considered the toll corn his to
dispose of.[19] Even as Quiney and others were trying to disentangle the
legal situation but they were well aware that matters were coming to a

head. It was at this point that Greville took it upon himself to enclose the most important of the town commons, the Bancroft. The Corporation reacted swiftly. On 21 January 1601, according to Greville's complaint, the aldermen

> broke into the Bancroft, drove in horses, cows, oxen and pigs and 'then and there did depasture, tread down and consume to the value of forty shillings; and forty willows did lop and the wood thereof (six loads to the value of six pounds) took and carried away' and other enormities to him did do.[20]

Next day they took away the toll corn as well.[21] Greville had them arrested for riot and conveyed to the Marshalsea prison in London, where they were released immediately on bail. With the help of solicitor Thomas Greene, Quiney struggled to get access to Sir Edward Coke, the attorney general, but, despite bribing a clerk and a doorkeeper, he failed.[22] The authorities were too preoccupied by the Essex Rising and no one of authority would make himself available to calm the storm in the Stratford teacup.

Back home in Stratford, Quiney made a list of the people he could rely on to have the courage to oppose the lord of the manor. They were John Jeffries, the steward of Stratford, his father Adrian Quiney, Thomas Barber alias Dyer, Simon Biddle, the bellringer George Clemson, the beadle John Hemmings and Ann's father-in-law John Shakespeare. The list being neither long nor impressive, the Quineys were pretty much on their own. Greville was suing the Corporation, for the toll corn and for the right to enclose the Bancroft. Fighting the action demanded money the Corporation did not have. A letter was written to Greville pointing out that the expenses of the suit would be far more than would ever be earned from the toll collection. Greville's reply was pretty typical of the man:

> Sir Edward at our humble suit said he would have it if it cost £500 and if we tried it we must either try it in the Exchequer, where his uncle Fortescue was or if in the country before his uncle Anderson, said also to Thomas Samwell about his land which he would challenge, what jury in Warwickshire dares go against him, if he would contend with him.[23]

The Corporation then elected none other than Richard Quiney as bailiff, and once again Greville refused his consent. Thomas Greene wrote to Quiney that the attorney general had agreed to act as counsel for Stratford, and that Greville's consent to his election was not required, but it boded ill. Panicked, the Corporation begged Chief Justice Anderson to arbitrate and sent him a gift of sack and claret, to no avail. Then the aldermen turned to Greville's wife, giving her £20 to intercede on their behalf. She took the money and said that she 'laboured and thought she should effect' only to have her husband declare that his side 'should win it by the sword'. Greville's agent Robert Whitney wrote a threatening letter to Quiney, who had him bound over. The Corporation was not to know that by this time Greville was a desperate man; despite his braggadocio he had not £500 to his name. The next year he would be forced to sell Alveston Manor to Richard Lane, who was eventually obliged to sue him for non-payment of a bond of a thousand pounds. In 1610 he would sell the manor of Stratford to two speculators.[24] Anthony Nash would sue him in 1615. Within a very few years Greville was to have no property left.

The show-down, when it came, was terrible.

On 3 May 1602 Richard Quiney spent the day supervising the sale and exchange of horses at the Stratford fair and entering each transaction in the toll book.[25] That night he was making his nightly round of the town when he came upon some of Sir Edward Greville's men who, having been drinking all day, had begun brawling. The following account was written by Thomas Greene in preparation for the eventual lawsuit.

> there came some of [Greville's men] who being drunk fell to brawling in their host's house where they drank and drew their daggers on the host. [It being] fair time the Bailiff was late abroad to see the town in order and coming by in that hurley-burley came into the house and commanded the peace to be kept but could not prevail and in his endeavour to stifle the brawl had his head grievously broken by one of [Greville's] men whom neither [Greville] punished nor would suffer to be punished but with a show to turn them away and entertained again.[26]

It seems that Quiney never recovered full consciousness, for he made no will, either written nor oral, and appointed no executor or guardian for his children. We can only imagine the anguish of Bess Quiney and her children as he agonised for three terrible weeks before death released him. On 31 May he was buried. Bess found herself a lone parent of nine children who must have been deeply traumatised by their father's terrible death, and more and more demoralised as it became clear no one would be brought to book for his murder, even though there were witnesses to the event and everyone in Stratford knew who was responsible. The Corporation had never looked so irrelevant or so feeble, as its mad landlord rode roughshod over the criminal and civil law.

Another person who must have been almost as affected by Quiney's murder was Thomas Greene of the Middle Temple, who as solicitor for the Corporation had helped him prepare his suits to the Exchequer and the lord chancellor. After Quiney's return to Stratford, Greene had continued to give the case his full attention. In September 1598 he had succeeded in gaining access to Coke, who confirmed the right of the Corporation in the matter of the toll corn, and advised that the consent of Sir Edward Greville was not necessary for the installation of the bailiff. In October he had a third consultation with Coke and advised Quiney to hasten to London with the charter so that work could begin on drawing up a new one. It may have been Quiney's murder that prompted Greene to interest himself particularly in Stratford's struggle. He was to make his home in Stratford for nearly twenty years.

According to Fripp, Greene was 'an intimate friend of William Shakespeare, resident with him for some years at New Place, and proud to call the Poet "Cousin" '.[27] Unfortunately, it is as difficult to find evidence of real friendship between Shakespeare and Greene as it is between Shakespeare and Quiney. Greene certainly lived at New Place but he was more likely to meet Shakespeare in term-time in London than out of term in Stratford. Though Greene called Shakespeare 'cousin' we have no evidence that Shakespeare ever acknowledged the relationship. Coney-catchers (or conmen) gained the confidence of their victims by claiming cousinhood, which is why the activity is called cozening. Greene was beyond doubt an honest man but it has been impossible to establish any blood relationship between him and Shakespeare. We should probably infer that he was a kinsman of Ann's rather than Shakespeare's. Greene's father was Thomas Greene, a mercer, of Warwick, who died in 1590, five years before his son entered the Middle Temple from Staple Inn, where his membership fees were guaranteed by John Marston of Coventry and his son John, who would later turn dramatist.

In 1602, after Greene was called to the bar, he accepted a retainer from the Corporation of Stratford; his patent to serve as the steward of the Stratford Court of Record was sealed on 31 August 1603. At about the same time he married Lettice Chandler, the young widow of a Leicestershire mercer, and brought her to live at New Place. Not long afterwards, on 8 November 1603, Bess Quiney's daughter Elizabeth married Lettice Chandler's twenty-six-year-old widower stepson, the mercer William Chandler, who went into partnership with Bess in the mercery business, using one of her houses known as the Cage as his headquarters. Greene's father, Thomas Greene of Warwick, had served as master of the Warwick company of mercers, grocers and haberdashers, so it seems likely that this interlocking pair of marriages was engineered through the network of trading partners in mercery. Bess Quiney was certainly involved, but Ann Shakespeare too may have played her part, for without the offer of decent accommodation for the newly-weds at New Place the marriage could hardly have gone forward. Though the marriage was apparently arranged, it seems that Thomas and Lettice were very happy together. When Greene died in 1640, he left most of his estate to his 'most dear and loving wife, being sorry that [he had] no more to leave to so good a woman'.

If there was anyone in Stratford who realised just how conspicuous a figure Shakespeare cut in London it was Thomas Greene. The young gentlemen of the Inns of Court were passionate playgoers. Even after he became Town Clerk of Stratford, Greene lived during the terms in his chambers in the Middle Temple. It seems impossible that he did not keep Ann informed of her husband's triumphs, if no one else did. Greene may have had literary pretensions of his own. He is probably the Thomas Greene who penned a poem on the accession of James I called *A Poet's Vision and a Prince's Glory*, and he is probably the same Thomas Greene who contributed a commendatory poem for the 1603 edition of Drayton's *The Barons' Wars*. The conceit is daring, if not entirely felicitous.

> What ornament might I devise to fit
> Th'aspiring height of thy admirèd spirit,
> Or what fair garland worthy is to sit
> On thy blest brows that compass-in all merit?
> Thou shalt not crownèd be with common bays,
> Because for thee it is a crown too low.
> Apollo's tree can yield [but] simple praise;
> It is too dull a vesture for thy brow,
> But with a wreath of stars shalt thou be crowned
> Which, when thy working temples do sustain,
> Will, like the spheres be ever moving round
> After the royal music of thy brain.
> > Thy skill doth equal Phoebus, not thy birth.
> > He to Heaven gives music, thou to earth.

The Greenes' first child was born at New Place, baptised in Holy Trinity on 18 March 1604 and given the name Ann. The son who was christened on 17 January 1608 was given the name William. If he was therefore Shakespeare's godson, he was passed over in his will, as were all the Greenes (and for that matter all the Hathaways). Though New Place is repeatedly given as Greene's residence, and he may have lived there for more than ten years, Greene did not become the official householder; we know from entries in the record that, all through the period of Greene's residence at New Place, the mostly absent Master Shakespeare was identified as the householder. We should probably conclude that Greene and his wife and children occupied the equivalent of a serviced apartment in the big house, while they tried to find a home of their own which, given the shortage of housing after the fires, was no easy matter. Ann and her maids must have provided the Greenes with accommodation befitting a gentleman and his family; even after Greene had secured the title to St Mary's House, he was happy to continue at New Place, while the outgoing tenant found excuses to delay his departure. In September

1609 Greene wrote to Sir Henry Rainsford that he had agreed to let the sitting tenant George Browne sow his garden: 'I was content to permit it without contradiction and the rather because I perceived I might stay another year at New Place.'[28]

In 1617 when Greene came to sell St Mary's House he implied that he had lived there for only six years. The deciding factor may have been Shakespeare's retirement to Stratford, which most scholars think happened in about 1611. If Greene moved out of New Place at that point, and it seems he did, we have to conclude that he never lived with Shakespeare and was no great friend of his. We should probably see Greene as Ann's kinsman and Ann's friend, if a wife may be allowed to have such a thing.

CHAPTER FOURTEEN

of Susanna and her match with a gentleman of London and a
midsummer wedding at last

In September 1601 John Shakespeare died and was buried in Holy Trinity churchyard. If he left a will we can find no record of it, no inventory, nothing in the probate records. His son and heir, William Shakespeare, apparently disposed of his effects. One thing he saw fit to do was to issue a new lease of the Henley Street premises to Lewis Hiccox. As we have seen, when Hiccox died in 1627, this lease had still sixty-three years to run and was valued at £65.[1] The reference in his inventory to 'houses' should make clear that the Maiden Head Inn occupied both the east and west houses; what the sixty-three years represent is not so clear. The property was already leased in 1583; it seems that when he inherited the property the Bard granted a new lease of ninety-one years, probably because he needed to raise money.[2]

On 1 May 1602 Shakespeare parted with £320 in cash to William Combe of Warwick and his nephew John Combe for four yardlands amounting to 107 acres with rights of common in Old Stratford; as he was not himself present at the sealing of the deed, his brother Gilbert acted for him. The witnesses included Anthony and John Nash. The tenant-farmers were Lewis Hiccox and his brother Thomas.[3] This transaction bears the stamp of William rather than Ann, for he would go on to cultivate friendships with the Combes and Nashes, with whom Ann and her family had scant sympathy. As Whitgift's ecclesiastical commissioner, a post which he held from 1601 till his death in 1610, William Combe was involved albeit distantly in the rooting out of Calvinism from the established church. His nephew John Combe had grown rich by lending money at 10 per cent. In

1605 when Shakespeare bought for £440 from Ralph Hubaud of Ipsley a half-share in the tithes of Stratford and Old Stratford, he appointed Anthony Nash as his manager.

> To try to make too much of these transactions is risky, but speculation is excusable . . . Was it at this time that Shakespeare ceased to act, on a regular basis at least? And if so, was it because he was hoping to spend more time in Stratford now that his elder daughter was well into her marriageable years? He was fast turning her into a bourgeois heiress and could hardly be blamed for wanting to be on the spot to vet her suitors. He cannot have earned less than £250 per annum from his income as a sharer in the Globe, a playwright and a property owner. It must, at the very least, have been a temptation to divide his year more equitably between London and Stratford.[4]

Shakespeare seems to have resisted the temptation for ten years. In May 1602 Susanna turned nineteen, which was by no means 'well into her marriageable years'. Thought had been given to providing her with some sort of education; she could certainly read and she wrote a neat hand.[5] And as for 'wanting to be on the spot' we don't know if Susanna was in Stratford between 1602 and the time of her marriage there in 1607. She may have been sent into service years before. Thomson may find nothing far-fetched in the idea that young gentlemen were beseiging New Place begging the Bard for his daughter's hand; some such wishful thinking probably inspires Schoenbaum's impression that John Hall, the man Susanna eventually married, was living in Stratford before the wedding. Though Schoenbaum states confidently that 'Around 1600 he [Hall] settled in Stratford where he soon had a thriving medical practice', there is no evidence of Hall's having been in Stratford at all let alone 'settled' there at any time before his marriage to Susanna.[6]

If Shakespeare acquired the Old Stratford yardland because he was thinking of a marriage, it didn't happen. We hear nothing of any marriage until five years later, which is not to say that negotiations might not have been afoot in 1602. Susanna's marriage was certainly no rushed affair. It has all the hallmarks of a carefully arranged match. The prime mover could have been her father or her mother or herself, or her bridegroom's father, or a more distant kinsman or well-wisher. In *The Merry Wives of Windsor* Page chooses one bridegroom for his daughter Ann, his wife another, and the girl herself yet another. As for whether Susanna and John Hall knew each other before a match between them was proposed, we know nothing of the matter. We know that Susanna was in Stratford in 1606, the year before her marriage, because at Easter her name appeared on the list drawn up by the churchwardens and sidesmen of Holy Trinity as one of those who had not received the sacrament. One of the churchwardens was her uncle Bartholomew Hathaway. The offence was not considered trivial; if she had no excuse Susanna would have been fined a swingeing £20. Because seven of the twenty-one names on the list were suspected of being Catholics, Susanna's presence on the list becomes another card in the house of cards that is the Shakespeare-was-a-Catholic hypothesis. Susanna was summoned to attend the Vicar's Court but when she appeared her case was dismissed. By appearing, she had acknowledged the vicar's authority over her; often appearance and a promise of reformation were enough to fend off punishment. Catholic recusants usually preferred to stay away and pay the yearly fine. Hamnet and Judith Sadler were also summoned, but did not appear. Hamnet was often in trouble for providing bread and cakes on a Sunday; as Sunday trading may have produced the bulk of his weekly takings, he may have preferred to be excommunicated rather than confess himself at fault, but he was also being pursued by angry creditors. From 1597 or so Sadler was being sued on all sides for failure to pay for goods supplied and for defaulting on bonds of obligation.[7] On 13 January 1603 he appeared at the quarter sessions on a charge of baking contrary to the statute.[8]

In his submission to the Privy Council in 1577, the Bishop of Gloucester had identified three kinds of recusants: 'the third sort, commonly called Puritans wilfully refuse to come to church, as not liking the surplice, ceremonies and other service now used in the church . . .'[9] Given the fact that Susanna was to marry a strict puritan a year later it seems more likely that hers was puritan recusancy than that she was a Catholic. If she was a puritan Susanna would simply have been following the tendency of her mother's family, but if the ritual as practised by John Rogers did not alienate her Calvinist uncle, it's hard to see how it could have alienated her. If Susanna didn't stay away from church for doctrinal reasons, it could have been because she was away from Stratford. She may have been housekeeping for her uncle Gilbert in London or even for her father. If, as I shall argue, her younger sister went into the service of Bess Quiney, it seems only logical to consider the possibility that Susanna too found work outside her mother's household, and perhaps outside Stratford. However, given the Hathaway family's closeness to the church, it seems unlikely that the church officials would not have known that she was not then living in Stratford.

Susanna could have just been a bad girl, like Joan Tante: 'she useth not to stay in the church in service time and sermon time . . . going out of the church with beckoning of her finger and laughing . . .'[10] Joan seems to have been going through a bad patch; a few years later she was considered sufficiently deserving to be received into the almshouse. Elizabeth Wheeler wouldn't go to church and was continually brawling and abusing her neighbours. In the Vicar's Court, when questioned about her behaviour, she shouted, 'God's wounds! A plague upon you all! A fart of one's arse for you!'[11] Susanna simply appeared, and was forgiven. If Susanna's reason for non-attendance was that she was a Catholic, she betrayed her faith utterly when she married a puritan as uncompromising as John Hall, but her epitaph of 1649 could be interpreted to mean that she had been converted to right religion by her husband.

> Witty above her sex, but that's not all,
> Wise to salvation was good Mistress Hall.
> Something of Shakespeare was in that, but this
> Wholly of him with whom she's now in bliss.[12]

Susanna's bridegroom John Hall was born in Carlton in Bedfordshire in about 1576, and with his elder brother Dive studied at Queens' College Cambridge, graduating BA in 1594 and MA in 1597. What he did after that is not known, but it has been suggested that he studied medicine somewhere on the continent. He was never licensed by the Royal College of Physicians, nor did he secure a licence to practise medicine from the Bishop of Worcester. As a man of pronounced puritan sympathies, Hall may have been unwilling to submit to the authority of either institution. He was the second son of the physician William Hall, who had ten children besides. Four of his sisters had already made good matches, and at the time of John's marriage his father was living in Acton, a village north-west of London. Abraham Sturley may be the link between Stratford and the Halls; when he went down from Cambridge in about 1580 he took the position of legal agent for Sir Thomas Lucy of Charlcote, who held an estate at Pavenham in Bedfordshire, only a few miles from where John Hall was born. If William Hall had sent out the word to old friends that he was looking for a bride for his son, Sturley in Stratford may have bethought himself of Susanna, and may even have handled negotiations for the match and helped draw up the settlement.

No record of such a settlement has been found or indeed speculated about; but given Hall's status as a rising physician and Shakespeare's as a gentleman of means, it would in fact have been more unusual if the parties had not made the customary provisions for the settlement of lands on themselves and their heirs and provision for a jointure in the event of widowhood.[13]

Though it was customary for heiresses to share their father's estate, as the Arden women had done, Susanna seems to have been made sole heiress for the purposes of the match, with Hall's father correspondingly making John his chief legatee, disinheriting his elder brother Dive. In Deloney's novel, wealthy Jack of Newbury married, as his second wife, his housekeeper. To make the match, her poor parents scraped together twenty nobles and a yearling calf to give with her, along with the assurance that her new husband would be her father's sole legatee.

'O my good son,' quoth the old woman, 'God's benison be with thee forever more, for to tell thee true, we had sold all our kine to make money for my daughter's marriage, and this seven year we would not have been able to buy more. Notwithstanding we should have sold all that ever we had before my poor wench would have lost her marriage.'

'I,' quoth the old man, 'should have sold the coat from my back, and
my bed from under me, before my girl should have gone without
you.'[14]

If the documentation of Susanna's marriage should ever be found it
would probably make sense of Shakespeare's will. By securing such an
advantageous match for Susanna, Shakespeare severely limited the
marriage prospects of his other daughter. Twenty-first-century observers might find this behaviour distasteful, but it was by no means
unusual. Once the match was made, Shakespeare was legally bound to
respect the terms of the contract. If he left the matter to Ann, he may
have been surprised and displeased at how little room had been left
him when it came to disposing of his property. Without a settlement
Shakespeare could have left his property to Susanna and the heirs of
her body, bypassing John Hall, but this is not what happened. John
Hall became the outright owner of Shakespeare's estate after his
death, with the right to dispose of it as he wished. Scholars have
assumed that this reflected a particular trust placed in Hall by
Shakespeare, and because Shakespeare could do no wrong they have
assumed that the trust was justified. Ensuing events suggest otherwise.

We can now only wonder if Shakespeare knew how radical a
puritan his son-in-law was. The religious passion that drove his life
must have rather compromised his freedom to enjoy the fruits of
purveying licentious entertainment. After Shakespeare's death he lost
no time in getting rid of the house in Blackfriars. On 1 March 1625, he
sold all but a small part of the half-interest in the tithes that he had
inherited from Shakespeare back to the Corporation for less than
Shakespeare paid for them in 1605.[15] He would later claim he agreed a
price of £400 which was £100 below its true value, trusting to a
promise on the part of the Corporation to use the rental income to
improve the stipend of the radical puritan vicar, Thomas Wilson, a
promise that was not fulfilled. Hall then joined forces with Wilson to
bring an ill-conceived action in Chancery. In 1629 Hall's brother-in-
law Michael Welles, heir to Hall's elder brother Dive, sued him in
Chancery for failing to execute his father's will of 1607. Hall's excuse
was that he had given up the executorship 'in regard it should be a
hindrance . . . in his profession being a physician'.[16] After Hall died in

1635 having made only a nuncupative will, debts to the tune of £77 13s 4d were not paid out of the estate, though apparently there was money to cover them. The result was that bailiffs broke into New Place and removed 'divers books, boxes, desks, monies, bills and other goods of great value', possibly including books and papers of Shakespeare's.[17]

Though he used the arms of Shakespeare impaled with those of Hall, Hall chose to pay a fine rather than accept a knighthood.[18] He presented Holy Trinity with a carved pulpit and served as church-warden in 1628–9. He was elected to the Corporation three times but did not agree to serve until 1632, and then he found himself in opposition to the bailiff and other aldermen and was dismissed within a year.

The Shakespeare–Hall wedding may have followed the old custom of bedding the bride first and going to church afterwards, for Susanna's only child was born thirty-seven-and-a-half weeks after the solemnisation.

Local tradition holds that the Halls lived in a handsome half-timbered house in Old Town, close to Holy Trinity, and even closer to New Place. The spacious dwelling had an ample garden in which Dr Hall could cultivate the herbs and simples he used in his cures. Today the house is called Hall's Croft, but I have been able to find no reference to it by that name earlier than the listing of Hall Croft in *Spenell's Family Almanack . . . for 1885*.[19]

For people sniffing for the spoor of Shakespeare 'Hall Croft' morphs easily into Hall's Croft. We can probably dismiss the idea of John and Susanna Hall's living in any such place. Hall did not need to grow his own simples, and would have been ill advised to sully his gentlemanly hands by doing anything of the kind. He did not after all supply the actual remedies to his patients – that was the jealously guarded province of the apothecaries. Every morning herb-women would have come into Stratford, bringing plant material they had gathered from cottage gardens, woodland, fields and hedgerows to sell to the townswomen who would use them in cooking and preserving, and in treating the everyday ailments of their families. If a Stratford apothe-cary had received a prescription from Hall that demanded fresh botanical material, and if he hadn't bought it fresh that day from a herb-wife, he would simply have sent an errand boy to the market to buy the necessary handfuls or off into the hedgerows and woodlands to collect it. The idea of Hall digging in his own version of the Chelsea Physic Garden is merely fanciful.

On 12 December 1607 William Hall called his lawyers, made his will and promptly died. On 24 December, in London, John Hall proved the will and came into possession of Butlers, his father's house in Acton. Though he kept the house, he did not choose to take over his father's practice. His father left him all his 'books of physic'; his assistant, Matthew Morris inherited all his 'books of astronomy and astrology' with instructions to teach John if he should 'intend and purpose to labour study and endeavour in the said art', and his books of alchemy.[20] Morris, who had Stratford connections, eventually settled in Stratford and married a local girl.

Hall's original intention may have been to live as a gentleman, pursuing his medical studies as Cerimon does in *Pericles*, which was entered in the Stationers' Register on 20 May 1608:

> 'Tis known I ever
> Have studied physic, through which secret art,
> By turning over authorities, I have,
> Together with my practice, made familiar
> To me and to my aid the blest infusions
> That dwells in vegetatives, in metals, stones,
> And so can speak of the disturbances
> That nature works, and of her cures, which doth give me
> A more content and cause of true delight
> Than to be thirsty after tottering honour,
> Or tie my pleasure up in silken bags
> To glad the fool and death. (III. ii. 31–42)

Stratford boasted a number of barber–surgeons, who amputated limbs, let blood, set broken bones and lanced boils upon occasion, while a proliferating array of pills and potions was supplied to patients who could pay their huge prices by a number of local apothecaries. Otherwise it was the duty of women to care for the health of all members of the household, and for any dependent poor. Experienced women like Ann Shakespeare attended childbeds and deathbeds and gave primary treatment and preliminary diagnoses of illnesses and accidents. Most people had to make do with unprofessional care, because doctors' fees were astronomical. When John Hall began calling himself 'doctor' Hall and riding all over the county and beyond to visit patients, he did it for money. In 'The Preface to the Reader' in his edition of his translation of Hall's casebooks, James Cooke provides an insight into how the matter was handled:

> Their Honours [the Greville family of Beauchamp Court], when Physicians were with them, were always ready to engage them to be helpful to their sick Neighbours, the advices for such being for most part entrusted in my hands. I hope what is made public can be no wrong to any of those physicians, having for their pains, prescriptions and directions, received generous pay and noble entertainment.[21]

In Act V scene iii of *Macbeth*, the doctor, who is silent until Macbeth interrogates him about his wife's health, can say little but that she is 'troubled with thick-coming fancies'. 'Cure her of that,' snaps Macbeth, and taunts him with a mock demand for a 'sweet oblivious antidote' to 'cleanse the fraught bosom'. The doctor replies, a little smugly, that the patient will have to do that for herself, and gets a response that many would have cheered: 'Throw physic to the dogs. I'll none of it.' Obliged to remain until he is dismissed, the poor doctor has to endure more of Macbeth's sneering at his profession, unable as he is to 'cast the water' (examine the urine) of Scotland or remove the English by resort to 'rhubarb, cyme or purgative drug'. As he slinks off-stage, the doctor tells us:

> Were I from Dunsinane away and clear
> Profit again should hardly draw me here. (V. iii. 39–64)

As an outgrowth of bardolatry, Hall's image as a country doctor has been sentimentalised; we are told that he would travel many miles to see his patients, that he treated puritan and papist alike and that he occasionally treated poor people. In fact Hall had to ride such long distances because he treated the far-flung gentry rather than the needy townsfolk. His surviving case-notes reveal that he rarely treated poor people (and never, I suspect, without a fee) and when he did he prescribed much cheaper medications than he did for well-heeled clients. He certainly treated papists, but he never failed to mark them in his casebook as such.

Hall's own case-notes reveal him to have been typical in that he prescribed a bewildering array of infusions, decoctions, juleps, linctuses, electuaries, fumes, plasters, purges, emetics, stomachics, stimulants, expectorants, poultices and sudorifics, made of ingredients drawn from all over the known world.

> The *Pharmacopoeia Londinensis* of 1618 in its *Catalogus Simplicium* listed 1,190 simples or crude drugs, a collection supported by centuries of medical tradition, superstition and credulity. They were arranged under the headings: roots, barks, woods, leaves, flowers, fruits, seeds, gums, juices, plant excrements (for example, tree fungi), whole animals, animal parts and excrements, marina (things belonging to the sea) and salts, metals and minerals (which included precious stones). In practice the range of drugs prescribed by the physicians and stocked by the apothecaries tended to be smaller in number than the pharmacopoeial lists. John Hall . . . used just under 300 vegetable drugs, thirty-nine animal drugs and thirty-eight mineral items.[22]

Hall made notes in Latin on all his cases; in 1644 Warwickshire physician James Cooke visited New Place and bought two manuscript books of Latin case-notes from Susanna Hall; one of these he translated and published in 1657 as *Select Observations*, with a second and third edition in 1679 and 1683. The second edition states on the title-page that the collection features 'Eminent Persons in Desperate Diseases'; the earliest of these cases dates from 1611, which suggests that Hall's rise to eminence as the physician preferred by the local gentry was fairly slow. He seems to have conformed to the stereotype of the physician as rendered by Sir John Davies.

> I study to uphold the slippery life of man,
> Who dies when I have done the best and all I can.

From practice and from books I draw my skill,
Not from the known receipts or pothecary's bill.
The earth my faults does hide; the world my cures doth see;
What youth and time effects is oft ascribed to me.[23]

Certainly, there is little in Hall's own account of his practice that seems likely to have been effective. The treatments he ordered, especially for the wealthiest patients, could contain anything from pills of amber, resins from the East Indies, powdered pearls and crushed coral, gold leaf, shavings of ivory, sassafras from north America, camphor from China, mechoacan from Mexico, an array of gums from the Middle East, powdered mummy, benzoin, grains of paradise, galingale, bezoar stone (found in the stomachs of Persian goats), bole from Armenia, and so forth. If any of these worked it must have been as shock treatment or aversion therapy, derived from the sheer complexity of the preparation and administration, together with the drama of cupping and purging, fasting and sweating, not to mention the enormous cost.

Throughout Hall's practice there runs a vein of something more practical, treatments that availed themselves of herbs to be found in every hedgerow. Even the Countess of Northampton was given a fancy version of Hall's humble 'Scorbutic Beer':

[Take] scurvy-grass [four handfuls], watercress, brooklime, each, [2 handfuls], wormwood, fumitory and germander, each [one handful], roots of fennel, borage, succory, each [an ounce], root of elecampane [half an ounce], licorice [an ounce], flowers of borage, bugloss, rosemary, each [two pinches]. Boil them all in five gallons of beer till one be wasted. After having the following ingredients in a bag, viz., sarsaparilla, Calamus aromaticus, cinnamon, mace, seeds of anise and fennel, each half an ounce, juniper berries eight. Let them be infused in the hot liquor, well covered till it be cold, after put it up, hanging the bag in it. After fifteen days she drank of it, using no other; this she drank in April.[24]

The fact that *Cochlearia officinalis* is known as scurvy-grass is a pretty good indication that herb-women knew of its usefulness in treating scurvy long before Hall began to write out Latin prescriptions for it. Scurvy-grass was cried every day in the streets of every town in England. Among the many responsibilities of the goodwife was that of caring for the health of her household, treating any injuries and preparing remedies for what might ail them. Gerard published his *Herbal* in 1597 for the use of 'virtuous gentlewomen'.

> I send this jewel unto you women of all sorts, especially to such as cure and help the poor and impotent of your country without reward. But unto the beggarly rabble of witches, charmers and such-like cozeners, that regard more to get money than to help for charity, I wish these few medicines far from their understanding, and from those deceivers whom I wish to be ignorant therein.[25]

For all we know to the contrary, Hall may have learnt a good deal from women like Ann Shakespeare before beginning his practice. He may have acquired the recipe for his scorbutic beer from the wise women of Stratford, perhaps even from Ann. The resulting liquor was rich in the Vitamin C necessary to fend off scurvy.

In 1585 William Clowes inveighs against quacks, people who daily rush into Physic and Surgery:

> And some of them be painters, some glaziers, some tailors, some weavers, some joiners, some cutlers, some cooks, some bakers, and some chandlers, etc. Yea, nowadays it is too apparent to see how tinkers, tooth-drawers, idiots, apple-squires, broom-men, bawds, witches, conjurers, soothsayers and sow-gelders, rogues, rat-catchers, runagates and proctors of Spittlehouses, with such other like rotten weeds do in town and country, without order, honesty or skill, daily abuse both physic and surgery . . .[26]

John Cotta, a Warwickshire MD (Cambridge) who practised in Northampton, was particularly irritated by roving amateurs like John Hall, who certainly trespassed on his preserves in Northamptonshire.[27] Though Hall's calling may seem exalted to us now, it was regarded by many of Shakespeare's contemporaries with deep suspicion. Master Caius 'that calls himself doctor of physic', in *The Merry*

Wives of Windsor, lists all the local nobility and gentry, 'the earl, the knight, the lords, the gentlemen', among his patients. Dr Caius may be a caricature of the lumpen Paracelsian practitioners of Europe, who had had no education in the liberal arts and could not read or write Latin or defend themselves in terms recognised by the medical establishment. As they were often Huguenots they also suffered religious persecution; we might expect Hall, as a dedicated protestant, to have come under the influence of the Paracelsians in Basel or Geneva, perhaps, or in any of a number of German and French cities. 'Paracelsian ideas, often of a debased kind, spread among herbalists and apothecaries and were adopted by unlicensed physicians.'[28]

However, there is no sign in Hall's account of his own practice in *Select Observations* of any receptivity to the radical doctrines of Paracelsus, who had come to medicine after serving as an army doctor, and actually dosed his patients and operated on them himself. Hall makes no use of 'chemical medicine' or of Paracelsian specifics such as antimony. Nevertheless, the fact that his practice is profoundly conservative need not exclude the possibility that he had returned to England aflame with the new ideas and spent years studying how best to put them into practice, before giving way to the expectations of his patients. Though his recorded practice begins in 1611, the year in which the renowned Paracelsian Theodore de Mayerne arrived in London to be welcomed by the universities and the Royal College of Physicians and favourably received by the king who made him his personal physician, it seems that Hall did not begin to write up his cases until 1622, when Paracelsianism was both out of fashion and out of favour.

If Dr Caius in *The Merry Wives of Windsor* is not a Paracelsian it is difficult to discern what the point is of making him French in the first place. He makes reference to simples in his closet that he would not for the world leave behind, which suggests that he is conflating the traditionally separate roles of physician and apothecary and, like many Paracelsians, he cannot read Latin. According to Parson Evans, who is admittedly a hostile witness, Caius 'hath no more knowledge in Hibocrates and Galen' than a mess of porridge (III. i. 61–2). Mine host of the Garter Inn joins in the ridicule of Caius' professional pretensions, calling him 'Euscalapius', 'Galen' and a 'Castalian-king-urinal'.

Testing of urine, holding it up to the light to judge transparency, viscosity and colour, as well as smelling and tasting it, was one of the few diagnostic techniques available to the early-seventeenth-century physician.

One of Sir John Davies's distinctly nasty epigrams is addressed to a gentleman who has turned physician:

> Philo the gentleman, the fortune-teller,
> The schoolmaster, the midwife and the bawd,
> The conjurer, the buyer and the seller
> Of painting which with breathing will be thawed,
> Does practise physic and his credit grows . . .[29]

Though scholarly debate seems to have come to rest on a date of 1597 for the first performance of *The Merry Wives of Windsor*, it first appears in the Revels Accounts for 1604. If the play was written before Hall entered Shakespeare's life, we have a mildly spooky incidence of foresight; if afterwards, the possibilities are rather more disturbing. Susanna was Shakespeare's heiress as Ann is Page's. Ann's outburst when she is threatened with Caius as a husband sounds something a real Stratford girl might have said:

> Alas! I had rather be set quick i'th'earth
> And bowled to death with turnips! (III. iv. 86–7)

It is Ann's mother who wants her to marry Dr Caius; her father wants her to marry Shallow's kinsman Abraham Slender. Perhaps it was Ann who was the chief mover of the match with John Hall.

As Susanna prepared for her wedding, the west midlands broke out in riots.

In the early summer of 1607 Warwickshire was disturbed by 'tumultuous assemblies' against the enclosure of commons and 'depopulations'. Landlord aggression was worse than under Elizabeth, and the commoners, despairing of redress from James's corrupt and weak government, took the law into their own hands. Cecil wrote to Winwood in Holland to reassure him against exaggerated rumours of riot, that the 'rabble' had done no 'harm to any person living but in pulling down hedges and ditches' and the Lieutenants of the Shires had been 'directed to suppress them by fair or foul means'. There was alarm in Stratford. Sir Edward Greville as lord of the manor was again to the fore. The gaol was put in order, and extra accommodation for prisoners, if needed, was provided at the Gild Hall, the town-chest being removed from the armoury. The stocks too were mended.[30]

Amid the uproar, on 5 June 1607, Susanna Shakespeare married John Hall at Holy Trinity. Midsummer marriages were rare; theirs was the only wedding in Stratford that June. Ann had a long summer day in which to regale the wedding guests with the best of her ale and wine, and the spiced cakes and comfits that were traditional, as well as more substantial fare. Flushed with her exertions all that long hot day, she must have been the original for the shepherd's wife in *The Winter's Tale*.

> This day she was both pantler, butler, cook,
> Both dame and servant, welcomed all, served all,
> Would sing her song and dance her turn, now here
> At th'upper end o'the table, now i'the middle,
> On his shoulder and his, her face afire
> With labour and the thing she took to quench it
> She would to each one sip. (IV. iv. 56–62)

The feast was for everyone in Stratford, including those too poor to own a wedding garment. Even the almsfolk and the paupers had the right to drink the bride's health. Everyone must have been there, the burgeoning Hathaway clan led by Susanna's uncle, the churchwarden, Mary Shakespeare and her bachelor sons, the Harts, the Quineys, the Sadlers, perhaps even the bride's father with the King's Men, whose musicians might have played for the dancing under the mulberry trees.

CHAPTER FIFTEEN

of Ann's reading of the sonnets

In the summer of 1609 a visitation of the plague closed the theatres and we may assume perhaps that Shakespeare was at home in Stratford. Meanwhile Thomas Thorpe, who specialised in notorious texts by celebrities, published *Shakespeare's Sonnets: Never before Imprinted*. The year before he had published Chapman's scandalous *Conspiracy and Tragedy of Charles Duke of Biron*, which had been suppressed by order of the king, and Jonson's *Masque of Blackness* and *Masque of Beauty* which had been sensations when they were performed at court. We should probably conclude therefore that in 1609 Shakespeare was a celebrity of the same magnitude. Ever since Francis Meres had referred to the 'sugared sonnets' that circulated among Shakespeare's 'private friends' in his *Palladis Tamia: Wit's Treasury* of 1598, there had been a good deal of interest and gossip about them. Someone into whose hands copies of the sonnets fell sold them to Thomas Thorpe; what Thorpe acquired is thought by most scholars to have been a complete transcript, probably copied out by more than one scribe, if inconsistencies of spelling and diction are any guide. The possibility that additional sonnets were obtained from other sources cannot be ruled out. Thorpe registered his copyright at the Stationers' Company in May 1609 and hired George Eld to print the copy. As was normal in those days, the author, unless he actually sold the copy to the printer himself, received nothing. What Thorpe and his printer eventually produced was a collection of 154 sonnets and a narrative poem in forty-seven stanzas of rime royal called 'A Lover's Complaint'. Only two of the sonnets had appeared in print before. In 1599 rather different versions of Sonnets 138 and 144 had been the only poems by Shakespeare that appeared in William Jaggard's compilation *The Passionate Pilgrim by William Shakespeare.*

It may be that with everybody keeping clear of plague-ridden London the Shakespeares didn't notice the liberty that Thorpe had taken. In August 1608 Richard Burbage acquired for the King's Men the lease of the Blackfriars Theatre. This was the same building that James Burbage had refurbished in 1597, only to be prevented from using it by a petition from local residents; his sons had then leased it to Henry Evans, the entrepreneur who managed the boy actors. Their performance of *The Conspiracy and Tragedy of Charles Duke of Biron* so scandalised the French ambassador that the theatre was closed down, and Evans was obliged to surrender his lease. When the theatres reopened that autumn Shakespeare was writing for two theatres, plus the command performances at court and wherever else their royal patron required. Busier than he had ever been before in his life, he probably had no time to deal with Thorpe's edition. He could have insisted on corrections, supposing the book was still in press, but he didn't.

Thorpe, the son of a London innkeeper, kept no shop of his own. Of the thirteen copies of the little quarto that now survive two lack title-pages. Of the other eleven, seven are advertised as to be sold by William Aspley and and four by John Wright at his dwelling at Christ Church Gate. What this means about the sales of the volume is uncertain; given the dog days and the plague they may well have sold slowly. There would be no second edition. Shakespeare might have used his influence as a leading member of the King's Men to have the book covertly withdrawn from sale. Certainly, compared to the splash made by *Venus and Adonis*, which was still being regularly reprinted, the sonnets made no impact whatsoever.

How long it took for the first copy to turn up in Stratford we cannot tell, but anyone who knows small-town mores will be certain that it was not long before some 'well-wisher' made sure that the book was placed in Ann's hands. Perhaps it contained no surprises. If Will had accepted a commission in 1590 or so from a noble lady who wanted him to write a sonnet sequence persuading her playboy son to marriage, Ann would have been unsurprised to find it at last in unauthorised print and amused perhaps by the riddling dedication

with which Thorpe tried to disguise his ignorance of the provenance
of his copytext.

> To the only begetter of these ensuing sonnets Mr. W. H. all happiness
> and that eternity promised by our ever-living poet wisheth the well-
> wishing adventurer in setting forth.

Nothing about this makes sense. Ann could have made sense of it,
probably, if she chose. If, as some scholars think, Mr W. H. is the
begetter in the sense that he made possible the printing by supplying
Thorpe with the copy, some have suggested that W. H. may stand
for William Hathaway, Ann's half-brother. If this were the case, then
William might well have had the copy from Ann or her husband.
Hathaway was certainly struggling; perhaps rather than giving him
money the Shakespeares had given him the copy to sell for what he
could get. It is even possible that Ann had done it on her own initiative,
a possibility – and a ground for Shakespeare's disliking her and cutting
all the Hathaways out of his will – that no scholar has ever considered.
There is a school of thought that holds that Shakespeare engineered the
publication himself. If he did he could have used William Hathaway;
however, before getting too carried away with this idea, we must take
account of the fact that William Hathaway was not entitled to be
addressed as 'Master'.

Whatever the truth of the matter, even if Ann had never seen the
poems before, there would have been no question of a sudden and
painful discovery that her husband was homosexual. In 1609 the word
'homosexual' did not exist. All non-reproductive sexual activity was
sodomy, whether carried out alone or with others of either or both
sexes. Though all kinds of sexual proclivities were known about in
the early seventeenth century and roundly discussed as examples of
human depravity, none was assumed to be pathological or congenital.
Unprincipled thrill-seekers would, it was assumed, draw the line at
nothing. Whatever form their lechery took it would damn their souls to
hell. No contemporary gossip associates Shakespeare with buggery,
although boy players were thought by puritans to act the part of
women off as well as on the stage. It would have been literally
unthinkable that William Shakespeare, commoner, would commit

to poetry his attempts to seduce a youth of higher rank than himself. If the sonnets had been interpreted as any such thing they would have been suppressed, and all known copies burnt. Thorpe would never have dared openly to publish them. Sodomy, if proven, was a hanging matter.

The most popular candidate for the role of beloved youth has for more than a century been Henry Wriothesley, Earl of Southampton. If Thorpe had meant to give a clue to the other party in a sodomitical relationship by his reference to Mr W. H., he must have been very sure that no one would understand it as referring to a real-life magnate of the rank of Southampton. Anyone who could be shown to have defamed a peer of the realm, whether the allegations were true or false, could be hauled before the Court of Star Chamber on a writ of scandalum magnatum and punished severely; the peer referred to also had the right of recovery of damages, whether he was materially affected by the allegations or not. The last thing that Thorpe intended by referring to Mr W. H. was to suggest that a peer of the realm with the initials H. W. was the catamite of a popular playwright. He is probably not referring to any such person. The only other evidence we have for an intimate relationship between the glover's son and the peer consists in the fulsome dedications of Shakespeare's epyllia which are nowadays barbarously interpreted as indicating genuine, real-life intimacy. The dedication of *The Rape of Lucrece* in particular seems to go beyond mere courtly compliment:

To the Right Honourable Henry Wriothesley, Earl of Southampton, and Baron of Tichfield,
The love I dedicate to your Lordship is without end, whereof this pamphlet without beginning is but a superfluous moiety. The warrant I have of your Honourable disposition, not the worth of my untutored lines, makes it assured of acceptance. What I have done is yours, what I have to do is yours, being part in all I have devoted yours. Were my worth greater, my duty would show greater. Meantime, as it is, it is bound to your Lordship, to whom I wish long life lengthened with all happiness.

Your Lordship's in all duty,
William Shakespeare.

The self-conscious eloquence of this has nothing to do with intimacy and everything to do with publicity. One is reminded of Sir Walter Ralegh,

> Our passions are most like to floods and streams:
> The shallow murmur, but the deep are dumb.[1]

Like Southampton, Ralegh fell in love with one of Elizabeth's maids of honour, twenty-seven-year-old Elizabeth Throckmorton; when the queen discovered the relationship in the summer of 1592, both were imprisoned in the Tower.[2] The love for which Ralegh brought to a catastrophic halt his meteoric career as a royal favourite inspired not a single line of poetry. In disgrace he penned 'The Ocean's Love to Cynthia', in twenty-two books, the longest and most extravagant love poem in the English language, dedicated not to the woman for whom he had sacrificed everything, but to his tormentor, Elizabeth I.

> But that the eyes of my mind held her beams
> In every part transferred by love's swift thought,
> Far off or near, in waking or in dreams,
> Imagination strong their lustre brought.[3]

The language of real love as distinct from the courtly affectation of love reads like this, Ralegh's letter to his wife on what he thought was the eve of his execution:

> You shall now receive, (my dear wife) my last words in these my last lines. My love I send you, that you may keep it when I am dead, and my counsel, that you may remember it when I am no more. I would not, by my will, present you with sorrows (dear Bess). Let them go into the grave with me and be buried in the dust. And seeing it is not the will of God that ever I shall see you any more in this life, bear my destruction gently and with a heart like thyself.[4]

Ralegh had in fact fifteen more years of married life. The letter was famous among his contemporaries and much copied.[5] In a similar case, thinking he was to pay the ultimate price for his role in Essex's Rebellion, Southampton wrote to his countess from the Tower, addressing her as 'sweetheart', 'doubt not but I shall do well [that is, meet death bravely] and bless yourself with the assurance that I shall ever remain your affectionate Husband'. The letter was endorsed, 'To my Bess'.[6]

In trumpeting his devotion in the dedication of *The Rape of Lucrece* the poet is actually reminding Southampton of his obligations towards him, because he has devoted his literary activity to him, not because he is devoted to him. Southampton was the most active literary patron of the 1590s; Shakespeare reminds his lordship, with a tinge of tartness, that, while he may have other protégés, under the terms of their past relationship Shakespeare is bound to a single patron, himself. The language may be the language of idolatry, but South-ampton is quite capable of registering the nuance and appreciating the irony. Similarly, extravagant though their language of love may be, no one who read the sonnets before the nineteenth century imagined their context to be a consummated sexual relationship between men. Idealistic friendship did not involve buggery, regardless of what classical scholars have always known about same-sex relationships in antiquity. In 1609 Southampton, who had been released from his second spell of prison by James I on his accession, was thirty-six years old, a highly visible and successful courtier and merchant adventurer, the attentive husband of a court beauty and father of five children. He was also notoriously quick to take affront. If there had been any suggestion that one of his erstwhile protégés was exposing him to potentially harmful gossip, Southampton would have had him si-lenced, probably for ever, and the offending books destroyed. If we are to understand the sonnets we cannot treat them as documentation of a real-life relationship and we may hope that Ann did not.

The sonnets as published by Thomas Thorpe begin straightfor-wardly enough. The poet urges a young man to abandon self-love, marry and procreate. For the first twelve sonnets the young man is addressed as 'thou', and suddenly in the thirteenth there is a change. The person addressed is 'you' rather than 'thou', and the poet dares to address him, or her, as 'my love'. In the following sonnet we revert to the 'thou' form of address, and back to 'you' for the next three. It is conceivable if not obvious that the 'thou' and the 'you' are not the same person and the relationship not the same relationship. In Sonnet 145 Ann would have encountered herself as Will's relenting mistress.[7]

John Kerrigan sums up the problems that this fact – if it is a fact – poses for the whole collection:

> Was [Sonnet 145] included for sentimental reasons? Did it find its way into Shakespeare's manuscript by mistake? Was it inserted by a scribe, by Thorpe, or by someone at Eld's printing shop? More than any other sonnet 145 casts doubt on the authority and order of [Thorpe's text].[8]

Indeed. If one of the 154 sonnets is written by Shakespeare for his wife, why should not others too be addressed to her? Some of the sonnets appear to date from the early 1590s; others seem later, some much later. If, as we have supposed, the boy Will courted the woman Ann with poetry – and the existence of Sonnet 145 is part of the case – then his may not have been the only poetry that Ann read. She may have been aware of the sonnet craze of the 1590s and had a much better understanding of the context and the rules of the sonnet game that is vouchsafed to us today. A man does not write sonnets to his wife; 'deep-brained sonnets' are part of a seduction game – unless we are to understand a context of estrangement and an attempt to repair a damaged relationship. All English love poetry – probably all love poetry – is about distance and disappointment. Gratified desire does not feel the need to versify.

The persuasion of the young man to marry gradually gives way to a boast by the poet that the young man will be known to posterity not through the issue of his loins but because he, Shakespeare, has made him immortal in his verse. What is absurd about this claim is that though everybody knows the verse, nobody knows the identity of the young man, who may be several interchangeable young men. As far as description goes he is generic, young, lovely, with bright eyes and hair like marjoram buds; there is no identikit portrait, no blazon of his physical charms, not even a pun on his name. There are some sonnets that don't seem to be about any 'him' at all.

> So is it not with me as with that Muse,
> Stirred by a painted beauty to his verse,
> Who heaven itself for ornament doth use,
> And every fair with his fair doth rehearse,
> Making a couplement of proud compare

With sun and moon, with earth and sea's rich gems,
With April's first-born flowers and all things rare
That heaven's air in this huge rondure hems.
O, let me true in love, but truly write,
And then believe me, my love is as fair
As any mother's child, though not so bright
As those gold candles fixed in heaven's air.
  Let them say more that like of hearsay well;
  I will not praise that purpose not to sell. (21)

So may a man celebrate the worth of his wife, whom he does not
wish to share with the rest of the world. We know from his extreme
reticence that, however hyperbolically he might write of a distant
patron, Shakespeare did not 'like of hearsay well'. If his brother
chaffed him about never praising the beauty of his wife, he might have
answered in this vein, slightly testily, recalling his commitment to her
and her children, and her equal status with him in the 'one flesh' of
wedlock. Some of the sonnets ask forgiveness for neglect, again in
terms that seem ill sorted for a relationship between a young and
lovely nobleman and a poeticising commoner. We can hardly
imagine the young Earl of Southampton complaining like a neglected
wife that the man Shakespeare never told him that he loved him.

As an unperfect actor on the stage,
Who with his fear is put besides his part,
Or some fierce thing replete with too much rage,
Whose strength's abundance weakens his own heart,
So I, in fear of trust, forget to say
The perfect ceremony of love's rite,
And in mine own love's strength seem to decay,
O'ercharged with burden of mine own love's might.
O, let my books be then the eloquence
And dumb presagers of my speaking breast,
Who plead for love and look for recompense
More than that tongue that more hath more expressed.
  O learn to read what silent love hath writ;
  To hear with eyes belongs to love's fine wit. (23)

There was no 'perfect ceremony' to bind Shakespeare to his lovely boy, but he was so bound to Ann. It is not fashionable to suggest that he cared what she thought of what he did, but what writer–husband would be totally indifferent to his wife's opinion? What husband challenged by his wife would not say that everything he did was for love of her, even is she was never mentioned in any of it?

> Let those who are in favour with their stars
> Of public honour and proud titles boast,
> Whilst I, whom fortune of such triumph bars,
> Unlooked for joy in that I honour most.
> Great princes' favourites their fair leaves spread
> But as the marigold in the sun's eye,
> And in themselves their pride lies burièd,
> For at a frown they in their glory die.
> The painful warrior famousèd for fight,
> After a thousand victories once foiled,
> Is from the book of honour razèd quite,
> And all the rest forgot for which he toiled.
>   Then happy I that love and am beloved
>   Where I may not remove or be removed. (25)

The only relationship from which Shakespeare could not 'remove or be removed' was the one he had with his wife. This may not have been what he meant, for he may have been crediting the ideal lover with ideal constancy, but it is the obvious significance of the words he chooses here. Perhaps what Ann read as she leafed through Thorpe's little book were versions of sonnets that had once been written to her and had been reworked for another purpose. In 1609 Ann was fifty-three and unlikely to have given too much importance to rhymes written so long ago, but she was still without her husband's company for most of the year. Stratford citizens visiting London probably brought back excited tales of the theatres and who knows that her daughters did not beg their mother to come with them to see their father's plays?

Perhaps Ann was moved by the travelling Sonnets 27 and 28,

remembering the early days when Will first rode off to London leaving her and his children behind.

> Weary with toil I haste me to my bed,
> The dear repose for limbs with travel tired,
> But then begins a journey in my head
> To work my mind when body's work's expired,
> For then my thoughts from far where I abide,
> Intend a zealous pilgrimage to thee,
> And keep my drooping eyelids open wide,
> Looking on darkness which the blind do see –
> Save that my soul's imaginary sight
> Presents thy shadow to my sightless view,
> Which like a jewel hung in ghastly night
> Makes black night beauteous and her old face new.
> > Lo, thus by day my limbs, at night my mind,
> > For thee, and for myself, no quiet find. (27)

When Will rode off to seek his fortune he was on his own for the first time in his life. He may well have suffered the loneliness and anxiety, the frustration and disappointment that resound from this group of sonnets. A similar note is sounded in Sonnet 50:

> How heavy do I journey on the way
> When what I seek, my weary travel's end,
> Doth teach that ease and that repose to say
> 'Thus far the miles are measured from thy friend'.
> The beast that bears me, tired with my woe,
> Plods dully on, to bear that weight in me,
> As if by some instinct the wretch did know
> His rider loved not speed being made from thee.
> The bloody spur cannot provoke him on
> That sometimes anger thrusts into his hide,
> Which heavily he answers with a groan
> More sharp to me than spurring to his side,
> > For that same groan doth put this in my mind:
> > My grief lies onward and my joy behind.

Scholars have preferred to think that these were the feelings that afflicted Shakespeare as he rode towards Ann and his family rather than away from them. There is no hard evidence either way. Even the term 'friend' in the third line does not exclude Ann. A friend for life was one of the promises made in 'The Bride's Goodmorrow'; the term hardly fits the master–mistress of the poet's passion, because friends are meant to be *similes inter pares*, of equal standing, in perfect reciprocity. Sonnet 52 refers to the infrequency of his visits to his 'friend', like feasts 'so solemn and so rare', which reminds us that he would return to Stratford for those very feasts. The imagery of the chest and the wardrobe and even the 'up-locked treasure' might be taken to imply his home rather than the rather cheerless lodgings he could expect in London. All of which is not to say that Shakespeare's sonnets are addressed to his wife, but that perhaps once, before they were prepared for publication, some of them had been meant for her. Praise of the beloved for constancy, as in Sonnet 53, seems ill directed towards the young man. If Shakespeare assumed different masks for different sequences and different imagined readers, it is no more than we should expect. It seems not unreasonable that one of his masks was the aspect that he showed to his wife.

Perhaps Ann had seen this sonnet long before it appeared in print:

> When in disgrace with fortune and men's eyes,
> I all alone beweep my outcast state,
> And trouble deaf heaven with my bootless cries,
> And look upon myself and curse my fate,
> Wishing me like to one more rich in hope,
> Featured like him, like him with friends possessed,
> Desiring this man's art and that man's scope,
> With what I most enjoy contented least,
> Yet in these thoughts myself almost despising,
> Haply I think on thee and then my state,
> Like to the lark at break of day arising
> From sullen earth, sings hymns at heaven's gate.
> > For thy sweet love remembered such wealth brings
> > That then I scorn to change my state with kings. (29)

Such a sonnet is barely fit for the eyes of a patron, or for that matter for a paramour of the moment. It speaks of solitude and distance self-imposed, of ambition thwarted, of disadvantage in the sphere of his endeavour, all to be expected of a half-educated young man taking on the London theatre industry at its own game. If it referred to a woman keeping a home for him, remaining true to her bond with him regardless of his uselessness as a provider, it would make sense. If instead of plaudits and profits he could send home only a sonnet such as this, Ann would have been more than satisfied. The same could be said of the sonnet that follows it in Thorpe's edition. After a catalogue of repinings it ends:

> But if the while I think on thee, dear friend,
> All losses are restored and sorrows end. (30)

The most direct of the sonnets is also the least applicable to a crush on a first, second or third young man, however seductive and brilliant. Sonnet 110 reads like an apology to his oldest and truest love:

> Alas, 'tis true, I have gone here and there,
> And made myself a motley to the view,
> Gored my own thoughts, sold cheap what is most dear,
> Made old offences of affections new.
> Most true it is that I have looked on truth
> Askance and strangely, but, by all the above,
> These blenches gave my heart another youth,
> And worse essays proved thee my best of love.
> Now all is done, have what shall have no end.
> Mine appetite I never more will grind
> On newer proof to try an older friend,
> A god in love, to whom I am confined.
>> Then give me welcome, next my heaven the best,
>> Even to thy pure and most most loving breast.

Shakespeare had chosen the life of a mountebank, a dealer in shadows and illusions. If Ann was anywhere near as puritan as her brother Bartholomew she must have detested the idea from the beginning and even Shakespeare's eventual success would hardly have mollified her. The devil being the father of lies, dissimulation is the beginning of all sin and it was this, less than the lasciviousness of the displays, that excited the ire of the puritan reformers. The sonnet sounds as if it is a mild defence against a passionate condemnation, beginning by freely admitting guilt, 'Alas, 'tis true,' 'Most true it is . . .' The poet proceeds to argue like a sophist, excusing his infidelities in terms that strangely presage the devilishly brilliant boy who has ruined the country maid in 'A Lover's Complaint'.

> To make the weeper laugh, the laugher weep,
> He had the dialect and different skill,
> Catching all passions in his craft of will.
>
> That he did in the general bosom reign
> Of young, of old, and sexes both enchanted,
> To dwell with him in thoughts, or to remain
> In personal duty, following where he haunted.
> Consents bewitched, ere he desire, have granted,
> And dialogued for him what he would say,
> Asked their own wills and made their wills obey.

The boy's sophistical argument, that experiencing inferior loves serves to convince a man of the superiority of his first love, is a tougher doctrine than that might seem, for it has little to do with a rebirth of passion or conjugal intimacy. The sonnets that follow 110 spell out the theme of repentance and reformation:

> O, for my sake do you with Fortune chide,
> The guilty goddess of my harmful deeds,
> That did not better for my life provide
> Than public means which public manners breeds. (111)

Though the sonnets claim to be plain-speaking all through, this is the plainest speech so far. We don't know when these lines were written, but it seems that they belong to a much later stage in the poet's life than the trickier sonnets of the 1590s. The ultimate statement of the doctrine of marriage as spiritual discipline is probably Sonnet 116.

> Let me not to the marriage of true minds
> Admit impediments. Love is not love
> Which alters when it alteration finds,
> Or bends with the remover to remove.
> O no, it is an ever-fixèd mark
> That looks on tempests and is never shaken.
> It is the star to every wandering bark,
> Whose worth's unknown, although his height be taken.
> Love's not time's fool, though rosy lips and cheeks
> Within his bending sickle's compass come.
> Love alters not with his brief hours and weeks,
> But bears it out even to the edge of doom.
>   If this be error and upon me proved,
>   I never lived, nor no man ever loved.

The final couplet contains the equivocation, for if God is love, mere man is not capable of it. Such heroic love is unattainable for fallible humans, but strive for it the poet must and will. The love he now finds true may not have been his original passion for Ann, and Ann may not here be meant. Then again she may: again the poem appears to answer an angry accusation, and once again it finds a sophistical excuse. Shakespeare could have written 'no one ever loved'; he wrote 'no man ever loved'. In his plays women are shown time and time again to be constant in love through months and years of separation. Ann may have been the model, and her steadfastness itself a reproach that grew more poignant with the passing of the years.

> Accuse me thus: that I have scanted all
> Wherein I should your great deserts repay,
> Forgot upon your dearest love to call,
> Whereto all bonds do tie me day by day,
> That I have frequent been with unknown minds,
> And given to time your own dear-purchased right,
> That I have hoisted sail to all the winds

> Which should transport me farthest from your sight.
> Book both my wilfulness and errors down,
> And on just proof surmise accumulate.
> Bring me within the level of your frown,
> But shoot not at me in your wakened hate.
>   Since my appeal says I did strive to prove
>   The constancy and virtue of your love. (117)

There can be no proof that this is a husband speaking to a wife, but there are strong hints. The person to whom 'all bonds' tie a man can only be the woman to whom he has been bound in marriage. Shakespeare had certainly spent his precious time with all kinds of riff-raff, leaving Ann to grow old without him. The cheek of the final couplet has its literary precedent in famous stories like that of Patient Grissill, who endured all kinds of torments without ever being heard to condemn the man who inflicted them upon her. The penitent mood continues until Sonnet 126, which lacks its final couplet, and seems otherwise oddly out of sequence. Kerrigan interprets it as an envoi, a deliberate ending of the sequence. The next sequence concerns the dark lady. In reading these sonnets Ann would have realised, perhaps for the first time, that her husband had been besotted with a courtesan who seduced one of his adored young men.[9] The matter was fairly recent; the poet describes his 'days as past the best'.

Michael Wood finds in Sonnet 145 a key to the mystery of Shakespeare's marriage:

> one can never judge a relationship from the outside . . . Reading between the lines [of Sonnet 145] she would be the rock on which he relied through his life, supporting his career in London. Perhaps he really did mean that she had 'saved my life'. Years later those words stood when he published the poem. And later still Ann would desire to be buried with him.[10]

Though some caution is in order – it was not Shakespeare who published the poem and we have only late-seventeenth-century gossip about where Ann desired to be buried – Wood's almost unconscious absorption of an impression of Ann as rock-like strikes me as justified. There are some who want to believe that she reproached her husband for blazoning abroad his infidelities, others that she nagged and railed and drove him further out of her life.[11] She is as likely to have refused to read the sonnets or to have them read to her. She was after all part of his reality, not his fantasy. My own feeling is that she was indeed given a copy of the sonnets and not by her husband, that at first she scorned to read them behind his back, and when she did begin to read them she was shaken, moved and impressed. Some she would have seen before, but not all. Then she would have tucked the little book deep inside the coffer where she kept her own possessions, opened her Bible and prayed for them both. If her husband had never raised the question of the sonnets with her, I doubt she would have raised it with him. She may have permitted herself the odd grim little smile.

> They that are rich in words must needs discover
> That they are poor in what makes a lover.[12]

CHAPTER SIXTEEN

*of the poet's younger daughter Judith and the Quiney family, of
Ann as maltster and money-lender, and the deaths of Mary and
Edmund Shakespeare*

Though Shakespearean scholars have not been much interested in
Judith Shakespeare, the novelist William Black found her so interesting that he spun his romance of Judith Shakespeare into three
volumes, though it is actually quite short. Black's Judith is the prettiest
damsel in Warwickshire, who trips about the leafy lanes gathering
flowers and occasionally slips up to Shottery to visit 'Grandmother
Hathaway', naying and forsoothing as she goes. She is tricked by
Leofric Hope into selling him the script of one of her father's plays and
almost pines to death under her father's displeasure. End of story.[1]

Scholars too, bereft of anything like fact, occasionally permit
themselves a little idle speculation. One thinks Judith was Shakespeare's favourite. Another decides that she was afflicted by guilt for
the death of her twin. Yet another that her father punished her for it:
'Judith, it seems, was not a favourite daughter. She may have suffered
in her father's eyes, from having had the insensitivity to stay alive so
many years after the death of her much-loved twin brother at the age
of eleven.'[2] No one would have loved Hamnet better than his twin,
or been more traumatised by his death, unless it was the mother of
both of them. If Shakespeare was so unjust as to shun his daughter
because of her bereavement, he cannot have been the man we think
he was.

What is undeniable is that Judith Shakespeare reached the ripe age
of thirty-one unmarried. As we have seen, in Shakespeare's time
fewer women married than do today. Many women were in service,
and unable to marry or even to entertain offers of marriage without

the permission of their employers. Others had no dowries or portions to put towards the establishment of a household. Still others, at their own disposal and earning an independent living, saw no reason why they should jettison their freedom and their property by submitting to the rule of a man.

One way of assessing Judith Shakespeare's life career is to look at what became of the cohort of girls born in Stratford in 1585. Holy Trinity register shows thirty-nine girls (besides Judith) born that year; three (including girl twins) were baptised and buried on the same day; three more lived two weeks, another five weeks, another nine months; twin girls died young, one aged one year and the other in the plague year of 1588, along with another of Judith's age peers; two more died at the age of twelve. One-third of the girls born that year did not reach marriageable age, which leaves twenty-six who might have. Of these only three were married in Holy Trinity Church: Katherine Rose married John Tipping in 1604, Margaret Moore married John Molnes in 1605 and Isabel Loxley alias Cockes married Thomas Mayhew on 31 May 1606. Joan Yate was buried unmarried in 1606. Which leaves twenty-two girls – slightly more than half of the cohort – who were christened but neither married nor buried in Stratford. Women of the same names can be found marrying elsewhere, in London, for example, but, failing further evidence, it would be foolhardy to identify them with the Stratford-born girls.

This is not the first time we have encountered the phenomenon of vanishing girls. Ann Shakespeare's sister Catherine Hathaway is one such, and her half-sister Margaret another. Their disappearance from the Stratford records is most likely the result of their going into service and marrying, possibly, and dying, certainly, elsewhere. In their case, the family survived in Stratford for generations; in the cases of many in Judith's cohort the families too disappeared, so we probably have to conclude that in a period of intense social disruption they moved away beyond our ken, to developing manufacturing and commercial centres, to Coventry and Birmingham and to London. One who remained was Eleanor Verney, who went into the service of Joan Bromley, widow of the carrier Edward Bromley who died in 1606. We know of Eleanor only because in 1609 she was sent by her employer to serve a subpoena on Sir Edward Greville's henchman

Peter Rosswell. In the Court of Requests she deposed that, as she handed him the writ, he 'did violently snatch from her the said writ and refused to redeliver it unto her, and delivered his staff he then had in his hand to a stander-by who therewith did assault and beat this deponent out of the house'.[3] Disturbingly enough, among those called to answer in the case was Gilbert Shakespeare.[4] Eleanor was probably placed in Joan Bromley's service in 1596 by the Overseers of the Poor, after her father's burial as a pauper.[5]

At every level of society, households could not be run without servants, who were often poor relations. Richer households took on servants of a higher class, better educated and better paid; the poorest households kept foot-boys and maids of all work on rations even harder than their own. Once in service a woman became a member of the family, and might seldom if ever hear her own family name. Time and again we encounter in the records references to servants by their masters' names; they may even be buried without their own names, which neither the clergy nor their parishioners could supply.[6] It would be no disgrace to the Bard to learn that both his daughters lived and worked in the houses of others; even the noblest families in the land would have to say the same. The most glamorous household to work in was, of course, the court of James I, where Shakespeare himself was a servant.

In 1611 when Judith was twenty-seven, she and Master Thomas and Mistress Lettice Greene witnessed a deed of enfeoffment for widowed Elizabeth Quiney and her son Adrian.[7] Lettice misspelt her own name in careful italic script that contrasts with her husband's beautiful signature (very different from the scribble of his memoranda), but Judith could only manage the kind of wobbly double squiggle that shows that she was quite unused to holding a pen. Widow Quiney did not sign either, but her mark, an E entwined with a dribbly Q, was a better effort than Judith's. Perhaps Ann's star boarders haled Judith along with them from New Place to make up the numbers for the necessary witnessing of the deed, which transferred ownership of the lease of a house in Wood Street to William Mountford in return for the very large sum of £131. The appearance of Judith's name on the document might be no more than coincidence but, as the family's private affairs were involved, it seems improbable that a stranger would have been chosen to act as witness.

Judith was unlikely to have been Bess Quiney's gossip; spinsters of twenty-seven are not often chums of widows of forty-seven. As a grass widow herself for so many years, Ann Shakespeare is a likelier candidate for that role. The Quiney house, which stood in the High Street, two streets away from New Place, housed no fewer than sixteen people. It seems as likely as not that at some point Judith did become one of them. She may have entered Bess Quiney's household in the sequel to the events of May 1602, or she may have already been there for years, nursemaiding the younger children, governessing or helping Bess Quiney continue the mercery business. It may seem odd that Ann Shakespeare would take on servants of her own, while her daughter worked for a wealthier woman, but it was not in the least unusual. In fact, the pattern is so universal as to constitute a principle of social organisation and mobility that can be seen at work in Tudor and Jacobean society from the top down.

If Judith Shakespeare had entered the service of the Quiney family it was probably long before 1602 when Richard Quiney was killed. By then she would have been seventeen. Usually girls of eleven or so, but sometimes as young as nine, were taken on for training in the special skills needed by the employers' household. Until at least the mid-1590s Shakespeare was certainly not a wealthy man, and no attention would have been paid to providing Judith with an education that she did not need. By the time the family acquired New Place, it would have been too late. We may be sure, I think, that Judith could read her Bible, and she evidently couldn't write with a pen, but she might well have been able to enter transactions in chalk on a slate or keep track of them with wooden tallies. Richard Quiney was a country mercer and Bess Quiney was a country mercer's daughter. If, as seems likely, Richard Quiney made use of his enforced sojourns in London to buy stock, it would have been up to his wife to keep track of it, and keep the 'mercer's book' up to date. Besides the fact that she was so often pregnant or recovering from a confinement, Bess Quiney had the additional challenge of her husband's working almost full-time for the Corporation, having to spend months on end in London, when she had to run the business single-handed. If Judith had been taken on as an assistant in their retail trade she should have had to serve an apprenticeship, in which case her parents would have had to pay for her indentures. If this was the case she would have become a member of the Quiney household at about the same time that her twin brother died, in 1596.

Perhaps Judith was employed to help care for the Quiney children. As we have seen, her mother's child-rearing skills were rather better than average, as she brought the twins through the hazard of multiple birth and all three of them through the annual visitations of epidemic disease. Bess's children were not strong. The spacing of her eleven pregnancies suggests either that she fed her children for a shorter time than usual or that she used wet-nurses. Either way, the consequences for the children could be serious. Bess's seventh child, William, was born in mid-September 1590 and was probably put out to nurse in the neighbourhood of Alveston because all we know of him is that he was buried there on 10 October 1592. Children who died at nurse were usually buried in the wet-nurse's parish rather than brought home for burial. When she buried her husband, Elizabeth had nine surviving children: Elizabeth was twenty, Adrian fourteen, Richard twelve, Thomas not yet eleven; Anne was ten; her second William was not yet nine; Mary was seven, John five and George two years old. A little more than a year later, in August 1603, John died. Ensuing events in Widow Quiney's family support the notion of a settled intimacy with the household at New Place. Soon after her husband's death, Bess began negotiations for the marriage of her eldest daughter, Elizabeth, to William Chandler, stepson of Thomas Greene's wife Lettice.

At about the time of Richard Quiney's death, in 1602, Shakespeare wrote a play about a poor young woman who entered the household of a wealthy widow and endeared herself to her. *All's Well That Ends Well* is a disturbing play, the text of which we know only from the 1623 Folio. As G. K. Hunter put it:

> Various palliatives and explanations for the peculiarity of the play have been advanced – ranging from anatomisations of Shakespeare's soul to analyses of his text – and these undoubtedly have their place . . . The problem that presents itself is: how are we to describe the genuine

effects of this play so that readers (or audiences) can see it as a whole, or at least as a work with a centre? The play has undoubtedly a strongly individual quality, but it is difficult to start from this, since it is mainly a quality of strain.[8]

Helena is the orphan daughter of a physician, who bequeathed her to the 'overlooking' of the Countess of Rossillion.

> I think not on my father,
> And these great tears grace his remembrance more
> Than those I shed for him. What was he like?
> I have forgot him. (I. i. 78–80)

So might a little girl say whose father left her for months, perhaps years, at a time to go to an unseen place called London. There were probably repeated scenes in the Shakespeare household like the one described by Thomas Deloney in *Thomas of Reading*:

> when I set toward this my last journey to London, how my daughter took on, what a coil she kept to have me stay, and I could not be rid of the little baggage a long time, she did so hang about me, when her mother by violence took her away, she cried out most mainly, 'O my father! My father! I shall never see him again!'[9]

The abandoned child in *All's Well That Ends Well* wins the love and esteem of the mistress of the household, so that the countess has no difficulty in forgiving her for her presumption in falling in love with the son and heir: 'Her father bequeathed her to me, and she herself, without other advantage, may lawfully make title to as much love as she finds. There is more owing her than is paid, and more shall be paid her than she'll demand' (I. iii. 96–101). It is a recurrent theme in the literature of women that they are abandoned by those with a duty of love and care and left to fend for themselves in households peopled by indifferent strangers who exploit and abuse them. Judith may be a precursor of the lonely governess of Victorian novels. Like many women raising children in the absence of their father, Ann may have found it very difficult to manage Judith's resentments and have been relieved when she left home to struggle for acceptance by another family.

It was only to be expected that all the effort would go into securing the most advantageous match possible for the Shakespeares' elder daughter, and smaller provision made for her younger sister. The lot of a younger sister in 1600 was almost as disadvantaged as that of a younger brother. Left to their own devices, younger daughters often came to grief. In service they were more likely to be seduced than courted. Abraham Sturley, gentleman, had ten children; among the disappearing women of Stratford are two of his daughters – Catherine, his fifth child, born in 1585, and Frances, his seventh, born in 1589. Hanna, born in 1591, reappears in the Holy Trinity register, not as a bride, but as the unmarried mother of a bastard daughter who was buried there on 23 December 1611, when she was twenty. Shocking as this may seem, it was not all that unusual even for eminent families; in every case the shamed woman is a younger sister. On 22 March 1598, the bastard daughter of thirty-year-old Joan Gilbert alias Higgs was brought to the font at Holy Trinity and five days later brought to be buried, much to the shame of Joan's father, the Curate of Holy Trinity. He had been married three times, and was the father of at least twelve children, two baptised at Wootton Wawen, and ten at Holy Trinity, of whom Joan was the fourth.

Judith Sadler, third last of Hamnet and Judith's children, born in April 1596, bore a bastard son Robert when she was twenty and buried him two years later; four years after that, in January 1622, she bore a second illegitimate child, a daughter Judith, and buried her ten days later. The court acts for 28 May reveal that she was cited for incontinence but did not appear.[10] The court acts also reveal that a William Smith of Bridgetown had been required to perform his compurgation on a charge of having committed fornication with Judith Sadler, which means that he had to provide a number of witnesses, neighbours of long standing, who would vouch for his conduct and character and swear that they believed him when he said that he was not guilty. On 19 July Smith was excommunicated for failing to produce his compurgators.[11] On 3 August Smith did appear in the Vicar's Court and brought witnesses to testify that 'the said Judith Sadler with whom the said Smith is accused of incontinency did in the house of Thomas Buck upon her knees swear and protest that the said William Smith had not ever or at any time carnal knowledge of her body, and the said Judith did acknowledge she had done him great wrong by raising such a fame, and did there with tears protest that she was heartily sorry she had done him that injury, and that one — Gardiner was the true father of her child'.[12] (The Gardner in question could have been a Hathaway.) In a side note to the original entry we find a clue to the unimaginable sequel: 'She went away.'

Though the Hathaways believed it their duty to find good husbands for all their girls rather than a rich husband for one of them, in January 1602 orphaned Rose Hathaway, the youngest child of Thomas Hathaway, sister of the little girls who were left a sheep each in Richard Hathaway's will, bore and buried illegitimate twin daughters. If Ann Hathaway grieved over this, and hoped that her younger daughter would not be ignored while a brilliant match was being put together for the elder, she was to be disappointed.

Shakespeare might have felt that he had short-changed Judith; rather than leaving her his expertise, as Helena's father did in *All's Well*, he seems to have left her defenceless. It is the more surprising then that the abandoned daughter married a son of her employer. It was not the son and heir, Adrian Quiney, who married an older woman in 1613, lost his wife in November 1616 and died in October 1617 aged only thirty-one, and it was not Richard, who became a merchant adventurer and made a fortune, who was to seal Judith's fate, but Thomas, who was an eleven-year-old schoolboy when his father was brought home unconscious and bleeding in May 1602. At that age the shock of his father's violent and agonising death could easily have shaken him so profoundly that he never recovered his equilibrium. For whatever reason, Thomas was to turn out to be a handful. Perhaps Judith had always loved him, and he her, but if her parents would not make the match for her, if they settled none of their property on her, there was no way the match could be made. She could have 'got herself pregnant', but manners were changing. Perhaps it would have seemed too great a betrayal of Bess Quiney to steal her boy away into a disadvantageous match. Judith remained, like so many other young Shakespeares, unmarried.

Judith may of course have been living and working at New Place, rather than at Bess Quiney's. We know that her mother's business entreprises had expanded to include the making of malt and lending of money. 'As local capitalists, moreover, brewers and maltsters often became the money-lenders of the rural community, and sometimes obtained a powerful hold over feckless tradesmen or husbandmen.'[13]

In 1608 'Shakespeare' brought an action in the Court of Record seeking recovery of £6 plus damages from a John Addenbrooke. Addenbrooke was apprehended but released when a Stratford black-smith called Thomas Hornby agreed to stand surety for him. The court awarded Shakespeare his £6 with costs and damages, but when Addenbrooke was nowhere to be found, they were obliged to attempt to recover the money from Hornby.[14] Addenbrooke may have been an associate of the Grevilles; in 1584 when Greville was buying up rectories all over Warwickshire, Addenbrooke bought the advowson of Tanworth as an investment and sold it the next year. In 1600 he is recorded as selling licences to make starch, in what was perhaps another of Greville's ill-starred ventures. How he could have come to be indebted to Shakespeare is unclear; it seems far more likely, as he was a businessman who came and went from Stratford, where he successfully sued a John Armstrong for forty shillings in 1594, that his business was with Ann.[15] Ann may have supplied him with malt or lent him money; she may even have become involved in the starch-making business. Unfortunately Hornby was not the right person to guarantee Addenbrooke's debt; when Margaret Smith, Hamnet Sadler's sister and widow of Alderman John Smith, died in 1625, Thomas Hornby still owed her the sum of £5 that he had owed since 1610, when because he defaulted she had been unable to pay the Corporation the £10 left to it by her son, Hamnet Smith.[16] In 1613 the Corporation sued him as surety for the bequest.

Ann's mother-in-law is supposed by most scholars to have been still living in Henley Street with her three sons and her daughter, her daughter's husband and their growing family. If I am right and most of the Henley Street property was leased away, her situation would have been uncomfortable enough without the addition of the Hart family, unless her sons had found themselves somewhere else to live. At some point Mary Shakespeare's youngest son took off for London, where he hoped to find success as a player. At the beginning of 1608 came the news that he was dead. Mary probably never knew that she had a baby grandson who had died six months before his father and was buried as 'Edward, son of Edward Shakespeare, player, base-born' on 12 August at St Giles, Cripplegate. On the last day of 1607 Edmund himself was buried at St Saviour's in Southwark 'in the church with a forenoon knell of the great bell' which cost the person who paid for it the considerable sum of twenty shillings. Peter Ackroyd is sure he knows who paid for it, and the other commentators would agree with him: 'The money for the bell no doubt came from the purse of his brother, who in the bitter cold accompanied the coffin to the burial place.'[17]

The other commentators would probably not agree with Ackroyd's notion that Edmund was living with his brother at Silver Street and working at the old Curtain Theatre in Shoreditch. If it was Shakespeare who paid for his brother's obsequies it is the more surprising that, when his mother died, nothing of the sort was arranged. As the King's Men were on tour it seems unlikely that Shakespeare could have been present when Mary was buried on 9 September 1608; the chief mourners were probably her bachelor sons, forty-one-year-old Gilbert and thirty-four-year-old Richard. The register records the burial of plain 'Mary Shakespeare, widow', as if there was no one to remind the clerk that this was the widow of Master Shakespeare, erstwhile alderman, let alone that her son's endeavours had made her husband a gentleman. Six weeks or so before her death Richard Shakespeare had been presented to the Vicar's Court: 'the said Shakespeare appeared, admitted, petitioned the favour of the court. And for the fault committed is admitted to pay before the next court twelve pence to the use of the poor.'[18] Two other men, Ralph Burnell and Richard Kelly, were fined the same amount at the same sitting. What they had all been up to is anybody's guess. As fines in the Vicar's Court went, twelve pence was rather steep. The tariff for ploughing with oxen on the sabbath, for example, was only one or two pence even though the worst offenders were rich landowners.

CHAPTER SEVENTEEN

in which Shakespeare returns to the town some say he never left and lives the life of an Anglican gentleman while Ann continues to live the life of a puritan townswoman

Scholars cannot agree on why or when Shakespeare returned to Stratford. Those who think that Thomas Greene and his family finally vacated their lodgings at New Place and removed to St Mary's House in 1611 believe that Shakespeare's return was probably the precipitating factor. In September 1611 Shakespeare is listed as one of seventy-one residents of Stratford willing to contribute 'towards the charge of prosecuting a bill in parliament for the better repair of the highways and amending divers defects in the statutes already made', and that too is taken as evidence that he was physically and permanently present; however, the name is entered in the margin and could well have been suggested by someone else, by Thomas Greene or John Hall, both of whose names appear in the list proper.[1] Shakespeare had after all been listed before at times when he is understood to have been in London. Some scholars interpret the fact that on 11 May 1612 Shakespeare was in London giving evidence in a lawsuit and did not reappear when recalled on 19 June as proof that he had withdrawn permanently to the country – or rather to Stratford, which is not the same thing – in the interim. Peter Thomson believes that Shakespeare remained a full member of the King's Men until 1613, writing *Cardenio, Henry VIII*, and *The Two Noble Kinsmen* in collaboration with John Fletcher, as it were training his successor as the company playwright.[2]

It is possible of course that Shakespeare never really left Stratford. Aubrey stated confidently that 'Mr William Shakespeare was wont to go into Warwickshire once a year . . .'[3] The trip from London to Stratford still took three days. William Greenaway, who organised the wagon trains in Shakespeare's youth, was dead, but trade had expanded and we should probably assume that from about 1600 goods left Stratford for London and vice versa most days of the week. The carriers also leased out horses so that gentlemen who had business in London could ride in convoy with them and so avoid the danger of being waylaid and robbed. Most scholars agree that Shakespeare returned from London for the funeral of his father in September 1601, for the issue of the fine for New Place in the summer of 1602, for the wedding of his daughter in June 1607, and for the funeral of his mother in September 1608, mainly because they think he should have. There's certainly no evidence that he did. To observers like Peter Ackroyd it seems obvious that Shakespeare sought the company of his family: 'There were of course many other neighbours – as well as his immediate family – living in close proximity. These were the people whom he saw every day, and with whom he exchanged greetings and small talk.'[4]

If Shakespeare did indeed return to enjoy the company of his brother Gilbert he must have been devastated when he died at the beginning of February 1612. A year later almost to the day Richard died. William had only one sibling left; Joan was apparently living with her husband William Hart and their three surviving sons at the old address in Henley Street behind the Maiden Head Inn.

We do not know whether Shakespeare was in Stratford in June 1613 when John Lane the younger 'reported' that his daughter Susanna Hall 'had the running of the reins and had been naught with Ralph Smith at John Palmer'.[5] What is meant is that she had contracted venereal disease causing a copious vaginal discharge by having intercourse with Ralph Smith at the house of a John Palmer. How Lane published this libel is not clear. One way of doing it was to pin a notice to her house door, or to make up a scurrilous rhyme and have people sing it. He may have scribbled it

as it were upon a table, or in a window, or upon the wall or mantel of a chimney in some place of common resort, where it was allowed every man might come, or be sitting to chat and prate, as now in our taverns and common tabling houses, where many merry heads meet and scribble, with ink, with chalk or with a coal, such matters as they would every man should know and descant upon.[6]

At the worst Susanna may have been balladed, that is her 'whole story sung to some villainous tune in a lewd ballad' so that boys in the street hooted at her.[7] Something of the sort must have happened for Susanna (or more probably her husband) to think it worth pursuing as far as bringing a suit in the Consistory Court at Worcester five weeks later. By that time the Globe had burnt down during a performance of *Henry VIII*, another event that is supposed by some to have precipitated Shakespeare's return to Stratford.

Truly destructive libels were brought before the Court of Star Chamber; less destructive libels were dealt with in the Vicar's Court.[8] The damage done to Susanna must have been somewhere between the two extremes. The offence was the graver because the Lane family were gentry. A week before the case was heard, John Hall and Thomas Greene were asked to act as trustees for John Lane's cousins, children of Richard Lane, Esquire, of Bridgetown, who, feeling his terminal illness upon him, had settled property on them. One of them, Edward Lane, was to marry twenty-one-year-old Mary Combe, sister of William and Thomas, a few weeks later. John Lane's sister Margaret was married to Thomas Greene's brother John, which makes it all the stranger that, in a weird re-enactment of the story from the Apocrypha, he should have chosen to libel Susanna. Ralph Smith, the man he implicated with her – and therefore accused of being poxed – was a haberdasher cum hatter, thirty-five years old, and nine years married to Anne Court. His mother was Margaret Sadler, sister of Hamnet. His father, the vintner John Smith, had served as Bailiff of Stratford in 1598 and had then apparently gone a little crazy; three months before his death in 1601 he lost his position as head alderman for 'obstinate and wilful hindering of the execution of process out of the Court of Record' and refused to surrender the mace or the keys to the cupboard where the Book of Orders was kept. According to Fripp, John Palmer was 'a gentleman of Compton' and a 'grandson of the late alderman William Smith', as was Ralph.[9]

Neither Susanna nor John Lane attended the Consistory Court hearing. The plaintiff's case was presented by Robert Whatcott, and Lane was duly declared excommunicate. Susanna might have been vindicated, but that was before the dons began chewing over the case. Here is A. L. Rowse on the subject: 'I dare say she had the running of the reins, for she was the member of the family who possessed something of her father's spirit.'[10]

Lane may have been nothing more than a loose cannon, firing at random, or his obscene libel may have been part of a growing antagonism between the Stratford puritans and the unreformed gentry. As well as obstructing the local gentry in their endeavours to fiscalise their estates, the Corporation was known to be a puritan brotherhood, sworn to be secret in its dealings and severe against the traditional sports and pastimes of the people. In attacking Susanna, Lane was probably aiming not only at her husband but also at her Hathaway cousins who were rising stars of the puritan meritocracy. What Shakespeare thought of the scandal is, needless to say, not known. Nowadays we would tend to think of the whole thing as a fuss about nothing, but in Jacobean Stratford a person whose credit was destroyed could not function as a citizen. Though Ann Hathaway had been living manless for nearly thirty years, no breath of scandal ever attached to her name, which, given the evidence of the surviving records of the Vicar's Court, is itself remarkable.

The usual view is that Shakespeare left the hurly-burly of London for peace and quiet in Stratford. Rowe sets the scene and most of his successors follow his lead.

> The latter Part of his life was spent, as all Men of Good Sense will wish theirs may be, in Ease, Retirement, and the Conversation of his Friends. He had the good Fortune to gather an Estate equal to his Occasion and, in that, to his Wish; and is said to have spent some Years before his Death at his native Stratford.[11]

Rowe's notion of a country gentleman is mildly anachronistic, though probably less so than our own. But Shakespeare was not living within landscaped acres far from the madding crowd of sectarians and troublemakers; he was living in the market town of Stratford, in Chapel Street, where butchers set up their stalls and cried their wares from daybreak every Thursday morning.[12] Certainly he would not be troubled with theatricals passing through and anxious to remake his acquaintance, nor would he be expected to attend theatrical performances. No plays had been performed in Stratford

since the Hall of 27 December 1602 when the Corporation 'ordered
there shall be no plays or interludes played in the Chamber, the Guild
Hall, nor in any part of the house or court from henceforward, upon
pain that whosoever of the Bailiff, Aldermen and Burgesses of this
borough shall give leave or licence thereunto shall forfeit for every
offence 10s'.[13] This order was renewed on 7 February 1612, with the
penalty, already heavy, multiplied twenty-fold.[14]

Perhaps a break with the theatre was what Shakespeare wanted.
Certainly it was what he needed if he were to pass himself off as a
gentleman. 'His pleasurable wit and good nature engaged him in the
acquaintance and entitled him to the friendship of the gentlemen in
the neighbourhood.'[15] If we may judge by Shakespeare's will, the
friendships he chose to cultivate in his retirement, if such it was, were
no mere tradesmen. Chief among them were the Combes. John
Combe, who with his uncle William Combe had sold Shakespeare
the land in old Stratford in 1602, was the richest man in Stratford. His
uncle, who died in 1610, had served as MP for Droitwich and
Warwick, reader in the Middle Temple, counsel for Stratford-
upon-Avon and ecclesiastical commissioner and had taken as his
third wife the widow of the Lord Keeper of the Great Seal, Sir John
Puckering. John Combe had concentrated on building up a fortune
by lending money at 10 per cent per annum; he had also invested in
land near Stratford and acquired a lease of Clopton Park from William
Clopton. The Shakespeare family had known him at least since 1598
when they appointed him one of their commissioners to examine
witnesses in their failed suit against the Lamberts. John Combe was a
bachelor; his brother Thomas, who died in 1609, had two sons,
William and Thomas, both in their twenties and both members of the
Middle Temple. They would have been well informed about current
developments in the London theatre, supposing Shakespeare had
wished to discuss them. As Thomas Combe lived at the College, he
was Shakespeare's nearest congenial neighbour.

Shakespeare also hobnobbed with the next richest men in Stratford, Anthony and John Nash. They were connected through their
grandmother to one of the most active enclosing landlords in the west
midlands, Sir John Hubaud. Hubaud not only depopulated the manor
of Hillborough and flattened all the houses; he knocked down the

parish church as well. John Nash was an old enemy of Richard Quiney, who was forced to seek sureties of the peace against him in 1588. Anthony Nash and Ralph Hubaud, brother of Sir John, who inherited the tithe-rights from him in 1583, made one serious mistake: in 1599 they sold part of Sir John Hubaud's lease of the tithes to Sir Edward Greville, who instantly mortgaged it for the full sale price and failed to service the loan, so that Nash had to sue him in the Court of Requests in 1615, probably to no avail. Richard Lane was another who was burnt by Greville, who defaulted on a bond for £1,000; after Lane's death his executors were instructed to sue but there was little point. Greville was to all intents and purposes bankrupt. After losing money on various get-rich-quick schemes, in 1607 Greville invested in a salt monopoly with Sir Arthur Ingram and Sir Lionel Cranfield; by 1610 he was £1,000 in debt to his partners, who took full advantage, appropriating his estates one by one. By retaining just enough of the equity to prevent his being evicted, Greville contrived to hang on at Milcote.[16]

Greville having become a veritable black hole in the local economy, his defalcations pushed his creditors to ever more desperate schemes to augment the profitability of their landholdings. Combe's nephew William Combe joined forces with Arthur Mainwaring, steward to the lord chancellor, with his cousin William Replingham of Great Harborough acting as his attorney, to form a consortium to buy up the remaining open arable fields in Milcote, Welcombe and Old Stratford with the aim of engrossing and enclosing them and selling them on at a profit.[17] The Corporation had a fight on its hands, for the consortium proposed to enclose the town commons as part of the scheme. The aldermen were well aware that Mainwaring's relationship to Lord Chancellor Ellesmere was not that of a mere steward; his mother was Elizabeth More, sister of Ellesmere's second wife. Her death in 1600 after only three years of marriage affected Ellesmere so deeply that in the years following he made various attempts to adopt one or other of her sister's children. As matters stood in 1614, as well as being Ellesmere's protégé, Mainwaring looked likely to inherit the bulk of his huge estates. In terms of clout the Corporation was David to the consortium's Goliath.

It made economic sense to enclose the clusters of yardlands, strips of land four rods wide by forty long, separated by turf balks or slades, that made up Welcombe, obliterate the divisions and operate the area as a single unit, whether for pasture or cultivation. Ideally, all those with rights in the land would be partners in the enterprise and would receive their due share of the yield, but the poor husbandmen of Stratford, who needed to pasture their few beasts on the common to survive, would have faced starvation. The Corporation, struggling to finance poor relief after the fire of July, feared the consequences if the townspeople were to lose their ancient right to the use of the stubble fields after harvest. Shakespeare seems to have expected to do fairly well out of the enclosure, but Ann, who may have acquired the land in the first place, may have had ideas more in line with the misgivings of her old tenant Thomas Greene, Town Clerk of Stratford, who, though he stood to profit by the scheme, opposed it.[18]

Ann and her children, who had lived all their lives in Stratford, seem at all times to have been closer to the puritan Corporation than Shakespeare was. Ann and Thomas and Lettice Greene must have enjoyed each other's company, having lived under the same roof for so long, but Shakespeare had no dealings that we know of with Greene and left him out of his will. There seems no reason to believe that Shakespeare exchanged much small talk with his brother-in-law Bartholomew Hathaway either. Hathaway had ceased serving as churchwarden under John Rogers in 1608 and was probably spending more time on improving the freehold estate he had acquired in Shottery, where he built an extra wing on to the old farmhouse. Shakespeare would have had even less in common with Bartholomew's sons who were working their way up through the Corporation and the parish. As Shakespeare's heir apparent, John Hall had to be involved in business arising from the estate, and so rode with him to London in November 1614 and stayed there with him until after Christmas, but it is hard to believe that Shakespeare found him particularly congenial company, or that he took him along when he visited the Combes and the Nashes. Ann Shakespeare is even less likely to have made one of the party. Husbands and wives did not go about as couples. Ann had her gossips and William had his.

Though Shakespeare evidently insisted on his rank as gentleman he never offered any of the public services that gentlemen were expected to provide. He neither witnessed the signing of a will nor oversaw the performance of its provisions; he drew up no inventory; he did not serve on the commission of the peace; he played no part in the affairs of the church; he examined no recusants. John Hall resented the time taken up by such chores and excused himself whenever possible, but even he ended up having to do them. If Shakespeare was never asked to render such services, it was probably because he was perceived to be incapacitated. He may have been asked and refused, but we would probably know about it in that case, because the Corporation had the power to fine citizens who refused to do their duty.

In the winter of 1613–14 Ann's old friend Judith Sadler was dying. The last years of her life had been miserable. At the time of her marriage she was a co-parcenary heiress of a wealthy businessman and Hamnet was a comparatively rich man with three houses in Church Street; in 1595 he had inherited the lease on the house in the High Street only to have it burn down. The cost of rebuilding it beggared him. Sadler was not an ambitious man; while others strove for public office and neglected their honest trade for more lucrative commerce, he had continued working as a baker, despite the constant inter-ference of petty bureaucracy which was continually harassing bakers who sold bread and cakes on Sunday. In 1597 he went collecting alms for Stratford with Richard Quiney, much to the alarm of Abraham Sturley who was aware that Sadler could not afford even the hire of his mare for twenty-four days at a shilling a day, for which he was eventually sued. By 1613 the house in the High Street, which had probably been rebuilt too cheaply if at all, was described as 'much out of repair'. Judith's surviving children had probably all been sent out to service, for there is mention of only one of them in the register and it seems that she had been working in Bridgetown. After fourteen pregnancies Judith was effectively childless. On 24 March 1614, Ann followed her bier to the churchyard.

On 9 July 1614 'a sudden and terrible fire' destroyed fifty-four dwelling-houses, 'besides barns, stables and other houses of office':[19] 'the force of which fire was so great (the wind sitting full upon the town) that it dispersed into so many places thereof whereby the whole town was in very great danger to have been utterly consumed'.[20] After the heroic attempts since the fires of 1594 and 1595 to rebuild

the housing stock and roof the new buildings with tile, there were still
too many thatched houses left standing: 'the wind taketh the thatch
and carrieth it very far off and there fireth other thatched houses . . .
very many fair tiled houses have been burned to the ground'.[21]

By luck and perhaps Ann's good management New Place sustained
no damage, but once again, for the third time in living memory, the
town was a stinking wreck. When the royal patent was issued in
December, authorising five citizens to gather contributions from
neighbouring boroughs for fire relief, one of those named was
Richard Tyler. When the collectors' accounts were examined by
Sir Richard Verney, Sir Henry Rainsford and Bartholomew Hales in
March 1616, each of the five was declared to have been 'preferring his
own private benefits over the general good' and was accused of
claiming more for expenses than he managed to collect. As Tyler later
took action in Chancery to clear his name, we may suspect that the
decision to inculpate the nominees of the Corporation for the poor
return from the appeal was not entirely disinterested. By March 1616
the gentry were determined to discredit the Corporation by any
means possible, legal or not.

The day after the fire John Combe died. He named as his executors
his residual legatee, Thomas Combe, with Sir Richard Verney and
Bartholomew Hales. He left more than £1,500 in bequests, including
£100 to be laid out in loans to tradesmen wishing to expand their
business, £30 to the poor, an endowment for a learned preacher to
give two sermons a year at Holy Trinity, £60 for his tomb in the
church – and £5 to William Shakespeare. Combe had drawn up his
will eighteen months before his death; Francis Collins wrote it out for
him on 28 January 1613, so Shakespeare must already have endeared
himself to the old man, but only to the value of £5. Lawyer Collins
received twice as much. Sir Francis Smith was left as much to 'buy
him a hawk' but his wife got £40 'to buy her a basin and ewer'.[22]

The threatened enclosure loomed ever closer. On 23 September
the council voted unanimously to oppose it. In October Shakespeare
and Thomas Greene entered into agreement with William Replingham that they and their heirs would be indemnified for any loss of
value in their tithe fields 'by reason of any enclosure or decay of tillage
there meant and intended' – damages to be assessed by 'four

indifferent persons'.[23] Our guide to what happened next is the sheet of memoranda written by Thomas Greene when he was preparing the case to be made by the Bailiff and Burgesses of Stratford to the lord chief justice and the Privy Council the following year.[24] By 15 November Greene was in London where he met with Mainwaring, who assured him that he 'should have no wrong' by the enclosure and that he 'would rather get a penny than a half-penny, and rather get twopence than lose a penny'. Mainwaring then offered to buy Greene's interest, whereupon Greene asked him 'whether he had ever thought with himself what they were worth', but Mainwaring was in a hurry to go into the Chancery court and promised to let him know.

Two days later, Greene wrote in his memorandum book:

At my cousin Shakespeare coming yesterday to town I went to see him how he did. He told me that they assured him they meant to enclose no further than to Gospel Bush and so up straight (leaving out part of the Dingles to the field) to the gate in Clopton Hedge and take in Salisbury's piece and that they mean in April to survey the land, and then to give satisfaction and not before, and he and Mr Hall say they think there will be nothing done at all.

Greene was right not to be convinced, for the land was surveyed within days, in December. If Mainwaring had come forward with an irresistible offer Greene would probably have sold, but as it happened nothing was concluded before he returned to Stratford. On 5 December the company agreed that six of their number should 'go to Mr Combe in the name of the rest to present their loves and desire he would be pleased to forbear to enclose and to desire his love as they will be ready to deserve it'. At a follow-up visit, Combe told the aldermen that he would be glad of their loves and that the 'enclosures would not be hurtful to the town that he had not to do with it but to have some profit by it and that he thought Mr Mainwaring was so far engaged therein as he would not be entreated and therefore he would not bestow his labour to entreat him in any sort saying if the frost broke the ditching would go presently forward'.[25]

On 10 December Greene found himself at the centre of the

dispute; somehow it had become known that Replingham and
Mainwaring were trying to do business with him. He assured the
Corporation that he knew his duty as town clerk to represent its
interest, only to be challenged by Alderman William Walford,
younger half-brother of Bess Quiney. Greene advised the aldermen
about the kinds of action they might lawfully take if Combe's men
began digging. They decided that, until he did, there was no need to
do anything. As luck would have it, the frost broke on 19 December
and Combe's men moved at once, digging a trench 275 yards long in
preparation for the hedging and ditching.

On 23 December Greene noted: 'Letters written, one to Mr
Mainwaring, another to Mr Shakespeare with almost all the company's hands to either: I also writ of myself to my cousin Shakespeare the
copies of all our oaths . . . also a note of the inconveniences that
would grow by the enclosure'. The letters, which went to the owner
of Bishopton, a Mr Archer of Tamworth, and to Sir Francis Smith
who owned land at Welcombe, as well as to Mainwaring and
Shakespeare, warned them that the enclosure would bring the curses
of the 700 almspeople of Stratford upon their heads. Shakespeare was
still in London. At New Place Ann oversaw the hospitality offered to
the Christmas preacher. The Christmas accounts of Chamberlain of
Stratford list twenty pence paid for 'one quart of sack and one quart of
claret wine given to the preacher at New Place'. Some have interpreted this as evidence that Ann had turned fanatical puritan, and even
that in a fanatical puritan way she had committed indecencies with the
visiting preacher.

As soon as the holidays were over the Corporation made its
counter-move. Acting on Greene's advice, two of the alderman,
Masters Chandler and Walford, managed to secure a lease at Welcombe giving them rights of common.[26] Chandler was Greene's
stepson and married to Bess Quiney's eldest daughter, Elizabeth. On
the evening of Saturday 7 January William Combe let it be known
that he had heard that 'some of the better sort would go to throw
down the ditch'.[27] Master Chandler was told by Master Bayliss that
Combe ground his teeth and snarled, 'O would they durst!' in 'great
passion and anger'. The following Monday Master Chandler went to
see Combe for himself and told Greene on his return that Combe

called them all 'factious knaves', 'puritan knaves' and 'underlings in their colour', threatening to 'do them all the mischief he can'. Undeterred Chandler and Walford sent spades to be hidden at the worksite in advance so that they could go in person and 'throw down some of the ditch'. Greene, concerned that they would find themselves in breach of the peace, advised them to 'go in such private manner as none might see them go lest others might perhaps follow in companies and so make a riot or a mutiny'. The conclusion was thus foregone. When the two aldermen turned up they were outnumbered by Combe's workmen who knocked them to the ground and beat them: 'the said Mr Combe for a long space sat laughing on horseback and said they were very good football players and bade the diggers get on for those that did set them on work would bear them out'.[28]

That afternoon an attempt was made to get Greene to come over to the side of the enclosers. He was offered £10 to buy himself a gelding, if he would intercede with Sir Henry Rainsford. Greene explained that he needed to remain impartial in the affair and to continue to do his duty by the Borough whether he agreed with them or not. He was startled to learn that the area of arable land to be laid down to pasture was as much as 600 acres. The next day Greene sought assistance from a justice of the peace in swearing out an injunction to prevent a breach of the peace. It was agreed that to avert public disorder the names of the members of the consortium would not be divulged to the public. By evening the Corporation had arrived at the following accommodation with them.

It is agreed for preventing of tumults and avoiding of meeting of the people of Stratford and Bishopton for the present:
    That any further ditching stay until the 25 of March next
    That there be no ploughing on the common or any part thereof
        until then
    And it is meant there shall be a cartway left under Rowley and other
        usual ways to lie open
    It is meant that there shall be no throwing down of the ditches
        already set up but after such ways as aforesaid until after the said
        25 March.

But they were too late. Greene's side note simply remarks: 'While this was doing as it stands, the ditches by women and children of Bishopton and Stratford were filled up again.'[29]

Greene's memoranda were intended for his use in the event of legal action; though they are not easy to follow it seems clear that he had no idea what was toward.[30] The women must have taken this action entirely on their own initiative. On one of the coldest nights of the year they had shouldered spades and mattocks, and led their children out of the town, across the bridge and down into the pitch-dark meadow of Welcombe, where they knocked down the hedge mound and back-filled the ditch. Either Combe's thugs were all at home in bed and not keeping watch, or they didn't dare lay hands on the women. When the 275 yards of mound and ditch were flattened, the women marched their troops back to Stratford and Bishopton and so to bed.

Astonishing as this action on the part of the women of Stratford may seem it was not all that unusual. In 1589 Sir Robert Wroth and Henry Middlemore enclosed 100 acres of pasture in the manor of Enfield:

> On 7 July . . . forty women, for the most part wives of artisans and labourers, destroyed the offending enclosures. Twenty-nine of the women were arraigned at a petty sessions before Robert Wroth and Middlemore, and twenty-four of them sent to Newgate Gaol to await trial . . . A number of them were pregnant and actually gave birth while in Newgate. They were still imprisoned on August 20 when they wrote to Lord Burghley seeking relief.[31]

In cases where it could be established that the women had been put up to it by their menfolk, the menfolk were as likely to be arraigned for causing a riot. But if women and children could be shown to have acted spontaneously the law was powerless: 'if a number of women (or children under the age of discretion) do flock together for their own cause, there is none assembly punishable by these statutes, unless a man of discretion moved them to assemble for the doing of some unlawful act . . .'[32]

Nevertheless the women of Stratford were taking a risk. In 1609, when the lord of the Warwickshire manor of Dunchurch enclosed eight acres and blocked his tenants' access to their common pasture, and fifteen women came by night and destroyed his hedges, Star Chamber prosecuted not only the women but the men responsible for them, whether fathers, employers or husbands, and rejected the women's claim to have acted spontaneously.[33]

Clearly someone must have organised the action at Welcombe, but that someone was not necessarily a man, or even a woman under the tutelage of a man. She was probably a woman without father, employer or husband. She was probably a widow. When Alderman Chandler arrived home after his drubbing, his wife, Bess Quiney's eldest daughter Elizabeth, must have been among the first to hear of the outrage perpetrated by Combe. It looks very much as if, as the Corporation tried to come to some agreement with their powerful opposition, the Widow Quiney sent her maidservants to knock on doors in Stratford and Bishopton, and mobilise her troops. One thing is certain: the women who destroyed Combe's earthworks that night were never arraigned on any charge in the Star Chamber or anywhere else. As he put together the case to be presented to the lord chief justice, Greene listed the crimes of Edward Greville against the Corporation, including the murder of Bess's husband, Richard Quiney.[34] Bess had gradually overcome the shock and grief of her husband's murder in 1602 and assumed the role of *de facto* leader of the Quiney gang. In 1612 when the bailiff and burgesses sued Sir Edward Conway and Francis Cawdry, the witnesses were examined at her house. Other occasions were celebrated by banquets at Mistress Quiney's.

There and then Greene feared that the women's intervention had made the situation worse, for he could see no way that the aldermen would not be held ultimately responsible for what was in effect a riot. On Thursday the Corporation met in emergency session at Bess Quiney's house; Masters Barker, Walford, Chandler, Henry Smith, Lewis Hiccox and Laurence Wheeler, plus Mistress Quiney, told Replingham 'to his face' that they disagreed with the intended enclosure. Replingham's only reply was that 'he would give names to Mr Bailiff for doing justice upon the women diggers' and he was promised in return that 'justice would be done'.

Ann must have been among the first to hear of the events at Welcombe, if indeed she wasn't directly involved. Both her daughters may have been part of the hedge-breaker gang, and perhaps even Judith Hart and her boys. And perhaps none of them.

The Corporation's petition to the lord chief justice was successful; he ordered a stay of enclosure. Combe and Replingham then resorted to their second strategy; the yardlands were all laid down to pasture, and four to five hundred sheep let in to graze it with four shepherds. Combe was still buying up land; Mistress Reynolds resisted his offers and even went so far as to defy him and plough her yardland, but Mistress Mary Nash was happy to pocket his fifty pounds. Combe then began to court Sir Edward Greville, sending him a 'fat wether' in order to get his favour in persuading Sir Arthur Ingram (who was buying up Greville's estates) to sell the manor of Old Stratford to the consortium. In August Master Barker died. He was another who had dared to infuriate Combe by ploughing his holding within the enclosure area. His executors were not so tough, and soon accepted a ten-shilling deposit against a full price of £40. In September Shakespeare told Greene's brother John Greene that Greene could not bar the enclosing of Welcombe.

Though the citizens of Stratford had the law on their side, they were helpless before the *force majeure* of the gentry. Workmen had appeared on the common again, this time claiming that they had instructions from Thomas Combe and Boughton, who would indemnify them against any action by the Corporation to prevent them from working. On 2 March 1616 Master Chandler sent his man 'to the place where Stephen Sly, John Terry, Thomas Hiccox, William Whitehead and Michael Pigeon were working', and they 'assaulted him so he could not proceed with throwing down the ditches and Sly said if the best in Stratford were there to throw it down he would bury his head in the bottom of the ditch'.[35] At this point Mainwaring, who had been anxious all along to be seen to do no wrong, withdrew from the consortium, which left William Combe effectively on his own.[36] Combe resorted to main force, using casual labourers to drive his tenants off the land by kicking and beating them. At the Lenten Assizes in Warwick in March the next year, the Corporation finally learnt that it had won.

Upon the humble petition of the Bailiff and Burgesses of Stratford-upon-Avon, it was ordered at these assizes that no enclosure shall be made within the parish of Stratford, for that it is against the laws of the realm, neither by Mr Combe nor any other, until they shall show cause at open assizes to the Justices of Assize; neither that any of the commons being ancient greensward shall be ploughed up either by the said Mr Combe nor any other, until good cause be likewise shown at open assizes before the Justices of Assize; this order is taken for preventing of tumults and breaches of his Majesty's peace; whereof in this very town of late there had like to have been an evil beginning of some great mischief.[37]

The victory was a real one; the Stratford town commons were never enclosed. Combe was not subdued, however; he continued to intimidate and beat his own tenants, impounded their livestock, and eventually succeeded in depopulating the village of Welcombe until only his own house remained standing.[38] By that time William Shakespeare was dead and buried, and Thomas Combe was the proud possessor of his sword, which Shakespeare left to him in his will.

CHAPTER EIGHTEEN

of Shakespeare's last illness and death and how Ann Shakespeare
handled the situation

Perhaps Shakespeare headed for New Place because his health was failing.

> Good broth and good keeping doth much now and then;
> Good diet with wisdom best helpeth a man.
> In health to be stirring shall profit thee best;
> In sickness hate trouble, seek quiet and rest.[1]

That his terminal illness was of long standing is suggested by the fact that four months before he did die, Shakespeare knew that he was dying. Most people who died in Warwickshire in April 1616 were bowled over by a catastrophic infection. Very few of Shakespeare's contemporaries were as long as four months a-dying, though there were a few who made a will as far in advance as Shakespeare did and some further. As we have seen, Shakespeare's friend John Combe made his will eighteen months before he died.

The Rev. John Ward, who settled in Stratford forty-six years after the poet's death, recalled gossip that 'Shakespeare, Drayton and Ben Jonson had a merry meeting and it seems drank too hard, for Shakespeare died of a fever there contracted.'[2] Ward is using the late-seventeenth-century version of the theory of plethora to explain the poet's death as a sort of melancholy accident. This won't fit with what we know of the poet's gradual decline, or for that matter with what we know of his rather awkward relationship with Ben Jonson.[3]

The existence of Shakespeare's will with its cancelled date of January 1616 gives the lie to the idea of a sudden eclipse. Fevers kill rapidly or not at all. Other terminal diseases, congestive heart failure for example, would have taken longer than four months to enter a terminal phase, and we would expect some evidence of illness to have manifested much earlier – which of course it may have. A possibly fatal circulatory disorder would probably not have been diagnosed. At fifty-two Shakespeare was young to be in the final stages of a disease of old age. For reasons that she does not divulge Duncan-Jones decides that Shakespeare was 'increasingly tired and unwell'. She believes too that Shakespeare was probably morbidly obese.

> As a man of considerable wealth he is likely to have indulged in the heavy diet of fat meat and sweet, or sweetened, wines habitual in his class. And if he was now spending longer periods in Stratford, he enjoyed greater access to the excellent veal and beef produced in the Forest of Arden. His 'mountain belly' may now have rivalled Ben Jonson's, making the three-day ride from Stratford to London increasingly uncomfortable.[4]

For the horse, presumably. Duncan-Jones appears unaware that there were such things as litters, or that the Bard could have hitched a ride on the carrier's wagon train. Coaches did exist, but they were too slow and cumbersome for a journey as long as from Stratford to London. Having created her Falstaffian Shakespeare, Duncan-Jones then turns him into a drunk.

> There are several reasons why, in the years 1615–16, he may indeed have been drinking more than was his wont . . . The first and most compelling reason is that he was already ill . . . If he 'drank too hard' towards the end, it was most probably in an attempt to palliate pain or distress.[5]

Michael Wood too entertains the idea that Shakespeare was an alcoholic, principally on the grounds of the shakiness of the signature on the first draft of his will.[6] Duncan-Jones prefers her own diagnosis 'that heart and circulatory trouble were now added to latent syphilitic infection'.[7] The syphilitic infection she takes to date from 'visits to Turnmill Street' in 1604–8. 'Going to Turnmill Street to beat up whores was a traditional pastime for high-spirited young men through-

out the Tudor period.'[8] What the apprentices and students liked to do
to the whores was, not to have intercourse with them without paying
(anglice, to rape them), but to smash their glass windows and kick their
doors in, as they do to the Bawd in *Northward Ho* (1607).[9] It is possible
but surely not probable that a successful businessman would turn
juvenile hoodlum at the age of forty-five. Contemporary physician
Philip Barrough was so used to finding the primary infection in very
young men that he refers to his generic patient as a young man, even as 'a
lad or a stripling of tender years'.[10] Duncan-Jones elaborates: 'Though
Shakespeare was to survive for nearly seven years more, his visits to
Turnmill Street may have left him with an unwanted legacy of chronic
and humiliating sickness.'[11]

Turnmill Street, which was as often known as Turnbull or Turnball
Street, was in Clerkenwell.[12] Shakespeare had small need to travel so far
when the Globe stood in the middle of the stews of Shoreditch and
Southwark. So close was the relationship between the theatres and the
stews that in 1593 the wife of the best-known tragedian Edward Alleyn,
Joan Woodward, Henslowe's stepdaughter, was carted through the
streets of Southwark as a bawd, probably because it was thought she
lived on the proceeds of prostitution, as perhaps she did.[13] Both the
Diocese of Winchester as landlord of parts of Southwark and Lord
Hunsdon, who was granted the manor of Paris Garden by the queen,
pocketed the rents of brothels in the theatre district without a qualm.
George Wilkins, who is thought to have collaborated with Shakespeare
in writing *Pericles*, besides penning the odd pot-boiler, owned an inn in
St Sepulchre's which was also a house of ill repute.[14]

One thing should be very clear: Shakespeare was vividly aware of
venereal disease from the beginning of his career; his revulsion at the
operation of lust was always expressed in terms of sickness, which no
more goes to prove that he had experienced the horror for himself than
that he hadn't. He is far more likely to have risked casual sex earlier in his
life than in middle age. If he did consort with prostitutes in his early years
in London, and had seen the signs of venereal infection upon himself, or
believed that he had been infected, we need seek no other reason for a
cessation of intimacy between Ann and William. Succumbing to a
momentary urge might have cost William the connubial comforts of his
marriage with Ann. Certainly Ann lived far too long to have been

infected by her husband with syphilis. However, the sixteenth century could not distinguish between syphilis (an imported disease) and gonorrhoea (which had been endemic for centuries). If William had contracted gonorrhoea and continued to cohabit with his wife after having been treated for it, she might well have contracted it and suffered sterilising disease as a consequence.

Syphilis was a spectacular disease when it first manifested at the end of the fifteenth century: 'This grief at the first was so extreme, cruel and so merciless, that it molested those who were infected therewith, even the head, eyes, nose, palate of the mouth, skin, flesh, bones, ligaments and all the inward parts of their bodies.'[15] Duncan-Jones follows the view rather casually adopted by recent historians that by the second half of the sixteenth century the disease had settled down and was showing the same pattern, with two long periods of latency, that it did from the late seventeenth century. A careful reading of contemporary medical texts does not corroborate this view. Though observers agree that the disease was not as virulent as it had been but a few years before, latency is not yet established. Time and again all through the seventeenth century we find that a sufferer has been identified as such and ostracised. Gough's report on a case brought as late as 1698 describes the dilemma of the Myddle parish authorities confronted with a supposed victim of venereal disease:

> The younger son of Charles Reve of Myddle Wood [who] had lived a year and more in Gloucestershire, came privately to his brother's house in Myddle Wood, for he had got the French pox and was not able to do service. His brother was not able to maintain him and because no one else would receive him, our officers were forced to give his brother 2s 8d a week to harbour and maintain him.[16]

In 1579 Ambrose Paré described the Lues Venerea thus:

> It partakes of an occult quality, commonly taking its original from ulcers of the privy parts and then further manifesting itself by pustules of the head and other external parts, and lastly infecting the entrails and inner parts with cruel and nocturnal tormenting pain of the head, shoulders, joints, and other parts. In process of time it causeth knots

and hard tophi, and lastly corrupts and fouls the bones, dissolving them, the flesh about them being oft-times not hurt . . .

Inner corruption became manifest in gross disfigurement:

Some lose one of their eyes, others both, some lose a great portion of the eyelids, other some look very ghastly and not like themselves, and some become squint-eyed. Some lose their hearing, others have their noses fall flat, the palate of their mouths perforated with the loss of the bone Ethmoides . . .

The effects of infection on the genitals could be catastrophic:

There be some who have the Urethra or passage of the yard obstructed by budding caruncles or inflamed pustules, so that they cannot make water without the help of a catheter, ready to die within a short time unless you succour them by the amputation of their yards.

Systemic effects were almost as spectacular:

Others become lame of their arms, other some of their legs, and a third sort grow stiff by contraction of all their members, so they have nothing left them sound but their voice which serveth for no other purpose but to bewail their miseries, for which it is scantly sufficient.

The terminal phases of the disease were often revolting.

Wherefore should I trouble you with mention of those that can scantly draw their breath by reason of an asthma, or those whose whole bodies waste with a hectic fever and slow consumption? It fares far worse with these who have all their bodies deformed by a leprosy arising thence, and have all their throttles and throates eaten with putrid and cancrous ulcers, their hair falling off from their heads, their hands and feet cleft with tetters and scaly chinks, neither is their case much better, who, having their brains tainted with this disease, have their whole bodies shaken by fits of the falling sickness, who troubled with a filthy and cursed flux of the belly, do continually cast forth stinking and bloody filth.[17]

Paré's last observation, however, slightly undermines confidence in his diagnosis: 'Lastly, there are no kinds of diseases, no sorts of symptoms, wherewith this disease is not complicate, never to be taken away, unless the virulency of this murrain be wholly taken away and impugned by its proper antidote, that is, *argentum vivum*.'[18] Historians of medicine are still unable to disentangle the venereal disease process from the cumulative effects of treatment with *argentum vivum*, literally 'quick silver' or mercury, which was in routine use for treating syphilis/gonorrhoea well before 1579. Paracelsus, alias his translator John Hester, insists that the initial infection was always accompanied by intense pain, 'great pricking and shooting between the skin and the flesh', which was so severe at night as to be unbearable; in our own time the initial chancre is held to be localised, painless and unaccompanied by systemic symptoms.

Understanding how the disease manifested in the last decades of the sixteenth century is complicated by the effects of a growing awareness of its shameful nature; at first physicians believed that it could be caught from close stools (that is, toilet seats) and sleeping in infected sheets, but gradually, as they came to realise the disease's entirely venereal character, the diagnosis went underground. Because it was rare to find an untreated case, it was impossible to disentangle the disease process from the dire consequences of the destructive therapies invented by the quack 'pockmasters'. More conservative Galenists preferred to treat syphilis with the resin of the Jamaican tree *Guaiacum officinale*. 'Of the kind of this hebenus is another strange and foreign wood, commonly called guaiacum, the powder whereof being filed off and boiled in water till three parts be consumed is most sovereign to cure the pox, and the loathsome infection gotten by lewd, filthy and lecherous life.'[19] Philip Barrough, whose *Method of Physic* was republished nearly every year by Shakespeare's first publisher Richard Field, observed that a disease of such long duration was bound to go through different phases, but the phases he describes are not the same as those described later. In his version too the signs of initial infection were neither localised nor trivial.

Straightways after a young man is infected, he feeleth in himself a certain lassitude or weariness . . . a lumpish heaviness in the whole body, a dullness, faintness, litherness or slowness to move in all the members . . . Moreover, there is a certain pain or ache which wandreth throughout all the body or parts thereof.[20]

Barrough also noticed a change in the complexion. Then within six months of the primary infection, or so Barrough thought, would appear 'hard pustules in the whole body and in the head and beard'. 'If the disease beginneth in the winter, it shall bring forth his crusts in the beginning of summer.'[21] There is also a typical hoarseness, caused by the relaxation of the soft palate, and intense pain at night and unseen 'corruption of the bones'. In Barrough's description the different stages of the disease follow so hard upon each other that they seem almost continuous. He arrives at a tenth development in relatively short order, with no periods of latency worth mentioning:

We may add here in the tenth and last place malign ulcers in all the parts of the body, which ulcerate the whole skin, head and all parts. To conclude there succeed this disease sometime their affects as asthma, which when it is come upon a patient, it declareth him to be past cure. Therefore never put such a one to pain by medicines or other means, for you shall never heal him.[22]

The description given by William Clowes is of a piece with Barrough and Paré. One of his patients was a smith, fifty years old:

for the space of twelve years he had been oftentimes in cure, both by the diet and by unction, and yet ever this disease did reverse, and return to the former state or worse. This infection was dispersed over all the parts of his body, namely, with hard swellings, prickings, with virulent and corrosive ulcers, and corruption of the bones and pains of the joints . . .[23]

Clowes provides various prescriptions for the ointment, all of them containing *argentum vivum*. Barrough was well aware that he was more likely to encounter loosened teeth, collapse of the roof of the mouth and bone-deep ulceration in patients who had been treated with mercury, but even he occasionally used it when all else had failed.[24] Eventually guaiacum was seen to be a symptomatic treatment and even the most hide-bound Galenists came to accept that the administration of mercury, though often destructive and dangerous, was the only effective way of treating venereal disease. Even an amateur gentlewoman practitioner like Lady Mildmay used mercury in her 'ointment for the great disease':

> Take an ounce of quicksilver and kill it with fasting spittle. Then put it into half a pound of boar's grease. Mix them well together. Then take an ounce of mastic, an ounce of wine, an ounce of camphor. Beat these to powder, every one by themselves, and [sift] them. Then take one ounce of saltpetre and mingle them with the boar's grease and quicksilver and anoint the party from the crown of the head to the soles of the feet, sparing no place but the eyes and ears.
>
> Then let the party keep his bed with moderate sweating 2 days and let him sit up for his ease the third day till night. Then anoint him as before and let him lie 2 days more and rise the third day. Take great heed for taking cold and use very good diet and warm drink. If the party take cold it is unto death. It will make the mouth to run very much.

Lady Mildmay's lotion 'for the cure of the pox', apparently used for affected members, is equally robust, being based on sublimate of arsenic, plus unsublimed arsenic. She also treated penile lesions 'and the carnosities in the neck of the bladder, specially . . . such as proceed from the pox and all running of the back, be it of man or woman'. Lady Mildmay, in common with all her contemporaries, had no way of distinguishing gonococcal from syphilitic infection.

Gervase Markham was addressing himself to humbler mortals, but even he includes specifics for 'the French or Spanish pox' in the opening section of *The English Housewife* and he too begins, 'Take quicksilver and kill it with fasting spittle . . .' A second ointment calls for 'white lead and mercury sublimed'. A third ointment is described and then a drink 'to put out the French or Spanish pox', by which is meant to cause the skin lesions to appear so that they can be treated with one or other of the lotions.[25]

If Shakespeare was infected for the first time in middle age when 'the hey day in the blood is tame and waits upon the judgment' he was a colossal fool. Still, if he had been in love with a professional courtesan, c.1600, as some think he was, he might have behaved recklessly. If the dark lady had made him a space on her crowded dance-card, he might have snatched at the opportunity and drunk disease and death with her kisses. If, on the other hand, the dark lady was Emilia Lanier, who lived to a hale old age, dying at the age of seventy-six in 1645, she seems far too healthy to have infected him. The casebooks of Simon Forman record that he examined her several times, without noting any symptom of the French disease. Indeed, his eagerness to 'halek' (his own jargon word for having sex) with her suggests indeed that he found her sound.[26]

The whores of London were not irresistible. Both Henslowe and Alleyn, who were brothel-keepers as well as theatrical entrepreneurs, had daily dealings with prostitutes and yet lived to a healthy old age. But William Jaggard, the printer of the First Folio, lost his sight through the ravages of syphilis. Shakespeare's old enemy Robert Greene may have met his premature end because of the effects of the pox, but his main symptom, massive oedema with virulent diarrhoea, suggests kidney and/or liver failure.

At least one person was being treated for settled venereal infection in Stratford at about the time that Shakespeare is thought to have returned for good. In the Court of Record a surgeon called George Agge brought an action for 'trespass on the case' against the apothecary Philip Rogers, who was at the time suing him for a debt of 35s 7d. We first hear of Philip Rogers in the spring of 1604, when Ann Shakespeare sold him twenty bushels of malt and advanced him two shillings in June. Rogers only ever paid six shillings of the debt so Shakespeare sued him for 35s 10d, plus ten shillings damages.[27] Rogers was probably a relation of William Rogers, sergeant-at-mace, who died in 1597. William Rogers was a victualler but, as his inventory contains distilling equipment, and a quantity of pharmaceuticals, we may conclude that he or someone else in his household worked as a druggist.[28] Philip Rogers married Elinor Saunder in Wroxall on 9 October 1597, and he may have lived for some time in Wroxall. The first of his children to be christened at Holy Trinity was a daughter, Frances, on 6 January 1605. Another daughter, Rose, was christened on 20 September 1607, and another, Margaret, probably an older child, was buried on 19 March 1609. A son went to

Oxford and obtained a licence to practise as a surgeon.[29] Rogers's wife Elinor was buried at Holy Trinity on 29 July 1613. Although he was not buried in Stratford, Rogers seemed to have remained there for some years, and probably filled prescriptions for John Hall. In 1621 Hall treated Frances Rogers for vomiting, jaundice, amenorrhoea and nose-bleeds with an emetic infusion and syrup of violets, purged her with a decoction of senna and sarsaparilla, and then gave her the white of hen's dung in white wine with sugar, which must have done her the world of good.[30]

George Agge seems not to have been a member of the well-known and extensive Ainge family of Stratford. According to the statement penned for him by the attorney William Tetherington he treated Philip Rogers twice, once in the summer of 1611 for 'an ulcer in virga ipsius' which he cured and again a year later for a great ulcer in his shin, which he also cured.[31] Both the penile ulcer and the ulcer on the shin are typical of venereal disease as it manifested at this time.[32] In such a case, the surgeon expected to be paid a substantial sum of twenty or thirty shillings per cure, but Rogers had given nothing in consideration. Agge had also provided Rogers with a cerecloth worth twenty pence, probably to be used as a plaster in his treatment or possibly for the burial of his daughter Margaret in 1609. For this too he had not been paid.

In a list of residents called to answer the commission of the peace Agge is identified as a surgeon.[33] The earliest mention of him in the Court of Record dates from 1605.[34] His presentment in the Court of Record was part of a series of actions involving Philip Rogers of which we know only that Rogers had sued Agge for a debt of 35s 7d, most of which was owed for materials supplied for what was clearly a treatment for the pox, including not only the aniseed, senna, hermodactylis, sarsaparilla and liquorice used in the diet drink, but also the guaiacum, sassafras, bark, venetian turpentine, burgundy pitch, mastic and sub-limate of mercury used in electuaries and ointments. It seems that, in common with most of the litigation that found its way into the Court of Record, the action was partly to establish the correct state of the financial relationship between two colleagues who were obliged to deal almost entirely without cash. So intricate was the mutual indebtedness that both parties agreed to go to trial by jury. The outcome is lost to history.

Agge's unusual surname may represent a German name transmog-rified; the drugs that Rogers supplied are more likely to be utilised in Paracelsian practice than, for example, in the far more conservative practice of John Hall. The administration of corrosive sublimate could mean that Agge was an unscrupulous quack. German candidates for a degree in medicine were at one stage required to take an oath that they would under no conditions prescribe mercury. Surgeons who made a speciality of treating venereal disease were not the most respected in their profession. They often set up lodging houses where their patients could hide out while they were undergoing treatment; poor house-holders could occasionally be prevailed upon to take patients into their houses and nurse them. In 1625 we find the receiver of the Earl of Middlesex, Thomas Catchmay, writing to tell his master that he had searched all over London for Sir Edward Greville only to find him 'in the hands of some chirurgeon for some venereal scars'.[35] We do not know whom Agge was treating besides Rogers.

We have no record of the Bard's ever being treated for the French disease, or exhibiting any of the symptoms of either syphilis or its treatment. If he was infected when he was first in London, at the age of twenty-two or so, he is likely to have had to undergo treatment at various times and ultimately to have been anointed or dosed with mercury or arsenic. What would have killed him, if this was the case, was not the spirochete or the gonococcus but the accumulation of toxins resulting from repeated treatment. Shakespeare's strange de-tachment, from his neighbours in the enclosure struggle, even his astigmatic will, could be explained by the effect of mercury and/or arsenic on his brain. When Shakespeare appeared as the chief witness in the Belott v Mountjoy case in the late spring of 1612, he could not remember the details of a match in which he had acted as chief negotiator. Though Schoenbaum goes easy on him for having no recollection of what had happened eight years earlier, it was no small matter for a 'friend' who had been trusted to handle such a business to claim under oath to have no recollection of the salient details.[36] It was Shakespeare's duty to provide evidence of what had transpired; that was why the Mountjoys had asked him to act for them in the first place. He was to be called for a second interrogation under oath and his name appears in the margin of a set of interrogatories, but he seems to have been excused. He certainly did not appear. I cannot rid myself of an uneasy feeling that when Shakespeare gave evidence on 11 May he was so obviously ill and confused that it was decided that there was no point in his making a second appearance on 19 June. If he had been undergoing treatment, that is, being systematically poisoned with mercury chloride, he would have passed through periods of acute illness of which a common symptom was mental confusion. For all those who wonder why Shakespeare stopped writing, the cumulative effects of successive episodes of mercury poisoning could provide a tragic and terrible answer.

Syphilis provides a possible answer to two more questions: why Shakespeare's career ended so early and why he died so young. To the first could be replied that no one showing signs of any infection was allowed to frequent the court; courtiers with obvious signs of any contagious disease upon them, even measles or smallpox, had to find alternative lodgings until a complete cure had been achieved. As for Shakespeare's dying so young, syphilis plus its treatment could kill at any age. And if the final phase had manifested in the form of an asthma or epilepsy Shakespeare would have known that he had at best only a few months to live.

Syphilis would also provide an explanation of the quatrain inscribed on Shakespeare's gravestone.

> Good friend, for Jesus' sake forbear
> To dig the dust enclosed here.
> Blest be the man that spares these stones,
> And cursed be he that moves my bones.

In his eagerness to prove that Shakespeare hated his wife, Greenblatt makes a nonsense of these undistinguished lines. What is stipulated is not that the grave not be opened, as Greenblatt has it, but that the bones not be disturbed. Hall and Dowdall both say that Shakespeare wrote the doggerel himself. I think it more likely that the stage management of Shakespeare's monument in Holy Trinity was the work of John Hall, who would have known only too well that, if Shakespeare's bones were ever to be exhumed for reburial in a more conspicuous place, posterity would see the lesions on them and know beyond the possibility of doubt that the man of the millennium died of terminal syphilis. As long as the bones are not disturbed, the question will remain moot.

Long-standing venereal disease was not the only condition that permitted the identification of a terminal stage. Certain tumours of the internal organs were pretty well understood to be impossible to treat, especially because the diagnosis could only be made very late in the disease process. Ambrose Paré, principal physician to Henri III, distinguishes four kinds of tumour or imposthume; as he is primarily concerned with curing such things he has little to say about the management of terminal disease, but there are some clues, as in his description of the management of the patient with a 'phlegmon':

> If he be of that age or have so led his life that he cannot want the use of wine, let him use it, but altogether moderately. Rest must be commanded, for all bodies wax hot by motion, but let him chiefly have a care that he do not exercise the part possessed by the phlegmon for fear of a new defluxion. Let his sleep be moderate, neither, if he have a full body, let him sleep by day, particularly after meat. Let him have his belly soluble, if not by nature then by art, as by the frequent use of glisters or suppositories. Let him avoid all vehement perturbations of mind, as hate, anger, brawling; let him wholly abstain from venery.[37]

Some such consideration might explain why Shakespeare seems so inert once we have him at New Place. He may not even have been told of Judith's sudden wedding in February or of the death of his brother-in-law at the beginning of April. As his condition deteriorated its management may have involved clumsy palliatives that would have intensified his inertia and even resulted in stupor. 'If the pain remain, and yield not to these remedies, we must fly to stronger, making use of narcotics or stupifactives, but with care lest we benumb or dead the part . . .'[38]

Paré's treatments for pain are all local, cataplasms and poultices of henbane, poppy and nightshade. In the case of the tumours called cancers, most physicians were well aware, as Paré was, that there was nothing to be done.

When it is increased and covers the noble parts it admits no cure but by the hand, but in decayed bodies, whose strength fail, especially if the cancer be inveterate, we must not attempt the cure, neither with instrument, nor with fire, neither by too acrid medicines as potential cauteries, but we must only seek to keep them from growing more violent or spreading further, by gentle medicines and a palliative cure. For thus many troubled with a cancer have attained even to old age. Therefore Hippocrates admonishes us that it is better not to cure occult or hidden cancers, for the patients cured (saith he) do quickly die but such as are not cured live longer.

If her husband's illness had been diagnosed as a cancer, Ann would have been advised to purge his melancholy humour.

Therefore thick and muddy wines, vinegar, brown bread, cold herbs, old cheese, old and salted flesh, beef, venison, goat, hare, garlic, onions and mustard, and lastly all acrid, acid and other salt things which may by any means incrassate the blood and inflame the humours must be eschewed. A cooling and humecting diet must be prescribed, fasting eschewed, as also watching, immoderate labours, sorrow, cares and mournings. Let him use tisanes, and in his broths boil mallows, spinach, lettuce, sorrel, purslane, succory, hops, violets, borage and the four cold seeds. But let him feed on mutton, veal, kid, capon, pullet, young hares, partridges, fishes of stony rivers, rear [soft-boiled] eggs, and use white wine, but moderately, for his drink.[39]

As the patient wasted, she would have been advised to procure asses' milk for him, for both internal and external application.

It is assumed that John Hall treated the poet in his last illness; if the diagnosis had already been made and the disease known to be terminal, there was small call for the services of a physician. In any case, Hall's use of botanicals was very close to the kind of medical treatment supplied by gentlewomen and well within the competence of Ann Shakespeare. She might have been able to reduce local inflammation by dressing the sores with leaves of mercury but, basically, beyond keeping her husband as clean and comfortable as possible, there was little to be done. If what was needed was palliative care and pain relief, the apothecary was of more use than the diagnostician. Most effective was opium. If Ann was game to dose Shakespeare with opium, he was lucky. Mostly it was considered too dangerous to use. Mary, Lady Hoby was shocked to hear of the death of her physician Dr Brewer, 'procured by a medicine he ministered to himself to cause him to sleep'.[40]

Once their patient was despaired of, all three, physician, surgeon and apothecary, probably took their costly selves off and left the poet to his nurse. Terminal nursing since the beginning of time has been women's work. As Adriana says in *The Comedy of Errors*:

> I will attend my husband, be his nurse,
> Diet his sickness, for it is my office.[41]

Mandragora was known to procure sleep; soaking mandrake root in sweet wine resulted in a reasonably effective anaesthetic.[42] In Joshua Cooke's *How to choose a good wife from a bad* Young Arthur attempts to murder his impossibly good wife by drugging her wine with what he takes to be a poison, which is actually a 'compound powder of poppy . . . and mandrakes', originally intended for use in anaesthetising a man whose leg was to be cut off.[43] Ann would not have intended to cast her dying husband into a 'dead sleep' so she is more likely to have used another analgesic, henbane perhaps, or syrup of poppies. Of all the simples in the New Place garth, henbane was the one most extensively used by old wives. The henbane of choice was the white henbane:

> The juice . . . drawn out of the dry seed bruised by itself and laid in warm water is better and releaseth the pain sooner than . . . the milky humour that cometh out of the herb by scotching or nicking . . . the first juice and that which is drawn out of the dry seed are conveniently put in the medicines that assuage pain.[44]

Preparations of henbane and poppy seeds 'drunken with mead' were also used:[45]

> the heads and leaves of poppies be boiled in water will make a man sleep if his head be bathed therewith . . . the juice of black poppy called opium

cooleth more, thicketh more and drieth more . . . it assuageth ache and bringeth sleep . . . But if a man take too much of it it is hurtful, for it taketh a man's memory away and killeth him. If it be put into the fundament after the manner of a suppository it bringeth sleep . . .[46]

White poppy brings a pleasant sleep, black poppy 'dull or sluggish' sleep.

Ann was less likely than a professional man to have dosed her dying husband with harsh purgatives and emetics to add to his miseries, and more likely to have concentrated her efforts on easing his pain as they both waited in patience for the end. She might even have told Hall to keep his ludicrous and astonishingly expensive prescriptions for more distinguished patients, because four months' care from physicians like him had been known to reduce the richest clients to penury. Perhaps it was Ann's expert care that kept Shakespeare hanging on for a whole month after he updated his will on 25 March. In those quiet hours in the sickroom, husband and wife may have drawn closer together, reliving the old days of their courtship and marriage, remembering the time of their children's innocence. Ann would certainly have read to her husband from her Bible. She would not have read to him from his own poetry, I fancy, for fear of agitating and distressing him, unless it was his fable of marital union between the phoenix and the turtle-dove.

> So they loved as love in twain
> Had the essence but in one:
> Two distincts, division none.
> Number there in love was slain.
>
> Hearts remote yet not asunder,
> Distance, and no space was seen
> 'Twixt this turtle and his queen,
> But in them it were a wonder.

When Hamlet had groaned, in his misery, 'Husband and wife is one flesh,' he was speaking, necessarily, anagogically. The union of marriage is not a union of bodies, but a union of souls, of which the

intercourse of bodies is merely an emblem. If Shakespeare had gone
here and there, defiling his body and compromising his compact with
his wife, her constancy now redeemed him.

> Property was thus appalled
> That the self was not the same.
> Single nature's double name
> Neither two nor one was called.
>
> Reason, in itself compounded,
> Saw division grow together,
> To themselves yet either neither
> Simple were so well compounded.

Once Ann would have had so many questions, but now that it was
too late to ask them she realised that she no longer needed the
answers. Her daughters may have remonstrated that she was doing too
much for the husband who had done so little for them, that the men-
and maidservants should undertake the heavier, dirtier tasks, but Ann
was a wife of the old school.

I have no better reason to believe that Ann slept in her husband's
chamber so that she would wake if he was restless at night than the example of Mistress Quickly watching by the deathbed of Sir John Falstaff:

> He parted even just between twelve and one, even at the turning of
> the tide, for after I saw him fumble with the sheets, and play with
> flowers, and smile upon his fingers' end, I knew there was but one
> way. For his nose was sharp as a pen and he babbled of green fields . . .
> he bade me lay more clothes to his feet. I put my hand into the bed and
> felt them and they were cold as any stone. Then I felt to his knees and
> so upward and upward, and all was cold as any stone.[47]

In peasant families it was usual for a family member to sleep alongside
the dying person, checking regularly that they were still warm,
chafing their limbs if they grew chill, ready to call the others if
the end appeared to be approaching. If Ann did as much for
Shakespeare it would not have been thought worthy of remark.

As her husband's health deteriorated, Ann may have been too preoccupied to notice what her younger daughter was up to. On 10 February Judith Shakespeare suddenly married Thomas Quiney, with no prior announcing of the banns. The match may have been mooted as long before as 1611, when Judith witnessed a deed of sale of a house belonging to Thomas's mother Elizabeth Quiney. With the proceeds Thomas Quiney had taken a lease on a tavern in the High Street, which might have been thought of as a prelude to setting up as a married man, but no wedding ensued. Now, suddenly, five years later, 31-year-old Judith and 27-year-old Quiney were in such a hurry to be married that they applied for a licence to permit their marrying in Lent, not from the Bishop of Worcester, as Judith's parents had, but from the Vicar of Holy Trinity Church, who claimed the right to issue licences as part of the privilege of the town charter or 'Stratford peculiar'.

In this case the spur may have been a pregnancy but not the bride's. When an unmarried woman called Margaret Wheeler was brought to bed in Stratford in mid-March and the midwives did their duty by refusing to assist her until she 'confessed the man', she named Thomas Quiney. The midwives may have delayed too long, for they lost both mother and baby. On 15 March 'Margaret Wheeler and her child' were buried in Holy Trinity. Duncan-Jones assumes that Margaret Wheeler is a connection of Alderman John Wheeler who was bailiff in 1565 and 1576, before resigning his office in 1586.[48] This Wheeler died in 1592, and his wife in 1596. Of their four sons none can be identified as the father or the grandfather of a Margaret. No fewer than five Wheeler families, as well as scattered Wheelers who appear unrelated, can be found in the Stratford registers of the time. The only possibility seems to be the daughter of Randall Wheeler, who was baptised Margaret at Holy Trinity Church in September 1586, which would make her three years older than Thomas Quiney. An Elinor Wheeler was the servant of Richard Pink, maltster and husbandman, who in his will in 1615 assured her of bed and board in his house for as long as she stayed in service or a legacy of £3 if she preferred to leave. Two more Wheelers bore illegitimate children, Joan Wheeler a son Robert in March 1617, and Elizabeth Wheeler a son John in January 1625. Perhaps there was a low-life clan of Wheelers living somewhere on the wrong side of the tracks, though Humphrey Wheeler, the shoe-maker, had a daughter Elizabeth born in 1601 who may have been the same Elizabeth who bore a base-born child in 1625.

By 15 March the newly-weds were in trouble. An apparitor called Walter Nixon informed against them to the Consistory Court of Worcester for marrying without the correct licence. Quiney did not attend the hearing, and was excommunicated. On 26 March, Quiney was called before the Vicar's Court in Stratford to answer the matter of Margaret Wheeler's pregnancy; in open court he confessed to having had carnal knowledge of her and was condemned for fornication. His penance was to stand at the church door arrayed in a white sheet for three Sundays in succession. For some reason, perhaps for fear of public disorder, the penalty was quickly reduced. Quiney was asked instead to make a gift of one crown to the poor of the parish, and to confess his fault to the incumbent of the chapelry at Bishopton. In the court record the clerk has entered against this mitigated requirement, 'dismissus', so perhaps even this mild punishment was eventually waived.[49] We need to infer, I think, that the truth behind this matter was more complex than appears. Somehow or other Quiney was able to convince the moral authorities that he was not the unprincipled lecher that he seems. He did after all attend the court, thereby acknowledging its authority; he did confess his fault, either because he couldn't do otherwise, if indeed Wheeler had named him, or because he was shocked and contrite at the price she and her child paid for their dalliance.

The whole business seems repellently squalid. We can now only wonder about Judith Shakespeare's motivation. Perhaps she didn't know of Quiney's relationship with Wheeler, which would be sad, but perhaps she did, which would be horrible. Perhaps she wanted him at any price. Judith had been at her own disposal for ten years, so there was little that Ann could say or do to influence her behaviour.

Fripp thinks that the occasion of the drinking bout that killed Shakespeare was 'doubtless that of his daughter's wedding'.[50] Others think that the shock of the scandal was what caused his decline in health. Given the present state of our understanding, neither case has merit. By 1616 official attitudes to premarital pregnancy had hardened and the parish authorities were less likely to allow Quiney to admit paternity and bear the costs of rearing the child than to force him to marry a young woman who claimed to be pregnant by him. The only way of preventing such an outcome was to be already married to someone else. If Judith had always been his chosen partner, and prevented from marrying only because her parents would not make the match or provide her with a portion, it would have made sense to persuade her to rescue him at this desperate juncture. The vicar, John Rogers, must have agreed that swift marriage was what was required; his curate Richard Watts would later marry Quiney's sister.

Quiney may have been fool enough to have sex with a woman who had had sex with other men, and she may have picked him out as the best candidate for provider for herself and her child. Judith Sadler did try something of the sort in 1622. Somehow in this miserable business Thomas came to be seen as the lesser offender. His confession to the Consistory Court strikes one as artless; a hardened sinner would, one feels, have denied everything. Ann cannot have regretted her younger daughter's marrying into Bess Quiney's distinguished family, but she may well have regretted that her daughter was married as it were in her smock, with nothing from her father as a portion, in winter and with no time for celebration. Ann must also have known that the marriage settlement between the Hall and Shakespeare families had effectively disinherited Judith. When Thomas married Judith that winter it must have been for qualities inherent in herself, and perhaps Ann was glad of that.

It seems from the rewriting of Shakespeare's will in March that it was already apparent that Shakespeare's brother-in-law Willam Hart was drawing close to death. He was buried on 17 April, a week before his brother-in-law. Ann must have walked behind both coffins. Her nephew Richard Hathaway was now a churchwarden and met them both at the entrance to the churchyard. Hart was buried in the churchyard. Shakespeare is supposed to have been buried in the chancel, according to Fripp because it was his right as lessee of the tithes.[51] The manner of it seems a little strange; the gravestone is too short, being little more than three feet long, and rather too obviously sited under the monument on the north wall.

CHAPTER NINETEEN

of Shakespeare's lop-sided will and Ann's options – dower right,
widow-bed or destitute dependency

Once her husband was decently interred, Ann had to endure the
opening and reading of the will. The will first became known to
posterity in 1747, the Vicar of Holy Trinity having come across a
copy of it transcribed in the mid-seventeenth century. The vicar,
Joseph Greene by name, expressed his disappointment in a letter to
James West, secretary to the Treasury:

> The legacies and bequests therein are doubtless as he intended; but the
> manner of introducing them, appears to me so dull and irregular, so
> absolutely void of the least particle of that spirit which animated our
> great poet, that it must lessen his character as a writer to imagine the
> least sentence of it his production.[1]

As Shakespeare is always thought of by bardolaters as standing alone,
it has never occurred to any of them to ask whether it was Shakespeare
himself who decided to call Francis Collins and instruct him to set about
the tedious business of drawing up his will. It happens often enough in
real life that carers have to take the initiative in this delicate business and
it may have happened in Shakespeare's case. We might wonder why
Thomas Greene did not take charge, seeing as he is supposed by
historians to have been Shakespeare's kinsman and close friend. He
was certainly a much better lawyer than old Francis Collins, a country
attorney who was in poor health and would die within months.

There are some who want us to believe that Greene's grief at
Shakespeare's untimely death was what prompted him to sell his
pretty house and flee to Bristol. In fact Greene had loved living at

New Place as long as Shakespeare wasn't there, when Ann was in complete control. Shakespeare had disappointed Greene by currying favour with the Combes; he was now to disappoint Greene again by authorising a shabby, poorly drafted, mean-spirited statement of his last wishes. Nevertheless it may have been Ann who insisted on setting something down in writing; her family were all will-writers. In Shakespeare's family, as far as we can tell, there were none. John, Mary, Gilbert, Richard, Edmund – none left a will, as far as we know.

The most obvious, and for some people the most unusual, thing about Shakespeare's will is that he did not appoint his wife his executor. As Sir Thomas Smith remarks:

> few [widows] there be that be not made at the death of their husband
> either sole or chief executrices of his last will and testament, and have
> for the most part the government of the children and their portions
> except it be in London where a peculiar order is taken by the city
> much after the fashion of the civil law.[2]

The job of an executor was onerous, both at the time of the administration of the will and, especially in the case of a will like Shakespeare's which reached into generations yet unborn, for years afterwards. At sixty Ann Shakespeare would have known herself to be too old to take on the responsibility. For all we know she begged her husband to excuse her and suggested Susanna and John Hall instead. Indeed, if she had had to listen to her husband's desperate attempts to identify male heirs generations down the line, she might have lost patience and told him she wanted nothing to do with it. Dreaming of a male child for thirty-three-year-old Susanna Hall who hadn't been pregnant in eight years was just soft-headed; projecting further into the reproductive career of an eight-year-old granddaughter was even less realistic. Who knows but Ann may have really objected to her husband's meanness to her younger daughter. Judith had thrown herself away on Thomas Quiney much as Ann Hathaway had on young Will Shakespeare. Ann may well have pleaded Judith's case with her obdurate father and retired defeated. More likely is it, however, that Collins's pernicketiness about the entail was necessitated by the terms of Susanna's marriage settlement.

When the first draft of Shakespeare's will was written by Francis
Collins in January 1616, Shakespeare was already conscious of
approaching death; a second draft was never written. All that Collins
could manage was to rewrite the first page; the rest had to stand. The
will was first published in Part I of the sixth volume of *Biographia
Literaria* with an interesting error in the transcription; instead of
'second-best bed' the transcriber read 'brown best bed'.

The will begins unremarkably:

In the name of God Amen I William Shakespeare of Stratford upon
Avon in the county of War[wickshire] gentleman in perfect health and
memory God be praised do make & ordain this my last will and
testament in manner and form following that is to say first I commend
my soul into the hands of God my Creator hoping & assuredly
believing through the only merits of Jesus Christ my Saviour to be
made partaker of life everlasting and my body to the earth whereof it is
made . . .[3]

The preamble as written by Francis Collins would make it clear that
Shakespeare died a protestant, if it were not simply the formulaic
preamble set out in law textbooks. To have departed from it, and
made reference to the intercession of the Blessed Virgin and the saints,
would have shown Shakespeare to have been a Catholic; simply
failing to depart from it proves nothing. If there is anything odd about
the will at this point it is that Shakespeare does not specify where he
wishes to be buried.

Shakespeare then addresses the problem of Judith.

Item I give and bequeath unto my daughter Judith one hundred and
fifty pounds of lawful English money to be paid to her in manner and
form following that is to say one hundred pounds in discharge of her
marriage portion within one year after my decease with consideration
after the rate of two shillings in the pound for so long time as the same
shall be unpaid to her after my decease & the fifty pounds residue
thereof upon her surrendering of or giving of such security as the
overseers of this my will shall like of to surrender or grant all her estate
and right that shall descend or come unto her after my decease or that

she now hath of in or to one copyhold tenement with the appurtenances lying and being in Stratford aforesaid . . . being parcel or
holden of the manor of Rowington unto my daughter Susanna Hall
and her heirs forever

Shakespeare gives his executors the option of paying Judith £10 a
year in lieu of her handsome lump sum. The £50 was compensation
for surrendering any right to the 'copyhold tenement', that is the
cottage in Chapel Lane, that had been acquired in September 1602:
'No doubt the cottage came in handy as quarters for a servant or
gardener.'⁴ One is surprised to find a scholar as scrupulous as
Schoenbaum writing 'no doubt' when he means 'perhaps'. With
New Place slap in the middle of Stratford, and the unemployed poor
all around, an employer in search of a 'servant or gardener' hardly
needed to offer the blandishment of a cottage. There is no hint in the
records that Judith, who was neither servant nor gardener, had any
claim on the Chapel Lane cottage, but she must have had. She
certainly surrendered it after her father's death, for the Rowington
Manor records show that Susanna took over the payments of the
yearly fine or ground-rent and became the official tenant. At the time
of the reading of the will Judith was living with her husband in his
tavern in the house called Atwood's, next to his mother's house. On
21 December 1615, a new lease of the house called the Cage had been
granted to Bess Quiney's son-in-law, Alderman William Chandler,
who seems to have been running his mercery business in partnership
with her. Chandler's wife, Bess's eldest daughter Elizabeth, had died
the preceding May and Chandler had lost no time in remarrying. The
new lease, granting him thirty-one years from 21 December 1615 for
an annual rent of forty shillings, was sealed on 1 March 1616, but
within weeks Thomas managed to agree with him a straight swap, of
Atwood's for the Cage. The exchange was not formally sanctioned
until 19 July, but the newly-weds probably moved in before that.
The next provision for Judith strikes a curiously callous note:

Item I give and bequeath unto my said daughter Judith one hundred
and fifty pounds more if she or any issue of her body be living at the
end of three years next ensuing the day of the date of this my will

during which time my executors to pay her consideration from my decease according to the rate aforesaid And if she die within the said term without issue of her body then my will is and I do give and bequeath one hundred pounds thereof to my niece [that is, grand-daughter] Elizabeth Hall & the fifty pounds to be set forth by my executors during the life of my sister Joan Hart and the use and profit thereof coming shall be paid to my said sister Joan and after her decease the said £50 shall remain amongst the children of my said sister equally to be divided amongst them but if my said daughter Judith be still living at the end of the said three years or any issue of her body then my will is & so I devise & bequeath the said hundred and fifty pounds to be set out by my executors and overseers for the best benefit of her and her issue and the stock not to be paid unto her so long as she shall be married & covert baron but my will is that she shall have the consideration yearly paid unto her during her life & after her decease the said stock and consideration to be paid to her children if she have any & if not to her executors or assigns she living the said term after my decease provided that if such husband as she shall at the end of the said three years be married unto or at any time after do sufficiently assure unto her & the issue of her body lands answerable to the portion by this my will given unto her.

If Judith 'or any issue of her body' is still living three years after Shakespeare's death, a further £150 is to be made available in the form of a trust, meaning that she and/or her child or children could enjoy the interest on it at the usual rate of 10 per cent. Her husband could claim the principal only if he settled on her lands to the same value. This he was under no obligation to do. If Judith should die with no surviving child within the three years, the £100 would go to Susanna's daughter Elizabeth, and the £50 to Shakespeare's sister Joan Hart and her children. Shakespeare succeeded in guaranteeing Judith and her children sufficient inalienable income to live on. At the same time he contrived a situation where his widowed sister would get her windfall of £50 only if his daughter and any child she might have both perished, possibly because he was only entitled to take out of the estate as entailed by the marriage settlement personal bequests to a certain value. If Judith survived (and she did), Joan had to make do with a mere £20 and her dead brother's old clothes. Her three sons were sixteen, eleven and eight. They would have looked very odd trailing round Stratford in their dead uncle's silks, but in any event they were not entitled to wear them. The Bard's wardrobe must have been turned over for sale by one or other of the Stratford mercers, who took his cut and gave Joan and her boys the rest, a shabby bequest if ever there was one. Again, we might infer that Shakespeare had very little room to manoeuvre. His clothes would be one asset that had not been considered in a marriage settlement. 'I do will and devise unto her the house with the appurtenances in Stratford wherein she dwelleth for her natural life under the yearly rent of 12 pence'. Shakespeare did leave each of Joan's three boys £5, which reflects interestingly upon the £5 that he got from old John Combe.

> Item I give will bequeath and devise unto my daughter Susanna Hall for better enabling of her to perform this my will & towards the performance thereof all that capital messuage or tenement with the appurtenances in Stratford aforesaid called the New Place wherein I now dwell and two messuages or tenements with the appurtenances situate lying and being in Henley Street . . .

To Susanna and her heirs male went all his other possessions in Old Stratford, Bishopton and Welcombe, plus the Blackfriars house, and to Susanna and her husband all the poet's 'leases', 'all goods, chattels, leases, plate, jewels and household stuff whatsoever', except his plate that went to Elizabeth and a silver-gilt bowl that went to Judith.

Shakespeare made no gift to the King's Men, but simply set aside £1 6s 8d for the purchase of mourning rings by three members of the company, John Hemmings, Richard Burbage and Henry Condell. To set Shakespeare's will beside that of the musician and actor Augustine Phillips, who died in May 1605, with its gifts of £5 to be shared among the hired men, twenty shillings each for five of his fellow shareholders, a thirty-shilling gold piece for Shakespeare and another for Condell, and silver bowls worth £5 for each of his three executors, is to be struck by the coolness and distance of Shakespeare's relations with the King's Men. He leaves the sword he had paid through the nose to have the right to wear to Thomas Combe. Six months later Combe came across Valentine Tant in the town common close to the Dingles, and beat him up. On 14 November Tant, who was nearly seventy, was buried.

Perhaps the most disappointing aspect of Shakespeare's will is his indifference to the plight of Stratford's poor, to whose use he left £10. Sterner men had been anxious that their death provide the poor with an occasion for celebration. Even Bartholomew Hathaway wanted the poor to enjoy a square meal on the occasion of his funeral. Cantankerous Alderman Robert Perrott left money to buy fuel to be sold on to the poor at cost. When the elder William Combe died in April 1610, by the will written six months before his death he left £20 to the poor of Warwick, and £10 each to the poor of Alvechurch, Stratford and Broadway. When John Combe died in 1614 his will provided twenty shillings for a learned preacher to make a sermon twice a year at Holy Trinity, money for ten black gowns for the poor at 13s 4d each, £20 to the poor of Stratford, and £100 to be lent to fifteen 'poor or young tradesmen' setting up in business, at the rate of twenty nobles a piece for three years, in return for a twice-yearly payment of 3s 4d.

Though Shakespeare may have been in perfect health and memory when he wrote his will, according to Greenblatt he was incapable of recognising the obvious – that he had failed to mention his wife – until someone pointed it out to him.

> Someone – his daughter Susanna, perhaps, or his lawyer – may have called this erasure, this total absence, to his attention. Or perhaps as he lay in his bed, his strength ebbing away, Shakespeare himself brooded on his relationship to Anne – on the sexual excitement that once drew him to her, on the failure of the marriage to give him what he wanted, on his own infidelities and perhaps on hers, on the intimacies he had forged elsewhere, on the son they had buried, on the strange ineradicable distaste for her that he felt deep within him.[5]

Some, like Charles Knight, Schoenbaum and Wood, have explained Ann's absence from her husband's will as a consequence of her entitlement as a widow to 'dower right', understood to be a third of the estate.[6] Later research has shown that such dower right applied only to London, York and Wales.[7] After 1590 in the Vale of Oxford, for example, dower right could only be enjoyed as long as a widow remained unmarried. At sixty Ann was unlikely to remarry. The truth seems to be that, in the case of intestacy, the ecclesiastical authorities could not assign to a widow less than one-third of her husband's estate but a husband making a will could reduce his wife's share to nothing, which is what Greenblatt and his ilk think Shakespeare did. Perhaps he did consign his wife to destitution and perhaps it was not the first time. Such behaviour would have been all things unbecoming and most unusual. It is to be hoped that the truth is less contemptible.

Though different notions of widows' entitlements prevailed in different areas, the general practice was probably as it is outlined in Burn's *Ecclesiastical Law* of 1763:

> widows have been tolerated to reserve to their own use, not only their apparel and a convenient bed, but a coffer with divers things therein necessary for their own persons; which things have usually been omitted out of the inventory of their deceased husband's goods, unless peradventure the husband was so far indebted, as the rest of his goods would not suffice to discharge the same.[8]

Much that was custom was not enshrined in law. Women did have property of their own that doesn't appear in wills and inventories, which seldom mention jewellery of any sort, even wedding rings. Weeks before her husband died, Ann might have chosen what she wanted for her own use. What she chose, being already given, would not have appeared in the will. The estate according to the will includes no theatre shares, and no books or papers of any kind. As a distribution of everything Shakespeare died possessed of his will doesn't make sense.

The matter of the bed may have been accidentally overlooked, or perhaps the bed Ann had chosen could not easily be removed before Shakespeare's death, perhaps because Shakespeare was himself lying in it, and so he had to make especial mention of it. If Ann had been seen to take or had been believed to have taken goods out of the estate after her husband's death, she could have been sued by his executors.

The absence of any mention of where Ann should live after she left New Place is not unusual, but often testators specify that a widow should be allowed free use of part of the estate, whether a gatehouse or a pair of rooms or an upper floor or a 'back-side', or that she be allowed to remain as tenant of leasehold property for the term of her life. Shakespeare's silence on the point is not remarkable but it is not particularly creditable either. It is possible that Judith had been made to give up any interest in the copyhold cottage in Chapel Lane because it was reserved for the use of her mother during her life.

Throughout this book I have argued that, as we can find no evidence of Shakespeare having supported his family, especially during the lost years, we must assume that Ann Shakespeare was financially independent and assessed for tax purposes as *feme sole*. If this is the (admittedly unusual) case she may not have been eligible for dower thirds. For commentators determined to interpret any and all evidence as proving that Shakespeare hated his wife, even this circumstance would be held against her. Even leaving her the bed is parlayed into a ruse to disinherit her, as if any such ruse would have been necessary.

It is for legal historians to debate whether by specifying a single object the testator was in effect attempting to wipe out the widow's customary one-third life-interest – that is to disinherit her. But what the eloquently hostile gesture seems to say emotionally is that Shakespeare had found his trust, his happiness, his capacity for intimacy, his best bed elsewhere.[9]

Greenblatt is following in the tradition of Malone who splutters: 'His wife had not wholly escaped his memory, he had forgot her, he had recollected her but so recollected her, as more strongly to mark how little he esteemed her; he had already (as is vulgarly expressed) cut her off, not indeed with a shilling, but with an old bed.'[10]

Ann's father in his will had made a strange stipulation about the bed he had caused to be made and set up at Hewlands:

Item my will is that all the ceiling in my Halls house with two joined beds in my parlour shall continue and stand unremoved during the natural life or widowhood of Joan my wife and the natural life of Bartholomew my son and John my son and the longest lived of them.[11]

What the motive can have been for insisting that his bed not be moved until the three lives had elapsed we do not know and can hardly guess. Mary Evelyn in her satiric poem *Mundus Muliebris* refers to the sturdy oaken bed that is meant to last 'one whole century through' as if it were typical of a certain kind of overbearing patriarch.[12]

Even a humble bed, consisting of frame, straw mattress, rugs and blankets, was a valuable commodity worth £2 or so, about as much as a cow. If the frame was posted and canopied and the mattress was stuffed with pure goose down, the value could rise to £10 or more. In any house, the bed was the most costly item of furniture and sometimes so massive and heavy that it could hardly be regarded as movable property. The actual wooden structure, which was usually erected *in situ*, plus its carving and gilding, was expensive; when down mattresses were added to the expenditure on hangings, a big bed could be worth as much as a small house.

In 1557, William Bracey of Snitterfield left his second-best bed to his son and heir with three pair of sheets. In 1573 William Palmer of Leamington left his wife all her wearing apparel and his 'second best bed for herself furnished and other meaner featherbed furnished for her maid' – and at the same time doubled the income she would receive from their original marriage settlement 'in consideration that she is a gentlewoman and drawing towards years and that I would have her to live as one that were and had been my wife'. Thomas Greene's father, Thomas Greene of Warwick, in his will of 22 July 1590 left his 'second feather bed furnished' to Thomas Greene.[13] The bequest of a bed was often a sign of particular affection: Francis Russell, Earl of Bedford, when he died in 1585, left his youngest daughter his 'best bed of cloth of gold and silver'.[14] By the will of Stratford Alderman Robert Perrott, drawn up on 8 March 1589, his wife is given a yearly allowance, and 'the bed which she brought unto me with all furniture thereto belonging'.[15] Walter Ralegh advised his son 'if she love again, let her not enjoy her second love in the same bed wherein she loved thee'.[16] One yeoman of the Sussex Downs, in his will of 1616, gave his wife Agnes Mockford the best feather bed in the 'great chamber' with all its 'appurtenances' or furnishings, but only on condition that she deliver to his son a signed and sealed 'deed of release in the law of all her dower', excluding £3 per annum. This was Agnes's only specific bequest from her husband, apart from the residual goods she received as executrix, and on first reading it appears to cheat her out of valuable land in exchange for a bed which might be of only sentimental value. However, the will went on to specify that if she refused to give up her dower lands she would then forfeit her right to the featherbed. Hardly a ferocious sanction, but it immediately suggests that the land and the bed were of comparable value.[17] When Alice Thornton was widowed in 1668 her brother-in-law told her 'That it was the law . . . the widow was to have her widow-bed first out of all her husband's goods . . .'[18]

Wills do not account for all the transfers of property that occur at the time of the testator's death. Often property is transferred by deeds, which are not registered and will not appear in probate records either.[19] Land was often transferred in the owner's lifetime by deed or court roll or directed to be sold off to pay debts. Shakespeare's will mentioned no books but he must surely have had books and have disposed of them by personal bequest. If they included papers of his own, they would have been of a different order of value to any of the trifling bits of plate and mourning rings and what-have-you that were distributed around friends and family. No one has ever suggested that he may have given them into Ann's keeping, but such a suggestion is no more unlikely than any other.

The key to Shakespeare's lop-sided will, if we could only find it, must be the settlement that was negotiated at the time of the marriage of John Hall and Susanna Shakespeare. If I am right, and both parties were made sole legatees of their parents, Shakespeare was not free to split his estate or devise any of it to Judith or, indeed, to Ann. Before deciding that he thereby disinherited his wife, we ought to consider the possibility that the marriage was actually promoted by Ann and accepted by Shakespeare as a *fait accompli*. Either Ann or William could have constructed the settlement in this fashion because Judith was understood to be contracted in some way to Thomas Quiney.

Contrariwise the terms of Susanna's wedding settlement could have left Judith without a portion, and have brought negotiations with Bess Quiney to a halt. Solemnisation could have been deferred indefinitely in order to force the Shakespeares' hand, or Judith may have been too proud to enter a marriage entirely unprovided for and totally dependent upon her husband's family.

Scholars who have considered the matter have assumed that Shakespeare conveyed the title of the Blackfriars gatehouse to trustees in order to prevent his wife's getting her hands on it. It is at least as likely, and to my mind more likely, that the trusteeship was instituted in order to prevent the gatehouse being swallowed up in the marriage settlement and becoming part of the Hall inheritance, in which case the King's Men could have lost the use of it. Hall lost no time in conveying his interest in it to different trustees, including the mysterious Matthew Morris, who had been his father's assistant and was now making a name for himself in Stratford.

If we assume that Ann had the widow's coffer to go along with her widow-bed, her future begins to look rather more interesting, worthier of Shakespeare's oldest, truest love.

CHAPTER TWENTY

*of burials, and monuments, widows' mites and widows' work, and
the quiet death of the quiet woman of Stratford*

When her husband died Ann was sixty, and free for the first time in a
third of a century. Both her daughters were married, for better or worse,
and the husband of one of them had been left her house. Tension in
Stratford was running high, as the Corporation continued the battle to
exert its right against the enclosing gentry. On Trinity Sunday, as he
came away from a meeting with Thomas Greene at St Mary's House,
Alderman Chandler was handed a threatening letter from William
Combe;[1] in September Combe abused his power as high sheriff to
impound the commoners' cattle.[2] Greene kept faithful note of all such
hostilities, even as he was preparing to leave Stratford for ever.
According to Fripp, 'Combe troubled him to the end of his Steward-
ship; but it was the loss of his great kinsman evidently, that decided him
to sell his house and interest in the tithes and remove to Bristol.'[3]

What is evident to Fripp is not necessarily evident to others ex-
amining the same material. Greene had had very little of his great
kinsman's company at any time. He had come to the end of the
possibilities for advancement afforded by Stratford. As the agent of the
Corporation he had accumulated powerful enemies and he was
probably losing sympathy with the Corporation's brand of puritanism
which, under persecution from the ecclesiastical commissioners, was
becoming rigid to the point of truculence. During the Bard's many and
long absences Greene had certainly protected Ann and her daughters to
the best of his ability, so he had ample reason to be disgusted with the
passing over of his children, twelve-year-old Ann and eight-year-old
William, in his great kinsman's will, even if he was unsurprised at the
omission of himself and his wife. He might have deplored the Bard's

treatment of Ann and Judith too. A career opening in Bristol offered him an opportunity to escape the drudgery and disappointment that seemed to be all Stratford had to offer. In losing him Stratford lost an able champion, and the most trustworthy chronicler of its struggle, but the Corporation gained St Mary's House and at a cut price. In the late spring of 1616 Greene wrote to the Corporation:

> I have received your letters of the 15 of this May, and do see, if we
> agree, I must lose a hundred marks of the true value of my things I sell,
> to the place which has more reason, if I may speak it without offence,
> to give me recompense to a greater value for my golden days and spirits
> spent in Stratford's service.[4]

Abashed, the Corporation upped its offer, but not by much, and Greene had no option but to accept. Among the aldermen who provided money to enable the purchase was Ann's nephew, Richard Hathaway, who lent £20.[5] The money for the second tranche of the payment was collected at New Place, where Greene came for the purpose on 3 February 1618. By that time his family was gone from Stratford; at the Hall of 8 October 1617 it had been decreed 'that Mrs Bailiff and Mrs Alderwoman shall be removed to the seat [in Holy Trinity Church] where Mrs Greene did sit'.[6]

Most commentators assume that during her widowhood Ann lived at New Place as a dependant of her son-in-law John Hall. If she had she would not have felt herself free in the least; if I am right, and she was used to being self-sufficient, she would have resented having to go cap in hand to John Hall for clothes, food, light and heat. She could hardly have worked for her son-in-law as some kind of menial or even as his housekeeper. Her daughter was thirty-three years old and had been mistress of her own house for nine years; she was hardly likely to have entered New Place as anything but the chatelaine. As there is no record of where the Halls lived before they took over New Place, they may always have lived in an apartment there, and the fact of ownership as conferred by Shakespeare's will may have made very little practical difference. Or they could have set aside the cottage in Chapel Lane for Ann's use or she could have taken over whatever lease they were relinquishing in order to transfer to New Place, or none of the above. As a widow Ann actually had more options than she had ever had in her life before.

Social historians have disagreed about the likelihood of widowed mothers eking out their days nodding by a daughter's or a daughter-in-law's fireside. Laslett was very clear on the point, saying that barely 5 per cent of households contained more than two generations. Spufford interpreted this as meaning that almost all surviving grandparents were accommodated with their children, as only 6 per cent of people survived to be grandparents. Later research has tended to support Laslett:

> The living situation of 211 widows is discernible from their own probate accounts or inventories and wills . . . only 16 per cent lived in someone else's house, usually that of a married daughter or son. The majority of widows whose estates reached the probate court (84 per cent) headed their own households . . . In parish lists of inhabitants in the early modern period . . . 74 per cent of all widows either headed households or were solitary (in their own house) and only 25 per cent lived in someone else's household.[7]

Ann might have chosen to live with her younger daughter. Susanna's breeding days were apparently over, but Judith was facing her first confinement at the ripe age of thirty-one. In July 1616 she and her husband moved from his small tavern to the Cage, in a prime position on the corner of Bridge Street and the High Street, where he set up his wineshop.[8] Susanna took over a well-run house, with established gardens and a trained workforce. Six months pregnant, Judith must have been glad of experienced help in organising the new establishment and training the staff. She bore her first child in November. Despite her father's coldness towards him, when Thomas Quiney took his newborn to the church on 23 November, the name that had been agreed upon was 'Shakespeare'. Ann's delight in her grandson was soon cut short; little Shakespeare was buried less than six months later, on 8 May 1617. Though Shakespeare could not have been weaned by then, Judith was already pregnant when he died, for her next baby, Richard, was baptised on 9 February, a bare nine months later. We should probably infer that little Shakespeare was put out to nurse, and we can imagine what Ann thought of this. But her daughter had gone up in the world. What Ann had done out of necessity was not fitting for a woman whose husband was described (wrongly) in the parish registers as 'Thomas Quiney gent'.

For those who could afford it, the rationale for putting children out to nurse was persuasive; first milk was universally condemned as bad for the child, and the newborn was usually fed instead on substitutes while the mother suffered for as much as a month before being allowed to breast-feed. It made sense to give the baby into the care of a woman with an established milk supply.[9] It seems that Richard, Judith's second-born, was nursed by his mother, possibly because Judith, having lost her first-born, heeded her mother's advice and allowed herself to be reassured as to the quality of her milk. Richard's little brother Thomas was christened on 23 January 1620, two weeks short of the two-year interval that is usual among births to women of the people in Stratford. Ann must have been delighted to watch these two babies grow up to be healthy boys.

Unfortunate though the circumstances of Judith's marriage had been, the marriage seems to have been a real one. Thomas may have been unreliable and impractical, but he might also have been fun. While Susanna busied herself in her huge house with her one daughter, living the life of a gentlewoman, Judith and Thomas seem to have lived at the Cage like lovers. As the babies came along the Cage must have been as lively as New Place was dull. And there was work to do. If Ann was, as I think, a skilled maltster and brewer, she would have made sure that the Cage sold good ale. As long as she lived it was possible to believe that Thomas Quiney had it in him to do well. The deaths of his brothers, one of whom married an heiress, must have improved his prospects, especially as his other brother Richard was building an impressive fortune of his own. In 1617 Thomas was named burgess, and later constable; in 1621 and 1622 he served as chamberlain, but he was no accountant. When he presented his accounts for 1622–3, he prefaced them with an inaccurate quotation from Saint-Gelais, an unwarranted piece of swank that made him no friends, especially as the accounts were then rejected as defective. Chamberlain was as far as he got. After Ann's death his standing and his business slid downhill. In 1631 he was presented in the Vicar's Court for swearing and fined a shilling, and for 'suffering townsmen to tipple in his house' which cost him 1s 6d. After his mother's death, he tried to dispose of the lease of the Cage. Eventually he was obliged to live on an allowance from his wealthy brother.

Ann may have been needed at Hewlands too. On 11 February 1617 Isabel Hathaway died, leaving Bartholomew and their seventeen-year-old son Edmund alone at Hewlands Farm. Their first-born, Richard, had been apprenticed to a baker; after completing his indentures he married Priscilla Kyrdall. As a master baker, based at the Crown in Bridge Street which he leased from the Corporation, he had risen in the world, though he incurred at least once the usual fine of twelve pence for sabbath-breaking.[10] We have no record of his attending school, but as he acted as one of the Overseers of the Poor in 1609, when thirteen-year-old Margaret Getley was covenanted to Anne Curtis to 'learn the trade of knitting and other housewifery', he must have been literate.[11] If I am right about the way Ann supported herself and her children, she would have been especially useful to her nephew when it came to finding the skilled craftswomen who could be trusted to take on small children as apprentices and to train them properly.[12] Richard had been elected a capital burgess in 1614. At Easter 1616 he was confirmed as churchwarden and officiated at the funerals of William Hart and Shakespeare.

Bartholomew's daughter Ann had been married to Richard Edwards, son of Avery Edwards of Drayton, since January 1610 and was busy filling her own house in Drayton with children. Bartholomew's second son John had married his sister's sister-in-law, Elizabeth Edwards, in November the same year, and they too had set about producing a numerous brood. Only Edmund remained living with his father. If Ann had decided to return to Shottery and housekeep for her beloved brother and his son, she would have found life more congenial than at New Place. Living with Judith or Bartholomew would have been less soul-destroying than staying on in her old house as a dependant of her son-in-law. The years of Ann's widowhood must have been happy times for the Hathaway clan, as the babies came thick and fast, ten of Ann's and nine of John's. Great-aunt Ann would have been kept busy attending family confinements, and arranging christenings and churchings. Nothing of the sort was happening at New Place.

The puritan Corporation was facing another crisis. For years it had been trying to control the activities of the Vicar of Stratford, John Rogers, who had been presented by Sir Edward Greville in 1605. In 1611 Rogers moved into the renovated Priest's House in Chapel Street, thus becoming a neighbour of the Shakespeares. His attempts to augment his income by pasturing cattle in the churchyard and keeping a pigsty in Scholars' Lane as well as pocketing the fees for burials were being vigorously resisted by the Corporation, but he seems to have been as popular with the common people as he was unpopular with the aldermen. When Rogers and Francis Collins were appointed trustees of a legacy of two houses left for the use of Stratford's numerous poor, Rogers contrived to cut Collins out, using the services of another lawyer, Thomas Lucas of Gray's Inn, to 'keep it from the poor unconscionably', much to the distress of Collins who attempted to clear his conscience by righting the matter in his will.[13] At the Hall of 30 January 1614 the Corporation agreed 'that there shall be a fit gown cloth of good broadcloth given to Mr John Rogers our vicar in hope that he will deserve the same hereafter and amend his former faults and failings'. Rogers paid the aldermen no mind, but went on lining his pockets by whatever means he could. Meanwhile Holy Trinity Church was in very poor repair. At the Hall of 4 December 1615 it was 'agreed that the Chamberlains shall discharge Mr Rogers from receiving any more benefit by burials in the chancel, and that the Chamberlains shall receive it from henceforth towards the repairs of the Chancel, the parish church, and also to demand of Mr Rogers so much as he hath received within this past year'.[14]

In 1619 the Corporation saw its chance. Rogers accepted a second benefice; on the advice of Lucas, who had taken over as town clerk, the Corporation begged the lord chancellor, acting as lord of the manor, to present Thomas Wilson, and its petition was successful. But Rogers refused to go.[15] The Corporation voted on 5 May 1618 to petition for confirmation of Wilson's appointment.[16] The petition was successful. On Sunday 30 May, the day before he was to be inducted, as Wilson walked to Holy Trinity to attend the evening service his way was barred by a frenzied crowd, brandishing a motley assortment of weaponry and yelling, 'Hang him, kill him, pull out his throat, cut off his pocky and burnt members, let us hale him out of the church!' His supporters dragged him into the church, and barred the door, while the crowd raged outside and hurled stones through the windows. Ann was probably present then and again when Wilson conducted his first service on 6 June; she had a choice of pews to sit in, either the Hathaway pew with her brother and nephews, and grand-nieces and -nephews, or the New Place pew or, if she was a member of the household at the Cage, the Quiney pew.

The uproar had been orchestrated, and the Corporation had a shrewd idea who was behind it, but as the people involved were gentry there was not much it could do. On 9 June the churchwardens had complained of the poor state of the way to the church at the point where it passed Master Reynolds's house, and it was duly repaired. At the entrance stood a may-pole which was adjudged, despite King James's Declaration concerning lawful sports, to be a nuisance and an obstruction of the way. The decision was taken to remove it in time for the autumn fair. When the fair opened and the removal of the pole was discovered, a yelling crowd appeared and re-erected the may-pole where it had been before, despite the bailiff's assurances that it would have been re-erected anyway but in a different spot. This time there was enough evidence against the ringleaders for Lucas to draw up a bill in Chancery naming them as John Nash and William Reynolds, aided and abetted by John Lane and Ralph Smith. John Nash and William Reynolds had both been left money in Shake-speare's will to buy a memorial ring; one wonders if they were wearing their mourning rings as they tore up the town or if they ever bothered to have them made. John Lane was the libeller of Susanna Hall, Ralph Smith the man who is supposed to have had relations with her. The literate among the rioters made sure that singable libels turned up all over town. The bitterest was in prose:

> all the old biting and young sucking puritans of Stratford are joined with their two Just-asses apiece maliciously to displace and utterly undo their minister [Rogers], and to bring in his place as arrant a knave as themselves, of purpose to assist them in their hypocrisy . . .[17]

The new vicar's most passionate adherent was John Hall. Wilson was a brilliant preacher; he was also a radical puritan who refused to allow the use of rings in wedding ceremonies, refused to anoint baptisands or the dying with the sign of the cross, wouldn't allow people to kneel in his church and not only refused to maintain the guild chapel, but let his children play ball in it.[18] Ann may have found Wilson's uncompromising religion challenging, exciting and worthy, but it was also a liability for Stratford, which had long been recognised as a little Geneva. From some points of view the unity of the puritan brotherhood was a source of strength, but it also laid the town open to discrimination and persecution, not to mention the ever-present threat of riot.

If Ann ran out of options, and one of the twenty-four places became vacant, she could have applied for admission to the almshouse, where, besides lodging and firing, she would receive four pence a week. When Elizabeth Ashwell became a widow in 1583, though she had living children, the Stratford Corporation granted her a place in an almshouse, where she lived until her death in 1596.[19] Margaret Grannams, widow of George Grannams, a weaver, entered the almshouses in 1602, fourteen years after her husband's death, and died there four months later.[20] Joan Tant, widow of the Stratford burgess Valentine Tant who died after being attacked by Thomas Combe in November 1616, entered the almshouses in February 1619 and lived there until her death in June 1625. Eady White was selected to enter the almshouses a month before her husband's death in April 1617; she lived there for ten months.[21] If Ann Shakespeare had applied for admission to the almshouses we would probably know about it from the surviving records. If she did not, she must have had, as most other widows did, other options; we should probably conclude that as a widow Ann was still a woman of independent means.

While Ann may have continued to make malt or to play some part in the mercery–haberdashery business, she may also have put her money to work. Widows who had some capital of their own usually lent the money out at 10 per cent interest per annum.

The most prominent economic function of the widow in English rural society between 1500 and 1900 was money lending. The constraints upon her disposal of income did not apply, as a rule, to the use of moveable or liquid assets inherited or accumulated by saving and investment. Every collection of wills and inventories, published or unpublished, contains examples of widows and spinsters in possession of sheaves of promissory notes or bonds of debt owing to them at death.[22]

Isabel Mecocke, who died a widow in Old Stratford in 1621, had lent £4 to Arthur Cawdry and £9 to John Sheffield, in bonds repayable on the Feast of the Archangel Michael.[23] When Alice Williams died in 1622 she was owed £100 'upon specialties'.[24] Mary Mills, who had lived as a widow for seven years before her death in 1624, was owed rather more than £60 in debts 'sperate' and £2 in debts 'desperate' when she died.[25]

Widows sometimes pooled their widows' mites and lived together. Alice Fletcher, widow of the toll-gatherer William Fletcher who died in 1600, shared a room in the almshouses with a Widow Bayliss, to which she brought the glass from the window of her old house, appraised at her death in 1608 as worth sixteen pence.[26]

Ann's forty-eight-year-old sister-in-law was widowed a week before she was. Shakespeare left her, rather than his wife, a life-tenancy of the western part of the Henley Street house, but once sixteen-year-old William, eleven-year-old Thomas and eight-year-old Michael were accommodated, there would have been scant room for Ann. The nest of Widow Quiney, being all but empty, would have provided plenty of room for Ann. Bess had married her daughter Elizabeth to Thomas Greene's stepson William Chandler in 1603, and had seen her buried in May 1615. Thirty-year-old Adrian had been married to Elinor Bushell since 1613, but no baby had been born. Richard Quiney had been in London since 1606, when he left Stratford with John Sadler the younger and went into business with him. By 1616 he was well on his way to becoming a successful importer of groceries from the new world where he and Sadler had acquired plantations. Thomas had been rather hastily placed in the capable hands of Judith Shakespeare, and was on his way to becoming mine host of the Cage. Mary, not yet twenty-two, may have been still at home, while young George, having come down from Oxford, was working as an usher at Stratford grammar school preparatory to taking orders. Widow Quiney was probably still economically active, with a busy household consisting as usual of employees, among whom Widow Shakespeare might have been counted.

Bess Quiney had endured, besides the murder of her husband, the deaths of two sons in infancy, of her eldest daughter at the age of twenty-one, and of another son aged six, but there was more anguish to come. Her second daughter Ann was married to the haberdasher

William Smith in May 1614 when she was twenty-two. She bore a daughter Elizabeth in January 1615, and probably set her out to nurse for in May the next year she gave birth to premature twins who died before they could be baptised. In November Elinor Quiney, the wife of Bess's eldest surviving son Adrian, died childless. In May the next year Ann followed her twins to the grave. A month later Adrian made his will; four months later he died and was buried, on 11 October 1617. In his will he simply asks his 'mother Quiney', whom despite her age he has named as an executor, and his widowed brother-in-law William Smith to dispose of his possessions as they think fit. William Chandler, now Bailiff of Stratford, helped to compile his simple inventory which included 'one parcel of lace with all books and other odd implements'. Adrian too had been money-lending; he was owed a total of £133 3s, including £30 lent to Sir Edward Greville and 'uncertain to be got'.[27] The next year Widow Quiney had the consolation of seeing her successful son Richard marry a Stratford girl, Ellen Sadler, but then he took her away with him to London where eleven children were baptised at St Stephen's Walbrook, and three of them buried. Bess's greatest success was in getting her youngest son George to Oxford. In 1620 he was appointed Curate of Holy Trinity but by 1623 he was ousted by Simon Trappe, and Hall was treating him for consumption to which he succumbed a year later. In 1623 Bess's twenty-nine-year-old daughter Mary married Richard Watts, who had served as Minister of Holy Trinity from 1613 to 1617. In March 1623 Watts had been appointed Vicar of Harbury, and it was there that Mary was married to him.

We know a good deal about the way that widows lived in Stratford from their wills and inventories. When Agnes Elliott of Stratford died in 1564, she was living in her own three-roomed cottage, and possessed of £18 15s 4d worth of chattels, most of it malt worth £12 6s 8d. In the main room or hall, where she cooked, there was a collection of pewter platters, porringers, salt cellars and a quart pot, ten candlesticks, four hanging cauldrons, brass pots and pans and two painted cloths. The bed chamber above, where a man- or maidservant might have slept, contained only an old feather bed and mattress. Agnes seems to have slept and worked in the lower chamber, where her malt was stored, alongside malting equipment and four loads of wood. She had moreover a cow in the keeping of Thomas Smart of Bridgetown, three frocks and a petticoat.[28]

In 1585 died Elizabeth Smart of Bishopton, possibly the widow of the same Thomas Smart, and her inventory shows that she too was living in a three-roomed cottage, with a 'back house' and a barn. In all, her possessions were worth £17 10s 2d, of which £4 was in wheat and barley. She too owned her own pewter and brass, and five flitches of bacon, probably of her own curing, for in her barn there were two 'store pigs', as well as a cow and a heifer, two geese and a gander, twelve hens and a cock. It seems that right up to her last days Elizabeth supported herself by selling her butter and eggs and bacon.[29]

Alice Bell was widowed in 1572 and survived until 1588; according to her will she was survived by three unmarried daughters and two sons-in-law whose wives may or may not have been living. Her inventory gives no clue to where she lived; her goods consisted of clothing, bedding, furniture and thirty-four pieces of pewter, valued at £10 17s. It seems likely that at least one of her unmarried daughters was living with her.[30]

Elizabeth Pace of Shottery is identified as a widow in her inventory of 1589, but as we do not have a will for her we have no way of knowing how she fits into the extended Pace family; she too lived in a three-roomed cottage consisting of hall, chamber and kitchen. She was comfortable, it would appear. Her apparel was appraised at twenty shillings, her linen at twenty-five shillings, but her real wealth was in horses, cattle and sheep, to the value of £11 6s 8d out of a total of £15 16s 8d.[31]

Elizabeth Nott's house was, again, three rooms, this time a hall, a chamber and a 'saller' or, more usually, 'soller', an upper room with a window in the gable. The appearance of a soller in cottages like Elizabeth's is probably an indication that some kind of craft is being carried out, mostly in the off-season, when light was low. When she died in 1596 Elizabeth had been a widow for nearly twelve years; but she was well supplied with furniture, linen (to the value of £5), brass and pewter.[32] Not all widows were so fortunate; Elizabeth Such of Shottery was left a widow in 1586; when she died in 1602 her few goods, as assessed by Fulke Sandells and Stephen Burman the younger were worth only £4 0s 16d. Her clothing amounted to no more than twelve shillings; she had an old cupboard and two coffers, an old vat, an old table board, a brass pot, an old cauldron, two pewter platters and one candlestick, one bed covering, a blanket and an old counter-pane, cattle and horse fodder worth thirty-two shillings, and her sown barley and peas.[33] The appraisers noted no firewood, no animals and no stored foodstuffs of any kind, which suggests that Elizabeth may have died of malnutrition.

Elizabeth's neighbour Alice Burman had been a widow for eighteen years when she died in 1608; Bartholomew Hathaway was one of the men who appraised her belongings, which were worth the considerable sum of £34 7s 4d, largely comprising 'her crop of corn' (£20), her cows and a heifer and her ten sheep. Her clothes were worth the unusually high sum of thirty shillings, her linen and bedding £3.

Widows might be left leasehold property to occupy in their own right, either with or without any of their children. Joan Biddle who died in 1614, seventeen years after her husband Robert Biddle the shoe-maker, inherited his lease of a commodious house in Sheep Street consisting of a hall, parlour, two chambers, a kitchen, stable, buttery, shop and yard, for which the Corporation charged eight shillings a year. In 1611 the Widow Biddle paid a fine of £9 to renew the lease in her own name for twenty-one years, leaving it at her death three years later to her son William, who was to share it with his brother Robert, or else to pay him £4, which suggests that both sons had been living there with her.[34] Biddle's goods were appraised at £20 8s 10d; his widow's at almost the same amount, £19 5s 2d.[35] In her will she left her great cauldron, her apparel, a sow and a pig to her 'daughter', Elizabeth, who may have been a daughter-in-law.[36] Almost all the items listed in her husband's inventory can be found in Joan's inventory, except the glass in the hall window and her husband's tools. In 1617 Mary Mills inherited her husband's lease of a house on Rother Street and later renewed it.[37] Her husband died worth £204 7s 4d; at the time of her death seven years later Mary's goods were assessed at £268 9s 4d. Mills was a yeoman who probably doubled as a maltster; the most valuable item in his inventory was £100 in malt; Mary's inventory too shows £72 in malt and barley. She had also lent out £60 and the lease of her house was worth £50. In the house was all the equipment needed to make malt, more of it than can be traced in her husband's rather

perfunctory inventory. Widow Mills must have been living in the
house alone except for servants; her son Thomas was dead, and her
daughter married to the son of a gentleman.

Ann probably knew about all of these women; she certainly knew
what befell Margaret Smith, the widow of John Smith, son of William
Smith, the mercer and haberdasher and mother of Ralph Smith the
hatter. Margaret was Hamnet Sadler's sister; she married in 1572 and
bore three sons and three daughters between 1574 and 1583; in 1592
she produced another son, John. One son, Henry, died at the age of
one. After her husband's death in late 1601 Mary was supposed to
share their house in Sheep Street with her eldest son Ralph, while a
house in Church Street which was sub-let was to go to John.[38] When
her son Hamnet Smith died in 1609, aged twenty-six, and left £10 to
the Corporation, Mary was unable to raise the cash until 1613, when
she paid it in two instalments.[39] In 1615 the Corporation decided, in
consideration of her poverty and the fact that her husband had served
as Bailiff of Stratford, to reduce the rent she was paying for a barn and
a garden attached to the house in Church Street, where she was then
living with her son Ralph, to a mere twelve pence a year, but even so
she couldn't pay it. (What became of John is not known.) In 1617 she
and Ralph accepted £13 16s 8d in return for relinquishing all their
rights in the Church Street property. The crushing blow fell in 1621
when Ralph died. When Mary made her will in 1625, she mentioned
no child.[40] In her inventory, out of a total estate of £16 19s 6d, her
clothing was appraised at the relatively high sum of £5, the lease of
the house she was then living in at £4, and she was owed £8 17s in
'desperate' debts, for which there was no hope of payment.

With no money or land settled on her, Ann still had to make her
own living. Susanna might have been able to queen it as a lady of
leisure, living on her rents and her husband's income, but Ann was a
woman of the old school, who was not used to sitting with her hands
folded in her lap. Her husband may have made himself a gentleman,
but Ann seems to have had no pretensions to be a gentlewoman.
Younger widows would take over a husband's business and run it
until the heir was old enough to take over. At first, after her husband's
death in 1591, Isabel Wotton continued in his trade as a weaver but in
1604 she secured a licence to sell ale. When her husband died in 1595,

Cicely Bainton was pregnant. Six months later she was listed as a victualler in Wood Street: 'Widow Bainton breweth two strikes of malt weekly having none other trade to live by. In house four persons', namely Cicely and her three surviving children. Margaret ap Roberts, who was widowed in 1592, was brewing eight strikes of malt a week by 1595 when she was licensed to sell ale.[41] Mary Green, widowed in 1603, survived by selling malt.[42] Joan Bromley, widowed in 1606, ran her own alehouse for twenty years.[43] We have surmised that Ann knew all about brewing that there was to know; perhaps she went on making malt and brewing, and perhaps she did it using the couch house and still rooms at New Place. It was possible to live at New Place without being a member of Susanna's household, by renting a self-contained part of the house.

Nowadays Shakespeare's remains are assumed to lie in the chancel of Holy Trinity Church. Certainly there is a stone for all to see in front of the communion rail to the left of the altar. This is not the original stone, according to Halliwell-Phillipps; in the mid-eighteenth century the original stone was found to be rotten and was replaced.[44] There was a belief among locals that Shakespeare had been buried 'full seventeen foot deep, deep enough to secure him'.[45] Schoenbaum comments, 'this seems unlikely so close to where the Avon flows'.[46] What is significant about this tradition is that if Shakespeare's burial stone had always been where it is now, no one could have imagined for a moment that he had been buried seventeen feet down. Graves that were dug in the chancel were of necessity shallow. The flagged floor had first to be broken, earth taken out, the coffin interred, the earth replaced, and left to settle before the pavement could be reinstated.

> Interment inside the church was disruptive as well as expensive. Churches were used almost daily for prayers and special services and routine worship could not have been improved by the presence of workmen's tools and open tombs. Uncovered graves inside the church were as common as ill-tended churchyards without, and too many families failed to finish the job or to pay all the necessary fees.[47]

We may discount the truth of the tale that Shakespeare was buried seventeen feet down even outside in the churchyard, if only because it would have taken at least a week, with pit-props and a winch, to dig such an enormous hole. Mining was a growing industry in northern Warwickshire in 1616, but not in the environs of Stratford. What we cannot ignore is the doubt such an enormously deep grave casts on the certainty that Shakespeare was buried in the chancel in the first instance. Shakespeare's will is odd in that he did not bequeath his body to Holy Trinity churchyard or anywhere else and he left no money for a tomb. Suppose that, as the wiser sort in Stratford realised that distinguished visitors were arriving to pay homage to Shakespeare, they decided that they had to provide a shrine. There would have been no point in digging up the churchyard, and no way of deciding which heap of rottenness was which. All that was needed was a stone in a convenient place in the chancel. However, in the last years of the seventeenth century there was the beginnings of a movement to re-inter Shakespeare with Chaucer, Spenser and Jonson in Westminster Abbey. The churchwardens would have been aware that any attempt to dig under the stone in Holy Trinity would have exposed their little stratagem. The churchwardens' accounts for 1616 have not survived. All we can be sure of is that the stone was in position by 1693 when Dowdall saw it and transcribed:

> Good friend, for Jesus' sake forbear
> To dig the dust enclosed here.
> Blest be the man that spares these stones,
> And cursed be he that moves my bones.

When Shakespeare was buried, John Rogers was still adding to his income by charging high fees, probably ten shillings a time, for burials in the chancel. To keep the money coming, more room was made by digging up the bones already there and removing them to the charnel house. The money Rogers made was supposed to maintain the fabric of the church, but he apparently kept it for his own use, though the church roof was leaking badly. Various levies were raised but little money was collected. On 13 October 1616 the churchwardens were summoned to attend the Episcopal Court at Worcester. By April of the next year they claimed to have spent £27 16s 10d on repairs, but the roof still leaked and the stonework was still crumbling. Richard

Hathaway had contributed four shillings to the fund, and John Hall only eight, even though as one of the lessees of the tithes he was legally obliged to invest some of the rental income in keeping the church in repair. Six months later the chancel was still unrestored and John Hall, William Combe and the other tithe-holders were presented. Still they dragged their feet. On 16 July the Corporation stepped in, and voted to 'bestow some charges' to keep the chancel dry. On 16 July 1621 George Quiney, who had been appointed curate the year before, and the churchwardens presented Lord Carew, the new lord of the manor, and Hall and Combe for failing to invest of their income from the tithes, and the bailiff and burgesses for not constraining them to do their duty. It was not until a year later that work was under way. If Ann was the woman I think she was, she can hardly have been impressed by her son-in-law's feebleness at this juncture. His parsimony and inertia were bringing her family into disrepute. Once again it was the Quiney gang to the rescue. William Chandler donated a new canopy for the pulpit and the Corporation directed and paid for the restoration work.

A Lieutenant Hammond, passing through Stratford in 1634, noticed Shakespeare's 'neat monument' on the north wall of the chancel.[48] Dugdale scribbled in an almanac of 1653 that the artist was 'one Gerard Johnson'.[49] This too is problematic; the elder Gheerart Janssen died in 1611 and the younger is not known to have sculpted anything other than a marble basin that is now untraceable. Art historians do not credit him even with the tomb of John Combe.[50]

> It occupied him in his workshop at Southwark near the Globe, where the Poet's old friends could drop in to criticize it, and eventually was brought down to Stratford and put up in the restored Chancel for the admiration of his relatives and neighbours.[51]

Combe had set aside £60 in his will, to pay for his tomb, Shakespeare nothing. Shakespeare's monument is more modest than Combe's full-length effigy atop a sarcophagus, but somebody must have paid for it. In his commendatory poem for the First Folio, Leonard Digges refers to Shakespeare's 'Stratford monument', which is taken to be this one. Ben Jonson, more teasingly, refers to Shakespeare 'as a monument

without a tomb'. Dugdale's original sketch, which was engraved by
Hollar for the *Antiquities of Warwickshire*, printed in 1656, is still in
existence in the possession of his family.[52] The fact that the propor-
tions are different from those of the monument now to be seen is
what one would expect in a hurried sketch, but one important detail
is not the kind of thing that is misrendered by an inexpert draughts-
man: both the poet's hands are shown resting on a fat woolsack. There
is no quill in the right hand and no leaf of paper under the left. At
some stage, perhaps when the monument was restored in the mid-
eighteenth century, the woolsack was greatly reduced in size and
made to support a hand with a pen in it, and another lying on a leaf of
paper. The putto that can now be seen holding an inverted torch was
then holding an hourglass and his other hand was not resting on a
skull. Both putti would seem to have been completely renewed. In its
present state the whole is an awkward assemblage, the putti too big for
the cornice they sit on, and the surmounting crest overbalancing the
whole. Perhaps the 'neat monument' Hammond saw in 1634 had yet
to acquire its outsize embellishments.

Most Jacobeans who erected monuments to their dead kinsmen
used the inscription to inform the world of their own identity. The
inscription on the Shakespeare monument is anonymous: the Bard is
referred to only by his surname,

> Judicio Pylum, Genio Socratem, Arte Maronem,
> Terra tegit, populus maeret, Olympus habet.
> Stay Passenger why goest thou by so fast?
> Read, if thou canst, whom envious death hath placed
> Within this monument: Shakespeare, with whom
> Quick Nature died, whose name doth deck this tomb
> Far more than cost, sith all that he hath writ
> Leaves living art but page to serve his wit.
>   Obiit An[no] Do[min]i 1616
>   Aetatis 53 Die 23 Apr[ilis]

Poets dwell on Parnassus rather than Olympus. The egregious error
chimes ill with the detail of the inverted torch copied from Roman
sarcophagi, which is typical of later neo-classicism. The other odd

thing about Shakespeare's likeness is that he is sporting the falling bands and shot white cuffs of a puritan. It is at least possible that the Shakespeare bust started life as something else.

Monuments like Shakespeare's are usually financed and the design specified by his survivors, who are keen to take the credit and claim the association. The strange silence of the Shakespeare monument on this point makes one doubt that it was John Hall, though he may have composed the inscription, which is inept enough. It could have been the silent woman of Stratford, the woman who was buried that year as plain 'Mistress Shakespeare'. In the parish register she is not identified as a gentlewoman, or even as a widow. She is just herself.

Ann was buried in the newly restored chancel beneath her husband's monument. Her epitaph was probably written by John Hall, ventriloquising for Susanna:

Ubera, tu mater, tu lac vitamque dedisti;
    Vae mihi, pro tanto munera saxo dabo?
Quam mallem amoveat lapidem bonus angelus ore!
    Exeat, ut Christi corpus, imago tua!
Sed nil vota valent; venias cito, Christe! resurget
    Clausa licet tumulo, mater et astra petet.

Breasts, mother, milk and life thou gavest me;
woe is me, for so great a boon must I give stones?
How much rather would I that the good angel remove this slab from
    the grave mouth,
and thine image come forth as did the body of Christ!
But prayers avail nothing – come quickly, Christ,
that though shut in the tomb my mother may rise again and seek the
    stars.

Hall can hardly have known what Ann's early life was like, when she nursed her first baby with her boy husband by her side, and they read in their Bible the injunction so dear to the uxorious puritans: 'Let thy fountain be blessed and rejoice in the wife of thy youth. Let her be as the loving hind and pleasant roe; let her breasts satisfy thee at all times, and delight in her love continually' (Proverbs, v: 17–18).

CHAPTER TWENTY-ONE

in which the intrepid author makes the absurd suggestion that Ann Shakespeare could have been involved in the First Folio project, that she might have contributed not only papers but also money to indemnify the publishers against loss and enable them to sell a book that was very expensive to produce at a price that young gentlemen could pay

A few weeks before Shakespeare died, on Shrove Tuesday 1616, a mob of apprentices converged on the Cockpit, Christopher Beeston's newly built indoor playhouse in Drury Lane,

> wounded divers of the players, broke open their trunks, and what apparel, books or other things they found, they burnt and cut in pieces . . . got on top of the house and untiled it . . . and would have laid that house . . . even to the ground . . . In this skirmish one apprentice was slain, being shot through the head with a pistol, and many other of their fellows were sore hurt, and such of them as are taken his Majesty hath commanded shall be executed for example's sake.[1]

As is only to be expected in official accounts, this rioting is presented as meaningless and unmotivated. Were the apprentices attacking Beeston's new theatre because it was private and expensive or simply because it was a theatre? Were they frustrated playgoers or indignant puritans? Christopher Beeston was a known whoremaster; in 1602 a woman condemned to Bridewell for bearing an illegitimate child accused Beeston of raping her and said that he boasted of having 'lain with a hundred wenches'. Though Beeston denied the charges he and 'his confederate players' were deemed guilty of unseemly and lawless behaviour.[2] When the Globe burnt down in 1613, the balladeers showed scant compassion, admonishing the players:

> Be warnèd, you stage strutters all,
>   Lest you again be catched,
> And such a burning do befall
>   As to them whose house was thatched.
>   Forbear your whoring, breeding biles,
>   And lay up that expense for tiles.[3]

The year of Shakespeare's death was also the year of the issue of Ben Jonson's grandiose folio, entitled *The Works of Benjamin Jonson*, for which as his own editor, in a bid to acquire gravitas, Jonson created literary versions of selected playtexts and added to the mix non-dramatic verse. In England writing for the theatre had never been a profession, let alone a respectable profession; the playwrights of the 1590s and 1600s strike one as rather like the writers of TV soaps in our own time, under pressure to produce endless variations on a limited number of themes, structuring dialogue to accommodate a fixed cast of players, meanwhile keeping bums on seats and sponsors and producers happy. Most playtexts were ephemeral. Thomas Heywood, to name just one contemporary playwright, claimed that over his sixty-year career he was author or principal part-author of 220 plays, most of which have not survived. By putting together improved versions of selected plays and a quantity of non-dramatic verse, all printed in a consistent style and prefaced by an extraordinary number of commendatory verses, Jonson's intention was to establish himself as a literary figure rather than an entertainer. *The Works of Benjamin Jonson* was a *succès* only *d'estime*; copies sold slowly and may actually have left him and his publishers out of pocket.[4]

Three months after Ann Shakespeare died, her husband's collected plays were published in a handsome folio. Scholars have never given any consideration to the possibility that the Bard's wife might have been involved in the Folio project. They prefer to believe that she was illiterate, had nothing whatever to do with Shakespeare's creative work and no interest in it whatsoever. The idea that she might be entitled to some of the credit for the preservation of her husband's work is apparently too ridiculous to contemplate, which is why we shall now contemplate it.

The suggestion that Shakespeare took advantage of peace and quiet at New Place to work on his plays is actually less preposterous than the commonly held belief that he never went near the place until he had given up writing them. Theatres were not allowed to open in the penitential season of Lent, which lasted from Septuagesima Sunday until Easter Sunday, quite long enough to justify the week lost in travelling to and from Stratford.

If Shakespeare did work at New Place, there must have been papers somewhere in the rambling house. Paper, being costly, was not disposed of lightly. Paper with writing on one side was good for writing on the other; paper that was entirely overwritten was good for wrapping anything from spices to gunpowder. The fact that no papers and no books were mentioned in Shakespeare's will doesn't mean that there weren't any to be found. Even if we had the inventory made at the time of his death, we might not find his books and papers listed. No dog has ever been listed in an Elizabethan inventory but that doesn't mean that Elizabethans didn't own dogs. If there was ever any significant accumulation of documents at New Place, it must have been assembled during Shakespeare's life, when Ann was chatelaine. It may have been Ann who tidied the sheaves of paper and put them away for safe-keeping, and perhaps, if and when she left New Place, she took them away in her widow's coffer.

The possibilities are many. Shakespeare may have done what other authors have done before him, forbidden his wife and her maids from entering, let alone tidying, his study, but the prohibition can hardly have held when he was not in residence. If no one had ever cleaned the room, mice and other vermin would have made short work of his papers. Shakespeare may have had his own faithful servant, who kept his wife and her industrious maids well away from his personal effects. One possible candidate for this role is the mysterious John Robinson who was present in Stratford to witness Shakespeare's will in March 1616. The name Robinson is not common in Stratford; none of the few Robinsons who can be found in the archives seems to fit the bill. In London, twenty years before Shakespeare's death, in November 1596, a John Robinson was one of the thirty-one signatories who protested against Burbage's opening of a public theatre in the Black-friars together with Shakespeare's old colleague Richard Field.[5] In 1613 a John Robinson was installed as the tenant of the gatehouse in Blackfriars and he was still the tenant when Shakespeare's will was made. If these John Robinsons and the witness of Shakespeare's will are all the same person, it is not inconceivable that he was Shake-speare's manservant. Boys initially trained for the theatre who didn't make the cut were usually retained by the company to work in other capacities. To have been the tenant of the gatehouse John Robinson must have had some connection with the company; he may, for example, have been Shakespeare's dresser. He may have been related to the actor Richard Robinson who married Richard Burbage's widow.[6] There would have been nothing unusual in Shakespeare's keeping a personal servant, and it may have been he rather than Ann Shakespeare who cared for Shakespeare in the last months of his life.

Ann's is the slightly better case. If Shakespeare had kept a man-servant in London, and wished to stay in the house in London, he would have. Part of the point of returning to New Place for good must have been to have the benefit of Ann's housekeeping and later her nursing. Whenever he went up to London, Ann and her maids might have moved in to set his chamber to rights, and she may have spent long hours sorting his papers, reading his plays and imagining what they would have been like in the theatre. Perhaps they had been read to her as they were written, and she read the revised versions with interest. Or perhaps she was ashamed and disgusted by her husband's connection with the theatre, and preferred to regard it as nothing to do with her or her daughters.

On the face of it, the person who concerned himself with Shakespeare's papers should have been Thomas Greene who was a student at the Middle Temple in the years of Shakespeare's greatest triumph, but in the last years of Shakespeare's life that relationship seems to have become distant, as he drew closer to two other Middle Templars, William and John Combe, either or both of whom could have been involved in the Folio project. John Hall was certainly aware of his father-in-law as the most successful playwright of his day, but he was surely too deeply imbued with Calvinist values actually to have risked exposing himself to the corrupting influence of the theatre, or to commit himself to the labour of keeping his father-in-law's playscripts intact and together. It would be pleasing to think of Susanna or Judith as fans of their father's work and eager to preserve his reputation but we don't know whether either of them ever travelled to London. It is not clear whether Shakespeare would have wanted them in a playhouse, given the promiscuous mix of people they were likely to encounter. Ladies of reputation, especially un-married ones, seldom visited the public playhouses. We should probably not exclude Susanna from consideration as her father's literary executor, but as she and her husband were already Shake-speare's chief and residuary legatees, he might well have bethought him of someone else. If Judith Quiney was illiterate – she certainly could not sign her own name – her husband was not.

Ann has as good a case as any of them. As good, but no better. Though the Folio was advertised as newly published in 1622 it didn't actually appear until the end of 1623, four months or so after Ann's death. For the earlier date to have been at all feasible, work on collating and standardising the texts would have had to have begun many months before, in 1620, say, or even earlier. Supposing Ann had had copies in her possession, she would not have surrendered them before she knew that someone she trusted was seriously committed to issuing the volume. That person could have been an old friend from childhood days in Shottery. What would have decided the issue would have been providing him with the funds to finance or part-finance the project. According to the colophon of *Cymbeline* in the First Folio it was 'Printed at the charges of W. Jaggard, Ed[ward] Blount, J[ohn] Smithwick and W. Aspley'. The printing was done in the Jaggards' shop, and Isaac Jaggard and Edward Blount seem to have been the publishers but whether they bore the whole of the considerable cost is unknown: 'they are unlikely to have been the prime movers. In fact it is doubtful whether they would have been much interested when it was first proposed unless offered substantial incentives, though not necessarily financial ones, by the players.'[7] It seems more likely to me that the printers and publishers would have needed indemnities rather than incentives – that is, as Charlton Hinman says in the introduction to the Norton facsimile, 'some kind of guarantee against disastrous loss'. The King's Men had absolutely nothing to gain and would have been ill advised to throw their money away. But somebody must have.

Scholars who need to think of Shakespeare as a self-conscious artist are rather too keen to find evidence that he was involved in the preparation of the volume. He may have had time between his retirement from the stage and the onset of his last illness to give some thought to such a project. The precedent had been set by Jonson, who was certainly the designer and leader of the project to publish his own 'works', which he undertook at about the time Shakespeare is thought to have left London to take up permanent residence in Stratford. The notion that Ben Jonson was a crony in the last years of Shakespeare's life and that Shakespeare would have wished to follow the precedent set by *The Works of Benjamin Jonson*, which Chambers and Greg both entertained, would be easier to countenance if Shakespeare had followed Jonson's example in anything else, which he didn't. There was no attempt to include non-dramatic verse in the Shakespeare Folio, as Jonson had done, and it was called simply *Comedies, Histories and Tragedies*. Again, if we try to put Ann in the picture, we can too easily understand why she would not wish for the sonnets to be reprinted, or even *Venus and Adonis* and *The Rape of Lucrece*. Other booksellers had rights in these, but a deal could have been done and those rights acquired. The narrative poems were obviously connected with Southampton, the sonnets rather less so. Another odd thing about the Folio is that it was dedicated not to Southampton, but to the puritan lords William Herbert, Earl of Pembroke, and his brother Philip, Earl of Montgomery. Southampton evidently accepted the role of patron to Shakespeare; he paid forty shillings to the company for reviving *Richard II* at the Globe in 1599 and had them perform *Love's Labour's Lost* before Anne of Denmark at Southampton House in 1603. In 1610 Southampton had fallen out with Montgomery at a tennis match, where they belted each other about the head with their wooden racquets, so the choice could be interpreted as a snub to Southampton.

W. W. Greg asks, more or less rhetorically, 'In the quiet evening of his days at New Place, did Shakespeare ever discuss the possibility of printing with the cronies who visited him there?'[8] Who can these cronies have been? It is usually presumed that they were Richard

Burbage, John Hemmings and Henry Condell who were each left £1 6s 8d each to buy mourning rings in Shakespeare's will. After the death of Richard Burbage on 13 March 1619, John Hemmings and Henry Condell were the leading members of the King's Men. Both men may have had Stratford connections. Malone certainly believed that the John Hemmings who edited the Folio was born in Shottery in about 1556, as was Ann Hathaway.[9] It will be remembered that a John Hemmings witnessed Ann's father's will in 1581.[10]

John was a popular name in the Shottery Hemmings family; John Hemmingses were christened in Stratford in 1565, 1571 and 1574. In 1574 an older Hemmings had been hayward of Shottery, with the two-fold duty of guarding hedges against cattle or people breaking them down and impounding stray animals. Though some of the sturdier yeomen managed to consolidate viable estates in the arden, the waste lands filled up with the hovels of masterless men, some of whom had lost even their identity. The parish register records a series of deaths as simply 'a poor young man from Shottery' in December 1599 and again in January 1600, and 'an infant from Shottery of a poor man's' (1607). By 1600, the presence of the Hemmings family in Shottery was much diminished. Like many others displaced by the engrossing of agricultural estates the Hemmingses may have gravitated to London.

The John 'Heminge' who collaborated with Condell in the compilation of the Folio is supposed to be the same John Hemmings who was a member of the Queen's Men when they visited Stratford in 1586. By 1587 he was living in London. After the actor William Knell was killed in a brawl with another player, 'John Hemminge, gent. of Cornhill' was granted a licence on 5 March 1588 at St Mary the Virgin Aldermanbury to marry Rebecca, widow of 'William Knell. gent.' From then on he was associated with Aldermanbury where Condell was a churchwarden and where he too eventually served as a sidesman.[11] The first of John and Rebecca Hemmings's fourteen children was christened John at Aldermanbury on 2 April 1588. A daughter Thomasine, born in 1595, was married to William Ostler, a player with the King's Men, in 1611; their son was christened Beaumont at Aldermanbury on 18 May 1612. As part of the marriage settlement, Ostler had been given shares in both

Blackfriars and the Globe. When Ostler died at the end of 1614, his widow tried to cash in the shares, and ended up in litigation with her father who denied her valuation of £600. Hemmings's ninth child, William, was educated at Westminster and went up to Oxford as a king's scholar. Hemmings died in 1630. The possibility that Hemmings had been a childhood playmate of Ann Shakespeare raises the further possibility that when her young husband set off for London to ply his poetry he knew where to go and whom to see about a career in the theatre. The very suggestion will raise guffaws in university common-rooms, but the possibility remains, nonetheless.

Not much is known about Henry Condell, who married an heiress in 1596, when he is thought to have been about twenty. One of the trustees of the Globe was another churchwarden at Aldermanbury, William Leveson. Aldermanbury, not far from the Moorgate, was as distant from the Bankside as it was possible to get and still be in London, and it was not much nearer Blackfriars; the Aldermanbury connection has yet to be fully investigated.

We know from a warrant of 2 October 1599 for payment of £30 'for three interludes or plays played before her majesty on St Stephens Day at night, New Year's Day at night, and Shrove Tuesday at night last past' to Hemmings and Thomas Pope that Hemmings was by then a shareholder in the Chamberlain's Company. At some point, between 1605 and 1608, Henry Condell joined as a shareholder in the Globe. Both bought a share of the Blackfriars in 1608. When Shakespeare bought the house in Blackfriars, and mortgaged it for part of the purchase price, Hemmings and Condell were trustees and co-tenants.

If Shakespeare had discussed with Hemmings and Condell the possibility of printing an edition of his plays, we might wonder what took them so long. They were representatives of the King's Men: the company owned the plays and had the sole right to sell the playtexts to a publisher. When we consider that for the company there was no advantage to be gained by printing their playtexts which then became available to every cry of players, we must ask ourselves why Hemmings and Condell undertook such a project when they did. What they said in their dedicatory letter was that they did it 'only to keep the memory of so worthy a friend and fellow alive, as was our Shakespeare'. The best way to keep his memory alive, one would have thought, would have been to stage his plays but, in the winter of 1620–1, of eleven performances at court by the King's Men, the only play by Shakespeare to be performed was an adaptation of *Twelfth Night*, called 'Malvolio', and apparently an anti-puritan satire.

Shakespeare's reputation was fading fast. Michael Drayton, writing 'Of Poets and Poesy' to Henry Reynolds *c.*1625, had more to say about Spenser, Sidney, Warner, Marlowe, Nashe, Daniel, Chapman, Jonson, Sylvester and Sandys than he did of Shakespeare.[12] Fifteen years or so later William Cartwright could assure John Fletcher:

> Shakespeare to thee was dull, whose best jest lies
> I'the Lady's questions and the Fool's replies,
> Old-fashioned wit which walked from town to town
> In turnèd hose, which our fathers called the Clown,
> Whose wit our nice times would obsceneness call,
> And which made bawdry pass for comical.
> Nature was all his art. Thy vein was free
> As his, but without his scurrility.[13]

In 1622 the King's Men visited Stratford and were paid six shillings not to perform. 'What brought them for once and now to Shakespeare's native town and home and burial-place? . . . but to pay homage to the man and his monument and to receive "papers" without a blot on them, from his Widow and Daughter and Son-in-law at New Place?'[14]

It would not have taken a company of twelve persons or more to collect Shakespeare's papers, or three people to give them away for that matter. What it would have taken to print the Folio was money. The printing of large-paper folios was expensive. Somehow money had to be made available up front for the acquisition of paper, still an extremely expensive commodity, and the setting of the print. The sales of such bulky and expensive volumes were bound to be slow. Later generations would deal with this problem by raising subscriptions, but Hemmings and Condell did not have that option. The mildly facetious letter 'To the great variety of readers' signed in full 'John Heminge and Henrie Condell' makes quite clear that the publishers were anxious to recoup what they had outlaid.

From the most able to him that can but spell, there you are numbered.
We had rather you were weighed, especially when the fate of books
depends upon your capabilities, and not of your heads alone, but of
your purses. Well! It is now public and you will stand for your
privileges we know, to read and censure. Do so, but buy it first. That
doth best commend a book, the stationer says. Then, how odd soever
your brains be or your wisdoms, make your licence the same and spare
not. Judge your sixpenn'orth, your shillingsworth, your five shillings
worth at a time, or higher, so you rise to the just rates, and welcome.
But, whatever you do, buy.

This is so strangely apologetic that the reader might be pardoned
for doubting the seriousness of the editors' commitment to the
project. Modern scholarship, assuming that the printers had to cover
their costs, has arrived at a retail price for the First Folio of £1, which
for most people would have been prohibitive. The poet's 'friends' are
credited with compiling and collating the works with 'care and pain',

and so to have published them, as where, before, you were abused
with diverse stolen and surreptitious copies, maimed and deformed by
the frauds and stealths of injurious imposters that exposed them, even
those are now offered to your view cured and perfect of their limbs and
all the rest, absolute in their numbers, as he conceived them.

Though the editors do not claim to have had autograph manuscripts for their copytexts, they imply as much: 'And what he thought,
he uttered with such easiness that we have scarce received from him a
blot in his papers.' Scribal copies are necessarily blot-free; a professional copyist who makes a mistake has to throw away his page and
start again. If the absence of blots is worthy of remark it is because
what the editors had was written in the poet's own hand, described on
the title-page of the Folio as 'the true, original copies'. They claim
elsewhere that their texts are 'truly set forth, according to their first
original. In the theatre the whole play was the copytext for scribal
copies of parts, and the platts listing entrances and exits that were used
by the stage managers. These multiple copies were costly to generate
and would not have been thrown away. Whether companies were as

careful with their copies of whole plays is not clear. Certainly, printers threw away their copytexts, whether they were autograph or not. The puzzle remains, if Shakespeare's texts were not all in one place, under the control of the King's Men, where could they have been? Some may have been in the Blackfriars house, though it seems that Shakespeare never lived there, but surely some must have been at New Place. If any papers had been at New Place or in Ann's keeping, it is most unlikely that they would have found their way back there after they had been used by the printer, so whatever papers remained in Stratford after the Folio appeared were not the Folio copytexts.

The Frankfurt book fair was already up and running in 1622, when it was held twice yearly, in spring and autumn. The English version of the catalogue for October 1622 lists 'Plays written by M. William Shakespeare, all in one volume, printed by Isaac Jaggard in folio'. Printing had in fact begun in the summer of 1621, and it is thought that the assembling of the texts must date from at least a year earlier. However, the Folio was not entered in the Stationers' Register until 8 November 1623. The point of entering copyright in the Stationers' Register was to prevent anyone else from uttering the same text; leaving the entry so late in the lengthy production process implies an absence of competition and no risk whatever of piracy.

In the First Folio of 1623 there are thirty-six plays, eighteen of them never before published. Of the others six had been published in bad quartos and the Folio text is superior; three had been published in doubtful quartos and the Folio text is no better; and in eleven cases the Folio text is based on the published quarto. It seems clear from this that there was no single source of the Folio copytexts. Textually the Folio had more than one begetter, but there may have been only one angel who provided the money to set it up and that could have been Ann Shakespeare, anonymous as usual.

The fact that the Folio was reprinted nine years later is usually taken to mean that the first print-run sold out, yet no mention of the Folio can be found in any documented contemporary collection. Indeed, the copy sent for deposit in the Bodleian was so little regarded that it was sold when the second edition appeared in 1632.[15] We have no idea what the original print-run can have been; 500 copies is considered too few because it would result in too high a unit cost, while 1,500 was the legal maximum.[16] Two hundred and thirty copies are known to survive. This fact itself suggests that the First Folio was not much read, certainly not as *Venus and Adonis* was, for example; as we have seen, virtually all of the copies of the more than eleven editions of *Venus and Adonis* were read to pieces. The First Folio is the kind of volume that is presented to all kinds of luminaries, who accept it with thanks but don't read it. One is reminded of the folios vanity-published by Margaret Cavendish, Duchess of Newcastle and sent to every educational institution in the country, where they are still, in pristine condition.

The cost of production having been assessed at about 6s 8d a copy, the retail price can hardly have been less than about fifteen shillings. As Stanley Wells points out: 'The publishers' investment in a massive collection of play scripts was a declaration of faith in Shakespeare's selling power as a dramatist for reading as well as for performing.'[17] The declaration of faith and the investment may not after all have been the publishers'. If the publication was subsidised, the print-run could well have been small. In 1633, William Prynne was scandalised to notice that 'Shakespeare's Plays are printed on the best crown paper, far better than most Bibles,' which suggests that for someone cost was no object.[18] Wells credits Hemmings and Condell with the actual editorial work; they commissioned a scribe called Ralph Crane to copy 'a number of plays specially for the volume' and chose 'which printed editions and manuscripts to send to the printer . . . copy which must have been a printer's nightmare'. What is obvious from the appearance of the First Folio is that a house style has been imposed on all this disparate material, which suggests to me at least that the editors did not take the risk of giving the printers jumbled papers or leaving them to impose a house style of their own. So far-fetched is the idea that Shakespeare's widow might have hired an amanuensis to prepare an edition of her husband's plays that no one has ever considered it.

As a widow Ann Shakespeare was entitled to make a will. If we could find it, and her inventory, we would know once for all whether she died a penniless dependant or whether she left money in trust to be spent on further publishing of her husband's work. If she did she would have left her executor no choice but to make available any funds remaining for a de-luxe second edition before he himself was gathered to his eternal reward.

All this, in common with most of this book, is heresy, and probably neither truer nor less true than the accepted prejudice. Ann Shakespeare cannot sensibly be written out of her husband's life if only because he himself was so aware of marriage as a challenging way of life, a 'world-without-end bargain'. The Shakespeare wallahs have succeeded in creating a Bard in their own likeness, that is to say, incapable of relating to women, and have then vilified the one woman who remained true to him all his life, in order to exonerate him. There can be no doubt that Shakespeare neglected his wife, embarrassed her and even humiliated her, but attempting to justify his behaviour by vilifying her is puerile. The defenders of Ann Hathaway are usually derided as sentimental when they are trying simply to be fair. It is a more insidious variety of sentimentality that wants to believe that women who are ill treated must have brought it upon themselves. The creator of Hero, Desdemona, Imogen and Hermione knew better. Ann might say like Lady Macduff:

> I have done no harm. But I remember now
> I am in this earthly world, where to do harm
> Is often laudable, to do good sometime
> Accounted dangerous folly. Why then, alas,
> Do I put up that womanly defence
> To say I have done no harm? (IV. ii. 75–80)

NOTES

ABBREVIATIONS

BL   British Library

CSPD   *Calendar of State Papers Domestic*

CSPF   *Calendar of State Papers Foreign*

DNB   *Dictionary of National Biography*

M&A   *Minutes and Accounts of the Corporation of Stratford-upon-Avon 1553–1620*, vols i–iv ed. R. Savage and E. I. Fripp, vol. v ed. Levi Fox (Hertford, Dugdale Society, 1921–90)

MS   manuscript

NA   National Archives

OED   *Oxford English Dictionary*

SBTRO   Shakespeare Birthplace Trust Record Office

SPD   *State Papers Domestic*

VCH   *Victoria County History*

INTRODUCTION

1. Jardine, *Still Harping on Daughters*, 103.
2. Chambers Bunten, *Life of Alice Barnham*, *passim*.
3. Bacon, 'Of Marriage and Single Life', *Essays*, viii.
4. Tasso, *Of Marriage and Wiving*, Sig. Blv.
5. *DNB*. His wife was Philippa de Roet, daughter of the Rienne king-at-arms and she bore him at least three children – two sons, Thomas who survived to adulthood and Lewis who didn't, and a daughter Elizabeth who became a nun. The marriage is presumed to date from *c*.1364 and Philippa is thought to have died in about 1387.
6. Moore, 'Notices of the Life of Lord Byron', 136n.
7. Schoenbaum, *Shakespeare's Lives*, 173.

8. *ibid.*
9. Malone, *Supplement to the Edition of Shakespeare's Plays*, i, 653.
10. Schoenbaum, *Shakespeare's Lives*, 247.
11. Thomas De Quincey, quoted in Schoenbaum, *Shakespeare's Lives*, 322.
12. *ibid.*, 312. The allegation was repeated in Rees's *Cyclopædia* (1819).
13. Moore, 'Notices of the Life of Lord Byron', 136n.
14. Hunter, *New Illustrations*, i, 51.
15. Joyce, *Ulysses*, 247.
16. Schoenbaum, *Shakespeare's Lives*, 765.
17. Holden, *William Shakespeare*, 63–4.
18. Guizot, *Shakespeare et son temps*, 22–3.
19. Greenblatt, *Will in the World*, 147.
20. Price, *Shakespeare's Unorthodox Biography*, 14.
21. Armstrong, *Shakespeare in Psychoanalysis*, 2–3.
22. *ibid.*, 3.
23. [Cooke], *How to chuse a good wife from a bad*, Sig. [A2v].

CHAPTER ONE

1. Rowe, 'Some Account of the Life &c of Mr. William Shakespeare', in Rowe, *Works of Shakespeare*, i, ii–iii.
2. Holy Trinity Parish Register, SBTRO, DR 243/1.
3. Eccles, *Shakespeare in Warwickshire*, 63.
4. The thirteenth-century *Legenda Sanctorum* of Jacopus de Voragine, printed by Caxton in 1483 as *The Golden Legend*.
5. Worcestershire Record Office, 008.7, 16/1601; Schoenbaum, *Documentary Life*, illustration facing p. 69.
6. Hoskins, 'The Rebuilding of Rural England, 1570–1640', 44–59.
7. NA, Prob. 11/64/31; Schoenbaum, *Documentary Life*, 60; complete transcript, Gray, *Shakespeare's Marriage*, 221–3.
8. Fripp, *Shakespeare*, 184.
9. According to the International Genealogical Index a Catherine Hathaway married a Henry Widdowes at Shipton-under-Wychwood, Oxfordshire, in 1590.
10. *M&A*, iii, 137.
11. e.g. Wood, *In Search of Shakespeare*, 81.
12. Warwickshire Corn Enquiry, *M&A*, v, 58.
13. *Henslowe's Diary*, 90.
14. *ibid.*, 89.
15. *ibid.*, 126.
16. *Belvedere or the Garden of the Muses*, Sig. [b2v].
17. *Henslowe's Diary*, 138.
18. *ibid.*, 65.
19. *ibid.*, 166.
20. Dulwich College MSS, vol. 1, Article 33 (*Henslowe's Diary*, 295).

21. *Henslowe's Diary*, 183.

22. *ibid.*, 193.

23. *ibid.*, 186–7.

24. *ibid.*, 206.

25. *ibid.*, 221.

26. *ibid.*, 208.

27. *ibid.*, 221, 222.

28. Vicar General's Book No. 4, f. 301v, Principal Probate Registry, Somerset House, in Gray, *Shakespeare's Marriage*, 233–4.

CHAPTER TWO

1. That is, if the first Joan Shakespeare in the baptismal register of Holy Trinity is his daughter, and perhaps even later if – as I suspect – Joan is the child of another John Shakespeare.

2. SBTRO, ER3/1923; Halliwell-Phillipps, *Outlines* (7th edn 1887), ii, 173; Hone, *The Manor*, 125, 310; Chambers, *William Shakespeare*, 30–1; *VCH: Warwickshire*, iii, 44.

3. SBTRO, Miscellaneous Documents, ii, 21; Halliwell-Phillipps, *Outlines* (7th edn 1887), ii, 173–6.

4. Wood, *In Search of Shakespeare*, 27.

5. *M&A*, ii, xlvi, xlviii, 110; iii, 14.

6. *M&A*, v, 149, 161.

7. Emanuel van Meteren, *Album*, quoted by Plowden in *Tudor Women*, 1–2.

8. *M&A*, iv, 12, 24, 28, 29, 34.

9. *M&A*, iii, 142, 154, iv, 89.

10. *M&A*, iv, 67, 128; Eccles, *Shakespeare in Warwickshire*, 100.

11. *Stratford-upon-Avon Inventories*, i, 195–6.

12. Dekker, *The Shoemakers' Holiday*, III. ii. 131–9, in *Dramatic Works of Thomas Dekker*, 54.

13. Prior, 'Women and the Urban Economy: Oxford 1500–1800', 95.

14. Deloney, *Jack of Newbery*, 68.

15. SBTRO, BRU 15/1/130, 178; Bess Quiney's mother-in-law also participated in her husband's business: *M&A*, iii, 14.

16. SBTRO, BRU 15/1/129, 177.

17. *M&A*, iii, 31 (Council Book A, 87).

18. *M&A*, iii, 19 (Council Book A, 186).

19. *M&A*, iii, 24 (Council Book A, 190).

20. Schoenbaum, *Documentary Life*, 60.

21. Ferne, *The Blazon of Gentrie*, 58–60.

22. *M&A*, iii, 68–9; NA, Court of King's Bench, Anglia 20b 21a Trinity Term, 22 Eliz.

CHAPTER THREE

1. Duncan-Jones, *Ungentle Shakespeare*, 17.

2. Browne, *Britannia's Pastorals*, Book I, Song iv.

3. *Corydon's Commendation*, The Second Part, in *Pepys Ballads*, i, 81.

4. *A New Ballad intituled, I haue fresh Cheese and Creame*, in *Pepys Ballads*, i, 48.

5. *Greenes Vision*, Sig. D2–[D2ᵛ].

6. 'he weeps like a wench that had shed her milk', *All's Well That Ends Well*, IV. iii. 110–11.

7. *Turner's Dish of Lenten Stuff*, in *Pepysian Garland*, 34.

8. Holden, *William Shakespeare*, 63–4.

9. *The Winter's Tale*, IV. iii. 9–12.

10. Fripp, *Master Richard Quyny*, 85.

11. *A Maydens Lamentation for a Bedfellow. Or, I can, nor will no longer lie alone*, in *Pepys Ballads*, i, 67.

12. 'Coridon's Song', in *Englands Helicon*, 114.

13. Laslett, *World We Have Lost*, 81.

14. Stone, *Family, Sex and Marriage*, 43–4; Wrigley and Schofield, *Population History of England*, 255.

15. Laslett, *World We Have Lost*, 82.

16. Brodsky, 'Widows in Late Elizabethan London: Remarriage, Economic Opportunity and Family Orientations', 127–8.

17. Deloney, *The Gentle Craft*, 12.

18. Deloney, *Jack of Newbery*, 9.

19. *ibid.*

20. *ibid.*, 19.

21. *DNB*.

22. Greenblatt, *Will in the World*, 125–6.

23. e.g. letter of 28 October 1598, Abraham Sturley to Richard Quiney, SBTRO, BRU 15/1/145.

24. The evidence for this is her signature in full on an indenture of 1647, reproduced in Fripp, *Shakespeare*, facing p. 905, as Birthplace Catalogue, No. 69.

25. Eason, *The Genevan Bible*, 1–12.

26. Weston, *Autobiography of an Elizabethan*, 164–5.

27. Quoted from the thesis of N. Evans by Spufford, *Small Books and Pleasant Histories*, 34.

28. Cressy, 'Education and Literacy in London and East Anglia, 1580–1700', 99–100, 111–13, 129–35.

29. Spufford, *Small Books and Pleasant Histories*, 21.

30. Cross, 'Great Reasoners in Scripture: Women Lollards 1380–1530'; Schofield, 'Illiteracy in Pre-Industrial England: The Work of the Cambridge Group for the History of Population and Social Structure'.

31. Rhodes, *The Countrie Mans Comfort*, quoted in Spufford, *Small Books and Pleasant Histories*, 10.

32. Spufford, 'First Steps in Literacy: The Reading and Writing Experiences of the Humblest Seventeenth-Century Spiritual Autobiographers', 407–35.

33. Bownde, *The Doctrine of the Sabbath*, 242. See also Baskervill, *The Elizabethan Jig*, and Brody, *The English Mummers and their Plays*.

34. Maden, ed., 'The Daily Ledger of John Dorne, 1520', quoted in Spufford, *Small Books and Pleasant Histories*, 14.

35. *ibid.*

36. Greenblatt, *Will in the World*, 55.

37. *The Poems of Sir Philip Sidney*, 211.

38. Dekker and Webster, *Westward Ho*, I. ii. 120–1, in *Dramatic Works of Thomas Dekker*, ii, 329.

39. *Westward Ho*, II. i. 75–105 (the whole exchange is rather longer than as quoted here).

CHAPTER FOUR

1. Gurr, 'Shakespeare's First Poem: Sonnet 145', 221–6.

2. *Joan is as good as my Lady. To the Tune of What care I how faire she be*, in *Pepys Ballads*, i, 159–60.

3. Kyd, *Soliman and Perseda*, I. ii. 6–9, 15–16, in *Works of Thomas Kyd*, 655.

4. *As You Like It*, V. iii. 21–6.

5. Gataker, *A Good Wife Gods Gift*, 11.

6. E.g. 4 & 5 Philip & Mary, c. 5, and 39 Eliz., c. 9.

7. Duncan-Jones, *Ungentle Shakespeare*, 217–18.

8. *Love's Labour's Lost*, IV. iii. 322–3.

9. Ascham, *The Scholemaster* (1570), in *English Works*, 205.

10. [Becon], *The golden boke of christen matrimonye*.

11. Googe, *Eglogs, Epytaphes and Sonettes*, 'Notes of his Life and Writings', 10.

12. *ibid.*

CHAPTER FIVE

1. *As You Like It*, V. i. 13–58.

2. Holden, *William Shakespeare*, 65.

3. Worcester Diocesan Registry, 28 November 1582; Gray, *Shakespeare's Marriage*, 204.

4. Steel, 323.

5. Holden, *William Shakespeare*, 65.

6. *ibid.*

7. Lee, *A Life of William Shakespeare*. Schoenbaum remarks: 'Lee allowed this passage to remain intact throughout his lifetime, despite the fact that twenty years earlier Gray had refuted Lee's inferences in *Shakespeare's Marriage* (1905) pp. 48–57' (Schoenbaum, *Documentary Life*, 65).

8. Collins, *Sidney Papers*, ii, 81.

9. *ibid.*, 90.

10. *CSPD*, Eliz. cclxviii.
11. *Henry VI, Part 1*, V. v. 11–13.
12. Brinkworth, *Shakespeare and the Bawdy Court*, 122–3; *M&A*, v, 97.
13. *ibid.*, 131.
14. *ibid.*, 132.
15. *ibid.*, 135.
16. *ibid.*, 142.
17. Greenblatt, *Will in the World*, 123.
18. Ingram, *Church Courts, Sex and Marriage in England*, 286.
19. Brinkworth, *Shakespeare and the Bawdy Court*, 127.
20. *ibid.*, 138.
21. Boswell, *The Kindness of Strangers*, 100–2, 186, 258–9, 261–4; Wrightson, 'Infanticide in the Early Seventeenth Century', 10–22.
22. Episcopal Register, Worcester Cathedral, f. 43v, 27 November 1582.
23. Eccles, *Shakespeare in Warwickshire*, 41.
24. Honan, *Shakespeare*, 81–2.
25. Fripp, *Shakespeare*, 191.
26. Burgess, *Shakespeare*, 57.
27. *Love's Labours Lost*, V. ii. 886–9, 895–8.

CHAPTER SIX

1. Perkins, *Of Christian Oeconomie*; Swinburne, *A Treatise of Spousals*, 219–20.
2. Laslett, *World We Have Lost*, 141–2.
3. [Bullinger], *The Christian State of Matrimony*, Sig. [H8]v.
4. [Watson], *Holsome and Catholyke doctryne concernynge the seuen sacramentes*, f. clxxii.
5. *View of Popishe Abuses, Puritan Manifestoes*, 34.
6. *ibid.*, 127.
7. Breton, *The Court and the Country*, 183.
8. *Pepys Ballads*, i, 77.
9. Ingram, *Church Courts, Sex and Marriage*, Chapter 7, *passim*.
10. *The Bride's Goodmorrow*, BL Roxburghe i, 15.
11. Spenser, *Amoretti and Epithalamion written not long since by Edmunde Spenser*, 'Epithalamion', ll. 19–30.
12. *ibid.*, ll. 151–8.
13. Deloney, *Jack of Newbery*, 26.
14. Browne, *Britannia's Pastorals*, Book I, Song ii.
15. *Greene's Vision*, Sig. D3.
16. Spenser, 'Epithalamion', ll. 137–8.
17. *ibid.*, ll. 43–4.
18. Brooke, 'An Epithalamium, or a Nuptiall Song, applied to the Ceremonies of Marriage', 220.
19. *The Bride's Goodmorrow*.
20. Fripp, *Master Richard Quyny*, 36.

CHAPTER SEVEN

1. Rowse, *Shakespeare the Man*, 272.
2. Fripp, *Shakespeare's Stratford*, 23.
3. Laslett, *World We Have Lost*, 90.
4. Greenblatt, *Will in the World*, 149.
5. Coram Rege roll, Halliwell-Phillipps, *Outlines*, (7th edn 1887), ii, 298.
6. Wood, *In Search of Shakespeare*, 72.
7. Eccles, *Shakespeare in Warwickshire*, 31.
8. Rowse, *Shakespeare the Man*, 36.
9. Eccles, *Shakespeare in Warwickshire*, 33–4; NA, Court of Common Pleas, Docket Roll 78, f. 8v.
10. NA, CP 40/1697 mem. 327, Hilary 31 Eliz.
11. Fripp, *Shakespeare*, 192.
12. Bearman, 'John Shakespeare: A Papist or Just Pennniless?', 418.
13. *Stratford-upon-Avon Inventories*, ii, 16: Worcestershire Record Office, 008.7 1627/04.
14. In 1642 the Corporation leased to Francis Ainge a messuage in Bridge Street supposed to be 'Henry Turbitt's [house], being the Maidenhead' (SBTRO, BRU 15/11/10).
15. Stubbes, *The Anatomie of Abuses*, Sig. [H5].
16. *The Countryman's Chat,* in *Pepys Ballads*, ii, 235.
17. Whateley, *A Bride-Bush*, Sig. [A6r–v].
18. *The Witch of Edmonton*, I. i. 5–9, 44–5, in *Dramatic Works of Thomas Dekker*, iii, 490–1.
19. Laslett, *World We Have Lost*, 90–1.
20. Statutes of the Realm, iv, 804–5; NA, DL 44, 398.
21. *The Private Life of an Elizabethan Lady*, 8.
22. Fripp, *Shakespeare*, 792.
23. [Dekker], *The Pleasant Comodie of Patient Grissill*, I. ii. 151–6, in *Dramatic Works of Thomas Dekker*, i, 220.
24. *As You Like It*, IV. iii. 80.
25. Sir John Davies, 'The Wife', in *The Poems of Sir John Davies*, 227.
26. Cary, *The Tragedy of Mariam* (1613), 113.
27. Greenblatt, *Will in the World*, 126–7.
28. *ibid.*, 130.
29. Overbury, *A Wife now The Widow*.
30. Greenblatt, *Will in the World*, 130.

CHAPTER EIGHT

1. Holden, *William Shakespeare*, 65.
2. Laslett, *World We Have Lost*, 141.
3. Deloney, *Jack of Newbery*, 76.
4. *ibid.*, 80.

5. Burgess, *Shakespeare*, 60.

6. Sharp, *Midwives Book*, 50–1.

7. BL Additional MS 29. 571, f. 83.

8. Sharp, *Midwives Book*, 145.

9. Raynaldes, *The Birth of Mankind*, 100–1.

10. Sharp, *Midwives Book*, 153.

11. Raynaldes, *The Birth of Mankind*, 101.

12. Sharp, *Midwives Book*, 153.

13. Boorde, *A Breviary of health*, 89.

14. Sharp, *Midwives Book*, 163.

15. Smith, *A Preparative to Mariage*, 84.

16. Coster, 'Purity, Profanity, Puritanism: The Churching of Women, 1570–1700'; Cressy, 'Purification, Thanksgiving and the Churching of Women in Post-Reformation England'.

17. Deloney, *Jack of Newbery*, 140.

18. Short, *The Biological Basis for the Contraceptive Effects of Breastfeeding*.

19. Duncan-Jones, *Ungentle Shakespeare*, 22–3.

20. *Romeo and Juliet*, I. iii. 26–8.

21. Sharp, *Midwives Book*, 76.

22. *ibid.*, 77.

23. In the register of baptisms, however, we find two separate entries; on 6 August 1559, we have a mysterious entry recording the baptism of a 'Richard Hathaway', with no father's name, and on 4 January 1562 a 'Richardus filius Richard Hathaway alias Gardner'. It seems at least as likely then that one of the Richard Hathaways buried at the end of March was Ann's full brother, and the other a nineteen-month-old cousin.

24. Sharp, *Midwives Book*, 58–60.

25. *Cymbeline*, II. v. 9–13.

26. Barrough, *The Method of Physick, 202.*

27. Raynaldes, *The Birth of Mankind*, 106.

28. Stone, *Crisis in the Aristocracy*, 283.

29. Fildes, *Breasts, Bottles and Babies*, 155.

30. *ibid.*, 159, quoting *The Private Diary of Dr John Dee* (1842) and F. G. Emmison, *Tudor Food and Pastimes: Life at Ingatestone Hall* (1964).

31. Muffett, *Health's Improvement*, 122–3.

32. Markham, *The English Housewife*, 39.

33. Dekker, *The Pleasant Comodie of Patient Grissill*, IV. i. 123–7, 129–34, in *Dramatic Works of Thomas Dekker*, i, 258.

CHAPTER NINE

1. Greenblatt, *Will in the World*, 124.

2. Honigman, *Shakespeare: The Lost Years*, 1–2, 128.

3. Manning, *Village Revolts*, 4.

4. Rowe, *Works of Shakespeare*, vii, v.
5. Eccles, *Shakespeare in Warwickshire*, 75.
6. Chambers, *William Shakespeare*, ii, 257.
7. Manning, *Village Revolts*, 38.
8. Schoenbaum, *Documentary Life*, 87.
9. Greene, *The Repentance of Robert Greene, Master of Arts*, Sigs C3, C3v, [C4].
10. Greenblatt, *Will in the World*, 124.
11. *ibid.*, 126.
12. SBTRO, ER1/115, f. 4.
13. Lady Mary Wroth, 'Pamphilia to Amphilanthus', Sonnet 13, in *The Poems of Lady Mary Wroth*, 94.
14. *CSPF*, 1569–71, no. 185.
15. Lehmberg, *Sir Walter Mildmay and Tudor Government*, 78.
16. Northamptonshire Record Office, W/A, Box 2, parcel xii, no I/D^9.
17. *CSPF*, 1578–9, nos 67, 82.
18. *CSPF*, 1581–2, no. 59.
19. Lehmberg, *Sir Walter Mildmay and Tudor Government*, 272.
20. Pollock, *With Faith and Physic*, 34.
21. Northamptonshire Record Office, W/A, Box 2, parcel xii, No I/D^{1}2.
22. *CSPD*, 1595–7, nos 51–2, 59–60.
23. [Cooke], *How to chuse a good wife from a bad*, Sig. [E3v–4].
24. Thomson, *Shakespeare's Professional Career*, 69.
25. Nashe, *Pierce Pennliess his Supplication to the Devil*, in *Works of Thomas Nashe*, i, 216.
26. Lasocki, *The Bassanos*, passim.
27. *The Diary of John Manningham of the Middle Temple*, 208–9. The story was first published in Wilkes, *A General View of the Stage*, 220–1; from BL, MS Harley 5353, f. 29v.
28. Quoted by Wells in *Shakespeare and Co.*, 47–8, without acknowledgement.
29. Dekker and Webster, *Westward Ho*, I. i. 198–9, 205–6, in *Dramatic works of Thomas Dekker*, ii, 324–5.

CHAPTER TEN

1. *Stratford-upon-Avon Inventories*, i, 96.
2. *ibid.*, 96–7; Worcestershire Record Office, 008.7 1588/76.
3. *M&A*, v, 112.
4. *M&A*, v, 111.
5. *Stratford-upon-Avon Inventories*,' 267–8, SBTRO, BRU 15/1/77.
6. *M&A*, v, 51, 52.
7. *M&A*, v, 59.
8. *M&A*, v, 60–1.
9. *M&A*, v, 61.
10. Parish Register, Welford-upon-Avon, *M&A*, v, 41.
11. Locke, journal, 1 March 1681, Bodleian MS Locke f.5.

12. *Stratford-upon-Avon Inventories*, i, 54.
13. Laurence, *Women in England*, 19.
14. Clark, *The Working Life of Women in the Seventeenth Century*, 131.
15. *M&A*, ii, 48.
16. *M&A*, ii, 116.
17. *M&A*, ii, 117.
18. *M&A*, iii, 96; iv, 16.
19. *M&A*, iii, 27, 28, 29, 43, 44.
20. *M&A*, iii, 79, 81.
21. *M&A*, iii, 95, 96.
22. *M&A*, iii, 135.
23. *M&A*, iii, 164.
24. SBTRO, BRT 3/1/63.
25. *M&A*, iv, 55.
26. *M&A*, iv, 73.
27. *M&A*, iv, 143.
28. Plowden, *Tudor Women*, 164–5.
29. Worcestershire Record Office, 008.7 1580/62; *M&A*, ii, 106, 115–16, 119; iii, 28, 84; SBTRO, BRU 15/7/107.
30. Deloney, *Jack of Newbery*, 65–6.
31. Clark, *The Working Life of Women in the Seventeenth Century*, 'Introduction', xxx.
32. Deloney, *Thomas of Reading*, 95.
33. *ibid.*, 127.
34. Worcestershire Record Office, 008.7 1560/184.
35. Worcestershire Record Office, 008.7 1564/33.
36. Worcestershire Record Office, 008.7 1570/18.
37. SBTRO, BRU 15/7/147.
38. SBTRO, BRT 3/1/15.
39. *Stratford-upon-Avon Inventories*, i, 332–4.
40. *Stratford-upon-Avon Inventories*, i, 107–8.
41. *M&A*, v, 115.
42. *Stratford-upon-Avon Inventories*, i, 24.
43. *Stratford-upon-Avon Inventories*, ii, 87.
44. *Stratford-upon-Avon Inventories*, ii, 43.
45. Markham, *The Compleat Housewife*, title-page.
46. Tusser, 'The Preface to the Book of Huswifery', *Five Hundred Points of Good Husbandry*, f. 29.
47. Sue Wright, ' "Churmaids, Housewives and Hucksters" '; cf. Weigall, 'An Elizabethan Gentlewoman: the journal of Lady Mildmay circa 1570–1617'.
48. SBTRO, BRU 15/12/63, 70.
49. SBTRO, BRU 15/12/74.
50. SBTRO, BRU 15/13/12.
51. Deloney, *Jack of Newbery*, 24.
52. [Cooke], *How to chuse a good wife from a bad*, Sig. [Cv].

53. Laurence, *Women in England*, 10.
54. Thirsk, 'The Fantastical Folly of Fashion', 51.
55. Stow, *Annales*, 948.
56. Thirsk, 'The Fantastical Folly of Fashion', 54.
57. Stow, *Annales*, 867.
58. *ibid.*, 869.
59. Holinshed, *Chronicles*, (1807–8), iv. 384; Nichols, *Progresses*, ii. 144.
60. *Joan is as Good as My Lady*, Campions's *Two Books of Airs*, i, 20, in *Pepys Ballads*, i, 159. See also Everitt, 'Cottage Husbandry and Peasant Wealth', 190.
61. Borough Justices 22–6–49, Wells Session Book, quoted in Quaife, *Wanton Wenches and Wayward Wives*, 150.
62. SBTRO, BRU 15/1/131, f. 179.
63. Stubbes, *Anatomie of Abuses*, Sig. Eiiiv.
64. *ibid.*, Sig. [Fviii]v.
65. SBTRO, BRU 12/6/107, 114.
66. Lille, Archives Départmentales du Nord, MS 20H9, 'The Lady Faulkland Her Life', f. 9r.
67. Everitt, 'Cottage Husbandry and Peasant Wealth', 190–1.
68. SBTRO, BRU 15/12/91, f. 116.
69. SBTRO, BRU 15/12/91.
70. SBTRO, BRU 15/13/21, 22.
71. Gough, *History of Myddle*, 132.
72. *ibid.*, 241. See also Erickson, *Women and Property*, 58.
73. Halliwell-Phillipps, *Outlines* (7th edn 1887), ii, 298; Eccles, *Shakespeare in Warwickshire*, 108.
74. Greene, *A Quip for an Upstart Courtier*, Sig. Fii.
75. *OED*.
76. Greene, *A Quip for an Upstart Courtier*, Sig. Fii–F[ii]v.
77. Stow, *Annales*, 869.
78. *OED*.
79. Cotgrave, *Dictionary*, 'mercerot'.
80. Statute of Apparel, 39 Eliz. 1.
81. Dekker and Webster, *Westward Ho*, II. ii. 108–9, in *Dramatic Works of Thomas Dekker*, ii, 340.
82. *M&A*, iii, 13.
83. *M&A*, iii, 45, 46, 47.
84. *M&A*, iii, 45, 46.
85. *M&A*, iii, 14.
86. *M&A*, iii, 118, 119.
87. *Stratford-upon-Avon Inventories*, i, 297–9.
88. SBTRO, BRU 15/6/170, 15/7/237.
89. SBTRO, BRU 15/7/244.
90. Brinkworth, *Shakespeare and the Bawdy Court*, 127.
91. *Stratford-upon-Avon Inventories*, i, 329–30. See also SBTRO, BRU 15/13/65, which

recognises her as 'of Stratford'. In *Northward-Ho* (1607) by Dekker and Webster, Doll masquerades as 'a country pedlar . . . that travels up and down to exchange pins for coney-skins' (V. i. 391–2, in *Dramatic Works of Thomas Dekker*, ii, 474).

92. *A New Ballad intituled, I haue fresh Cheese and Creame*, in *Pepys Ballads*, i, 50.

93. Lippincott, ed., *'Merry Passages and Jeasts'*, 44.

94. Dekker, *The Shomakers Holiday, or The Gentle Craft*, I. i. 207–11, in *Dramatic Works of Thomas Dekker*, i, 29.

95. Jones, *Family Life in Shakespeare's England*, 86.

CHAPTER ELEVEN

1. He signed the Holy Trinity Registers in those years; see also Brinkworth, *Shakespeare and the Bawdy Court*, 63, 67, 68, 69–70, 109, 118.

2. *ibid.*, 22–3; cf. Ingram, *Church Courts, Sex and Marriage*, 324–9.

3. *Stratford-upon-Avon Inventories*, i, 74–5.

4. *ibid.*, 268–9.

5. *ibid.*, 295–6.

6. Worcestershire Record Office, 008.7 1636/103.

7. *Stratford-upon-Avon Inventories*, i, 116.

8. *The First Part of the Return from Parnassus*, ll. 1200–3, in *The Three Parnassus Plays*, 192.

9. *The Second Part of the Return from Parnassus*, ll. 301–4, in *The Three Parnassus Plays*, 244.

10. Freeman, *Rubbe and a Great Cast. Epigrams*, Sig. K3.

11. D[avies], *A Scourge for Paper Persecutors*, Sig. A3.

12. Forman, 'Diary', Bodleian MS Ashmole 226, ff. 93v, 95v, 110v, 122v, 201, 222v, 236.

13. Stow, *Summarie*, 399.

14. SBTRO, BRU 2/1–5, A. 233.

15. *M&A*, iii, 156.

16. SBTRO, BRU 2/1–5, B.; account of sums received BRU 2/1–5, B. 7.

17. *M&A*, v, 1593–8, xx.

18. 'Warwickshire Buyers of Corn', Warwickshire County Record Office, CR 1886/BB711/2663.

19. *Agricultural History Review* xii (1964), 39; also table facing p. 29.

20. 'Buyers of Corn', *M&A*, v, 49–50.

21. Duncan-Jones, *Ungentle Shakespeare*, 90–1.

22. *Venus and Adonis*, 'To the right honourable Henry Wriothesley, Earl of Southampton and Baron of Tichfield'.

23. Halliwell-Phillips, *Outlines* i, 299–304.

24. Ackroyd, *Shakespeare*, 270.

25. MacDonald, *Mystical Bedlam, passim*; see also Macfarlane, *The Family Life of Ralph Josselin*, and his *Marriage and Love in England*; Houlbrooke, *The English Family*; Pollock, *Forgotten Children*.

26. 'On my first daughter', *Epigrammes*, xxii; 'On my first son', *Epigrammes*, xlv.

27. 'On my dear son, Gervase Beaumont'.

CHAPTER TWELVE

1. Duncan-Jones, *Ungentle Shakespeare*, 91.
2. Ferne, *The Blazon of Gentrie*, 58–60.
3. Andrew Gurr, personal communication to Duncan-Jones, quoted on p. 85 of *Ungentle Shakespeare*.
4. Carter Sutherland, 'The Grant of Arms to Shakespeare's Father', 384.
5. Greene, *A Quip for an Upstart Courtier*, Sig. A[iii] v.
6. Duncan-Jones, *Ungentle Shakespeare*, 86.
7. Thomson, *Shakespeare's Professional Career*, 144–5.
8. Jones, 'Lewis Hiccox and Shakespeare's Birthplace', 497–502.
9. Ackroyd, *Shakespeare*, 373.
10. Revels Accounts, *passim*.
11. SBTRO, BRU 15/1/45.
12. Schoenbaum, *Documentary Life*, 173.
13. Thomson, *Shakespeare's Professional Career*, 99.
14. Wells, *Shakespeare and Co.*, 107.
15. Leland, *Itinerary*, ii, 49.
16. Halliwell-Phillipps, *An Historical Account of the New Place*, 10; Eccles, *Shakespeare in Warwickshire*, 86–9.
17. BRU 12/5, 200, Writ of capias to Roland Wheler to answer William Bott 7 December 6 Eliz.
18. NA, 1 STAC 5, Proceedings Court of Star Chamber, Alford v. Greville and Porter, 1571.
19. NA, SP 12/79.
20. For whom see above, p. 224.
21. *M&A*, iii, 79.
22. SBTRO, MD 15/68. 69, 184, 186; NA, Star Chamber 5 H9/22; Bellew, *Shakespeare's Home at New Place*, *passim*.
23. Eccles, *Shakespeare in Warwickshire*, 88–9.
24. *M&A*, iii, 127, 143–4, 156.
25. Schoenbaum, *Documentary Life*, 237.
26. SBTRO, BRU 11/145/55; Rée, *The Shrieve's House*, *passim*.
27. The Sharers' Papers, NA, LC/5/133, 50–1.
28. Aubrey, *Brief Lives*, 21–2.
29. *Works of Ben Jonson*, i, 57–8.
30. Stow, *Annales*, 895.
31. Silk weaving was not to become an important industry in Britain until the influx of Huguenot refugees after the revocation of the Edict of Nantes in 1685.
32. Tusser, 'Of Brewing', *Five Hundred Points of Good Husbandry*, f. 31.
33. *ibid.*, f. 33v.
34. *ibid.*, f. 30v.
35. *ibid.*, f. 31v.
36. *The Private Life of an Elizabethan Lady*, *passim*.

37. Worcestershire Record Office, 008.7 1601/16.
38. NA, Prob. 11/64/31.
39. Smith, *Examination of Usury*, 49.

CHAPTER THIRTEEN

1. Thirsk, 'The Farming Regions of England', 89; see also Gay, 'The Midland Revolt and the Inquisitions of Depopulation of 1607', 212–14, 240.
2. *M&A*, v, 115–16; SBTRO, BRU 15/7/62, DR 140/26.
3. Warwickshire County Record Office, CR1618/W/21/6, 269.
4. NA, PPC, vii, 263, 273, 278, 313.
5. *SPD*, Eliz. cvii, 89. Also NA, V269/T161.
6. *DNB*, 'Conway, Sir John'. See also NA, STAC 7/18/48, and SBTRO DR 362/14.
7. Dugdale, *Antiquities of Warwickshire*, 497.
8. Chancery Inquisitions Postmortem, (Ser. 2), ccxxvii, 89, 192.
9. *ibid.; VCH: Warwickshire*, v, 200; cf. *Hamlet*, V. ii. 189–90.
10. *M&A*, v, 18, 20 (3), 31 (3), 96, 97, 120, 121, 123 (3).
11. *M&A*, v, 162–3.
12. SBTRO, ER3/678.
13. Abraham Sturley to Richard Quiney, 24 January 1598, SBTRO, BRU 15/1/135.
14. 'A Note of Corn and Malt in the Borough of Stratford-upon-Avon', SBTRO, BRU 15/1/106, *M&A*, v, 137.
15. SBTRO, BRU 15/2/2, 255.
16. SBTRO, ER 27/4.
17. SBTRO, BRU 15/1/136.
18. SBTRO, BRU 15/2/2, 69, 95, 356.
19. SBTRO, BRU 15/2/2, 70, 72.
20. SBTRO, BRU 15/2/2, 83.
21. SBTRO, BRU 15/9/3 15/5/20, 15/6/161.
22. SBTRO, BRU 15/5/216, 15/7/124.
23. SBTRO, BRU 15/1/144.
24. SBTRO, BRU 15/1/123; *CSPD*, 1603–10, 590.
25. SBTRO, BRU 15/7/40.
26. 'Sir Edward Greville's menaces to the Bailiff, Aldermen and Burgesses of Stratford', SBTRO, ER 1/1/50.
27. Fripp, *Shakespeare*, 168.
28. SBTRO, BRU 15/12/103.

CHAPTER FOURTEEN

1. *Stratford-upon-Avon Inventories*, ii, 16.
2. Jones, 'Lewis Hiccox and Shakespeare's Birthplace', 497–502.
3. Thomas Hiccox is listed as the occupant in 1590 (*M&A*, v, 111).

4. Thomson, *Shakespeare's Professional Career*, 145.
5. Fripp, *Shakespeare*, 904.
6. Schoenbaum, *Documentary Life*, 235.
7. SBTRO, BRU 15/3/155, 156 (Thomas Rogers); 15/6/12, 21 (John Rogers); 15/3/89 (Robert Roberts); 15/4/198, 15/6/5 (William Walford); 15/5/57, 15/6/26, 33, 15/8/34, 178 (John Roberts); 12/7/334, 12/8/89 (John Combe); 15/8/140 (Thomas Merrell); 15/4/52, 69, 63, 164, and so on.
8. SBTRO, BRU 15/12/71.
9. *SPD*, Eliz. cxvii, 12.
10. SBTRO, ER 1/115, 7.
11. Brinkworth, *Shakespeare and the Bawdy Court*, 128.
12. Dugdale, *The Antiquities of Warwickshire*, ii, 686; 'wise unto salvation': Geneva Bible, 2 Timothy iii: 15.
13. MacDonald, 'A New Discovery about Shakespeare's Estate in Old Stratford', 89.
14. Deloney, *Jack of Newbery*, 27.
15. SBTRO, BRU 15/1/95, 15/3/18, BRU 15/2/2, 445, 467; Schoenbaum, *Documentary Life*, Fig. 155, facing p. 192; original, SBTRO, ER 27/2.
16. Schoenbaum, *Documentary Life*, 237.
17. 'The Joint and Severall Answers of Susan Hall, widow & Thomas Nashe gent.', Marcham, *William Shakespeare and his Daughter Susannah*, 66–71; SBTRO, BRU 15/8/1, 303; Halliwell-Phillipps, *An Historical Account of the New Place*, 92–108; Halliwell-Phillipps, *Outlines* (7th edn 1887), i, 247, 271, ii, 61, 99, 322–3; *Vestry Minute-Book*, 33–6.
18. Eccles, *Shakespeare in Warwickshire*, 85, 105 and note.
19. Schoenbaum, *Documentary Life*, 291.
20. Marcham, *William Shakespeare and his Daughter Susannah*, *passim*; Gray, *The Genealogist's Magazine*, 350.
21. Hall, *Select Observations*, Sig. A5–A5v.
22. Lane, *John Hall*, xvii.
23. *Poems of Sir John Davies*, 226.
24. Hall, *Select Observations*, 2–3.
25. Gerard, *Herbal*, 288.
26. Clowes, *Proved Practiser for all young Chirurgeons*, 33.
27. Cotta, *A Short Discoverie of the Unobserved Dangers of severall sorts of ignorant and unconsiderate Practisers of Physicke in England.*
28. Trevor-Roper, 'The Paracelsian Movement', 167, 34–6.
29. Davies, 'In Philonem', *Epigrammes* 38, in *Poems of Sir John Davies*, 146.
30. Fripp, *Shakespeare*, 670–1, from the Stratford Chamberlain's Account, 8 January 1608.

CHAPTER FIFTEEN

1. 'Sir Walter Ralegh to the Queen', in Ralegh, *Poems*, 104.
2. Rowse, *Ralegh and the Throckmortons*, *passim*.
3. 'The Ocean's Love to Cynthia', Ralegh, *Poems*, 80.

4. Ralegh, *Letters*, 263.
5. The version of the letter used here is based on the copy made for Sir Robert Cotton of a lost original, BL MS Sloane 3520, ff. 14v–171.
6. Stopes, *Southampton*, 206.
7. For which see above, p. 58.
8. Kerrigan, *The Sonnets; and, A Lover's Complaint*, 376.
9. de Grazia, 'The Scandal of Shakespeare's Sonnets', 104–7, 135–41.
10. Wood, *In Search of Shakespeare*, 87.
11. e.g. Middleton Murry, *Shakespeare*, 32, 41–3.
12. 'Sir Walter Ralegh to the Queen', in Ralegh, *Poems*, 104.

CHAPTER SIXTEEN

1. Black, *Judith Shakespeare, passim*.
2. Duncan-Jones, *Ungentle Shakespeare*, 268.
3. NA, Requests 1/28, Affidavit; Eccles, *Shakespeare in Warwickshire*, 109.
4. NA, Requests 2/431.
5. Holy Trinity Register, 7 November 1595.
6. e.g. 'a maid of Thomas Wotton's', 'John Lane's maid', *M&A*, iv, 14; 'Mr Underhill's maid', *M&A*, iii, 116; 'Elizabeth, Mr Quiney's maid', *M&A*, iii, 134.
7. SBTRO, ER 27/11.
8. G. K. Hunter, Introduction to the Arden edition of *As You Like It* (1983), xxix
9. Deloney, *Thomas of Reading*, 136.
10. Brinkworth, *Shakespeare and the Bawdy Court*, 151.
11. *ibid.*, 153.
12. *ibid.*, 156–7.
13. Thirsk, 'The Farming Regions of England', 556.
14. Eccles, *Shakespeare in Warwickshire*, 107, and n. SBTRO, BRU 15/5/116, 127, 139.
15. SBTRO, BRT 3/1/67.
16. SBTRO, BRU 2/2, 202.
17. Ackroyd, *Shakespeare*, 431.
18. Brinkworth, *Shakespeare and the Bawdy Court*, 141; Act Book, Kent County Archives Office, Sackville MS U269 Q22.

CHAPTER SEVENTEEN

1. SBTRO, BRU 15/1/4 (came before parliament in 1614, April and June, failed).
2. Thomson, *Shakespeare's Professional Career*, 190.
3. John Aubrey, 'Mr William Shakespear', Bodleian Library MS Arch.F.c.37; facs. Schoenbaum, *Documentary Life*, Fig. 57, facing p. 59.
4. Ackroyd, *Shakespeare*, 477.
5. BL, MS Harley 4064, f. 189.
6. Puttenham, *The Arte of English Poesie*, 44.

7. Charmont to Lamira in Massinger, *The Parliament of Love*, IV. v.
8. Fox, *Oral and Literate Culture in England*, 303–34.
9. Fripp, *Shakespeare*, 813. Smith was often in the Court of Record between 1606 and 1609, mainly suing defaulting clients for payment (SBTRO, BRU 12/7/3, 71, 103, 127, 180, 195; BRU 12/8/272).
10. Rowse, *Shakespeare the Man*, 450.
11. Rowe, 'Some Account of the Life &c of Mr. William Shakespeare', in Rowe, *Works of Shakespeare*, i, xxxv.
12. *VCH: Warwickshire*, iii, 237.
13. SBTRO, BRU 15/2/2, 95.
14. SBTRO, BRU 15/2/2, 220.
15. Rowe, 'Some Account of the Life &c of Mr. William Shakespeare', in Rowe, *Works of Shakespeare*, i, xxxv–xxxvi.
16. Prestwich, *Cranfield*, 69–70, 78, 401–8.
17. SBTRO, BRU 15/7/10.
18. SBTRO, BRU 15/1/94.
19. Eccles, *Shakespeare in Warwickshire*, 135.
20. *ibid.*, 135–6.
21. *ibid.*, 136.
22. NA, Prob. 11/126.
23. SBTRO, BRU ER 27/3.
24. SBTRO, BRU 15/13/26a–9: Petition of Bailiff and Burgesses to the Lord Chief Justice and Privy Council; SBTRO, BRU 15/13/5, draft in Thomas Greene's hand, also 8, 9, 11, 18.
25. SBTRO, BRU 15/1/107.
26. SBTRO, BRU 15/5/18, 15/13/13; BRU 2/1–5, B. 274–9, B. 281–4, B. 307, 310, 323–4, 358, 367, 369, 380.
27. SBTRO, BRU 15/5/162.
28. SBTRO, BRU 15/7/2, 3.
29. SBTRO, BRU 15/5/156.
30. *pace* Manning, *Village Revolts*, 92.
31. *ibid.*, 69.
32. Lambarde, *Eirenarcha, or of the Office of Justice of the Peace*, 169–70.
33. NA, STAC 8/16/14, Sir Henry Hobart, Attorney-General v. John Chaundeler.
34. SBTRO, BRU 15/5/155–6.
35. SBTRO, BRU 15/8/2, 182, 15/8/175.
36. SBTRO, BRU 15/7/23.
37. SBTRO, BRU 15/7/8–9; also 15/7/21, 15/8/1275, 15/7/28.
38. SBTRO, BRU 15/7/24, 27.

CHAPTER EIGHTEEN

1. Tusser, *An hundreth points of good husbandrie lately maried unto a hundreth good points of Huswifry*, 'The good huswifely physicke'.

2. Folger Shakespeare Library MS V. a. 292, f. 150, facs. Schoenbaum, *Documentary Life*, 242.
3. The best discussion of this is Ian Donaldson's 'Jonson and tother youth' in his *Jonson's Magic Houses*, 6–25.
4. Duncan-Jones, *Ungentle Shakespeare*, 258.
5. *ibid.*, 263.
6. Wood, *In Search of Shakespeare*, 336.
7. Duncan-Jones, *Ungentle Shakespeare*, 266.
8. *ibid.*, 206.
9. Dekker and Webster, *Northward Ho*, IV. iii. 77–8, in *Dramatic Words of Thomas Dekker*, ii, 459.
10. Barrough, *Method of Physick*, 369.
11. Duncan-Jones, *Ungentle Shakespeare*, 222.
12. Pinks, *History of Clerkenwell*, 338, 695.
13. Fripp, *Shakespeare*, 346.
14. Thomson, *Shakespeare's Professional Career*, 70.
15. Barrough, *Method of Physick*, 361–2.
16. Gough, *History of Myddle*, 255.
17. *The workes of that famous chirurgion Ambrose Parey*, 723–4.
18. *ibid.*, 724.
19. Newton, *An Herbal for the Bible*, 120. The use of 'hebenus' as a generic term should dissipate the extraordinary confusion evinced by annotators of *Hamlet*, I. v. 62.
20. Barrough, *Method of Physick*, 362.
21. *ibid.*, 363.
22. *ibid.*, 366.
23. Clowes, *A Short and Profitable Treatise touching the cure of the disease called Morbus Gallicus by Unctions*, Sig. Dlr.
24. Barrough, *Method of Physick*, 381, 382–3.
25. Markham, *The English Housewife*, 50–1.
26. Simon Forman, 'Geomantica', Bodleian MS Ashmole 354, f. 222v, 250.
27. SBTRO, ER 27/5.
28. *Stratford-upon-Avon Inventories*, i, 160–6.
29. Chambers, *William Shakespeare*, 99–101; Fripp, *Shakespeare's Stratford*, 37; Fripp, *Shakespeare*, 620, 792–3.
30. Lane, *John Hall*, 177.
31. SBTRO, BRU 12/7/63, 12/8/286.
32. Barrough, *Method of Physick*, 362.
33. SBTRO, BRU 15/4/190.
34. SBTRO, BRU 12/6/205; cf. BRU 12/7/221, 223, 341, 365.
35. Prestwich, *Cranfield*.
36. Schoenbaum, *Documentary Life*, 213.
37. *The workes of that famous chirurgion Ambrose Parey*, 256.
38. *ibid.*
39. *ibid.*, 280–1.

40. *The Private Life of an Elizabethan Lady*, 13.
41. *The Comedy of Errors*, V. i. 99–100.
42. Turner, *Herbal*, f. 46.
43. [Cooke], *How to chuse a good wife from a bad*, Sig. [L1v].
44. Turner, *Herbal*, f. 35v.
45. *ibid.*, f. 36.
46. *ibid.*, f. 77v.
47. *Henry V*, II. iii. 12–25.
48. Duncan-Jones, *Ungentle Shakespeare*, 270–1.
49. Brinkworth, *Shakespeare and the Bawdy Court*, 143.
50. Fripp, *Shakespeare*, 825.
51. *ibid.*, 829.

CHAPTER NINETEEN

1. BL, MS Lansdowne 721, f. 2.
2. Smith, *The Commonwealth of England and the Maner of Gouernment thereof.*
3. NA, Principal Probate Registry, Selected Wills, Prob. 1/4.
4. Schoenbaum, *Documentary Life*, 192.
5. Greenblatt, *Will in the World*, 145.
6. Knight, *The Pictorial Edition of the Works of Shakespeare*, ii, 192; Schoenbaum, *Documentary Life*, 248; Wood, *In Search of Shakespeare*, 338.
7. Stone, *Family, Sex and Marriage*, 195–6.
8. Burn, *Ecclesiastical Law*, ii, 38; cf. Brodsky, 126–7.
9. Greenblatt, *Will in the World*, 146.
10. Malone, *Supplement to the Edition of Shakespeare's Plays*, i, 657.
11. NA, Prob. 11/64/31, facs. Fig. 60, Schoenbaum, facing p. 66; transcript Halliwell-Phillipps, *Outlines* (7th edn 1887), ii, 195–6 etc.
12. [Evelyn], *Mundus Muliebris*, Preface.
13. Fripp, *Shakespeare*, 827.
14. Fowler, 'The Earl of Bedford's "Best Bed" ', 80.
15. *M&A*, iv, 61–2.
16. Ralegh, *Remains*, 86.
17. Erickson, *Women and Property*, 65.
18. *The Autobiography of Mrs Alice Thornton of East Newton Co. York*, 247.
19. Erickson, *Women and Property*, 67.

CHAPTER TWENTY

1. SBTRO, BRU 15/1/108.
2. SBTRO, BRU 15/7/1, 2, 3, 4, 5, 6, 11, 16, 175.
3. Fripp, *Shakespeare*, 833–4.
4. SBTRO, BRU 15/7/125.

5. SBTRO, BRU 15/1/126–7.

6. SBTRO, BRU 2/1–5 B. 336.

7. Erikson, *Women and Property*, 187.

8. SBTRO, BRU 8/9/18, 22; 15/12/119.

9. Fildes, *Breasts, Bottles and Babies*, 83–5.

10. SBTRO, BRU 15/13/15.

11. SBTRO, BRU 15/12/116.

12. SBTRO, BRU 15/13, 42.

13. Eccles, *Shakespeare in Warwickshire*, 135; SBTRO DR 37/83/52–4, 60.

14. SBTRO, BRU 2/1–5, B. 349.

15. SBTRO, BRU 15/13/81.

16. SBTRO, BRU 2/1–5, B. 372.

17. The libels were produced in evidence in a Star Chamber suit brought by the attorney general on Wilson's behalf: NA, STAC 8/26/10, January 1621.

18. SBTRO, ER 1/1/97.

19. *M&A*, iii, 131, 135.

20. SBTRO, BRU 4/1/1602.

21. SBTRO, BRU 2/2, 324.

22. Holderness, 'Widows in Pre-Industrial Societies', 435–6.

23. *Stratford-upon-Avon Inventories*, i, 321.

24. *ibid.*, 326.

25. *ibid.*, 337.

26. SBTRO, BRU 17/3 and 4/1; *M&A*, iv, 126.

27. Worcestershire Record Office, 008.7 1618/174b.

28. *Stratford-upon-Avon Inventories*, i, 23–4.

29. *ibid.*, 59–60; Worcestershire Record Office, 008.7 1585/13c.

30. *ibid.*, 95–6; Worcestershire Record Office, 008.7 1588/95.

31. *ibid.*, 96–7; Worcestershire Record Office, 008.7 1588/76.

32. SBTRO, BRU 15/1/24.

33. SBTRO, BRU 15/1/46.

34. *M&A*, v, 76.

35. Worcestershire Record Office, 008.7 1614/55.

36. Worcestershire Record Office, 008.7 1614/77.

37. *Stratford-upon-Avon Inventories*, i, 303; SBTRO, BRU 8/10/13.

38. NA, Prob. 11/101/54.

39. SBTRO, BRU 2/2, 202, 298.

40. SBTRO, BRT 13/1/69.

41. Warwickshire Record Office, BB 711/2663; SBTRO, BRU 15/3/23.

42. SBTRO, BRT 3/1/18.

43. SBTRO, BRU 15/12/71, 93.

44. Schoenbaum, *Documentary Life*, 250.

45. Bodleian Library, MS Rawlinson D. 377, f. 90, William Hall to Edward Thwaites, [1694].

46. Schoenbaum, *Documentary Life*, 251.

47. Cressy, *Birth, Marriage and Death*, 463.
48. BL, MS Lansdowne 213, f. 332v.
49. *The Life, Diary and Correspondence of Sir William Dugdale*, 99.
50. See, for example, Theime-Becker, *Allgemeine Künstlerlexikon*, 'Gerard Johnson'.
51. Fripp, *Shakespeare*, 849.
52. Price, 'Reconsidering Shakespeare's Monument', Fig. 3a.

CHAPTER TWENTY-ONE

1. Gurr, *The Shakespearean Stage*, 14.
2. Salkeld, 'Literary Traces', 379–85.
3. Schoenbaum, *Documentary Life*, 227.
4. Herendeen, 'A New Way to Pay Old Debts', 41 and n.
5. Fripp, *Shakespeare*, 455.
6. Schoenbaum, *Documentary Life*, 223, 248, 250.
7. Charlton Hinman, Introduction to the Norton Facsimile of *The First Folio of Shakespeare* (London, Paul Hamlyn, 1968), x.
8. Greg, *The Shakespeare First Folio*, 2–3.
9. *DNB*.
10. See above, p. 20.
11. There is another John Hemmings who was married at much the same time at St Clement Dane's. It may be he who served an apprenticeship in the Grocers' Company and became a freeman of the city.
12. Drayton, *Poems*, i, 51–6.
13. Cartwright, *Comedies, Tragicomedies*, 273.
14. Fripp, *Shakespeare*, 852.
15. West, *The Shakespeare First Folio*, vol. i: *An Account of the First Folio based on its Sales and Prices*, 6.
16. *ibid.*, 4.
17. Quoted in *ibid.*, 'Foreword', v.
18. Prynne, *Histrio-mastix*, 'To the Gentle Reader'.

WORKS CITED

The spelling and punctuation of all sixteenth- and seventeenth-century texts, including the works of Shakespeare, have been modernised by the present author.

Ackroyd, Peter, *Shakespeare: The Biography* (London, Chatto & Windus, 2005)

Armstrong, Philip, *Shakespeare in Psychoanalysis* (London and New York, Routledge, 2001)

Aubrey, John, *Brief Lives*, ed. Oliver Lawson Dick (London, Secker & Warburg, 1958)

The Autobiography of Mrs Alice Thornton of East Newton Co. York (Durham, Andrew, 1875, Publications of the Surtees Society, No. 62)

Bacon, Francis, *Essays* (London, George Newnes, 1902)

Barrough, Philip, *The Method of Physick containing the causes, signes and cures of inward diseases in man's body* (1601)

Baskervill, C. R., *The Elizabethan Jig and Related Song Drama* (Chicago, University of Chicago Press, 1929)

Bearman, Robert, 'John Shakespeare: A Papist or Just Penniless?', *Shakespeare Quarterly* lvi, No. 4 (2005), 411–33

[Becon, Thomas], *The golden boke of christen matrimonye newly set forth in English by Theodore Basille* (1542)

Bellew, J. C. M., *Shakespeare's Home at New Place, Stratford-upon-Avon* (1863)

Belvedere, or the Garden of the Muses (1600)

Black, William, *Judith Shakespeare: A Romance* (1884)

Boorde, Andrew, *A Breviary of health* (1575)

Boswell, John, *The Kindness of Strangers: The Abandonment of Children in Western Europe from Late Antiquity to the Renaissance* (New York, Pantheon Books, 1988)

Bownde, Nicholas, *The Doctrine of the Sabbath* (1595)

Breton, Nicholas, *The Court and the Country or a Brief Discourse betweene the Courtier and the Countryman* (1618), in W. C. Hazlitt, ed., *Inedited Tracts* illustrating the Manners, Opinions and Occupations of Englishmen during the Sixteenth and Seventeenth Centuries (New York, 1868)

Brinkworth, E. R. C., Shakespeare and the Bawdy Court of Stratford (London and Chichester, Phillimore & Co., 1972)

Brodsky, Vivian, 'Widows in Late Elizabethan London: Remarriage, Economic Opportunity and Family Orientations', in The World We Have Gained: Essays Presented to Peter Laslett on his Seventieth Birthday (Oxford, Basil Blackwell, 1986)

Brody, Alan, The English Mummers and their Plays: Traces of Ancient Mystery (London, Routledge & Kegan Paul, 1971)

Brooke, Christopher, 'An Epithalamium, or a Nuptiall Song, applied to the Ceremonies of Marriage', England's Helicon. Or the Muses Harmony, ed. Hugh McDonald (London, Routledge & Kegan Paul, 1962)

Browne, William, Britannia's Pastorals (1613)

[Bullinger, Heinrich], The Christen state of Matrimonye (1546)

Burgess, Anthony, Shakespeare (London, Jonathan Cape, 1970)

Burn, Richard, Ecclesiastical Law (2 vols, 1763, 1765)

Carter Sutherland, Raymond, 'The Grant of Arms to Shakespeare's Father', Shakespeare Quarterly xiv (1963), 384

Cartwright, William, Comedies, Tragicomedies, with other Poems . . . 1651

Cary, Elizabeth, The Tragedy of Mariam, the Fair Queen of Jewry, with The Lady Falkland: Her Life, ed. Barry Weller and Margaret W. Ferguson (Berkeley, University of California Press, 1997)

Chambers, E. K, William Shakespeare: A Study of Facts and Problems (Oxford, Clarendon Press, 1930)

Chambers Bunten, A., Life of Alice Barnham (1592–1650), Wife of Sir Francis Bacon Viscount St Albans (London, Page & Thomas, 1919)

Clark, Alice, The Working Life of Women in the Seventeenth Century (London, Routledge & Kegan Paul, 1982)

Clowes, William, Proved Practiser for all young Chirurgeons (1591)

Clowes, William, A Short and Profitable Treatise touching the cure of the disease called Morbus Gallicus by Unctions (1579)

Collins, Arthur, Letters and Memorials of State, in the reigns of Queen Mary, Queen Elizabeth, King James, King Charles the First, part of the reign of King Charles the Second, and Oliver's Usurpation. Written and Collected by Sir Henry Sydney . . . (2 volumes, London, T. Osborne, 1746)

Collins, Sidney Papers

[Cooke, Joshua], How to chuse a good wife from a bad. A pleasant conceited comedie as it hath been sundry times acted by the earl of Worcester's Servants (1602)

Coster, William, 'Purity, Profanity, Puritanism: The Churching of Women, 1570–1700', in W. J. Shiels and Diana Wood, eds, Women in the Church (Oxford, Basil Blackwell, 1990)

Cotgrave, Randle, *A Dictionary of the French and English Tongues* (1611)

Cotta, John, *A Short Discoverie of the Unobserved Dangers of severall sorts of ignorant and unconsiderate Practisers of Physicke in England* (1612)

Cressy, D. H., 'Education and Literacy in London and East Anglia, 1580–1700', PhD thesis, University of Cambridge, 1973

Cressy, David, *Birth, Marriage and Death: Ritual, Religion and the Life-Cycle in Tudor and Stuart England* (Oxford, Oxford University Press, 1997)

Cressy, David, 'Purification, Thanksgiving and the Churching of Women in Post-Reformation England', *Past and Present* 141 (1993)

Cross, C., 'Great Reasoners in Scripture: Women Lollards 1380–1530', in D. Baker, ed., *Medieval Women: Studies in Church History* (Oxford, Basil Blackwell, 1978)

D[avies], J[ohn], *A Scourge for Paper Persecutors* (1625)

de Grazia, Margreta, 'The Scandal of Shakespeare's Sonnets', *Shakespeare Survey* 46 (1994), 104–7, 135–41

Deloney, Thomas, *The Gentile Craft. The second part.* (1639, written before 1600)

Deloney, Thomas, *The pleasant Historie of Iohn Winchcomb, In his yonguer yeares called Iack of Newbery . . .* (1626; first published 1597), in *Shorter Novels: Elizabethan*, introduced by George Saintsbury (London, J. M. Dent & Sons, 1960), 1–80

Deloney, Thomas, *Thomas of Reading* (1612; first published 1597), in *Shorter Novels: Elizabethan*, introduced by George Saintsbury (London, J. M. Dent & Sons, 1960), 83–162

The Diary of John Manningham of the Middle Temple, 1602–3, ed. Robert Parker Sorlien (Hanover NH, University Press of New England, 1976)

Donaldson, Ian, *Jonson's Magic Houses: Essays in Interpretation* (Oxford, Clarendon Press, 1997)

The Dramatic Works of Thomas Dekker, ed. Fredson Bowers (Cambridge, Cambridge University Press, 1953)

Drayton, Michael, *Poems*, ed. John Buxton (2 vols, London, Routledge & Kegan Paul, 1953)

Dugdale, William, *The Antiquities of Warwickshire* (1765)

Duncan-Jones, Katherine, *Ungentle Shakespeare: Scenes from his Life* (London, The Arden Shakespeare, 2001)

Eason, Charles, *The Genevan Bible: Notes on its Production and Distribution* (Dublin, Eason, 1937)

Eccles, Mark, *Shakespeare in Warwickshire* (Madison WI, University of Wisconsin Press, 1961)

England's Helicon, ed. Hugh McDonald (London, Routledge & Kegan Paul, 1962)

English Professional Theatre, 1530–1660 (Cambridge, Cambridge University Press, 2000)

English Works, ed. W. Aldis Wright (Cambridge, Cambridge University Press, 1970)

Erickson, Amy Louise, *Women and Property in Early Modern England* (London and New York, Routledge, 1993)

[Evelyn, Mary], *Mundus Muliebris: or, the Ladies dressing-room unlock'd and her toilette spread. In burlesque* (1690)

Everitt, Alan, 'Cottage Husbandry and Peasant Wealth', in Christopher Clay, ed., *Rural Society: Landowners, Peasants and Labourers, 1500–1750* (Cambridge, Cambridge University Press, 1990)

Ferne, Sir John, *The Blazon of Gentrie* (1586)

Fildes, Valerie, *Breasts, Bottles and Babies: A History of Infant Feeding* (Edinburgh, Edinburgh University Press, 1986)

Forman, Simon, 'Diary' (Bodleian MS)

Fowler, Elaine W., 'The Earl of Bedford's "Best Bed" ', *Shakespeare Quarterly* xviii (1967), 80

Fox, Adam, *Oral and Literate Culture in England 1500–1700* (Oxford, Clarendon Press, 2000)

Freeman, Thomas, *Rubbe and a Great Cast. Epigrams* (1625)

Fripp, Edgar I., *Master Richard Quyny, Bailiff of Stratford-on-Avon, and Friend of William Shakespeare* (Oxford, Oxford University Press, 1924)

Fripp, Edgar I., *Shakespeare: Man and Artist* (London, Oxford University Press, 1938)

Fripp, Edgar I., *Shakespeare's Stratford* (London, Oxford University Press, 1928)

Gataker, Thomas, *A Good Wife Gods Gift* (1624)

Gay, E. F., 'The Midland Revolt and the Inquisitions of Depopulation of 1607', *Transactions of the Royal Historical Society* xviii (1904)

Gerard, John, *Herbal* (1597)

Googe, Barnabe, *Eglogs, Epytaphes and Sonettes* (1563), ed. Edward Arber (1871)

Gough, Richard, *The History of Myddle* (Harmondsworth, Penguin Books, 1981)

Gray, Irvine, *The Genealogist's Magazine* vii (1936–7), 344–54, 478–9

Gray, J. H., *Shakespeare's Marriage, his Departure from Stratford, and other incidents in his life* (London, Chapman & Hall, 1905)

Greenblatt, Stephen, *Will in the World: How Shakespeare Became Shakespeare* (London, Jonathan Cape, 2004)

Greene, Robert, *A Qvip for an Upstart Covrtier: Or, A quaint dispute between Veluet breeches and Cloth-breeches . . .* (1592)

Greene, Robert, *The Repentance of Robert Greene, Master of Arts* (1592)

Greene's Vision: Written at the instant of his death. Conteyning a penitent passion for the folly of his pen [1592]

Greg, W. W., *The Shakespeare First Folio: Its Bibliographical and Textual History* (Oxford, Clarendon Press, 1955)

Guizot, François, *Shakespeare et son temps: étude littéraire* (1821)

Gurr, Andrew, *The Shakespearean Stage, 1572–1642* (Cambridge, Cambridge University Press, 1992)

Gurr, Andrew, 'Shakespeare's First Poem: Sonnet 145', *Essays in Criticism* xxi (1971), 221–6

Hall, John, *Select Observations on English Bodies of Eminent Persons in Desperate Diseases First written in Latin by Mr John Hall, Physician* (1679)

Halliwell-Phillipps, J. O., *An Historical Account of the New Place, the Last Residence of Shakespeare* (1864)

Halliwell-Phillipps, J. O., *The life of William Shakespeare Including many particulars respecting the Poet and his family never before published* (1848)

Halliwell-Phillipps, J. O., *Outlines of the Life of Shakespeare* (printed for the author's friends, 1881; afterwards Longmans and Co., 1883)

Henslowe's Diary, ed. with Supplementary Material, Introduction and Notes by R. A. Foakes and R. T. Rickert (Cambridge, Cambridge University Press, 1965)

Henslowe Papers: being documents supplementary to Henslowe's Diary, ed. W. W. Greg (London, A. Bullen, 1907)

Herendeen, W. H., 'A New Way to Pay Old Debts', in Jennifer Brady and W. H. Herendeen, eds, *Ben Johnson's 1616 Folio* (Newark DE, University of Delaware Press, 1991)

Holden, Anthony, *William Shakespeare: His Life and Work* (London, Little Brown, 1999)

Holderness, B. A., 'Widows in Pre-Industrial Societies: An Essay upon their Economic Functions', in Richard M. Smith, ed., *Land, Kinship and Life-cycle* (Cambridge, Cambridge University Press, 2002), 423–42

Holinshed, Raphael, *Chronicles of England, Scotland and Ireland* (6 vols, 1807–8)

Honan, Park, *Shakespeare: A Life* (Oxford, Oxford University Press, 1998)

Hone, Nathaniel J., *The Manor and Manorial Records* (Port Washington NY, Kennikat Press, 1971)

Honigman, E. A., *Shakespeare: The Lost Years* (Manchester, Manchester University Press, 1985)

Hoskins, W. G., 'The Rebuilding of Rural England, 1570–1640', *Past and Present* 4 (1953), 44–59 (revised by R. Machin, *Past and Present* 77 (1977), 33–56)

Houlbrooke, Ralph, *The English Family, 1450–1700* (London, Longman, 1984)

Hunter, Joseph, *New Illustrations of the Life, Studies and Writings of Shakespeare, Supplementary to all the Editions* (1845)

Ingram, Martin, *Church Courts, Sex and Marriage in England, 1570–1640* (Cambridge, Cambridge University Press, 1987)

Jardine, Lisa, *Still Harping on Daughters: Women and Drama in the Age of Shakespeare* (Brighton, Harvester, 1983)

Jones, Jeanne, *Family Life in Shakespeare's England: Stratford-upon-Avon 1570–1630* (Stroud, Sutton Publishing, 1996)

Jones, Jeanne, 'Lewis Hiccox and Shakespeare's Birthplace', *Notes & Queries* ccxxxix, No. 4 (December 1994), 497–502

Joyce, James, *Ulysses* (London, The Bodley Head, 1962)

Kerrigan, John, *The Sonnets; and, A Lover's Complaint* (Harmondsworth, Penguin, 1986)

Knight, Charles, *The Pictorial Edition of the Works of Shakespeare* (Originally self-published, [n.d.]; 2nd edn, 2 vols, 1811)

Lambarde, William, *Eirenarcha, or of the Office of Justice of the Peace* (1602)

Lane, Joan, *John Hall and his Patients: The Medical Practice of Shakespeare's Son-in-Law* (Stratford-upon-Avon, The Shakespeare Birthplace Trust, 1996)

Laslett, Peter, *The World We Have Lost* (London, Methuen, 1965)

Lasocki, David, with Roger Prior, *The Bassanos: Venetian Musicians and Instrument Makers in England, 1531–1655* (Aldershot, Scolar Press, c.1995)

Laurence, Ann, *Women in England 1500–1760: A Social History* (London, Weidenfeld & Nicolson, 1994)

Lee, Sidney, *A Life of William Shakespeare* (London, Smith, Elder and Co., 1898)

Lehmberg, Stanford, *Sir Walter Mildmay and Tudor Government* (Austin, University of Texas Press, 1964)

Leland, John, *Itinerary*, ed. Lucy Toulmin Smith (2 vols, [s.l.], Bell, 1907–10)

The Life, Diary and Correspondence of Sir William Dugdale, ed. William Hamper (1827)

Lippincott, H. F., ed., *'Merry Passages ands Jeasts': A Manuscript Jest Book of Sir Nicholas Le Strange, 1603–1655* (Salzburg, Salzburg Studies in English Literature: Elizabethan and Renaissance Studies 29, 1974)

Locke, John, *Journal*, 1 March 1681, Bodleian MS Locke f. 5

MacDonald, Mairi, 'A New Discovery about Shakespeare's Estate in Old Stratford', *Shakespeare Quarterly* xlv, No. 1 (1994), 87–9

MacDonald, Michael, *Mystical Bedlam: Madness, Anxiety and Healing in Seventeenth-Century England* (Cambridge, Cambridge University Press, 1981)

Macfarlane, Alan, *The Family Life of Ralph Josselin, a Seventeenth-Century Clergyman: An Essay in Historical Anthropology* (London, Cambridge University Press, 1970)

Macfarlane, Alan, *Marriage and Love in England: Modes of Reproduction 1300–1840* (Oxford, Basil Blackwell, 1983)

Maden, F., ed., 'The Daily Ledger of John Dorne, 1520', in C. R. L. Fletcher, ed., *Oxford Historical Society, Collectanea I*, V (1885)

Malone, Edmond, *Supplement to the Edition of Shakespeare's Plays published in 1778 by Samuel Johnson and George Steevens* (1780)

Manning, Roger B., *Village Revolts: Social Protest and Popular Disturbances in England 1509–1640* (Oxford, Clarendon Press, 1988)

Marcham, Frank, *William Shakespeare and his Daughter Susannah* ([s.l.], Grafton, 1931)

Markham, Gervase, *The English House-wife, containing the inward and outward virtues which ought to be in a complete woman* (1649)

Massinger, Philip, *The Parliament of Love* (1624)

Middleton Murry, John, *Shakespeare* (London, Jonathan Cape, 1936)

Moore, Thomas, 'Notices of the Life of Lord Byron', Byron, *Works*, ed. Thomas Moore (1832), iii

Muffet, Thomas, *Health's Improvement* (1584)

Newton, Thomas, *An Herbal for the Bible* (1587)

Nichols, John, *Progresses and Public Processions of Queen Elizabeth* (4 vols, 1788–1821)

Overbury, Sir Thomas, *A Wife* (1614)

The Pepys Ballads, ed. Hyder E. Rollins (Cambridge MA, Harvard University Press, 1929)

A Pepysian Garland: Black-letter Broadside Ballads of the Years 1595–1639, ed. Hyder E. Rollins (Cambridge, Cambridge University Press, 1922)

Perkins, William, *Of Christian Oeconomie* (1617)

Pinks, W. J., *The History of Clerkenwell*, ed. E. J. Wood (1881)

Plowden, Alison, *Tudor Women: Queens and Commoners* (London, Sutton Publishing, 2002)

The Poems of Lady Mary Wroth, ed. Josephine A. Roberts (Baton Rouge, Louisiana State University Press, 1983)

The Poems of Sir John Davies, ed. Robert Krueger (Oxford, Clarendon Press, 1975)

The Poems of Sir Philip Sidney, ed. W. Ringler (Oxford, Clarendon Press, 1962)

Pollock, Linda A., *Forgotten Children: Parent–Child Relations from 1300–1900* (Cambridge, Cambridge University Press, 1983)

Pollock, Linda A., ed., *With Faith and Physic: The Life of a Tudor Gentlewoman, Lady Grace Mildmay, 1552–1620* (London, Collins & Brown, 1993)

Prestwich, Menna, *Cranfield: Politics and Profits under the Early Stuarts: The Career of Lionel Cranfield, Earl of Middlesex* (Oxford, Clarendon Press, 1966)

Price, Diana, 'Reconsidering Shakespeare's Monument', *Review of English Studies*, New Series, xlviii, No. 190 (1997), 168–82

Price, Diana, *Shakespeare's Unorthodox Biography: New Evidence of an Authorship Problem* (London, Greenwood Press, 2001)

Prior, Mary, 'Women and the Urban Economy: Oxford 1500–1800', in Mary Prior, ed., *Women in English Society 1500–1800* (London and New York, Methuen, 1985)

The Private Life of an Elizabethan Lady: The Diary of Lady Margaret Hoby, 1599–1605, ed. Joanna Moody (Stroud, Sutton Publishing, 1998)

Prynne, William, *Histrio-mastix* (1633)

Puttenham, George, *The Arte of English Poesie* (1589)

Quaife, G. R., *Wanton Wenches and Wayward Wives: Peasants and Illicit Sex in Early Seventeenth Century England* (London, Croom Helm, 1979)

Ralegh, Sir Walter, *The Poems*, ed. Agnes C. Lathem (London, Constable and Co. Ltd, 1929)

Ralegh, Sir Walter, *The Remains of Sir Walter Raleigh* (1675)

Ralegh, Sir Walter, *The Letters*, ed. Agnes Latham and Joyce Youings (Exeter, University of Exeter Press, 1999)

Raynaldes, Thomas, *The Birth of Mankind* (1598)

Rée, Peta with Richard Harris, *The Shrieve's House, Stratford-upon-Avon* (Stratford-upon-Avon, Stratford-upon-Avon Society Papers, No. 2, 1987)

Revels Accounts: Extracts from the Accounts of the Revels at Court . . . from the Original Office Books of the Masters and Yeoman (London, Malone Society, 1842)

Rhodes, John, *The Countrie Mans Comfort* (1588)

Rowe, Nicholas, *The Works of Mr. William Shakespeare* (1709)

Rowse, A. L., *Ralegh and the Throckmortons* (London, Macmillan, 1962)

Rowse, A. L., *Shakespeare the Man* (London, Macmillan, 1973)

Rowse, A. L., *William Shakespeare* (London, Macmillan, 1963)

Salkeld, Duncan, 'Literary Traces in Bridewell and Bethlem, 1602–1624', *Review of English Studies*, 56 (June 2005), No. 255

Schoenbaum, Samuel, *Shakespeare's Lives* (Oxford, Clarendon Press, 1970)

Schoenbaum, Samuel, *William Shakespeare: A Documentary Life* (Oxford, Clarendon Press, in association with the Scolar Press, 1975)

Schofield, R. S., 'Illiteracy in Pre-Industrial England: The Work of the Cambridge Group for the History of Population and Social Structure', in E. Johanssen, ed., *Literacy and Society in a Historical Perspective* (UMEA Educational Reports)

Sharp, Jane, *The Midwives Book: or the Whole Art of Midwifery discovered. Directing childbearing women how to behave themselves in their conception, breeding . . . and nursing of children* (1671), ed. E. Hobby (New York, Oxford University Press, 1999)

Short, R. V., *The Biological Basis for the Contraceptive Effects of Breastfeeding*, background paper, WHO Workshop on breast-feeding and fertility regulation (Geneva, WHO, 1980)

Smith, Henry, *An Examination of Usury in Two Sermons* (1591)

Smith, Henry, *A Preparative to Mariage* (1591)

Smith, Sir Thomas, *The Commonwealth of England and the Maner of Gouernment thereof . . . with newe additions of the chiefe court in England and the Gouernment thereof* (1609)

Spenser, Edmund, *Amoretti and Epithalamion written not long since by Edmunde Spenser* (1595)

Spufford, Margaret, 'First Steps in Literacy: The Reading and Writing Experiences of the Humblest Seventeenth-Century Spiritual Autobiographers', *Social History* 4, No. 3 (1979), 407–35

Spufford, Margaret, *Small Books and Pleasant Histories: Popular Fiction and its Readership in Seventeenth-Century England* (London, Methuen, 1981)

Stone, Lawrence, *The Crisis in the Aristocracy 1558–1641* (Oxford, Oxford University Press, 1967)

Stone, Lawrence, *The Family, Sex and Marriage in England 1500–1800* (London, Weidenfeld & Nicolson, 1977)

Stopes, Charlotte Carmichael, *Shakespeare's Environment* (London, George Bell & Sons, 1914)

Stopes, Charlotte Carmichael, *The Life of Henry Third Earl of Southampton, Shakespeare's Patron* (Cambridge, Cambridge University Press, 1922)

Stow, J., *The Annales or General Chronicle of England* (1615)

Stow, John, *A Summarie of the Chronicles of England . . . abridged and continued unto . . . 1604* (London, 1604)

Stratford-upon-Avon Inventories 1538–1699, ed. Jeanne Jones (Stratford, Dugdale Society in association with the Shakespeare Birthplace Trust, 2002)

Stubbes, Philip, *The Anatomie of Abuses* (1583)

Swinburne, Henry, *A Treatise of Spousals* (1686)

Tasso, Ercole, *Of Marriage and Wiving. An Excellent, pleasant and philosophicall controuersie, betweene the two famous Tassi now liuing, the one Hercules the Philosopher, the other Torquato the Poet* (1599)

Thirsk, Joan, 'The Fantastical Folly of Fashion: The English Stocking Knitting Industry, 1500–1700', in N. B. Harte and K. G. Ponting, eds, *Textile History and Economic History: Essays in Honour of Miss Julia De Lacy Mann* (Manchester, Manchester University Press, 1973)

Thirsk, Joan, 'The Farming Regions of England', in *The Agrarian History of England and Wales*, vol. iv, ed. Joan Thirsk (Cambridge, Cambridge University Press, 1967)

Thomson, Peter, *Shakespeare's Professional Career* (Cambridge, Cambridge University Press, 1992)

The Three Parnassus Plays (1598–1601), ed. J. B. Leishman (London, Ivor Nicholson & Watson, 1949)

Trevor-Roper, Hugh, 'The Paracelsian Movement', *Renaissance Essays* (London, Fontana Press, 1986)

Turner, William, *The first and seconde partes of the Herbal of William Turner* (1568)

Tusser, Thomas, *Five Hundred Points of Good Husbandry* (4th edn 1580)

Tusser, Thomas, *An hundreth points of good husbandrie lately maried unto a hundreth good points of Huswifry* (1571)

View of Popishe Abuses, Puritan Manifestoes, ed. W. H. Frere and C. E. Douglas (London, SPCK, 1907)

[Watson, Thomas], *Holsome and Catholyke doctryne concernynge the seuen sacramentes* (1558)

Weigall, Rachel, 'An Elizabethan Gentlewoman: The Journal of Lady Mildmay circa 1570–1617', *Quarterly Review* 215: 428 (July 1911)

Wells, Stanley, *Shakespeare and Co.* (London, Allen Lane, 2006)

West, Anthony James, *The Shakespeare First Folio: The History of the Book*, vol. i: *An Account of the First Folio based on its Sales and Prices, 1623–2000* (Oxford, Oxford University Press, 2001)

Weston, William, *William Weston: The Autobiography of an Elizabethan*, trans. and ed. Philip Caraman (London, Longmans, Green & Co., 1955)

Whateley, W., *A Bride-Bush: or, A Direction for Married Persons* (1619)

Wilkes, Thomas, *A General View of the Stage* (1759)

Wood, Michael, *In Search of Shakespeare* (London, BBC Worldwide, 2004)

The Works of Ben Jonson, ed. C. H. Herford and Percy and Evelyn Simpson, (11 vols, Oxford, Clarendon Press, 1925–52)

The workes of that famous chirurgion Ambrose Parey Translated out of Latine and compared with the French by Th. Johnson (1634; the Latin originally published in 1579)

The Works of Thomas Kyd, ed. F. S. Boas ([Oxford], Oxford University Press, 1901, reissued 1955)

The Works of Thomas Nashe, ed. R. B. McKerrow (Oxford, Basil Blackwell, 1958)

Wright, Sue, ' "Churmaids, Housewives and Hucksters": The Employment of Women in Tudor and Stuart Salisbury', in L. Charles and L. Duffin, eds, *Women and Work in Pre-industrial England* (1985)

Wrightson, Keith, 'Infanticide in the Early Seventeenth Century', *Local Population Studies*, 15 (1975), 10–22

Wrigley, E. A. and Roger Schofield, *The Population History of England 1541–1871: A Reconstruction* (London, Edward Arnold, 1981)

ACKNOWLEDGEMENTS

The author's thanks are due to all the people who have let her bang on at them over the years about Shakespeare's attitude to marriage and, much more recently, about Shakespeare's wife. They include late greats L. C. Knights, Peter Laslett, M. C. Bradbrook and the much-lamented Jeremy Maule, as well as, among the living, Her Majesty the Queen, Professor Anne Barton, Dr Peter Cochran, John Kerrigan, Anthony Holden, my sister Jane Burke and the odd taxi-driver.

As should be apparent from the documentation of my case, my greatest debt is to everyone at the Shakespeare Birthplace Trust Record Office. While there can be no doubting their utter loyalty to the maintenance of the reputation of England's greatest poet, they are also committed to the patient eliciting of the truth from the scattering of hard evidence that they so carefully preserve. Every year new biographies of Shakespeare rework the same set of assumptions and presumptions, their authors not having deigned to avail themselves of the services the staff at the SBTRO so generously offer, which include patient listening to misled hypotheses and gentle direction towards better information. I hope I have avoided mistaken certainty; if I have not it will not be the fault of Dr Robert Bearman or Mairi MacDonald or anyone at SBTRO.

This study could not have been contemplated if I had not had access to the Cambridge University Library, and if the library had not been as well-run as it is. The resources of the British Library are unparalleled, but they are unnecessarily difficult for out-of-town scholars to use, as no more than ten volumes may be ordered on any day, and usually fewer than those ten will actually be delivered. The author is grateful for the courtesy and helpfulness that the BL staff somehow manage to show to even the most bewildered and frustrated readers.

INDEX

Edwards, Avery, 330
Edwards, Elizabeth, 330
Edwards, Richard, 330
Eld, George, 252, 258
Eliott, Agnes, 167
Eliott, John, 165
Elizabeth I, Queen, 26, 76–7, 150, 162, 171,
    175, 250, 256
Ellesmere, Lord Chancellor, 283
Elliott, Agnes, 335
enclosure, 138–40, 222, 224, 231, 250, 282;
    Stratford dispute, 283–93, 326; women
    oppose, 290–1
Enfield, Middx., 290
England's Helicon, 48
English Housewife, The (Markham)
epyllion
Essex, Earl of, 76–7, 223, 225, 228, 256
Essex, 53, 136
Essex Rising, 231
Evans, Henry, 253
Evelyn, Mary, 323
Evesham, Worcs., 173

Faerie Queene (Spenser), 189
farming, *see* agriculture
Fasti (Ovid), 187
Faversham, Kent, 197
feme coverte, law of, 69, 207
Field, Henry, 146, 187–9
Field, Margery, 122
Field, Richard, 134, 180, 183, 187–9, 191–
    2, 299, 347
Field, Ursula, 180
Fillongley, 210, 212
Fleet prison, 77
Fletcher, Alice, 334
Fletcher, John, 215, 278, 352
Fletcher, William, 334
Flixton, Suffolk, 53
Florence, 4
food, rising prices and shortages of, 109,
    138–9, 193–4, 225–8; *see also* grain prices
Ford, John, 110
Forest of Arden, 14, 295
Forest of Arden, Warks. (*As You Like It*),
    112–13
Forman, Simon, 302
fornication, 87, 95, 124, 274, 312
Fortescue, Sir John, 225, 231
Foster, Margery, 78

Fotheringay Castle, Northants., 150
France, 76, 112, 149–150, 217
Frankfurt book fair, 354
Freeman's Epigrams, 191
French, 188
Freud, Sigmund, 9
Friedrich, Elektor, 9
'friends', 71, 99, 304
Fripp, Edgar, 16, 20, 100, 103–4, 106, 219,
    233, 280, 312–13, 326
Frith, John, 84
Fulham, Surrey, 216
funerals, 198

Garter King of Arms, 202–3
Geneva, 249, 333
Gentle Craft, The (Deloney), 48
George, Alice, 159
Gerard's *Herbal*, 248
Germany, 150
Getley, Margaret, 175, 330
Gilbert, Ann (Agnes), 12
Gilbert, Joan, 274
Gilbert, William, 12, 16, 20, 161, 219, 274
Globe theatre, 214, 238, 280, 296, 341, 345,
    349, 351
Gloucester, Bishop of, 239
Gloucestershire, 11, 224, 297
glove-making, 32, 36, 46, 70, 104, 162, 177
godparents, 74, 129, 197–8
Golden Book of Christian Matrimony, The, 65
Golden Legend, The, 12
Golding, Arthur, 188
gonorrhoea, *see* venereal disease
Goodere, Sir Henry, 215
Goodyear, John, 135
Googe, Barnabe, 67–9
Gough, Richard, 175, 297
Grafton, *see* Temple Grafton, Warks.
grain prices, 138–9, 193–4, 228
Grannams, George, 333
Grannams, John, 228
Grannams, Margaret, 333
Gray's Inn, 150, 331
Great Harborough, Warks., 283
Green, Mary, 339
Green, Thomas, 6, 12, 156
Greenaway, William, 278
Greenblatt, Stephen, 52, 56, 80, 104, 109;
    and Shakespeare's marriage, 6, 8, 114–16,
    118, 120, 133, 138, 145–6, 196; and